Alternative Australia: *celebrating cult*

Alan Dearling with co-pilot Brendan Hanley

CW01521646

Nude not Rude © John McCormick

An Enabler Publication

Alternative Australia: *celebrating cultural diversity*
first published in the Year 2000 by Enabler Publications
3 Russell House,
Lym Close
Lyme Regis
Dorset DT7 3DE
UK

Compiled by Alan Dearling with co-pilot Brendan Hanley.

A catalogue record of this book is available from the British Library.

BIC subject classifications:
1MB Australasia; YJMB9 Alternative lifestyles; JBWF Protest; GTS Cultural Studies; RNA Environmental thought; YJPX1 Rebels, revolutionaries etc; YLNY Sustainability; YJBH2 Indigenous people; JBKC Social and cultural anthropology.

ISBN *0 9523316 4 0*

Printed in the UK by Hobbs the Printers, Totton, Hampshire. on paper derived from sustainable resources.

Credits

Cover design: Alan Dearling, aided and abetted by Andy Wood. Photos on cover: Front cover: Last days of Giblett Camp, supplied by Emma, Chris Lee and Leith Maddock of The Lorax. Back cover photos: Entrance to the Labyrinth by Orryelle Defenestrate; Alan selling his dodgy books by Howie Armstrong, and Mook by Alan.

Specific credit is also accorded to: Peter Russell for graphics used to illustrate Denis Kevans' poem, and on pages 2, 16, 109, 112, 161, 227 and 142; John McCormick, PO Box 210, Mullumbimby 2462, Australia. Phone 02 66841600, for photos on the title page, and pages 10; 12, 26, 38, 43, 133 and 248; Julie Baigent for illustrations on the Acknowledgements page and page 245; Brendan Hanley (Mook) for illustrations on pages 23, 24, 25, 46, 48; David Hallett for photo on page 24; Kim Downs for photos on pages 34, 35 and 36; Peter Cock for photos on pages 57, 58 and 59; Sophie for photo on page 60; Ben Last photo on page 63; Orryelle Defenestrate for photos on pages 61, 62, 64 and 65; Janice Newton for photos on page 82; Graham St John for photos on pages 83, 84, 85, 86, 88, 89; Geoff Williams painting/logo for John Seed on page 94; Ted Trainer for photo on 103; Neil Pike/PLC for images on pages 105, 106 and 108; John Englart, Helen Lee and the Bread and Roses Collective for photos on pages 113, 114, 116, 118, 120, 122, 123, 125; JP Bell for photo on page 128; Gubby for illustrations on pages 130 and 131; Oms not Bombs collective for photos on pages 142, 143, 144, 145 and 146; Mark Barnes for illustration on page 147; Rak Razam for photos on pages 152, 153, 154, 156 and 158; Killian for photos on pages 160, 161, and 162; Chris Lee, Leith Maddock and Emma for photos on pages 162, 163, 164, 166, 167, 168, 169 and 170; Raja Ram for photos on pages 170 and 172; Liz Hall-Downs and Kim Downs for photos on pages 173, 175, 177, 197 and 199; Northern Star, Lismore for photo of David Hallett on page 175; Daevid Allen for photo on page 176; Merrill Findlay for photo on page 195; Sylvie Shaw/Peter Cock for photo on page 204; Realm of Shade website for photo on page 211; Graham Meltzer for photos on pages 216, 218 and 219; Wild Releasing for cover artwork on page 220; Gaia Films for cover artwork on page 223; Ray Castle for photo on page 226; Warwick Roe for protest photo on page 237; Em for photos on page 239; Tatiana for illustration on page 240; John Ellis for photo of Benny Zable on page 241; Jackylyn Wagner for photo of Alana Light on page 241; Hansen Planetarium for Solar Systems graphic on page 243. The majority of the other pics and graphics are by Alan Dearling.

Ah, white man, have you any sacred sites?
Denis Kevans

Ah, white man, I am searching for the sites, sacred to you,
Where you walk, in silent worship, and you whisper poems, too,
Where you tread, like me, in wonder, and your eyes are filled with tears,
And you see the tracks you've travelled down your fifty thousand years.

I am searching around Australia, I am searching, night and day,
For a site, to you so sacred that you won't give it away
For a bit of coloured paper, say a Church you're knocking down,
Or the Rocks, your nation's birthplace, by the Bridge, in Sydney town.

Your cathedrals I have entered, I have seen the empty aisles
Where a few knelt down in sorrow, where were all the children's smiles?
Big cathedrals, full of beauty, opal glass, and gleaming gold,
And an old man, in an overcoat, who had crept in from the cold.

Your schools, I drifted through them, heard the sound of swishing canes,
Heard the yell of angry teachers crushing flowers in their brains,
Heard the bark up on the rostrum where the powers had their say,
Wouldn't children's hearts be sacred, though they're made, like mine, of clay?

Where's your wonder? Where's your worship? Where's your sense of holy awe?
When I see those little children torn apart by fear of war,
What is sacred to you, white man, what is sacred to your clan?
Are your totems rainbow-feathered? Is there dreaming in you, man?

Sacred…sacred…sacred…gee you chuck that word about,
And when the echoes answer sacred…sacred louder still you shout,
And the echoes come in patterns, and then, louder, every one
Till they meet, like waves together, and go bang! Just like a gun.

Sacred…hesitating…now, a film is reeling through
My brain, and through my memory, of our sacred rendez-vous,
Of our meeting, of our parting, of my tears, as sweet as ice,
Of my numb incomprehension of a shattered paradise.

Sacred, oh so sacred, was our sacred rendez-vous,
And your ferocious anger when you found we weren't like you,
But if I should make an act of faith, in a voice, both firm and clear,
That there's something sacred to me, you start drowning in your beer.

What is sacred to you, white man, what is sacred to your heart?
Is Australia just a quarry for the bauxite belts to start?
Where the forests are forgotten, and the tinkling of the bell
Of the bell-bird in the mountains, is just something more to sell?

Ah brother, I am searching for the sites, sacred to you,
But the rivers, clear as crystal, smell like sewerfulls of spew
From the pipe and pump pollutors, and the nukes that fleck the foam,
Would you let a man, with dirty boots, go walking through your home?

Sacred means that…sacred…it's a place where spirits rise,
With the rainbow wings of sunset, on the edge of paradise,
Sacred…that's my father, that's my mother, that's my son,
Sacred…where the dreaming whispers hope for everyone.

In the silence of the grottoes of Australia's mighty land,
Stand together with the kooris, stand together, hand in hand,
Open eyes to endless beauty, and to spirits, far and near,
For Australia is my country, it is sacred to me here.

Ah, white man, I am searching for the sites, sacred to you,
Where you walk, in silent worship, and you whisper poems, too,
Where you tread, like me, in wonder, and your eyes are filled with tears,
And you see the tracks you've travelled down your fifty thousand years.

With especial thanks to Denis Kevans for allowing the use of this poem. His website is well worth a visit at: www.pnc.com.au/~dts.studio/denis_kevans/
Check out his 'City of Green – Green Ban Songs and Beyond' CD.

Contents

Acknowledgements and a few observations

There's lots of people who deserve a pat on the back. At the top of the list are Mook (Brendan Hanley) and Shanto (Julie Oliver). More hugs due there than pats! They were involved with me near the beginning of my quest; they looked after me as friends and taxi drivers while I was in the Rainbow Region, and they have kept on looking after me and sharing their web of friends with me via the Net ever since I have returned to the UK. My old mate, Harry Blagg, and his friend Sally Droosh, showed me the ropes and introduced me to their friends in Fremantle. Bill Metcalf and Peter Cock also deserve a special mention, since it was them that gave me an entry route into the world of Australian and international intentional communities, and introduced me to other colleagues like Sylvie Shaw and Susan Forde. Thanks are also due to Maryanne Larkin and Alan Tasker at the Mitchell Library, Sydney, and Christy and Ros at Bent Books, Brisbane for helping me obtain some of the more obscure literature I wanted for my research. Ray Castle networked me into a number of useful nooks and crannies of the trance and techno world; Graham St John introduced me to Down to Earth and the ConFests, and the weird and wonderful Orryelle Defenestrate. Liz Hall-Downs has also been particularly proactive in sending me material on street poetry and introducing me to other people. Hopefully, all the many other contributors – writers, photographers and illustrators – will be happy with the introductions and thanks I've offered in interweaving the pieces together. If I've missed anyone, it's senility rather than on purpose!

I'd also like to mention a little bit about how I met some of the other contributors. You'll be introduced to them during the course of the book. I'm keen on using the Internet to meet people, to find out about places, events, what's on offer, and to assemble information for publications. This book has taken just over 18 months to put together and in addition to my own 'real' travels around Australia and the people I met, I've spent many hours in 'virtual Oz', surfing in and out of sites throughout Australia. One contact has often led to another through personal networking and hyperlinks, and especially in the final stages of putting the book to bed, quite a lot of new contributors have come on board through earlier contacts.

Finally a word or two about the words, if you see what I mean! Language is both universal and at the same time highly personal. Australian English differs from UK English, but even more rich variety exists in the writings of the contributors to this collection. I've tried, together with Phil Bayliss and Julie Harvey, who've helped me with proofing, to, wherever possible, leave contributors' language as their own personal constructs. Words are in themselves an art form: diverse, colourful, as plain or intricate as their creators wish them to be. This means that you're in for a slightly bumpy, but hopefully more exhilarating ride through the contributions in this book.

I hope you enjoy that ride as much as I have done.

Luv and respect.

Alan

Ending at the beginning

It was thirty years ago, more or less today, that a late sixties adolescent lad called Alan was studying Australasian social history. And he wasn't even doing it in Australia. This was the University of Kent at Canterbury, England.

Sad; what a sad way to start a book.

But perhaps, just maybe, those pages of Anglo-centric history sowed a few seeds. Here we are in the new millennium, what one of my contributors, Ray Castle called the 'Age of Aquarious Themes'. Somehow that seems to sum up this book. It really is a variety performance. The topics covered are a big stage, and the actors represent all sorts of facets of Australian Alternative culture. These are the voices of the wise tribal elders and having-it young braves. This is a book about ritual and about the celebration of cultural diversity across the Australian continent.

Mook and Alan in Byron Bay

I made the collection of these contributions a very personal quest. They are bound together by my own travels around Australia and my electronic media travels via the World Wide Web, admirably aided and abetted by co-pilot, Mook Bahloo (Brendan Hanley). His personal web of friends and contacts through the Rainbow Region of New South Wales and beyond, made the collecting and nurturing of the project both vastly more fun and more effective.

Now the collection is complete, my aim is for you to make the journey with me. Here you will find a kaleidoscope of new friends. Weird tales from the edge of normalised society, much magic and not a little wisdom, especially in respect of our environment and the ways in which we live and organise our lives. As Jim Morrison of the Doors fame said,
"Enter in, the show is about to begin."

Hitting the West End

Just about 40 hours after leaving my seaside base at Lyme Regis in Dorset, UK, I arrived soon after sunrise for 5 a.m. in Brisbane's airport. The customs' officers didn't seem too impressed by the fact that I was a university researcher and writer. After twenty minutes of searching through my gear and not finding any drugs, they reluctantly let the 47 year old 'hippy' type into their country.

A 'long haul' it certainly is, especially if you're a big framed six foot three, rather than designed to fit a British Airways' air-gnome space! I'd booked into somewhere called an Education Lodge, in Brisbane's West End, but no one could let me in until 10 a.m. I was so tired, eyes straining, and almost hallucinating, but there was no way I could sleep. I tried after I received the key to my room, but went for a first walkabout back to the city's famous South Bank area. My first phone call in Australia was to Bill Metcalf to arrange a meeting for the following day.

Bill had exchanged e-mail correspondence with me about this book for about six months, and I had already read his books, *Social characteristics of alternative lifestyle participants in Australia (with Frank Vanclay)* and *From Utopian dreaming to Communal reality.* Bill is a nice mix of human warmth and intellectual monolith. Some of our e-mail exchanges had been a shade tetchy. Bill expected me to have a stronger set of expectations of what I wanted as contributions for the book. *"What will make it into saleable book, rather than a string of interesting stories?"* he politely enquired. Meanwhile, I was busy describing myself in terms of helms-person, rather than editor. Neither did I want to write an Alan's adventures in alternative Australia. Though, as you can see, there is a bit of that!

So, something like a year after Bill and I met on the Net, below you get Bill's personal story of his involvement and commitment to intentional communities. Thank you, Bill, for the contribution and your time while I was in the West End. I still remember you telling me about your arrival in Australia from Canada, and being asked by Immigration, *"How long will you be visiting for?"* and you replying, *"I don't know; if I like it I might stay."* Back in

1970, in those days of the White Australia policy, that was enough to give Bill a resident's stamp in his passport! Thirty years on, Bill is a genuine tribal elder.

Alternative and Communal Australia?
Or
The Education of Young Bill
Dr Bill Metcalf

Is there an alternative Australia?

That was the burning question for me when I arrived in Australia as an immigrant from Canada in late 1970. I had completed an Honours Degree in Agricultural Economics at University of Guelph, Canada, and worked unhappily for a financial firm, then spent a couple of years as a 'hippie' roaming North America and Europe. I experienced much of the communal, countercultural fervour of the late sixties – and I then saw the rot of hard drugs, sexism and violence set in and subsequently destroy the so-called 'Summer of Peace and Flowers'.

Australia in 1970 seemed to me like North America of five or ten years earlier. I soon became re-enthused about the possibility of developing a radically different society, of avoiding the moral abyss of serial monogamy, of overcoming loneliness and selfishness, of living within loving, communal families rather than as isolated nuclear families or singles, and of moving past rampant consumerism through learning to share.

In the lead-up to the general election of late 1972, Australia was still a profoundly conservative place; still with military conscription, still involved in the Vietnam War, and still acting politically like a poor cousin to USA, following an earlier Prime Minister's sycophantic promise to go 'All the Way with LBJ'. The Australian Labor Party, under the simple slogan 'It's Time', won that election with an overwhelming mandate for radical change, and Gough Whitlam became our Prime Minister.

Like most of my friends, I worked hard for the '72 Labor victory. That night, December 2, 1972, it really seemed as if Australia was fundamentally changing. I recorded in my diary simply, *"Exhausted but very happy and content"*. A new and brighter day appeared to be dawning, and the dreams to which so many of 'my sort of people' clung, seemed to be about to be realised. John F. Kennedy's election as US President in 1960, and Pierre Trudeau's election as Canadian Prime Minister in 1967, both had the same impact on me and on others of my generation. We naively thought that dramatic social change could and would come from the top down. It did not because it can not!

As an intellectual, I have always operated first and foremost through my head. I therefore enrolled in a Master's Degree in sociology at University of Queensland, in order to study the social change movements of environmentalism and communalism, of which I was, of course, already very involved. I slowly started to uncover my naive, blinkered eyes, and to see countercultural social change, and my own and my friends' communal experimentation, within a far wider historical and theoretical context. On the personal front, I had developed an urban commune here in Brisbane in which I lived with a number of other brave social experimenters. I fully appreciated and implemented the idea that social thinkers must live their altered reality – not just theorise about it. Like most communards, however, I soon found that day-to-day communal practice was much harder than the theorising. In spite of our purest intentions, jealousy, possessiveness and pettiness crept into our naively idealistic communal hearts and hearth.

In May 1973, I temporarily left the secure academic world to become part of the famous Aquarius Festival, at Nimbin in northern New South Wales. Here is part of what I wrote about this experience in my subsequent PhD Thesis (yes, Virginia, one can write about these things in academic works!).

My first view of the 1973 Aquarius Festival was when I arrived late on the afternoon of the first day. Car parks were organised on each side of Nimbin, and a regular shuttle bus service provided surprisingly efficient transport. The main (and almost only) street of Nimbin was packed with colourful people, dancing, singing and playing. The paddocks to the north and east were filled with tents, domes and assorted experimental housing forms. The whole area was covered by a haze of smoke from hundreds of small cooking fires. Music from exotic, unknown instruments wafted over the hills, and as I walked to our pre-arranged 'tribal site', the acrid odour of marijuana was frequently encountered. For ten days, we participants (estimated from 5,000 to 10,000) took part in serious workshops and discussions, swam and paraded in the nude (much to the consternation of townsfolk), smoked dope, listened to music, and talked incessantly of new social experiments.

By the end of the Aquarius Festival, we participants had learned that we were not alone in our dreams and faltering social experimentations. Far from being alone, participants began to recognise that we were part of a new, utopian social movement. A 'Full Moon Celebration' was held. This semi-structured event saw perhaps 1,000 people on a barren knob of a hill, and as the sun went down we took part in a pageant or dance. With hands linked, we chanted and sang as the moon suddenly appeared over the Nightcap Range. A sense of social solidarity seemed to develop within the crowd who had taken part. This intense feeling of one-ness, … [or] 'we consciousness', seemed all-pervasive. Because of the affective nature of this event it was only interpretable to a full participant like myself, with no ulterior motives, who became fully involved, then later in reflecting on the experience analysed its social significance.

Bill in hippie gear at Aquarius Festival, Nimbin, 1973

Perhaps the greatest achievement of the 1973 Aquarius Festival was its symbolism. It came to symbolise the alternative lifestyle movement, to provide a geographical focus, and, over time, it became an important aspect of the collective mythology of that movement. To have been at Nimbin in '73 came to be a source of pride for participants. Even today, I am frequently asked to describe the sensation of the Aquarius Festival by new participants who appear to regard it with a degree of awe.

Before the Aquarius Festival finished, posters appeared, asking, 'After Nimbin: What?'. A meeting to answer this question was convened on the final Sunday of the festival, and several hundred people (including myself) attended. There was a strong sentiment that the spirit of the festival must live on, and find expression in a continuing, living alternative lifestyle community. Several people volunteered to seek suitable land which would provide a permanent home base in the area, for participants in the alternative lifestyle movement. As we retreated from Nimbin in late May 1973, many participants must have felt (as I did) that it was only a temporary retreat, and that we were now part of a 'new' alternative lifestyle movement – with a utopian vision of the world in which we wished to live.

Late in 1973, notices began to appear in the developing network of alternative lifestyle media describing a large block of land at the head of Tuntable Creek, near Nimbin. Suggestions were put forward for the formation of a large land settlement co-operative. The formative ideology for Tuntable Falls (Co-ordination Co-operative) community, in early 1974, was unabashedly utopian!

Trying to be true to my dreams, I became an early member of this famous (or infamous, depending on your perspective!) Tuntable Falls communal group, and lived there for part of its first year. But the illness and squalor, the mindless use of drugs in a hedonistic frenzy, and the hopeless poverty were just not for me. Neither was Nimbin by that time. We were so self-indulgent, so precious about our beliefs, so silly, that our inability to implement those dreams is hardly surprising. We, the children of Aquarius, had to grow up before we killed ourselves! As have many social activists before me, I discovered during those heady, communal times that society consists of individuals, more or less like me, and that most of us really had, when push came to shove, feet of clay. I came to understand and implement the notion of 'Revolution by Lifestyle', wherein one must change oneself first, and only then social change might follow. That led me from an active political period into a time of introspection and exile.

I spent three years living and working in Papua New Guinea under the patronising belief that 'native peoples' could serve as a model for countercultural social change. Like most of my generation, subsequent experiences led me to abandon this naive notion.

I came back to Australia, determined 'To-Thine-Own-Self-Be-True', returning to academia, my natural home, and to the sociological study of radical social alternatives. Of course, as was popular at the time with young academics, I was determined not to follow the traditional rules of objective science, but to be fully involved in my research subject and with my fellow participants. I was adamant that my research would not exploit, but would support Australian communards. On that front, I hope this is what has happened with my research. Perhaps, at long last, I was not so naive? Since then, I have written and had published four books and innumerable scholarly and popular articles about communal living, have served as an adviser to the Australian Prime Minister on communalism, and have spoken at innumerable meetings and advised all sorts of individuals and local councils. I would like to think that I have achieved at least some good for this social movement to which I have devoted my life.

During the past twenty years, I have lived for much of my time in two urban communes. I have striven to live the ideal, communal life – but admit that I have fallen far short. I am now much more modest and realistic about what I can achieve in my life. I have seen too many new-age, ego trips, too much wasted effort, and too much personal damage – all in the name of supposed countercultural reform.

I continue to be appalled at the ignorance of many of my well-intentioned fellow travellers about the historical context of our utopian quest. Just as we in the 60s thought we had discovered sex and hallucinogenics, so too do most of today's Australian would-be communards think that communal living is a notion and practice unique to the later years of this century. I thought that also, until I started to research the matter. What I have found has profoundly changed me and my understanding of utopian communalism. Australia's first attempt at developing an intentional community was near Hahndorf, South Australia, in 1839, barely fifty years after European occupation of this continent. In 1853, Johann Krumnow established Australia's

first commune, Herrnhut, near Hamilton, Victoria. These fifty pioneer communards explored alternative sexual patterns, provided safe haven for Aborigines and other social outcasts, and developed a thriving, self-sufficient lifestyle. Like many contemporary, charismatic communal leaders, Krumnow had his 'odd' side. He believed that he was in direct communication with God (although just who listened to whom was unclear!). When God told Krumnow that he could fly, he promptly climbed to the top of the barn roof and leapt off, in full faith that he would fly away. He fell and broke his leg instead!

Herrnhut commune thrived until Krumnow's death in 1880, after which it slowly withered. Under the leadership of Frau Elmore, one of Krumnow's disciples and, according to critics, also one of his several wives, Herrnhut commune slowly collapsed in acrimony and lawsuits. In my research, I have discovered, so far, another 130 communal ventures in Australia prior to 1970, roughly when our so-called Aquarian Age started. I have found that these historical communal groups were in cities, suburbs and rural areas, were religious, spiritual and secular, followed traditional and radical sexual mores, and ranged from communist to right-wing in their political orientations. But what they all have in common is that they no longer exist – they have all collapsed.

That led me to wonder why communal groups collapse. My research shows that of those communal groups which have been planned, the overwhelming majority simply never start. Of those groups that actually do start, about half of them collapse within the first two years, and about half the remainder collapse within the next two years – not a very good success rate! But then I found, much to my surprise, that roughly the same failure rate applies to small businesses. So, while I have found that communal ventures in Australia are often unstable and short-lived, they are no more so than are most other, comparable social forms.

Another misconception is that communards are fickle and unstable people, and that communal groups have a very high turnover of members. Research, however, shows that while communal turnover is high, it is not all that high when compared with membership turnover found in other organisations. For instance, nurses and factory workers turnover a bit faster than commune members, while academics, prison wardens and civil servants all turn over a bit more slowly.

But then, on the other hand, my overseas research tells me that the Hutterites have been living communally in Canada and USA for over three centuries, and that several Israeli Kibbutzim go back almost a century. The oldest commune still in existence is Bon Homme, a Hutterite commune founded in USA in 1874. The communal groups described in my two books, *From Utopian Dreaming to Communal Reality: Cooperative Lifestyles in Australia* (1995), and *Shared Visions, Shared Lives: Communal Living Around the Globe* (1996), average about 35 years longevity, with the oldest commune starting in 1934. Communal groups can and do endure. They can be sustainable, but it is damned hard to do! The next phase of my life-long engagement with Australian counterculturalism and utopian communalism has been to intensively study several historical communes. To this end, I recently researched Bon Accord, Resolute and Byrnestown, three utopian socialist communes, with over 500 members, which were established here in Queensland, in 1894. These communal groups even received government support – although their demise was also orchestrated by that same corrupt political system. This fascinating and tragic story of three Australian countercultural communes of last century can be read in my 1998 book, *The Gayndah Communes*.

All of this research and writing has led me to be seen in Australia as something of a 'translator' or 'go-between', with one foot in the field of legitimate academia and the other in the world of 'the weirdos', as one reporter termed it. I enjoy this role, and feel that I have been able to serve a very useful purpose. Whenever the media drums up a 'cult' scare, I will be interviewed, and I try to dampen the hysteria. I have been able to advise several local governments which were worried about intentional communities in their midst, and through my writing and media appearances, have been able to inform many Australians that it really is possible to live a radically different life. This has only been possible because I can be seen as coming from the mainstream, not dismissed as being just some 'loopy hippie'.

So where does that leave me today?

I reflect upon, with the greatest admiration, earlier Australian communards and countercultural thinkers such as William Lane, Harry Head, Horace Tucker and Catherine Spence. William Lane was a wonderful writer and orator who inspired many communal ventures in Australia before taking several hundred followers with him to Paraguay where they established New Australia commune in 1893. Harry Head was the young and highly motivated leader of Resolute commune in Queensland in the 1890s. Horace Tucker wrote one of Australia's best utopian novels, *The New Arcadia*, and then founded seven communes with a combined membership of almost 2000, in Victoria. Catherine Spence, from Adelaide, wrote two powerful and influential utopian books, *Handfasted* and *A Week in The Future*, both of which had a dramatic impact on Australian radical social thought. I also admire several contemporary

Bill working on his next book, in rainforest, Brisbane 1999

Australians who have done so much for this movement, such as Peter Cock, Don and Estelle Gobbett, Jill Jordan, Jim Cairns, Enid Connochie, Bill Smale, Dik Freeston and Glen Ochre. They have all spoken and written clearly and persuasively about countercultural communalism, and each, in his or her own way, continues to serve as a beacon to young Australians, showing what can be achieved.

Also, of course, I continue to honour and respect those thousands of Australians who persist in starting new, communal ventures. From my position of age and experience I may doubt their chances of success, but I admire their determination and enthusiasm – and I certainly wish them well. For me, personally, the future looks like finding me devoting ever more attention to my researching and writing about historical communes in Australia. I will continue in my role as International Correspondent for the American magazine, *Communities*. I am the current world President of the International Communal Studies Association and, in that capacity, find that I have an ever greater formal role overseas, dealing with governments, universities and institutions, plus with many of the great communal groups in the world such as Findhorn (UK), ZEGG (Germany), Damanhur (Italy), Twin Oaks, The Farm and Padanaram (USA) and L'arche (France).

So far, I have been able to visit about 130 communal groups around the globe. While some enthuse and impress me, others are, quite honestly, simply appalling. Some communal groups support their members and provide healthy, growing, living environments, while others are havens for the abuse meted out by charismatic leaders onto their socially and emotionally crippled followers. I would 'modestly' claim to be widely recognised by both academics and communards as a world expert on utopianism and communalism. That feels good! Am I optimistic or pessimistic about the future of this social movement in Australia? Until recently, Australian communards were an ageing breed with not enough young people joining. More groups were planning cemeteries than schools, and old age pensions were becoming an ever more important source of income. Some groups were in danger of becoming 'hip' geriatric ghettos! Over the past five years or so, this seems to be changing, with more young people interested in communal living and more communal groups willing to facilitate their joining. Perhaps the 'greying' of Australian communal groups is reversing? In general, this social movement continues to become ever less radical, perhaps being slowly subsumed into the mainstream culture? But then I am heartened whenever any new social activists come forward to reinvent radical communalism. I am unsure, however, what will work out, on balance.

So I guess I am optimistic about countercultural communalism

in Australia, having faith that those who mix intelligence in with their enthusiasm will predominate over those whose enthusiasm is based on the worst excesses of new-age nuttiness.

Finding Ourselves

"In Aboriginal Australia, there are specific rules for 'going back' or, rather, for singing your way to where you belong: to your 'conception site', to the place where your tjuringa is stored." Bruce Chatwin

While searching out material to put into this book, I contacted a lot of people, travelled well over 12 thousand kilometres in Australia, plus the return journey from the UK. I rummaged around in many new and second hand bookshops and spent quite a few hours in libraries in Alice Springs, Cairns, Perth and especially the Rainbow Archives in the Mitchell Library, New South Wales. Sure, I was researching a book, but I was also trying to make sense of my own very personal experiences. I like the way Jorge Luis Borges put it when he said:
"The outward course of my life has been a common one, but in my dreams I always saw tigers."

Certain key themes kept on recurring. I can remember them buzzing around in my head as I travelled in and out of many different lives and locations across Australia. Some were echoes from my own past and books I'd read and compiled.
Identity and culture
New beginnings and a new consciousness
Nomadism
Global action and connectedness
Youthfulness, energy and enthusiasm
Tribalism
Dreamings
Aboriginality
Diversity
were among them.

Many of these subjects are central to the lives of the contributors of this whole book. One of my pre-occupations in the UK and beyond has been campaigning alongside others who are fighting for the right of people to be free to enjoy and celebrate their own cultural diversity. For thirty years and more this has led me into clashes with other friends,

colleagues and even my parents. *"Why do you want to live like you do?" "Why don't you settle down properly?" "What do you want to mix with people like them for?"*

Or, maybe, as Germaine Greer at 50, said:
"I'm growing old without ever having grown up." (Vogue, January 1989)

Perhaps my journey to Australia was, in a sense, an attempt to find out some of the answers to those and other related questions. My life has flitted between the straight culture of working with young people, social work, universities, publishing, the local pub, sport, and the alternative culture of Europe's equivalents of the ferals, the new Travellers, plus festival goers and protestors. I suppose I belong in both worlds and neither. My Australian experiences were similar. I could have been a Martian trying to untangle the myths of Oz. On the other hand, the fact that I was an outsider meant that I was sometimes without the baggage of preconceptions, which an Australian, say from Perth, would have when visiting Daintree in FNQ, or Byron Bay and Sydney in NSW.

I have talked at least another book the length of this one, with the people who have contributed to *Alternative Australia*, before, during and after my trip. As compiler and editor, the godhead role can become burdensome. On the next pages I've tried to interweave some of the thoughts, ideas and observations which struck me as being a part of the webwork of this book. I hope these word-bites assist in making connections between other contributions. Maybe, they'll even provide a new spark or two for your own adventures in the richness which is our historic and cultural diversity.

No apologies for including some largish chunks of words and ideas from Peter Cock and Brendan Hanley!

A sense of place and of community
"Like the Kooris before them, in time, white communities tend to take on spirit of place too. We begin to relate more directly to nature around us, naming rocks, trees and other creatures, talking to plants and animals, writing songs and poems and

painting pictures from nature.

Burnum Burnum, the late great Koori Ba H'ai Ambassador to the world, sat in our circle at Terania and gave us a 'clever' stone, telling us to love and protect the land and the forest, because we were the new Kooris. It was a great honour on one hand, and a massive obligation on the other. One thing is for sure, after all those years of doing it, they might be able to teach us a thing or two about sharing and caring for this land...and oh yeah...how to live in a tribe!" Brendan Hanley. "What began as a search for life in a beautiful environment is

A sense of place

now for me far more an exploration of eco-spirituality. The development of deep connections with the land is exciting and is a balance to connections with human community. I have but tasted our human need and potential for community. This taste feeds and drains me: it cushions me from the harshness and threats of the dominant world, while being a mirror to the wonders of human capacities. If you should take the risk to venture into community then be assured that you will learn more about yourself, about us and living with this planet than you dreamed. I have and I am thankful for the continuing journey." Peter Cock.

Diversity, challenge and difference
"How do we reach across the divide we have created between us and the rest of nature?" Peter Cock.

"It's not enough to change people's heads – though that's important. You have to change structures as well." Dennis Altman.

"The Aboriginal race would have been better off if the white man had never come to Australia. We have been kept on the fringes of your society, absorbing its evils but denied many of its benefits. A quarter of a million of my people have been killed off in the process." Billy Motogori.

"The history of Australia, to a large extent, is based around conflict, and much of this conflict has been of a positive nature. Whether it was the Eureka Stockade, the first Aboriginal push for land rights or the Franklin River Dam campaign, many seminal events in our nation's history revolved around the push for social change. Inspirationally, all of these actions began with one or two determined people who decided to speak out." Phil Thornton, Liam Phelan and Bill McKeown.

"We have been through the bright lights of the 70s, the downer of the 80s and the resurgence of the 90s. We are wiser, more pessimistic now of our capacity to generate alternatives and to transform the dominant paradigm. We have seen the co-opting forces at work through the marketing of alternatives to sell orthodox consumption. We have come face to face with our own limitations. The need for transformation is great but our capacity limited." Peter Cock.

(About Helen Garner, feminist school teacher at Fitzroy High School, Melbourne, 1972) "The idea that a female school-teacher was encouraging teenage girls to ask questions such as, 'Can a girl ask a man for a fuck?' – and then answering in the affirmative – was mind boggling." Gerster, R and Bassett, J.

"Beginning with prisoners and soldiers, and moving onto refugees, opportunists, dreamers and adventurers, we've made a society from the flotsam and jetsam of the world...Until recently it seemed that Australia was going to show the world that you can build something enduring out of the materials that washed onto our shores. A nation built from driftwood. Why not? Little multicoloured tiles can be transformed into majestic mosaics. Apparently conflicting shapes can be parts of a coherent jigsaw.

Let us hope that we can wait patiently, even proudly, for the picture to emerge – that we can save it from the Hansonites who pound at the pieces with their fists." Philip Adams.

"I was testing the boundaries of reality." Jim Morrison.

"I piss towards the dark skies, very high and very far." Arthur Rimbaud.

Bridges

"If a flash of insight can green the desert or save the dolphin, maybe a collective vision can change the world." Richard Neville.

"They (the contributors to 'The Way Out' book, published in 1975) work from an assumption that man is an endangered species...They want to find a way out of this dead-end future. Their signposts point in many directions: liberation movements, communal living, conservation, drugs and spiritualism, community action, self-help...But it should be realised that the alternatives discussed here have not been dreamed up for the fun of it. They are a cry of hope in a situation of profound cultural turmoil. I myself believe that political action is needed to deal with social and institutional forces. But I also recognise that there are some regions of the human spirit which politics cannot reach." Moss Cass, then Minister for the Environment and Conservation.

"Culturally we are so narrowly centred on a cult of individualism that species survival is taken for granted. However within nature, while the individual is unique, it is nearly irrelevant. The rise of the **sacred self** and the **victim self** parallels the denial of the group as sacred and the denial of nature as kin. Each person is an expression of the whole, and the attributes of others more or less replicate our own, as is true with nature in general. However we are not capable of holding all within our own hands; we need the diversity of others, human and non-human; to enrich the scope of our person. We need the comparative reference of other expressions of being as mirrors of our own being and as stimulus for our becoming.

In short, our difficulty is, that western culture has created **I** in bold. As a consequence we need a bridge to 'we', which creates the need for a bridge to 'them' and from them to alien 'others'.

When from natures perspective, we are all one anyway." Peter Cock.

"The Community/Tribe/Family spirit that dominates at protests like Terania, Nightcap, Franklin River and more recently Timbarra, Chaelundi and the Kakadu Park 'Jabiluka' anti-uranium rally, is a highly addictive heady drug! Make no mistake! Surrendered and focused on saving the forest or whatever, some part of the individual ego moves over to allow the collective to take a greater role...and magic happens as a result!" Brendan Hanley.

Aboriginality

"Trying to describe Aboriginal cosmology briefly is like trying to explain quantum mechanics in five seconds. Besides, no amount of anthropological detail can begin to convey Aboriginal feeling for their land. It is everything – their law, their ethics, their reason for existence. Without that relationship they become ghosts. Half people. They are not separate from the land. When they lose it, they lose themselves. This is why the land rights movement has become so essential. Because, by denying them their land, we are committing cultural and, in this case, racial genocide." Robyn Davidson.

"The dormitories stood there. We had numbered blankets on a hard wood floor. I was number six. The manager sent his dog to find us when we tried to hide. At 9 p.m. they locked us up." Alma Wason.

"To an Aborigine a sacred site is a story or song passed down. A personal mythology – that defines not just a place but a man, his family, his clan. That's not just a mountain: it's a quail that walked from Aurukun to Coen. That's not just a river: it's the coiling path of a rainbow serpent. To forget such stories of one's Dreaming turns a land to 'rubbish country'.

To go bush. To escape, for a while, into nature. To draw sustenance from the land. Physical sustenance. Spiritual sustenance." Cathy Newman.

"What we are is spiritual survivors. It was the only form of survival we had." Aboriginal elder quoted by Cathy Newman.
"My vision of the Aboriginal role in the Australian scheme is that we will be custodians of the country's ecological heritage." Noel Pearson.

Intentional communities/retribalisation

"I think for my own part communes will function best where they are seen less idealistically and more as a practical economic, domestic and fraternal arrangement – a sensible way of reducing overhead costs, of sharing cooking and cleaning, and a way of avoiding isolation and loneliness, where people can care for each other in many small practical ways and share a variety of experiences and friends. Seen more functionally, too, I think communards should not feel they have to love, or even like, everyone they live with, but that, as in a nuclear family, a whole lot of sensible balances can be made in order to get on with daily necessities, and in order to protect and maintain and stabilize the group as a whole." David Potts.

"Over the last twenty years the order of priorities in alternative communities has slowly shifted so that environmental concerns have become secondary to desires for individual autonomy and material pursuits. Although participants have a low per capita consumption of resources, there is the tendency towards greater privatisation of consumption. This means a gradual increase in their demand for resources, which has been reflected in a number of ways. Creeping materialism results from the tendency for duplication of facilities, largely due to psycho/social reasons rather than to practical considerations. The sharing of consumer durables and equipment becomes limited to items that cannot be afforded in any other way. Sharing is often seen as a necessity rather than a virtue, the alternative to doing without rather than as connected to a shared environmental ethic. Without a strong group value system to the contrary, sharing declines as incomes rise. The loser is often the community's shared vision of the land.

Collective strength comes through clarity of shared purpose, sustained through an organisational structure which is explicit while having supportive mechanisms to ensure its sustainability. That is, it is backed up by social pressure for individuals to participate and to carry out their agreed tasks, with clear lines of responsibility and areas of authority. It is a choice to join, or to leave, but within that there needs to be real community boundaries that limit the scope of diversity.

A major cause of this (privatisation of responsibility) propensity is that

John McCormick ©

Australian society is so polarised between our experience of the private and the public. We have been socialised to live essentially private lives within impersonal worlds. We are devoid of the experience of intimate sharing beyond family whether it be of our feelings, friends, flesh or things. The power of this socialisation has been denied and attempts to overcome it severely limited by an understandable desire to hang on to what we know and the security it brings. Re-tribalisation from our present cultural base will involve struggle, pain, letting go and reaching out. In our culture we don't know what a 21st century tribalisation means and we therefore have so much to learn from other cultures who have a long experience of village/tribal living." Peter Cock.

"There is a danger in overly romanticizing new life-styles, which only creates too many expectations and leads people to become totally disheartened by the inevitable problems. Anyone who has been involved in alternative movements knows that there is no magical way to deal with problems of envy, competitiveness, conflict and ambition." Dennis Altman.

"It can be argued that the (alternative lifestyles) movement may no longer be as radical as was once the case, but it has become part of the wider society, albeit a society catering for greater cultural diversity. The large numbers and diverse nature of the current and intending participants shows that the alternative lifestyle movement has gained maturity and is now truly a complex mass movement." Bill Metcalf and Frank Vanclay.

Uncritical cross-cultural celebration
"In the early seventies, when I first chugged into town (Byron Bay) in a Valiant station-wagon, it was a place of NOT DOING. Like white Aborigines, lured by the spirit of the place, we just wanted to soak it up; eat the mushrooms and gaze at the sunsets through tea-tree lakes, prolonging our stay till the money ran out." Richard Neville.

"In the name of multi culturalism however, there is also the risk of the other extreme of no limits to inclusion of difference. Cross-cultural encounters can lead to eco-cultural idealisation without seeing, let alone confronting difficult issues. While this is understandable given the previous attempts for example, to wipe out Aboriginal culture, it is in danger of going to the other extreme of uncritical celebration of the others. But what is the legitimate role of challenge? Cross-cultural exchange means not just a willingness to accept diversity but to use it as a basis for challenge. A risk of multi culturalism is repressive tolerance of destructive actions which for the sake of intercultural harmony goes unchallenged." Peter Cock.

Paradigm shift/Gaia
"We need to re-learn trust in Gaia's power and in life's ability to empower the future beyond the efforts of a particular group in a particular place and time. This position does not advocate that we don't have to do anything, rather it is an antidote to the other extreme of doom and gloom.

What we share in common is freedom, that comes from recognition that the earth's wellbeing or our own, isn't all in our human hands. Our awareness of our choices matter but, they are only one player in a bigger picture. Probably because of earthly pressures necessity will probably be the prime mother of invention for sustainability." Peter Cock.

Tribe vibe
"No matter where we come from, what we look like, what language we speak,what religion we follow or who we imagine we are, evidence suggests that we humans once lived in tribes, or large extended families.

Some still do, despite the odds.

Some have done until recently.

The rest of us did so way back in time."
Brendan Hanley.

"Totally isolated from our own culture for long periods, we became vulnerable to forgotten times and tribes re-awakening in us……it was an odyssey of self-discovery." Lawrence Blair.

Spirituality/festivals
"As humanity evolves, NEEDS change. We NOW can see the way in which festivals of this new era are becoming focusing points of the human interaction necessary for our REAL NEEDS, for a more healthy and joyfilled future." Dik Freestun.
"Since shortly after the first Down-to-Earth confest in 1976, New-Age groups of various persuasions have been holding workshop gatherings…these are not festivals in the accepted

John McCormick ©

It might be an Afro singing workshop, a yoga class, a protest, a football match, a rock concert or a spontaneous mass-singing of their latest TV jingle by all the Woolies staff and customers one day in the Deli section…it doesn't matter…being part of a cohesive and dedicated group experience is always a buzz. The bigger the buzzier!" Brendan Hanley.

"Dear Mardi Grass organizers
Bjorn and me come from Sweden. We come to film Northern NSW for a promotional film for a tourist company. On our third day we come to Nimbin just before Mardi Grass. We are very excited many times. We find everything here, culture, colour and many interesting people, games, parades, cookies, fashion show, music, seminars, markets and the Mardi Grass cannabis cup. We filmed everything and help judge the cannabis cup also we eat many cookies

sense; rather they are wonderful opportunities for people who want to learn more about themselves to explore many avenues not normally available or widely disseminated." Adrian Rawlins.

"Seasonal gatherings, festivals and holy day rituals are babies that have been tipped out with the bath water. Bath water that used to be Tribal Ways was already leaking badly at the hands of the Colonisers and Church over the centuries … when the Industrial Revolution came and up-ended the bath-tub completely!

But it was decreed that the newly-created, conveniently-packaged nuclear family had no need of gatherings of any sort, except where people are allowed to be organised and orderly paying bums on seats in some commercial venue.

The goosebump-caused-by-music thing is a very visceral manifestation of the principle I am trying to describe. The combined sound of the group is an excellent metaphor for the overall thing I'm talking about.

It is unquestionably a step towards enlightenment to have the privilege, even if only for a few short bursts, of real Community.

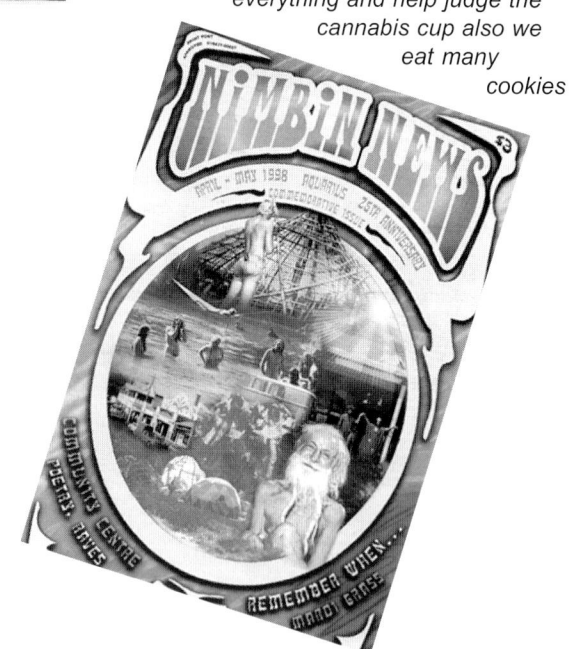

and we are the Swedish team in the HEMP Olympics. We took little film of the rest of NSW, as it did not interest us. When our film is developed we think our boss will be happy with our work. But he is not only unhappy with bad focus of the film but dislikes what we film as well. He cut out all the best bits about Mardi Grass, which left him with less than 1 minute of film suitable for his tourist company. We have been fired. We do not care. We have best time in our lives. We show the film to our friends and they all want to join our Swedish team at the next Mardi Grass. See you in May." From Nimbin Hemp Embassy Calendar, 1999.

Sacred sites

"Communities tend also to find or create Sacred Sites within or close to their boundaries, establishing the possibility of gatherings at these hot spots for ritual, meditative or other higher purpose...or just for plain fun.

Rosebud Farm, the legendary Community of Kuranda's hippie hey-day, had a tree, a giant jungle fig tree which was the power spot on the property. It was a massive tree, hollow inside like a cave where the forest-giant host tree had long-ago died and rotted, it was a tangle of roots and vines and its upper branches were great aerial beds of giant birdsnest and staghorn ferns. If you stayed at Rosebud for even a short while, it was an unspoken and inevitable rite-of-passage to climb to these lofty heights from whence one could look across rainforest canopy to the distant hills to the West of the Atherton Tablelands.

The bravado and stamina needed to reach the top of the tree was usually fired by a previous encounter with a Rosebud Gnome called Magic Peter and his latest bong, and/or the recent ingestion of several local fungi of the psilocybin cubensis variety." Brendan Hanley.

A small step into alto-Oz

I met Doug through the half obscured bottom of a glass of the amber nectar. It was my first taste of a 'watering' hole in Oz. Prior to our meeting, I'd been poking around in the local bookshops of Brisbane's West End, particularly in Emma's and Bent Books and had spent quite a few dollars. I'd already enjoyed conversations with Christy and Roz at Bent Books – a great collection of counter cultural books, and spent a couple of hours at Emma's – the downstairs home of Brian Laver and upstairs, Hamish Alcorn and the West End Neighborhood News.

Definitely a main anarcho-politico-eco-bohemian hub of Queensland's principal city.

The pub in question was the Boundary Hotel and Doug was part of a small, quite vocal crowd in the side bar. They were talking about things that were of obvious interest to me: Aboriginal celebrations, music, environmental issues and intentional communities. Having enjoyed reading through Bill Metcalf's accounts and commentaries about Australian communes and communities and talking with Peter Cock, Estelle and Don Gobbett and Frank Vanclay about their experiences, it seemed something more synergy-ful than mere coincidence to bump into Doug. He had lived at the Mount Oak intentional community – that's the one of Jim Cairns and Junie Morosi fame, and, more importantly, he was willing to pen some words about it for this book!. The others that I remember from a fairly 'serious' drinking session were Craig Darlington, heavily involved with rainforest action, and Tony Wellington, an artist, and like Doug, active in Murri (Aboriginal) events in Queensland. It was a long, informative (it led to other contacts with environmental activists and west coast poets), and enjoyable evening – I only wished that I hadn't got to get up at 5.30 the next morning to fly down to Sydney!

Mt Oak
Doug Broad

He asked me to write about Mt Oak.

Not a history, for I demurred at that; it is something which should be writ by someone other than I, someone with a sense of perspective, who could write dispassionately, with the fine hand of the historian, the observer, objective and removed from the events, but he asked me to write about it, about how I felt as an ex-resident, now the land had been handed over to the local indigenous people, now I had left, now that the house had been burned down. Ah, well, I'll get back to that. The burning. The arson. I'll get back to the anger, the outrage, the violation, the desire for vengeance, the pissed-offedness, the how-dare-you-you-scumbag-arsehole. I'll leave that for the moment, just for the moment. Like General Douglas, I shall return – you're not off the hook yet, mate. Not by a long chalk.

So, this is not going to be a history of Mt Oak. As I have said, others more competent than I, more dispassionate than I, will write that in the fullness of time. Suffice to say I lived at Mt Oak from 1987 until I left, under not the most pleasant of circumstances, in 1991. The reasons for that are not the provenance of anybody who didn't live there at that time.

What mattered, over and above the internal arguments and conflicts the community had, (and there were many, as any community or group of individuals trying to live together based around a political ideal has), was the overlying commitment of all the community members to the larger picture; economic and environmental sustainability, democracy among the community, and ultimately freed land, available to all people who would work within the ecological guidelines; land freed from ownership by an individual, free for all who would take up the stewardship. A hard row to hoe, believe me, a hard row to hoe.

The community did it. I don't know how, other than we all believed in what we were doing and made enormous sacrifices, sometimes to the detriment of the wellbeing of not only

individuals, but the community as a whole, but we did it. The evidence stands, and the defence rests – Mt Oak exists – we did it!

It was not my intention to digress, but a few words of explanation are necessary to give some sort of background to this singular event in the history of the Australian alternative movement. I will stand corrected by others who may have been present at events prior to my arrival at Mt Oak, but this is a Table of Events as I understand it, and the sequence of events from my time at Mt Oak I can vouch for, as can others.

Mt Oak came into existence at the *Down To Earth Festival* at Bredbo, N.S.W., in 1977. A festival which celebrated the emerging alternative lifestyle and political thinking of young Australia.

Young Australia, not in just terms of age, but in terms of emerging from the old colonial paradigm; from the mind set which had embraced the White Australia Policy, the forcible removal of Aboriginal children from their natural parents, (we can give them a better life!), and which had, willy-nilly, seized lands, expropriated them without recompense, and gifted them to pastoralists. A mind-set which was being challenged in multitude of ways all over the globe, which embraced a glittering array of new possibilities and attitudes; ecological responsibility, sustainable agriculture, permaculture, alternative technology, renewable energy source, alternative lifestyles and social parameters.

These ideals needed a home, some place to manifest other than in the pages of polemic, or the rhetoric of yet another talkfest or seminar, somewhere where the word could be made flesh. In a spirit of youthful optimism, in the strength of a young movement uniting a disparate collection of aims and ideals it was decided at a public forum to purchase, by public subscription and donation, a parcel of land on which these ideals could be put into practice.

The land on which the Bredbo Festival was held was ultimately purchased by public donation, by the collection of monies in plastic buckets, given by the committed 'freaks' who believed a new world and a new Australia, which could be built this way. A new Australia, a new Jerusalem, in which all racial differences would be obliterated, all economic powerlessness would not matter, in which those who really cared about the welfare of Australia and the planet could work, practically, for the betterment of all humanity and could show the way forward to a world lost in the miasma of consumerism and under the ever-present threat of nuclear war, could show the way, whereby all humanity could live in harmony without depleting the finite resources of the planet. A shining example to all. And they collected the money! Enough dosh to purchase 2,800 acres of marginal, over-grazed, ring-barked, tree-stripped, drought-stricken, high-country, exhausted, dust-bowl land. Bless them, they did it! Poor deluded souls, they did it! Out of the torn pockets of their jeans, out of the notes secreted in the bra, out of the hoarded stash in the bank account, out of the plea to Mummy or Daddy, the race winnings, the money they would have spent on beer, or sex, or drugs, or fuel, or food, or whatever, bless them, they did it! And it stunned Australia!

Some gave their life savings, not inconsiderable amounts, only to be ultimately disillusioned. Some gave only what they had in their pockets or their purses, a dollar or two, only to be disillusioned, some gave their labour and their commitment, years of work, only to be disillusioned. One man gave his life. But all were ultimately vindicated for their faith and belief, even if they were not present to witness it. Mt Oak survived, against all odds, it survived and came into being.

There were many disputes over the land and its purchase. Some argued the Bredbo block was too marginal, too overgrazed and degraded, too harsh with its Death Valley climate, (minus 15C in mid-winter and 40C in summer, with an average of 14.5 inches rainfall!), others argued this was just the place to practice permaculture and land reclamation – if it could work at Mt Oak, it could work anywhere.

There were legal disputes too, involving the Alternative Life-style guru and one-time Deputy Prime Minister of Australia, Dr Jim Cairns, his charismatic assistant and personal secretary, Junie Morosi and her family and their 'community' and the Mt Oak Community Assn (Inc), the Mt Oak Trustees, (amongst whom the redoubtable Burnum-Burnum was numbered), and the many Friends of Mt Oak.

It was a long, protracted and bloody battle. It ended in a war of legal attrition, move and counter-move – a nightmare chess game for those on the land defending its freedom from those who would wrest ownership of something bought with public monies and turn it to their own ends.

The story of the community of Mt Oak, of those who stayed after that seminal festival, of those who came later having heard from various sources of the project, (and I was one of the latter), of those who gave from a distance and close up, of those who lived there, who worked there, who gave birth there and who died because of their faith in it, is legion.

Suffice it to say this is not the forum to examine all the weaknesses or the strengths of the community which arose from the debacle, from the ashes, of that event, other than the Mt Oak Community arose and fulfilled the enormous geas placed upon it; to defend the faith, to stand true to the concepts and precepts of its inception, to care for the land and see to its regeneration, to attempt to build a community of disparate souls who had only one thing in common; i.e. the defence of people's freed land, and the defence of the environment. All of this the Mt Oak Community acquitted beyond reproach.

They built dams. They key-lined slopes ravaged by over-grazing and planted native trees indigenous to the area, they erected propagation houses with irrigation systems to grow native plants specific to the area, they refused, in the face of official pressure to use pesticides and herbicides on the land to control the spread of exotic weeds, and when the shouting and screaming was over, the Government authorities brought their mandarins onto the property to show them just how native pasture could flourish when left to combat imported weeds. In short they succeeded.

There is not enough space to list all the achievements of the Mt Oak Community both on the land and within the broader community. One notable involvement was in the kampongs to save the Southeastern Forests in Coolongoobra and Tantawangalo. In these battles with the NSW Government, Mt Oak provided infrastructure for the forest camps, food and produce from its community gardens, and activists on the ground. It was a great effort.

Now I am no longer a member of that community. I left for personal reasons and the community as I knew it no longer exists in the forms I knew, but has developed into the forms it needs to meet its needs. Other people live there now and I am glad of that, I am glad the community continues.

Now that the issue of legal ownership has been resolved and the title vested in the Trustees, they and the Community Association are in the process of gifting the land to the local Koori people.

Personally I am in favour of this for a number of reasons. First, it places the land permanently in a 'no ownership' state. Even though there must be a 'legal owner' under Australia's British-based legal system and that will be the local Koori Land Council, the reality of the situation is, European legal niceties aside, that the Koori relationship to land is such that they consider themselves not to be 'owners', but rather

stewards. Second, and perhaps more importantly, it is a clear message to the people and the governments of Australia. We all know that Australia desperately needs reconciliation with its past. It needs some public act of reconciliation with the indigenous people of Australia, and, if our Prime Minister, the leader of the elected Federal Government of Australia cannot find it in his heart to say a simple *"sorry"* on behalf of the European invaders of this land, then I rather like to think the gifting of Mt Oak to the local, D people as a public act of reconciliation, as an example for our political masters to follow because it represents an acknowledgement of prior ownership. It is a gift given in peace from one people to another.

At the time of writing this, (7/10/99), I don't know what the final resolution of Mt Oak has been. I hear things from time to time on the grapevine via my family connections, but I have no direct contact with the community. As to the arson? Well, it was an alcohol inspired act of domestic violence which was, in reality, attempted murder. This was the house which my daughter Morgan's mother Rita, had built herself to house herself and her three children long before Morgan was born. She built it herself, from planing to roofpeak; it was sound, made from recycled materials, was solar powered and water self sufficient; it was weatherproof, warm and friendly and, as were all the houses at Mt Oak, was a statement of commitment to the land, the ecological guidelines, and to the spirit of the place. It was built with love and it didn't need to die that way, in a fit of rage and loose cannon passion.

It was the first home my daughter ever knew. She was on holiday with me here in Brisbane when she got the news, and I wish that bloke had been standing here to hear my daughter's keening, her grieving and mourning for the loss of her dreaming. Her wooden cradle, her hand made birthgift, had been in that house. I wish he could have heard that. No charges, perhaps tribal law will hold sway, who knows.

In some ways perhaps it is indicative of the new realities of Mt Oak, a shift into a new status, a new reality with all its attendant weaknesses and strengths. Who knows. Anyway I for one am glad it exists. The world is a better place for it, I'm glad I had the privilege of living there. Thankyou Mt Oak! Cheers I say!

Douglas Broad,
Brisbane, Australia.
7th October, 1999.

Going On Om 'bout Mook n' Shanto

Mook, the Merry Mookster, Be-Bop Bahloo, Mukki, Brendan Hanley. All his names; all aspects of his personality, rich, multi-faceted and a wild rovin'. And Shanto his partner; Earth Spirit and Gaia goddess, a flowing, flowering, deep and embracing being from the depths of Aquarius rising. I thought I'd love them when I first met through the Rainboweb internet site. And so it was when I saw the bearded one and his first lady a-waiting on my arrival on the Greyhound bus.

Mook n'Shanto

A meal, wine, much talk later and I was in their car heading for four days at their Bangalow home. A house and home redolent of their past. The site of many small festivals, the remains of a May-pole still lying in the barn at the bottom of their pasture. Our days together were a blur of miles travelled through the Rainbow Region, people met, places visited, words and ideas exchanged and many songs played, sung and shared. For those four days a kaleidoscope of their friends and experiences were replayed for me. People speaking of things much larger than life, or it felt that way. In American literature terms it would be like spending ninety hours with Timothy Leary, Ram Dass, Paul Bowles, Ken Kesey and William Burroughs with a bit of Janis Joplin and Joni Mitchell thrown in for good measure. It felt like stepping back in time. Here again were the sixties, alive and well, but peopled by many elders along with the braves. For the most of me, I couldn't help thinking that I'd travelled back to a home I knew so well, but somehow had just missed visiting.

I made the brief acquaintance of exquisite, almost imaginary places. The foreshore of Byron Bay, true surfie paradise, palm beaches and sweeps of white water surf. Byron Bay, originally called Cavanbah – the meeting place. Main Arm, deep in the rainforests, with its impeccably built hippy homes, on stilts, lush greens, strange stones, all accompanied by the constant cacophony of the forest's other inhabitants. One fabulous eccentric man-of-the-forest, Jim, even showed me his collection of stones complete with the faces in them – they held the spirits of the people and place, he told me.

In and around Nimbin (Nmbngee, small, wise old man in the native Bundjalung), artists, poets and musos people every crevice. Sure, there's the downside of dodgy drug deals and some pretty messed up lost souls on the streets, but the tolerance and enthusiasm of the region still catches the imagination, almost thirty years on from the original hippy invasion in the early seventies. Even in frontier town, Nimbin, there's a real sense of visiting a mystical space.

And Mook truly took on the role of co-pilot. Quite literally, driving me around the haunts and homes of the Rainbow Region's most colourful, together, independent and vital communards. True to their adopted Buddhist and Aboriginal names, Mook and Shanto Bahloo shared the essence of their adopted home area and its culture. Throughout the book, you're invited to join the trip, and journey inside that world through both their own tales and those of their friends and fellow voyagers.

On Om
Alan

Farewell to Byron

Brendan Hanley

We first moved to Byron Bay in 1976.

We were musician Brendan Hanley (now Mook) and singer Julie Oliver (now Shanto) and both of us had been successfully involved for many years in the jazz/rock – folk – Beatles-and-beyond music scene in Melbourne. We had known each other in this professional sphere and had worked in many bands and studios together over the previous eleven years. We were the very best of friends.

Now, both being free of our earlier marriages we met at a recording session, fell in love completely, got pregnant, sold up, packed up and headed North for the hills to have our baby. Shanto was well pregnant when we set off from Melbourne on April Fool's Day 1976. We had an engine blow up on us on the journey North from Melbourne. We were marooned for almost two weeks in an engineless small Luton-peak taxi-truck-converted-to-mini-campervan in a caravan park in the Southern New South Wales coastal town of Eden.

I remember looking across the once-pretty view at an oil refinery on the hill across the bay. The big BP sign dominating. Eden? I don't quite think so! But the long-term and totally rancid commercial exploitation of incredibly beautiful seaside towns was yet to really dawn on us. We had yet to encounter Byron Bay.

The history of Byron Bay which was to unfold itself to us over the next twenty or so years makes Eden's ugly oil refinery look like paradise indeed. Anyway we got our engine fixed and arrived in Byron Bay on April 19th 1976. It was pissing rain and didn't really stop until August that year. Our tiny 4lb 10oz baby daughter Nuro arrived on May 3, feet first in nearby Lismore base hospital. There was just one midwife up here at the time and she had only delivered two babies to date, so we thought it best for the safety of mother and child to have her in hospital, knowing she was in breach position. No humidicribs were available at Byron, hence the move to Lismore.

After a week in Lismore, and because she was too tiny to be allowed to leave the Hospital, we had her moved back to Byron Hospital which now had a free humidicrib. So we parked our campervan in the First Sun Caravan Park opposite the hospital to be close to her, and that van was to be her home for the first seven months of her life. The First Sun is also opposite the Police Station, and that later became extremely relevant.

At that time in Byron Bay, there were four cops, three pubs and a meatworks which employed about half the men and women in a town with a total population of 3,000. There were fables afoot about dope barons and big deals in the surrounding hills, and the in-crowd gathered nightly in a bar-restaurant in town called Dinty's, later to be Julian Rocks and still later for many years the home of Earth and Sea, Byron's famous pizza house.

The Dole Officer, a Murwillumbah Real Estate Agent, would come to town every two weeks and take your forms from a back office in a local shop. He insisted on footwear being worn, and you had to give him good reasons why you wouldn't take a job at the meatworks. Some days when the wind blew across town from the Belongil killing fields, the smell would almost make you retch. Work there? We were vegetarians! It was against our religion! Allergic to blood and guts! Besides we were purchasing the first four-track studio in the area and planning to set up a Singing, Music and Performing Arts Studio/School in the Literary Institute Hall, with our recording facilities as part of the deal. We were hoping to offer an option other than the meatworks when kids were making career decisions, and to establish a self-supporting business.

The Literary Institute Hall, by the way, was a huge tropical theatre, all open along the top of the walls with latticework. It had a full stage, cinema screen and those wonderful canvas deck chair seats that you could once find all over Australia's tropical North in similar buildings, all of which have been pulled down and replaced with air-conditioned modern complexes. At the front of the Literary Institute were two floors of office-type rooms and a smaller hall, all of which still remain as of the writing of this article, but which are earmarked for the wrecker soon in the face of a new Community Centre. A hot subject around town!

Despite concern over the loss of the old Literary Institute facade, a most welcome Performance Theatre has been included in plans for the new complex and we performers see that as extremely overdue good news for the town, locals and visitors alike. We had a band that we formed in Melbourne and we reformed again in Byron. We called ourselves 'BAHLOO' which is a Goori (Goori or Koori – a word local Native Australians use to describe themselves) word for 'Moon God'. A benevolent male figure we understood, whose job it was to protect women and children. We asked permission from an elder to use the name and it was granted.

We wanted to run our own gigs and so we purchased a lightweight Yamaha PA system on the never-never from a Murwillumbah music retailer who liked us. To run a gig in Byron meant you had to deal with the local Sergeant, whom I'll call Sergeant Bone! Now this subject calls for a little history. Not many years prior to this time, it was quite common to see headlines and photos on the front pages of the more lurid daily rags – with feature articles exploiting bloody gang wars in the streets of this obscure little Northern NSW abattoirs town called Byron Bay. Because not only was it a meatworks town but it just happens to have at least seven top surf beaches which are world acclaimed, and because some of the beaches face different directions due to the geographic shape of the cape, there's nearly always a break somewhere that can pull a crowd...regardless of wind direction or weather conditions.

So surfers have always congregated here, especially on weekends. And so did aggro bikie gangs. And blood would be shed on the streets of Byron outside the top pub, and the gutter press loved it: 'GANG WARS IN SMALL TOWN!' and it became an issue...and they sent in Sergeant Bone!

Stories say that Bone was the 'Dirty Harry' of the NSW Police Force. A top marksman and karate expert, it is alleged that he arrived in town and straightaway strode up to the biggest bikie and the biggest surfer and banged their heads together, putting them both in hospital and putting an end to the Byron street wars once and for all. He was later to remind me on many an occasion that is was 'his' town, but I'll get to that in a minute.

Our particular saga started with a free concert we held in the Beach Park next to the Surf Club. We set up our new little P.A. and cruised off onto some cool sounds by the seaside. A small appreciative crowd gathered and sat on the grass beneath the big pine trees and we got off together for a while. After one set of beautiful tropical music had drifted out through the trees and into the town and the surf we were approached by a uniformed Council Officer and ordered to shut down or face being arrested. We were told there had been complaints about 'noise'. The pub over the road had the loudest bands in the area raging most nights. We were playing sweet songs and light rock through miniature equipment in a park in the middle of the afternoon!

After that, we sought permission to run dances for youth in a string of halls around town, but were always moved on after the event for some curious reason or other. We began to run out of halls. I would wait in the police station for an interview with the Sergeant each time we decided to try another venue. On many occasions he would stand up and bang the table with his fist, literally going purple in the face and screaming his absolute edicts into the air: *"Don' t try selling drugs in this town and don't ever try to get the Literary Institute off me! This is MY town!"*

I would assure him that I intended to do neither of those things, get his permission for our latest venture and then go about getting posters up and articles in the paper for the new gig. I also began to write a weekly column for the *Byron News* which was owned by Reg Wright, a renowned local musician. We had become friends with his son John, who had a band locally and the whole thing was working out well. I had a column called *North Coast Music Notes* and used the name BeBop (as in BeBop Bahloo!). This name still surfaces once or twice a month even to this day, especially in Nimbin where BeBop and Julie were to have such high profiles in the years after the events described here.

In my column, I would review all the local music, flog gigs (especially ours) and forecast bigger better days for music in the area. 'Australia's Nashville' in fact was where I was constantly heading with my scenarios. We were befriended at this time by a remarkable old man who was a true part of Byron's history, Tony Kibblewaite, whose story is too long and complex to deal with here, but who nevertheless played a key role in our first encounter with Byron Bay and the powers that be.

Tony, imported long ago from Brit at age 14, was by now a village elder, and had an eye open and a hand out to help people find suitable cheap accommodation when settling in the area. He was known as the 'hippy-lover' by the more red-neck element in town and suffered indignities and torment at the hands of the local cops, who obviously saw any new hippyish person or behaviour in town as a potential threat to their drug monopoly among other things.

This is quite normal in NSW particularly. It has always been the case, beginning with the original police who were known as the 'Rum Corps' because they controlled the rum and liquor supplies, the popular drugs of their day. Nothing much has changed! Bone and his henchman Giblet were alleged to have committed many an outrage on vulnerable little people in the cells late at night, and their treatment of Tony Kibblewaite and others that we met certainly supported this allegation.

Early one morning, we found an 18-year-old boy crying, all curled up in a foetal position on the beach. We took him home and comforted him, and he told us that he had been picked up drunk the night before by Bone and Giblet and beaten all night in the cell. He was a mess.

When the Bone and Bahloo thing was at its peak we were in the nearby town of Lismore one day in a secondhand furniture store which is now Harts Restaurant, when a young woman approached us from behind.
"Are you the people who are having all the trouble with Sergeant Bone?" she asked.
"Yes."
"I just want you to know that he killed my girlfriend!"
"WHAT????"
"They got her in the cells and raped her over and over one night. The next morning she began a crusade of standing on

the corner (where Rockmans is now) and when the police would drive by she would point at them and scream hysterically to all and sundry 'They raped me! Those Fucking Bastards raped me!' She disappeared and was found dead 'drowned' up near the meatworks a few days later."

I'm not making any accusations, just reporting what we were told, but if she's right, there will be a reported drowning of a girl near the meatworks in late 75 or early 76 in the *Byron News* or the *Northern Star* or even the now defunct *Advocate*, if any investigative journo wants to dig up some dirt.

Anyway the cops burnt down old Tony's sheds and huts where he was allowing 'hippies' to live, and they left this dear old man locked in the back seat of one of those cars with only front doors, so he couldn't get out and couldn't open any windows. He told us that he wondered how he was going to survive the six-hour ordeal – he thought he was going to die of heat and suffocation! More on Tony in a moment, but it was through him that we found out that a committee, which included Tony, administered the Literary Institute…and of which committee Bone was only one voice. So we rather naively contacted the chairman and put in a written request for the hire of the theatre for the aforementioned purposes of music/recording/performing arts etc.

This of course was to be our undoing – a fatal mistake as you will see! We got a letter in reply from the committee asking us to appear in person and present our case to them all, and await their decision. Because we had been whipping it all up in the paper every week, quite a little crowd had gathered in support outside the building on the night of the meeting. We arrived, went inside when called, and presented our full game plan for the almost disused centre (except for ZZZ grade movies on alternate weekends nothing ever happened there!). The committee included Bone sitting right at the back and avoiding eye contact with us.

I felt good vibes and good eye contact with the most of the committee, especially the women who were obviously thinking of their kids' futures in that smelly town. There was a question time and we got grilled but it was cool, then we were asked to go outside and await the decision. We stood outside for maybe twenty minutes surrounded by fans, band members and assorted supportive souls when the lawyer who was their spokesperson came out and announced to us all that the request to use the theatre had been denied by the committee. He turned on his heel and left us on the street, dumbfounded and without any more cards to play in this town.

The next day a friend turned up with some GoldTop mushrooms (Psylocibin) and we were all tripping the light fantastic around the Caravan Park (where by now, we had gathered a whole gypsy/hippy camp around us) when we saw two shiny unmarked cars arrive at the Police Station – which is coincidentally just across the road from where we were camping. Old Tony, who had been at the meeting turned up at our van with tears in his eyes. He knew we weren't long for this town.

He told us:
"After you gave your talk and went outside last night, Bone got up and told the committee that you (pointing to Shanto) are a big time drug dealer from Melbourne, and he's going to run you out of town!"
He had $200 cash in his hand, which he offered us to assist our soon-to-be forced relocation. We refused the money and talked with Tony for a while. It was obvious that Bone had decided to target Shanto because he knew that my father was a retired Police Superintendent and that I could cover my tracks with all my know how and know who! Shanto on the other hand was a gentle little woman with a brand new baby girl, fresh out of the humidicrib, so she was almost an icon of vulnerability. Right up these big bullies' alley!

That afternoon there was a knock on our van door and I opened it to confront three characters looking like rejects from the Mod Squad casting couch, saying they were busted on the way up from Sydney and could I do the right thing and sell 'em a deal of grass because you know how it is and you wouldn't let a fellow dope smoker down would you and all that bullshit!!! From the surreal heights of the Goddess Cilla I looked straight through these alien vapours drifting around my van and suggested that it was well known that the cops did the drugs in this town, and seeing as their cars were parked over there they were obviously friendly enough with the local boys in blue they ought to go and cut a deal with them!

The next day, tripping again, I picked up the *Byron News* and

opened to the editorial article. The lines on the page slithered evilly like snakes even before I got to read a single word. Anticipating and assisting our demise, Reg Wright, the good editor had done a complete turnaround, and despite many letters to the editor in support of us and our bid on the hall, Reg excused what was about to happen to us with the following words:
"Let it be said that prejudice always exists between us all – and this applies especially to strangers before they can establish their bona fides or prove to the locals that they are fair dinkum! This prejudice is often heightened if our lifestyles are different and we are sorry that Brendan and his associates feel as they do. Let us assure Bahloo we welcome all newcomers, whether their interest is community or commercial – but we must be sure it is for the good of us all. This is not always easy to determine."

My trip suddenly died in the arse and survival stuff started gripping my insides. The Caravan Park Manager called me into his office.
"I've been told by Sergeant Bone to tell you to move on out of here pronto!"
"What will happen if we don't?"
"They usually find drugs in your campsite the next day!"

So we panicked and headed for the hills, ending up in Nimbin on and off for the next seven years before returning to the coast, but that's a whole other story. Bone had the hall demolished and removed under some fire regulation, so it could never happen again. The town has been without a large community-access performance space ever since. Sergeant Bone's reputation got worse and more widespread and he was kicked upstairs somewhere and died of a stroke or heart attack not long after. Que sera sera. Giblet? Still out there I guess.

Song: Farewell to Byron
©Hanley/Oliver

Chorus:
And I'm sittin' around
In this meatworks town
Watchin' the seabirds play
It's rainin' again
And the sea's closed in
And it's farewell to old Byron Bay

Now the cops in this town
Keep the young people down
And nobody questions why
It's the same old rerun
Of the man with the gun
And the people with fear in their eyes
With their pubs and their clubs
And their RSLs
And the churches all empty and dark
And the kids on the corner
With nothin' to do
And no place to hang but the park

Chorus

Now the man come round
From the Council Hall
And he says that there's been a complaint
From the citizens
Of this one horse town
Who don't like the music that we make
But those same good folks
Who called in the cops
To break up our sunshine show
Put up with all the noise
From the pubs every night
So – who's foolin' who I'd like to know?

P.S. In case you're interested in a potted history of Byron Bay our website http://rainboweb.com has Eric Wright's (yes brother of Reg) famous Old Byron collection online – and in this case, a picture is truly worth a million words.

The Nimbin Allstars
Nimbin Music Halcyon Days 1978
Brendan Hanley

Nimbin Country Sheilahs
©Hanley/Oliver

Chorus
How I love those Nimbin country sheilahs
Goddesses in three part harmony
Far away from the noise and the wheeler dealers
Stone the crows it's Nimbin girls for me

Now Nimbin girls are good at homebirth babies
In the scrub or up a Mango tree
They can cure the mumps or even rabies
With lots of love and cups of herbal tea

Now this Nimbin sheilah took me in the moonlight
She sat me down and landed on me knee
She raised her pretty skirt and grabbed her banjo
And sat till sunrise serenading me

Now when I die and make me way to heaven
At those pearly gates I know I'll see
The angel choirs are packin' up and leaving
The Nimbin sheilahs are there on God's TV

Fleeing from the cops in Byron Bay in late 1976 we landed at the Garden House (an old farmhouse on the property used for communal purposes) at Tuntable Falls Community. This was the Community that sprang up as a by-product, or rather to some extent a continuum of the Aquarius Festival and the first Multiple Occupancy (MO) experiment in the country.

We had our portable recording studio and had been invited by Terry McGee, a Tuntable pioneer, to join the Community and move into the Garden House (at least temporarily) until something more appropriate was found.

A $500 share meant you could find a spot on the Community holdings, erect a flag to the height of your proposed building, and providing nobody objected, attending any one of three subsequent monthly Tribal meetings, you could build a house there.To say this idea has been abused over the years would be a gross understatement, and except for small numbers of families, say 4 to 8, the MO is not a recommended method of land sharing…certainly not by this writer!

Many new settlers came in the wake of the Festival, and in fact continue to do so to this day, in ever increasing numbers. They rented old farmhouses and refurbished old disused dairy sheds (known locally as cow bails), and banana sheds, chook pens, pig sties, you name it. Caravans, campers and tents were the home of many a family while the labour and love of building the first hippy homes took place. Nobody had television or videos, satellite TV, Internet or even a local cinema.

We had come fresh from Byron Bay where we had been, albeit unsuccessfully, involved in lots of entrepreneurial activity. The most successful of our Byron ventures had been the Folk Club which we co-founded with local singer-songwriter Ray Sorenson, and which had produced some great nights of music despite all the difficulties we had had with increasingly unavailable venues.

We were told that we had been misinformed as to the availability of the Garden House for our purposes and were forced to leave Tuntable three days after our arrival there. Our Tuntable time was yet to come!

A friend was vacating a rented farmhouse which nestled in the valley below the nearby misty mountain they call Blue Knob. Here we set up our four-track studio and dug our first garden. The rent was $12 per week and the garden kicked arse! We kept a fairly low profile and met very few people for many months, but then one day Ray Sorenson, whom we had left behind during the Byron debacle, turned up at Blue Knob and took up residence out in the cow bails on the property.

It was the height of gold-top mushroom season.

It wasn't long until we were jamming again with Ray and an expanding bunch of musical hippie friends. We soon found ourselves making plans for a Nimbin Folk Club. One night Ray turned up and said that he had put up signs around town for the opening night on the following Tuesday. We weren't happy with his choice of nights but took the PA along on the appointed evening and set up the show.

A good crowd turned up, but we had a lot of trouble with drunks lurching in from the pub next door and ruining many a fine performance…and making it impossible to get a clean recording of a night's music for radio play and possible product cassettes. This problem was to plague us for many months until we decided to change to Sunday nights, when the pub was shut.

Crowds began to increase and the quality of the music grew in step with audience attention and participation. People seemed to get enraptured by singing along. It turned the whole thing into something much more than a performance. By combining our spirits and harmonising together we would always invoke that 'heavenly' ambience and loving feeling that churches continue to usurp and make money and wield power out of over the centuries.

We were doing what tribes have done and do to this day; realigning and revitalising our personal and collective vibrations with music, made mostly with our own voices and percussion. Since throwing the church away as a generation we have inadvertently thrown the baby out with the bath water, and except for the odd choir recital or the odd Festival or Workshop, it doesn't happen much in people's lives any more – if at all!

I miss those days like mad!

I began writing songs for crowds to learn and sing instantly, and hung a sign in the Folk Club venue window. The venue was an ex-general store now called the Tomato Sauce, because of the advertisement left on one of the top windows from former days.

My sign said, 'Nimbin State Choir meets here. Members wanted. Wednesday 2pm.'

About 18 women and 5 men turned up and we had a ball. Weekly numbers of similar size would show up and a core group began to develop. Now the Folk Club nights would end traditionally with a big jam, consisting of a few guitars and mandolins and usually me on banjo, We'd have bass, percussions galore and the odd tin whistle or saxophone...and usually a dozen or so voices...and the audience joining in as familiarity and spirit would allow. It was incredible!

The Folk Clubs, dress-up balls and fundraisers were nothing short of religious happenings. Pagan rituals of immense power and community value. Some friends of ours came over one night at our invitation to a ball we were throwing in the Town Hall as a fundraiser to buy a car for popular midwife Carol Eliot and her partner Norman.

They commented halfway through the night in the illegal haze that pervaded that it looked like a scene from a story like *Alice in Wonderland* or some other such fairytale. Tripped out princesses floated Ophelia-like around the edge of the dancing throngs. As the band pumped out reggae-with-a-pinch-of-Nimbin, jesters and fools, gnomes and elves, kings and warriors, funkies, spunkies and no junkies, did court and spark merrily with goddesses, princesses, bawdy bitches, nasty nuns, pretty pretty flower power maidens, fairies and witches, spacey lacey's and good time country mamas...Nimbin country sheilahs!

**David Hallett
(a little later in life!)**

The colour, the vibe, the music was magic. We were undergoing our usual Australian 10-year time lag on the rest of the world. We were having the 60's in Nimbin in 1978. It was still before the ultra-materialistic 80's and hope was still alive that maybe all you DO need is love, and that we could still save the world.

High times, halcyon days, golden age, cosmic events...it all happened and practically nothing remains on record! And the crowds grew to overflow as the reputation of the Folk Club grew. Assured of a good audience, travelling acts from the likes of ABC's Musica Viva circuit would drop in for a spot and blow our minds. Assured of a great night of spirit and music, punters would come from the Gold Coast or Grafton, up to two hours or so drive away from Nimbin.

Then someone suggested we take the whole thing to Sydney! Dudley Leggett put up the first $100 and David Hallett jumped on the phone and began hustling gigs in Sydney! Great leaping Leos!

Easter Sunday 1978 was the big night. Most of the afternoon a certain un-named trio sat rolling dozens of joints out of a big bag of primo buds. The Folk Club burst its seams that night. People sat on every inch of the floor and stood where necessary, spilling out onto the street. This night was the inspiration for my song 'Ned' and the story and lyrics are built on the description which follows.

The first half of the night, the solo, duo and trio spots went well. We took our interval and prepared to set up the big group that was to go to Sydney, about twenty on stage as I recall. So while

this is a line of no relevance at all

Alternative Australia.... 24

stagehands started shifting microphones and such around, many dozens of joints made from the finest buds, were thrown into the audience like sweets thrown by the clown at a pantomime.

And like kids at a pantomime people scuffled, shuffled and scruffled each other in a childlike frenzy to be an early recipient of this sudden bounty. The place went berserk, and into uproar. Then the blue smoke began to fill the air, the odd cough rang out, and bit by bit the noise diminished to a murmur and beyond into reverent stoned silence.

We had the perfect audience…and they had the perfect show. And we all had real communion. No bread or wine, no bullshit and no collection plate. Well not usually that is, but this night was a fundraiser to help move a large group of local people to Sydney, which was over 800 kilometres away. It was a most memorable night of music and spirit…and if you can remember it…you weren't there!

And so was born the 'Nimbin Allstars'!

In broken down cars, kombis and campers we shuffled down the Pacific Highway to Sydney. We were a motley crew, all 35 of us, musoes, singers, masseurs, cooks, tarot readers, children and their minders and several pounds of local greenery in a pillowcase hidden inside the bass drum!

The car we had been loaned to drive down began to fall apart about halfway through the journey, and finally coughed and spluttered to a halt 100 metres from our city destination. Most of us took up temporary residence on the floor of an old empty brick Church Hall in Balmain before David Hallett pulled off yet another of his amazing entrepreneurial coups…Hawthornden!

Somewhere in the backblocks of inner suburban Woollahra, Hallett stumbled over an old castle-like mansion set in treed grounds avec tennis court, owned by a Porsche-driving man called Sam. It was currently inhabited by about twenty city dwellers who together paid the massive rent for the privilege of living in one of the myriad rooms, maids or servants quarters, attics, cellars or cubby holes that tunnelled the place like a rabbit warren.

Hallett knew somebody here and somehow got them to agree to us – *maybe kinda you know – a few of us – camping for a night or two…nothin' serious, know what I mean?* It was a fait accompli that confronted the hapless residents of the old mansion. By the time most of them got home from work one fateful day back in 1978, the house had been invaded by a tribe of musical hippies, and the captured ballroom was littered with blankets and sleeping bags, kids, guitars, bongo drums…and we spread out into the kitchen and lounge-room and bathrooms and in and out of the rabbit warren.

The dazed residents had an emergency house meeting and after registering their shock and disappointment at not having been consulted prior to our sudden arrival, they graciously moved over spiritually and let us share their old place in true communal style. The music, the parties, the interaction, the events physical, mental and spiritual that took place between them and us, (and the mobs of visitors who flocked in over the next two weeks) would fill a book on their own. Suffice it to say that it was a totally wild, neo-tribal, mostly harmonious musical moment in all our lives. A neverending party basically centred around the mostly musical meeting and meshing of all the different personalities and a certain pillowcase full of primo sinsemilla, imported all the way to the city from the foothills of Nimbin.

Hallett and Paul Joseph dug up primo gigs as well.

Somehow, with practically no notice and no resources we were working at the Paddington Town Hall (first ever Marijuana Party Green Ball), Paddo Church Hall, Martin Plaza at lunchtime to maxi-crowds, the New Awareness Centre...gigs were miraculously manifest...and we blew 'em away every time, if only by sheer weight of numbers!

The Green Ball was memorable to say the least! We were twenty-three colourful people on stage, a mini-community with mega-goodvibes and the cohesion that comes with singing together regularly! All this fresh country energy was pumped to

© John McCormick

a large and freaky wondercrowd through a massive PA that was later in the night to deliver mega-loud Punk and Hard Rock to the punters!

It was such a blast!

Australia's favourite actor, Jack Thompson came backstage to meet us and was extremely enthusiastic, especially about our songs and Shanto's immeasurable qualities. We have remained good friends ever since, and I am proud to say that to this day, Jack is an enthusiastic supporter of our music and even performs several of our songs. I am fantasising doing a CD with him one of these years!

So back in Sydney, the impact of such a large group of fresh-from-the-country hippies, all groovy guys and gorgeous girls, playing and singing their hearts out about stuff they believed in, was overwhelming! And people rose to the occasion as individuals within the format of the overall show. Everyone who took a solo spot, with only the odd exception, was fantastic. And together we were awesome!

And after the gigs we would end up around the big fireplace at

Hawthornden, jamming late into the night, and swapping stories and laughs with the residents and visitors. Then out of nowhere Sam the owner turned up, black Porsche and all, and announced that we ALL had to leave. He had Hawthornden up for sale, to be demolished and redeveloped!

So most of the Allstars drifted back home to Nimbin. We stayed on in Sydney, singing in the streets, and ended up getting somewhat involved in the war on busking that was going on. But that's another story.

Johnno – the last of the Dope Barons?

An article/interview by Brendan Hanley

When I first came to the Rainbow Region in 1974 my search for 'the real thing', was fed by rumours of fabled, legendary, even mythological creatures living in the hills...dingoes in the McKellar Ranges, yowies on the Black Butt Plateau...and dope barons in Main Arm, Mullumbimby. Not that you'll meet many these days, although if you try really hard, it's possible to come across the odd ex-dope baron. They're pretty pathetic cases, as you would expect of defrocked Royalty, usually addicted to alcohol, self-hatred and the unproductive TV consumer lifestyle. Normal sort of people really!

On the other hand there's people who sell and use cocaine and other crap, or who own hotels, or medical clinics, chemists, tobacco retailers...they're the only drug dealers who can claim the 'Baronial' title these days. The Halcyon days of 'Mullumbimby Madness' are over. No longer do the descendants of Ned Kelly, Captain Starlight and Lightning Jack reap the vast bounty of mega kilos of primo red-haired sinsemilla and smuggle it over for a small fortune to the bottomless marijuana marketplace. The baby-boomers, who have been the mainstay of the bush-buds market are either dead or dying or feeling like dying or smoking a lot less, if at all, in an effort to keep from being dead or dying –for a little while longer.

Ecstasy and hydroponic buds have completely cornered the city and youth markets that used to devour tonnes of local produce. Someone told me that there are about 20 different brands of grow-your-own-hydro kits currently available in Sydney. Also, you can click up a website or two in Amsterdam that will supply by airmail, seeds chosen from a downloadable catalogue listing 2,000 different varieties of Cannabis. Strains can be short term, long term, Hawaiian, Skunk, Thai Buddha, Durban Poison...specially bred hydro supershit...a veritable smorgasbord of mindblowing choices to make! The seeds arrive...into the wardrobe, in with the chemies; on with the lights...set your watch...three months to the day you harvest! Easy to control market supply and demand! No random factors like drought, wallabies, thieves, helicopters, floods, weed inspectors, bushfires, termites and all the rest! Just watch your electricity bill. If it starts to equal the local movie theatre or arc-welding workshop you might look a bit suss!

Meanwhile, back in the bush, frequent, incessant helicopter attacks, fanatical policing and hanging judiciary have reduced the average dope plot size to a level that could only be considered 'for personal use only'! As I write, two police choppers are combing the local countryside at great public expense, scaring the shit out of people and their kids, needlessly harassing thousands of innocent families, traumatising animals and chasing terrified chooks into the bush never to be seen again...and the guys in them are acting like macho dickheads out of some Rambo remake...and guess what? It's not 1930 any more!

Droughts and other natural hazards have further trimmed these small plots to even smaller yields. So real present day barons with substantial holdings are hard to find. There are consistent stories about one particular baron in a local valley hereabouts who seems to have pulled off the impossible dream...he's been able to buy up most of the valley around him without ever having been seen to do a tap of work in the outside world, although it's common knowledge he arrived up here over 20 years ago with nary a cracker to his name. Like some hippy hideaway Howard Hughes, he has built himself a dream house with a plethora of state-of-the-art electronic gadgetry and other expensive trivia on board. Apparently he has never been busted in all these years, helicopter intensives and all, although all of his dope-growing (share-cropping for him) neighbours have! He refers to himself as the 'Mayor' of his valley!

Anyway the closest I could get to a real dope baron was a bloke I'll call Johnno, who used to hire local people in the season to come and clean and manicure his legendary heads for a hundred bucks a day...plus you got to keep your favourite bud of the day! Johnno has spent whatever money he made on trips to Bali and red wine as far as I can tell. He's a shadow of his former self really, but a great guy to interview.

"How long have you been growing dope up here Johnno?"

"Aw, about 18 or 19 years!"

"So how come you're not a millionaire dope baron like the cops reckon?"

As Johnno had been toking rather intensely on a giant scoobie when I asked this question, he laughed for a second, caught his breath on the smoke, then totally lost it in a paroxysm of coughing, wheezing, sneezing, burping and farting great clouds of smoke simultaneously from every orifice in his body, lying in a foetal position in the middle of his dope patch, kicking and gasping, struggling for breath...dying, in fact, of laughter! So much for my attempt at a serious interview with a dope baron! What emerged instead was more like a tragi-comedy of Ned Kelly proportions, probably being acted out by thousands of other Johnnos and Jillos around these hills, and by millions around the globe.

Johnno is a middle-aged ex-advertising man who grew his first dope plant in his Balmain backyard in the mid sixties when people wore 'Legalise Pot' badges, bought and sold primo buds for $30 per ounce and believed that marijuana was not only safe and fun, but that it was one of the main solutions to all the problems besetting humanity...AND that its liberation was just around the corner.

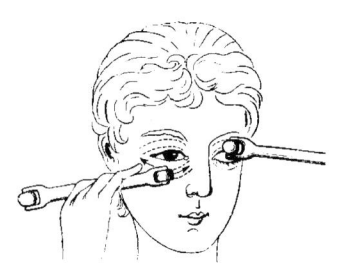

Two ingenious systems for smuggling dope

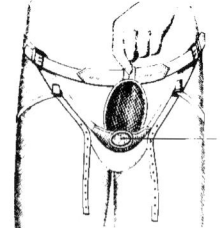

Now, going on 40 years later and almost 70 years after hemp's corporation-instigated prohibition, a teary-eyed Johnno claws himself upright on the trunk of a 15 foot heading female Hawaiian skunk plant, snorts a deep sniff on one of the big purple buds and gathers enough chi to unfold his tale of fear and loathing in the hills. It is the tale of a global war waged by a massive private army against harmless people, and against what is widely believed to be the world's most useful plant...a plant that many native tribes and most stoned hippies believe could easily have come from another planet.

"This plant's unreal", he croaks, *"Fuggin' unreal man! And if it wasn't for us Hippies and Rastas, a few Babas, Pygmies and Paysanos, the bloody plant'd be wiped off the face of the Earth by the Americans by now. Even as we speak the D.E.A. are spraying the shit out of Africa, having already rooted Mexico and South America with squillions of gallons of Paraquat! Some chemi-company is making a mint out of toxing all that land and all those people."*

"But hang on – everyone's talking about decriminalisation these days. You should be happy about that!"

"No way mate! What they'll do is fine everybody say $100 or so for being caught with a bud or two. That way they make a fortune without court or jail costs...then they get righteously heavy and do things like death penalties and shit like that for 'drug pushers' Then they define drug pushers as anyone who sells anything at all illegal – including the old herb – and WHAMMO! They've got the market sewn up, and they've got us all tagged as dangerous criminals. They'll nuke us!"

"What about the idea of being able to grow a few plants for personal use, like in Canberra?"

"Yeah sure! 5 fuggin' plants! Big deal! That's just part of the plan to screw the gene pool and exterminate the species! Anyway, out of five miserable bloody plants, three will be male and therefore useless, one will get eaten by termites, grubs or wallabies, and the fifth will turn hermaphrodite at the last

moment in order to fertilize itself and continue the line. HOW INBRED CAN YOU GET? Five plants is fatal for the gene pool, no sweat!"

"What's all this about turning hermaphrodite?"

"Well it's just my theory but I reckon in a good wet year you'll get lots of females and a few big males whose job it is to spoof pollen all over the females to create seeds. Because it's a fertile, wet season, they get lots of seeds out of lots of females...a year of plenty! But in these mega-dry years, the plants freak out and lots of 'em turn male, or hermaphrodite – a bit of both, with male and female flowers so it can produce its own seeds. This also makes sure that the few females left get plenty of pollen; insuring some fertilized seeds to keep the strain alive. It's a fail-safe!"

"What does this mean to the dope grower?"

"Disaster mate! Males aren't worth a pinch of shit! They flower up – SPOOF! – and waste away. Real blokes mate! Useless after they come! And this year, everyone I know lost heaps of good big females to this process. It was a disaster!"

"Was the rain too late?"

"Mate! The bloody rain really capped it off. A couple of weeks of pissing down on your almost mature heads, the plants drooping into mud puddles, the great buds all black and soggy, the hash all washed off the polyps, seeds sprouting on the plants – the bloody grubs, rotting buds – and then picking in the pissing rain and then trying to dry the stuff and cure it during the floods. People everywhere in sheds, bails, houses, cabins, tents, chook pens and caravans – hanging it up, spreading it out on paper, with fans, radiators, pot-belly stoves, gas heaters, paper bags on the clothesline full of mull pegged out in the occasional scarce sunshine! Shit mate, it's a miracle there's any ganja this year at all!"

"So it wasn't a good harvest?"

"Well any harvest is a good one – but it's getting tough enough with wallabies and termites, cops and helicopters and ripoff merchants pinching crops without having to deal with droughts

and floods in the same bloody season."

"Are you saying that there's no big crops, no fabled fortunes, no dope barons any more?"

"Yeah there's still a handful, like in any game, who kick goals consistently. The rest of us just plod along. Anyway I don't know how anyone gets away with having too much cash lately. They'd be onto you! As it is, the local Chambers of Commerce computer sales figures must go through the roof this time of year – the D.E.A. must be watching all this fiscal activity. I know

so many people who buy brushcutters and chainsaws, cars, washing machines and fridges, solar panels – all kinds of shit – world holidays – I know one bloke who goes overseas every year – takes his family and a few mates with him if he's had a good year. I know another bloke who lives out there in his nice owner-built house – looks pretty normal on the outside – open the door and it's like Dr. Who's bloody laboratory inside! Computers, faxes, videos, betacams, hi-f4 giant TV. screen, microwaves, big fridge/freezer – the works! He'd have a hard time explaining where he got all that shit!"

"And the business houses around here must love this time of year. I remember going to a well-known local restaurant a few years back. I met the owner at the door and asked him if I could negotiate a dinner for two in exchange for a baggy of mull. He grinned, grabbed the bag and said, 'God I love it up here this time of year. Look!' He stepped aside to let us in. The place was nearly full. At every table sat a hippy couple in conversation over a bottle of wine – and this was Wednesday night – and it happens every year! We should be famous for it, exploit it, like the wine harvest in France or the German beer fests. It'd be a hoot!"

"How would it work?"

"Like Amsterdam mate. Civilized! You know! You rock up to the Channon Market or Bangalow – and me and me mates are there – we've got our own stalls – and you come and browse – have a try. You know! Leaf for cooking and herb teas, leaf and tip for the timid smoker, buds, nuggets, seedless sinsimilla, deals of kiff, and even hand-rolled hash man! Boy! Watch the local economy jump then! Oh yeah and I've got this other mate who makes awesome hash oil!"

Johnno reached into his camouflage overalls pocket and pulled out an old Erinmore tobacco tin. He squatted down on his haunches and rolled a neat little one-paper racehorse out of dark green and bright orange mango-smelling 'buds of doom',

which he had chopped up religiously with a pair of mini-scissors.

"Look! Hemp papers!" He held up the packet.

"Unreal mate! Fuggin' unreal! They can make any fuggin' thing out of this plant mate! But paper's the big one. Not one more tree ever needs to be cut for paper. Do you realise that? And hemp seeds man...they contain chlorophyll, protein and fatty acids essential for the human immune system. Hemp oil is totally missing from the planetary diet – and look what's happening. We don't need antibiotics man – we need hemp seeds! Jesus man, the critters know what's good for 'em. If you've got seedy dope around the house, bush rats and mice'll eat nothing else until all the seeds are gone. No wonder they're so bloody healthy!"

Johnno lit up, took a big toke, held his breath, then exhaled into the foliage around his face. He raved on about people in cattle trucks being dragged away at dawn during the infamous Tuntable Falls bust, the Main Arm Mullumbimby chopper raids and intensive road blocks, smart arse cops shooting holes in people's water tanks, the naked guy running into the bush they shot dead in Kuranda, the insane local magistrate who froths at the mouth when a dope case appears in his court – how he'd love the death sentence – the set-ups and busts, the narcs, weed inspectors, choppers, 4 wheel drives and trail bikes, the D.E.A. and the black-uniformed, armed-to-the-teeth, scare police from the 'Plantation Squad'. All this aimed at ordinary people with a few proven-harmless plants in their backyards, while the smack and crack and coke and speed and bad acid, eccys, booze, tobacco and myriad legal pills and thrills flood the world and injure and kill millions of people every year.

Police likeness of Johnno?

Almost to himself, he mused: "Every mate of mine in Sydney has a dead friend from smack...and it's top quality now and *much cheaper than marUana...they're killing our kids mate..."*

Sitting in his dope patch with six or seven heading female cannabis sativa plants ingeniously hidden in lantana and backed in under a big old Sally Wattle, I had to agree with Johnno that it looked a trifle crazy...lopsided...dishonest even, the way this particular plant was getting clobbered all over the planet when it can provide so much, and when so many people love it and use it regularly instead of more harmful chemical stuff and particularly smack. But then that's the way it is with everything, isn't it?

"You know" he concluded, smoking the roach which he held to his lips in a split match.
"They say there's a little jigger in the brain which is only activated by one outside agent –THC (the active ingredient in cannabis). Nothing else does anything to it or affects it in any way. Only mull! It's called the 'Anand Centre' You've been around the Sanyassin scene mate. You know what Anand means don't you?"

He held the roach out to me.

"If I'm not mistaken"...I said out of the corner of my mouth while trying to hold my breath...*"Anand means BLISS...!"*

Bamboo Fever...Surfing the Internode
More from Brendan

Eeeeek! What's happening? I think I've gone troppo! All my friends are buying bigger computers, CD ROMs, mega-gigabyte hard disks and inte-grated fax/modems to surf the Internet, while I'm grovelling naked in the scrub, on hands and knees, counting the 'babies' on my brilliant Bambusa Oldhamii. After the recent rain, it's sending up three metre shoots, and the clump will top 18 metres in the next three to five years. Last night we had Oldhamii shoots with dinner, and tonight Shanto is weaving a beautiful basket out of dried banana plant, saloom sheaths and fine canes from the 'multiplex' bamboo Golden Goddess! (multiplexes are smallish, hedgy pretty bamboos that fill out and droop delightfully when it rains.)

Like hemp, bamboo lays claim to being the world's most useful plant, and like hemp, its list of uses is impressive. Apart from providing food and shelter, shade and grace for a significant proportion of the world's population, bamboo is used decoratively for fences, gates, trellises, screens, ceremo-nial artefacts, musical instruments and woodwind reeds, toys, styli, cooking and eating utensils, furniture, hunting weapons, carrying and storage baskets, lampshades, ropes and strings, bridges, roof tiles, hats, futon bases and fishing rods. Many Asian medicines are derived from bamboo. Even the didgeri-doo is said to have been made from Bambusa Arnhemica (Arnhem land bamboo), one of the five indigenous Australian species.

So how come bamboo has such a bad reputation as a runa-way eco-disaster in the bush and wears a very short-term 'throw-away' label as a building material?

Apart from the five fairly rare indigenous types, the main bamboo introduced into this country by British settlers was the potted northern Chinese species known as Phyllostachys Aurea and its black cousin, P. Nigra, which when planted out, tend to go berserk and take off over the countryside – which it has done magnificently and continues to do – but unlike the ubiquitous Lantana, running bamboos, when established, can be extremely difficult to halt or remove. Grown collectively bamboos grow out of a collective lump which consists of root mat and rhizomes, which are underground woody masses with the nodes (joins) and buds packed in place ready to telescope out into the familiar bamboo pole, or culm, when the time comes.

On running bamboos (monopodial), the rhizome forms a long cane-like structure that travels long distances underground, then striking buds to form a multiplicity of new shoots in your neighbour's garden or halfway down the hill. Stories exist of areas in India and other places where hundreds of square miles of runaway giant bamboos are bombed by the airforce with napalm in order to halt its progress.

However, all is not lost, because bamboo has a second category known as sympodial, or clumping bamboos, which send out rhizomes in a tight-packed circular shape, which makes them safe, predictable and easily-controlled, not to mention their breathtaking beauty and outstanding usefulness. And wow do they grow! Forget palms! A couple of well-chosen, well-placed bamboos and your yard is a jungle in no time. Bamboos come in very small, small, medium, large and gigantic! As well, they come in green, black, gold, yellow, pink, lime, striped, mottled, Buddha-bellied, thorny, long or short internodes (distance between the bumps, or nodes), thin-walled, thick-walled, solid (some with almost the tensile strength of steel are already being used as reinforcement in concrete construction). It comes tall and short, droopy, straight, bendy, mop-top, wild, spread-out and ground-creeper. All of it is predictable and safe to plant and available locally.

It is true that bamboo is a very temporary building material, unless the right sort of bamboo is correctly harvested (with regard to which poles to take and which to leave), at the correct seasonal time, and then properly cured. Also, bamboo should never be buried below ground level, nor directly exposed to rain or other water. Getting the correct advice on all procedures is essential and has not been readily available in the past.

In 1983, we were conned by a local bamboo 'expert' whom we paid to build us a bamboo house. He had me trying to drill and inject every chamber on every pole on the entire structure with salt water, which is falsely attributed with curing properties, supposedly keeping borers and bugs and moulds at bay, guaranteeing a long-term structure. This is simply untrue!

Actually we never got to find out because due to shoddy building procedures, the whole house fell over in the wind one night, and the next day in our absence, as if to remove the evidence, our man came and stole all the bamboo we had gathered, been given, or bought. He's built a few houses for other people since, but they've all rotted away after a few years because he doesn't know what he's doing. That's been pretty much par for the course for bamboo 'experts' up until now.

Fortunately these days there are people who not only know how to deal with bamboo they import, but also propagate, grow and sell bamboos from all over the world, including 80 or more of these safe, predictable sympodial clumping wonder plants. Beauty and versatility. A trip through the Bamboo World (near Nimbin) display gardens is just that...a trip! Especially during wet summers when all the keyline dams are full, the rows and rows of mango trees are in full fruit and full blush, and all the wondrous bamboos are shooting everywhere you look, thrusting up at the sky...small pretty canes right through to giant 20 metre spears! And at ground level, you find the shoots six or seven inches round, say a foot long. You snap off a giant cone, take it home, peel it, steam it, cut it up and into the wok with the stir fry, and you're into what millions of Asians have been into for centuries – bamboo shoots for tucker!

It's deliciously crunchy and maybe a trifle bland, so you can lean on the gamazio (roasted ground sesame seeds with salt) and tamari (soy sauce), or cook it with flavourful onions, garlic and ginger. Nutritionally bamboo shoots are the ideal food for the diet conscious, being low in fat, protein and carbohydrates, but very high in hard-to-get vitamin B complex, calcium, phosphate, iron, magnesium, sodium, thiamine, riboflavin, niacin, Vitamin C and choline.

Bamboo was a dietary life saver for Australian prisoners of war during World War II. They gained enough sustenance to survive by adding bamboo shoots to the poor rations of white rice doled out by their Japanese captors. It has also properties of special benefit to menopausal women.

Australia consumes over 4,000 tonnes of tinned, imported bamboo shoots per annum. A separate market already exists on the Gold and Sunshine Coasts and beyond to provide the growing Asian tourist industry with fresh bamboo shoots. Last year some friends at a nearby community were getting $18 per kilo for shoots of Moso, a running bamboo that is the most popular in Japan (although I'm told it's not the best by a long shot!)

A contagious future-primitive industry. So we're into it. I'm growing it as a windbreak, as a giant hedge to block out neighbours, to bind a steep creek bank together, to beautify as nothing else can, to build with, to make things with and to eat. I've made models, fences, gates, trellises, tomato and bean frames, stakes and poles, a tree house, a puppet theatre; and Shanto weaves with it.

Bamboo World have begun workshops that range from species identification and selection to teaching the spiritual aspects of the 'great grass'. You will be able to learn any aspect of bamboo-ology, from growing to making furniture, baskets and musical instruments. Future

houses will use bamboo when timber becomes too scarce. Costa Rica is already using bamboo in standard housing development. Bamboo is now pressed into building sheets and laminated into beams of enormous strength. Like hemp, it makes a great paper and rapidly outgrows trees as a permanent renewable source. Japan's most common bamboo, Ma-dake, can grow four feet in 24 hours. Trees can't compare with such growth.

It is a brand new contender on the Oz scene and my hot favourite for 'Sunrise industry of the decade', or should I say millennium?

What's that? Your hard disk went down and you're off line until further notice? Not me! I'm a bit bamboozled but I know future-primitive when I see it. I'm a true believer – I got de bamboo fever!

(In memory of beloved Arihanta - who loved his 'boo.)

As you will see later, in the section on the 'Performance Poets', it was good to get Kim Downs and his partner, Liz Hall-Downs, involved in the book. The next piece from Kim is a nicely personal, alternative view, of the Rainbow Region. It complements some of Mook's reminiscences.

Life on the Fringe in Northern New South Wales

Kim Downs

The following is a purely personal vignette. It is a day-in-the-life type sketch with no attempt to paint in the background of the larger 'alternative lifestyle' movement peculiar to northern New South Wales. The events described below take place in the summer of 1985.

Kim Downs, July 1999

I emigrated to Australia in 1980, a frustrated California hippy-wannabe escaping the ligatures of the American Dream. Up to that point an 'alternative lifestyler' more in mind than in practice, I naturally gravitated towards the spiritual hub of the movement, northern New South Wales. 1985 found me living on a friend's property near the small township of Burringbar. I rented one of several small 'humpys' erected midst a rugged rainforest retreat. The 'Spring House' was a 10 foot x 14 foot pole shack boasting running water as its sole concession to civilization. Rent was ten dollars a week.

Having recently extricated myself from an acrimonious relationship, I chose this hideaway as my emotional recovery zone. I wanted solitude and quiet. The Spring House was ideal. A goat track winding through the forest for some 300 metres was the sole access. The other end of this track led to the only substantial flat area on the property large enough to accommodate a car. Moving in had been a major effort as everything had to be carried in on foot through the forest. The upside was that this difficulty precluded visits from all but the most intrepid

and determined friends; particularly during the frequent rainy spells where a brisk three minute walk up the slippery path would ensure the would-be visitor arrived at my verandah with 10-15 leeches on each shoe! Appalled at first by this phenomenon, within months I had grown used to it to the extent that the leeches seemed less bothersome than mosquitoes. I learned to get about in thongs. This way the leeches were easily spotted and brushed off the feet before they could attach.

The Spring House perched along the side and halfway up a steep dead-end valley. Flocks of lorikeets, yellow-tailed black cockatoos, rosellas, crows, and sea-eagles wafted by at eye level. The forest floor teemed with life; possums, bush-rats, mice, snakes, blue-tongued lizards, echidnas, myriad spiders and the loathsome leeches scurried amongst the leaf-litter and rocky gorges. At night, the forest crackled and squeaked with nocturnal pursuits and Lilliputian ground campaigns. Being largely a city creature, it took me several months to grow comfortable with this night-time clatter.

I was 32 years-old when I moved into the Spring House. Up to that point I had worked in a dizzying variety of jobs including restaurant kitchen-hand, cook, athletics coach, shoe salesman, builder's labourer, gardener, tuna fisherman, oil exploration worker, fencing contractor, and most recently – a solo singer-guitarist. I had certainly spent years toying around the outer edges of conventional society, but usually just within the confines of the mainstream. Now, I felt myself suddenly casting off the innermost layer to reveal the feral bohemian who had always lurked within.

I held no proper job when I moved into the Spring House, bar a once-a-week music gig on Friday nights at Julian Rocks Restaurant in Byron Bay. (Mook and Shanto had the Saturday night spot. I didn't know them personally at this point. Ten years later we would share stages at the Maleny-Woodford and Lismore Folk Festivals) I subsisted on the dole and whatever cash I could scrounge from piece work. My rent was so low and my general habits so frugal, I could live pretty comfortably with this arrangement. Thus, I fell into the habits of a recluse.

It was not unusual for me to have no interaction with anyone at all for the week between gigs. I busied myself extending the verandah of the Spring House with timber salvaged from the Byron Bay tip (right in town in those days, now closed) and poles cut or found in the surrounding forest. In the evenings, I read by candlelight and kero lamps, practised guitar, and soaked up the healing ambience of forest life. I fell into a pattern of going to bed at 8:00 p.m. and arising at dawn to begin another day of de-nailing, handsawing, and hammer and chisel work.

On Friday nights, I would shave, put on my best clothes, tart myself up a bit, and, grabbing my guitar, walk with trouser legs rolled up through the muddy track to my 1976 Leyland Mini Van. There, I would de-leech my legs, towel off my feet, put on proper shoes, and drive the 35 minutes to Julian Rocks. The restaurant was an up-market eatery catering for tourists with exotic tastes and bulging wallets. I could never have afforded to eat there on my income. 'Incongruous' probably best describes how it used to feel playing 70s cover songs to passing yuppies. My 'pay' for this gig was a beautiful meal, twenty bucks, and as much wine or beer as I felt inclined to inflict on myself. Often as not, I would finish the evening at the restaurant bar, getting quietly drunk with some Melbourne developer and his wife. I was naturally shy about divulging too many details of my lifestyle in these exchanges as it inevitably led to bemused incredulity on the part of the squares. Byron Bay in the mid-eighties had only just turned the corner onto the path of 'trendyness' then. Within a few years the 'real big money' would flow in and the dreaded 'Californication' would begin in earnest. I had watched my beloved childhood beach suburb in San Diego undergo this same change twenty years before and it was a depressing deja-vu to see Byron Bay catch the same disease.

I remember well a particular night when I had lingered at the bar for as long as the boss would let me. A vicious summer electrical storm had blown up during the evening. Torrential rain lashed at the windows, Johnson Street was fully under water, and apocalyptic lightning and thunder flashed and roared nearly continuously. Fairly drunk on the house red, I ran

to the Mini Van with my guitar. Sneaking out of town up the back way through Bangalow to avoid any spontaneous breath-testing by the local fuzz, I drove cautiously back to Burringbar through swollen creek beds and causeways. The final half mile of the drive to my friend's property consisted of a steep gravel track called ominously (and appropriately!) Snake Gully Road. Narrow and pitted, it wound upwards adjacent to avocado and banana orchards which graced the steep hillsides. My friend's driveway cut acutely back from Snake Gully Road, forcing drivers wishing to enter to execute a two-point turn in the middle of the road. Blind corners on either side of the driveway added a degree of urgency to this manoeuvre. The farmers up the hill were wont to fly down Snake Gully Road in their Toyota Landcruisers. The Mini's tight turning circle helped, but its low clearance demanded careful inspection of gutters and pot-holes. The side of the road opposite the driveway fell away precipitously downhill into the orchards with

Forest track to the Spring House

nothing but a dilapidated barbed-wire fence to stop a car from rolling several hundred metres into the tangled undergrowth.

This night, a little sauced on wine, I misjudged the driveway and ended up having to back up and pull forward several times. The gravel road was nearly a river itself. With every attempt to right myself, I slipped sideways down the hill and closer to the edge of the road and the fearsome abyss. Back and forth I crabbed down the hill expecting any moment to be collected by a stray Landcruiser or to slip quietly over the edge and roll like a metal sausage down the embankment. Perseverence, sweaty palms, and a lot of cursing saw me eventually right the Mini and drive to the head of the track to the Spring House.

Rain still fell in sheets and the electrical storm howled and lit the night at frequent intervals. At this point I discovered I had forgotten my torch. A torch was absolutely essential to traverse the forest track at night. The density of the trees rendered the forest quite dark even on a night boasting a full moon. On a night such as this, it was utterly black inside the tree-line, except for the brilliant lightning flashes which strobed nearly continuously. I sat for awhile and pondered my choices. I could crawl in the back of the Mini van and try to sleep until daylight on the thin rug placed over cold metal, sans blanket and pillow. Or, I could brave the track using the frequent lightning to illuminate the way.

Fuelled by the adrenaline rush of my recent victory over the driveway and too much red, I opted for the latter. Removing my shoes and grabbing my guitar, I headed for the edge of the forest. I was soaked to the skin inside two minutes, but cautiously optimistic that my intimate knowledge of the trail and the lightning would see me through. At first, things went well. I made good progress the first hundred metres as the trail was quite straight and the lightning accommodatingly frequent. I stood motionless in inky blackness during the breaks and rushed forward in 20 metre bursts as the light afforded.

View over the valley from the Burringbar property

About halfway through, the trail began to snake and dip. Forward progress became possible only in smaller and smaller tentative dashes. Worse, the storm seemed to be suddenly abating, the lightning flashes becoming less frequent and sustained. During long moments of standing – shivering, wet, blind, and helpless – I had plenty of time to ponder my situation. Drunk, clutching my guitar, barefoot, leeches swarming over my calves, I stood for long moments unable to either retreat or advance. The night sounds seemed to press in and real fear of some surreal un-nameable horror rose like bile in my throat. Pressing ever forward in smaller and more infrequent bursts, I finally managed to make the verandah of the Spring House some 45 minutes after I had entered the forest. What was essentially a three-minute walk had taken three quarters of an hour.

Both shins teemed with leeches, which, being removed, were replaced by dozens of small rivulets of blood. I changed into dry clothes, patted my legs with tissues until they stopped bleeding, and eventually rolled myself a well-deserved nerve-calming joint. Later, I fell into bed sweaty and spent, only to arise the next morning to a perfect azure sky with nary a cloud in sight. Ah, summer on the North Coast!

Thus concludes my little personal vignette. I believe that my lifestyle during this period reflects a common scenario for fringe dwellers on the north coast over the past twenty years. Social misfits living in illegal dwellings just off the tourist track, subsisting on the goodwill of friends and the dole, engaging in conventional society at particular entrepreneurial junctures like markets, music gigs, festivals, but remaining largely outside the mainstream with like-minded friends, accessing money from the system where possible, often as not through cash or barter arrangements which produce no records and attract no taxes – that is how I would loosely define your garden variety 'fringe dweller' on the north coast.

I have written a poem entitled *Scarfhead*, which paints one of the sadder cases I have encountered over the 14 years I lived in Byron Shire. Luckily – for me – it was a seminal and care-free time in which I had the 'space' to grow and come to terms with some old demons. I still consider myself a 'fringe dweller' in spirit. It is an attitude and philosophy as much as a lifestyle and one I am not likely to abandon no matter the outer trappings of my daily existence.

Scarfhead

Scarfhead! Scarfhead! Don't pick her up!
She looks good from a distance but not close up.
She's ugly and weird, man, she scares me to death.
Don't pick her up!
That's Scarfhead, I'm tellin ya!
Don't pick her up! That's Scarfhead, okay?

Scarfhead squats in a dairy shed one mile from Byron Bay.
She sleeps in her clothes on a mouldy mattress,
Wears pink tights and a golden scarf,
Hitchhikes up and down the coast.
She's rough as guts old Scarfhead.

Scarfhead gropes through a foggy mist of Serapax, ciggies, and gin.
Bloated, pale, with a whiskered chin,
She's smothered in makeup like an old drag-queen.
She flags your car down, steps inside.
You're just another john for Scarfhead.

Scarfhead puts the seatbelt on. Rolls the window down.
"You got any drugs?" she says with a laugh.
Her wrinkled mouth is a crimson gash,
You stare at the road to avoid her gaze.
The expectant gaze of Scarfhead.

Scarfhead! Scarfhead! Don't pick her up!
She looks good from a distance but not close up.
She's ugly and weird, man, she scares me to death.
Don't pick her up!
That's Scarfhead. I'm tellin ya!
Don't pick her up! That's Scarfhead, okay?

Scarfhead speaks in demented streams of confusion, anger, and fear
Her words are fishhooks, baited and thrown.
She wears desperation like a cheap perfume.
She touches your arm with a brittle claw.
The grasping claw of Scarfhead.

Scarfhead says, "Aye, fancy a headjob? It'll cost you less than a carton of beer."
She's ocker and loud and laughs like a horse.
She slurs her approval of your music and hair.
She asks you back for a nip of gin.
A nip of gin with Scarfhead.

Scarfhead lives in a thousand sheds one mile from
                                        everywhere.

Abandoned, lonely, half insane,
She sleeps alone with her madness and pain.
We don't like to believe that we're all to blame.
Blame for a legion of Scarfheads.

Kim Downs

Staying with Mook and Shanto in their Rainbow Region house was a real launching pad for this book. You've already met Mook (Brendan) and hopefully enjoyed his sparky humour and wit. As a complement to Mook's role as Puckish Tribal Elder, Shanto is the Wiccan Earth Mother. She brings brings with her a very special harmony. In these next extracts she shares with us some of her own rituals and offers glimpses into two of her own particular artistic endeavours – forming and singing with the all-women's Gaia Choir and feltmaking.

Rituals, rites of passage and celebrations for all occasions
Shanto

I have always considered myself a spiritual person...as a kid, I loved going to Sunday School...loved all the stories about Jesus...even joined the Salvation Army in my teens...and was even deflowered on a pew in one of their churches...I can still play a mean tambourine!

But as I grew up and joined in the world's universal disappointment with Christianity and all its hollow meaningless male-oriented bullshit...I began to feel a desperate need for some form of Spirituality in my life...something real and tangible and easily accessible to ordinary people like myself, my family and friends...without the need to join some self-aggrandizing Church group and pay homage and money to some faceless hierarchy.

I began to study wiccan and pagan religious celebrations and rituals...especially my own Celtic inheritance. The first rituals we performed were with a group of about a dozen women or so...and we celebrated the Spring

Equinox with flowers, chants, newly baked bread, circles, dancing, self-blessings and healing prayers for the Earth. For the first six years we would do the larger (public) rituals with only women...to celebrate the seasons.

Slowly we entered into personal rituals that we would do with family and close friends i.e. puberty rituals, baby namings, house blessings etc., and I began to do my own personal growth ceremonies on a daily basis. After the first six years we opened the seasonal celebrations to men and boys...especially Beltane where the men get to play lots of percussion and the whole family has fun!

I believe it is of utmost importance to reclaim our lost cultural heritage through the use of rituals and ceremonies in our everyday life, bringing friends and community together for personal and group healing and nurturing. Healing of the planet can be done through these practices. All tribal peoples have used them since the beginning of time. Ritual fulfils the need to acknowledge our higher consciousness

Sitting in a circle we tune in to our hopes, wishes and dreams...and each other.

© John McCormick

Ritual for Young Elders – Entering the Wise Age

This ritual occurs when one has reached the point of life when Saturn returns for the second time to the natal position (around 56 years of age). Saturn is the teacher planet and this ritual signifies the time of becoming an elder in our community. Now it is our responsibility to help guide the community with love and wisdom and to impart our knowledge and experience to the younger ones.

We gathered for Lili's elderhood ceremony on the beach at sunset and the sky put on a great light show for us. As we stood in the circle and sang, *"Listen, listen, listen to my heart song"*, Lili stood in the centre tuning into the power of this ancient rite of passage. The celebrant smudged the group with sacred sage to purify, then blessed and anointed Lili. After being told the importance of this special time, Lili then performed her *'Dance of Life'* for us all and especially herself. It was beautiful and ecstatic to behold. She was then presented with a necklace with a purple stone in it – her Elder Jewel (purple is the colour of Spirituality, synthesis, royalty, learning and power), to remind her that she is our teacher, our beloved sister, our Elder. We all sang and danced around her kissing and hugging, then we feasted and partied on into the night.

Baby Naming Ceremony

Naming a child is an important and joyous occasion for all the family and if not performed as a Christening or such in the church this is an alternative way to do so.

All the family gathers in a circle, the baby being held by either parent with the baby's guardian/s standing beside them. After purifying with incense or smudge we sing a song of welcome and the celebrant says why we are gathered and then blesses the baby. She then places a tiny garland of flowers on the baby's head and asks the mother and father to name their child and to publicly give their dedication to her/him.

Another song is sung then the guardian/s step forward to give the child their dedication. A gift from the parents and guardian/s should be given at this time and the baby carried around the circle for everyone to give a wish and a present. It's very powerful to have a medicine bag for these tiny power objects to go in, as from time to time during the child's life this can be brought out to remind them of their origin. (A power object can be a special stone, shell, feather, jewel, figurine or anything precious). A tree can be planted in honour of the child and often the placenta is planted beneath it. After the ceremony there is much joy and celebrating with family and friends

Beltane

Beltane is of course the notorious Maypole fertility festival traditionally held in Spring in the old world.

Living in the Southern Hemisphere our seasons are the opposite of Europe and America. So every year in Spring, we get together for Beltane to weave the Maypole on the eve of October 31st...and so we celebrate the most fertile time of the year. A time of planting crops and planting our own seeds of creativity for the coming year. A time of rejoicing, when we weave the spiral web and all of nature is being renewed.

We meet in the time of flowering to dance the dance of life. This is our favourite seasonal celebration – one that is fun for all the family.

Preparation

To prepare a couple of weeks before the event is a good idea. We usually find a thick bamboo pole the best and easiest to deal with although this year we snapped off a dead Camphor Laurel sapling and it worked fine. It needs to be 4 meters (12 feet) long and approximately 12mm diameter at the top. Saw six-inch deep slots in the top of it so that knotted ribbons can easily be slipped in.

A hole is dug at the centre of the circle about one foot deep. Leave the dug out dirt in a heap to tamp back in when the pole is erected.

The invitations ask each woman to bring 7 meters of unjoined ribbon, (if it has knots in it, it will catch the other ribbons when weaving and snarl them all up!) The choice of colour can represent what you are wishing for in your life – garlands of flowers in hair and colourful party clothes and food to share... men to bring drums and percussion.

Traditionally both men and women wove together. At first we did our Beltanes with just women and girls (no men at all)

when we were learning to reclaim our lost culture...later when we invited the men to join in, we found it suited everyone best when the women and girls wove...and the men and boys kept time with drums and percussion – so here's how it goes:

The Ceremony
Women sing and weave the pole while men play drums and percussion. Everyone (men, women, boys and girls) forms a circle around the Maypole which is lying on the ground by the hole it is to be set up in. We hold hands and begin humming which tunes us into each other while someone goes around anti-clockwise and smudges everyone with sage and cedar.

The celebrant gives the Beltane Rave so people really get the feeling of why they are there...keep it short and sweet. The directions are called in to create a sacred space. Then we all write what we wish for on a piece of paper and place it in the hole the maypole will sit in.

I then sing *'The Charge of the Goddess'* (any appropriate song will do, a good time for people to sing a song together). The men step outside the circle and prepare to drum while the end of the Maypole is held up so that the women, in clockwise order, can place their ribbons in the slots...and when each one has done this, she steps back to the edge of the circle and holds the ribbon tautly by its end. This stops confusion and tangling. The Maypole is then set upright, the earth filled in and tamped down.

In a clockwise direction we start walking quite sedately, while singing, *"We All Come from the Goddess"* until the ribbons have spiralled down about 40 cm from the top of the pole. Then we all face each other as couples. Starting together we begin to weave. The women facing in the clockwise direction will start off by going under the ribbon of the anti-clockwise woman, then over the next anti-clockwise woman etc. going over and under in turn (and vice-versa for the anti-clockwise women).

At this stage everyone is moving in their particular direction. If there is an odd number then don't worry, follow the woman in front...it's all a bit confusing at first...that's the fun of it all. The chant *"Weave, weave, weave, weave, weave the web of life"* is set up making sure it is held taut and not tangled with another.

When we can no longer bend down under each others' ribbons, we all cluster around the pole (some on our knees) and with much chaos, fun and hysterical laughter we willy-nilly pass and snatch each other's ribbons around doing the final wild-woman weaving of the loose ribbons. This is my favourite part. We then invite the men into the circle to admire our handiwork and all sing a song to raise the cone of power, which we usually send to some sacred place which is under threat.

"Earth am I, water am I, fire and air and spirit am I."

When the energy is at its highest during the singing and dancing around the Maypole, the celebrant stops it and we all throw our arms up in the air and direct our healing energy to the sacred place with a loud whoop and a holler. All hands are placed on the earth to give back any unearthed energy...then we all get to jump the Beltane fire.

Bangalow site for the Maypole

The Beltane Fire
The fire is a small one just outside the circle. Keeping in order in our circle we run and jump the fire as an act of purification and good luck. As we jump we make a wish (silent or out loud) for ourselves or to banish anything undesirable from our lives. Lovers can jump the fire together to release any disharmonies in their relationship or just to make a love-wish.

We can make as many jumps as we like. If it's a large group usually two jumps each is enough, one to banish and one to wish. The celebrant opens the circle and we all feast and play music to our hearts content.

Burial Rites.

Soon after my mother died, my family (Dad, 2 kids and partner Mook) went down to the Pass, a very special power spot in Byron Bay, where we scattered some of her ashes, with flowers, into the sea. My Mum, a Pisces would have loved that!

Dad gave me the rest of her ashes to bury at the foot of a very large and special boulder on our property called 'Grandmother Rock'.

Because we had performed the sea ceremony just after Mum's death, thereby fulfilling our own needs to lay her to rest at that time, I was able to wait for the 'right time' to do this

Two and a half years later it felt just right to do this ceremony.

Eight wonderful friends with Mook and I, formed a procession from our home to the rock, myself in front holding the ashes in a hand-painted heart-shaped box, the others in single file and Mook bringing up the rear playing my ritual drum (aptly called 'Grandmother Shanadi' after a Native North American grandmother we met in USA. A special rock she gave us is buried at the base of Grandmother Rock.)

We made our way down through the orchard, around the pond-like dam we call our 'Frog Resort', past stands of bananas and bamboos to the 'Sunset Rocks', a West-facing group of boulders, dominated by the giant Grandmother. We formed a circle at the foot of her, I smudged everyone with incense and called in the directions. I sang a favourite song of my mother's - called 'Mother'.

Mother
(by Fantusi adapted by Shanto)

Mother you're darkness…Mother you're light
You're Shiva Shakti in and beyond all sight
Oh Mother please open our hearts tonight
Mother please lead us from darkness to light

Chorus
Mother you're beyond the beyond
Mother you're where we all come from
Mother you're beyond the beyond
Mother you're where we all come from

You're Rhada, you're Kali…you're Mary too
Oh Aphrodite we all are you too
Oh Mother oh Mother I'm singing to you
Oh Mother Gaia oh how I love you

Chorus

Beyond the beyond is not far from this place
Beyond and right here become one with some grace
And everywhere I look I see your face
Mother I thank you for all of this race

Chorus

I blessed her spirit, asked her to let go of all worldly possessions and asked that she may never know fear again. *"May you rest in peace in the arms of the Great Mother, with the protection of Grandmother Rock."*

I spoke of her loving ways and thanked her for being my Mum. I then sang a song to send her Spirit on its way…

"Within the stillness of the heart,
The White Dove flies.
From soul to soul she rides the wind.
She's born and never dies.

Sweet soul, your journey's just begun
Sweet lover of the light, your time has come.
Sweet soul, your journey's just begun
Sweet lover of the light, your time has come."

This ritual was very moving for us all and there were many tears shed, every one of us thinking about our own dear mothers. I placed the box of ashes in the ground, covered it over and put a white feather on the East side to symbolize freedom and rebirth. We all took a handful of flowers from the basket. I put my flowers on the earth over the ashes, said a prayer…and the others, very movingly, one by one, placed their flowers there and paid homage to the great spirit that she was.

After that I passed around a large crystal that I had dedicated to her on the day she died, and we all put our own special healing vibe into it, then wedged it in a hole in the rock face, faceted side facing in, to empower this very sacred rock even more. The circle was opened and as I was feeling very shaky and in need of a really big cuddle, we all had a group hug, with me in the middle (YUMMMM!) and did a big HUMMMM, and whooped and hollered. We then sat up on Grandmother Rock to ground our energy, take in the scenery, and feel the rock's very special vibe.

This has been my most powerful and moving ceremony so far which I was most honoured to share with my partner Mook, our newfound friends from Japan, and Echan from Canada.

Blessed Be.

Felting – an ancient art revisited
Shanto

The instant I saw my first felted garment I knew I was passionate about it and would just have to learn this amazing age-old craft. The use of felt goes back as far as 6500 BC in Turkey and today, still has many uses, from yurts, saddles, cushions, floor coverings, boots and clothing to intricate wall-hangings. Felt is a strange and unique fabric. It has no warp or weft like woven materials, no right or wrong side, no beginning and no end.

Using simple techniques, a strange alchemy takes place between wool, moisture, heat and friction, creating a fabric which is warm and hard-wearing and in densities ranging from very light and floaty to the thickness of a piece of sculpture.

Some women in this northern NSW region have developed a very light felt suitable for our sub-tropical climate in Summer, felting wool lightly into fine cotton material backings – we call it Tropical Felt. It is so light it can be worn on a warm Summer's night.

Australian Merino wools dyed in rainbow colours form the basis of the felt. Into this wool base we set hand-dyed silk threads, bits of exotic materials, lurex – in fact any material that will give the garment its own special appearance, texture and dimension. The whole layout is then wet with soapy water and rolled up in either a bamboo blind or bubble wrap, then rolled hundreds of times back and forth. This process compacts the wool, adhering the fibres to themselves and setting the silks etc. into the body of the wool which is becoming felt.

At a certain stage the garment-to-be is removed from the roll, folded and immersed in hot water, then literally thrown hard onto the table again and again until it is shrunken into the size and shape required. This shrinking completes the felting process. The garment is then laid out on towels, pulled into shape and left to dry.

I belong to a felt-making group and we get together every month or so to exchange ideas and different methods of felting. There is no competitiveness at all between us as each individual felts in her own unique and original way – no two pieces ever turn out the same! Our creations range from haute couture garments, dresses, jackets, coats, hats, shawls, scarves, slippers, bags, boots, tabards, vests and capes to glove puppets, tea cosies, masks, headbands, bookmarks, cushions, pelmets, wall-hangings and rugs. The list goes on. We have put on several fashion shows and exhibit at local art galleries and boutiques.

As the renaissance of this wonderful art form emerges I am excited to be part of an ever-widening circle of felters who are demystifying this ancient skill and educating people in the making, wearing and caring of these unique creations.

The Gaia Choir
Shanto

I had a vision in 1989 of 1000 people in 'The Gaia Choir' singing green songs of love and peace at the Sydney Opera House via satellite to the world. This hasn't happened yet but at that time we did a smaller Gaia Choir for Environment Day in the Lismore Town Hall.

Two years later I was feeling a great need to sing with other women. I put ads in the local papers and put posters up. Women began coming to these weekly singing groups, some of whom had never sung before. They were really a mixed bag, a few good voices but mainly just bathroom singers. They were mostly mothers, artists and healers (who mainly populate this area). We met regularly and would have a great time singing together. We sang songs of the Earth, love songs, Goddess songs…WOMANSONGS!…and we all grew and blossomed into our power through the experience.

Sometimes there were 23 of us and the energy was pretty wild. It was often more of a transpersonal workshop than a choir rehearsal – Did we go through some stuff! Very nurturing and often confronting.The music had a life of its own and sounded pretty tribal …sort of Pacific, but most of all, heartfelt and REAL.

After a while we started to sound good enough for a performance. Hardly any of the women had performed in front of an audience before, so it took a lot of gruelling rehearsals to groom them into some sort of an act. Most of them had never worn make-up or stage wear so I had to hold workshops and teach them these arts.

The Gaia Choir
WOMANSONG

Well we took off! Something very magical happened when we were all on stage together singing our songs of love…a sort of tribal thing that we and our audiences hadn't experienced before in that form. Women energy…very transformational stuff! Soon we were performing at all sorts of functions – at this stage for free! The first gig was the Spring Equinox Celebration with a dance/theatre group, then the Lismore Women's Festival where we brought the house down. We did benefits everywhere, for local schools, old people's homes, the midwive's conference, workshops and seminars.

The world needed to hear the joy and love we expressed so we decided to make the WOMANSONG album….rehearsing for two months (twice a week). On a friend's farm we found a huge old disused concrete Mushroom storeroom with great church-like acoustics. With producer Mook and engineer friend Darmin, we set up a huge altar of flowers, crystals, goddess images and incense, with stereo microphones in the centre. We gathered around it and held a ritual to invoke the muse and to send out healing vibes to the world through the music

© John McCormick

we were to make. We recorded about 9 songs on the first night.

Two months later (more bi-weekly rehearsals) we recorded the second half of the album in the same manner, and when we finished we all got naked and whooped and hollered in a circle like wild tribal women, dancing around the altar with our recently woven maypole. A month or so later the Gaia Choir opened the Maleny Folk Festival and had our album launch there. What a thrill for performers and audience!

I ran this group for two years and due to me moving away from the area for a while, and my need to do my own thing, I left the group. As soon as I left, most of the women started writing their own songs and becoming lead singers in their own right. Before this I had always led the singing, using all the other voices in harmony blocks...because no-one had the confidence or experience to fill this role...even though I encouraged them to do so and offered to privately coach anyone with such aspirations.

With their own original material now being featured the whole style and presentation took on a different flavour. Many members left, a couple died...new women were brought in. Five of the original members plus three extra women are now in a group called 'The Voices of Gaia', still doing wonderful performances in the area . They have produced a self-titled CD. The Gaia Choir 'Womansong' Album that we made back in 1991 is still being played by women all around the world and especially in Australia where it has spawned many women's singing groups.

Occasionally I get to sing with the 'Voices of Gaia' and our next exciting adventure together is to sing for the women in Grafton Jail. It would be a good thing if we inspired some women to form a singing group in prison, not to mention bringing a bit of joy and love into their lives. I still receive many letters from women all over Australia and beyond, saying how much they love this album and how it has changed their lives...may it continue to do so !

The Bangalow Festival Fiasco
By Brendan Hanley
The names of contentious characters have been changed for obvious reasons

Bangalow is a small town just southwest of Byron Bay. It bears the same name as a beautiful local palm tree, which is almost identical to the North Queensland Alexandra Palm. Green and straight and elegantly pretty, the Bangalow Palm is a favourite of forest regeneration devotees and home gardeners alike, especially in the surrounding districts.

It was January 1991. Bangalow's little timber town with verandahs and poles, nestled into a hillside, but was divided right through the middle, down the main street, by what at the time of this story, was the busy Pacific Highway. So that you may appreciate the impact of this fact on town life at that time, let me explain what it was like.

We played music over many pre-highway-bypass years in Bangalow's main street venues. When those big interstate semis would change down a gear not 20 metres away on the highway outside to take the Bangalow hill, the building would shake and no music would be audible at all for 20 seconds or so in the wake of each truck. Conversation was out of the question, and this would happen all day and night, over and over in a continuous great roar of leviathan machinery and clouds of diesel fumes.

This stream of Hell monsters roared its noisy black-fumed course directly through the heart of Bangalow like a planetary icon of separation. From the air it would have looked like two towns either side of a black river which had fire-belching monsters lurching up and down its length and breadth daring any brave soul to try to cross over. And unbeknownst to us when we set out on the little adventure I am about to relate, there were seven different churches in this tiny town. I am told this statistic and the population of Bangalow are the same as

Salem was in USA at the time of the infamous witch trials. You will see the relevance of this as the story unfolds.

Bangalow was so divided they even had (still have I guess) two war memorials for their sons who went to war. I wonder if their souls are in a divided Heaven? And this was the town in which we innocently chose to have a Festival.

This area is famous for many things. Near the top of the list for great happenings in this region would have to be the local Sunday Markets, and of them all (except when it's wet and swampy) rules the Bangalow market, if only for its magnificent people-friendly venue – the Bangalow Showgrounds. Giant spreading camphor laurel trees and pines dominate the upper area, providing a huge green canopy and shade for a large amount of people, stalls etc. This shady area fringes several well placed (if not well drained at times) sports arenas, sheds, amenities and parking spaces.

At the top end of the whole showground near the front gate is the magnificent old tropical theatre (complete with massive stage and choir gallery) known as the A&I hall. (Agriculture and Industry). At the time floor space was being rented cheap, and it was divided up into several small businesses, which included an op shop among others. The whole showground complex was (and still is) the absolute perfect place for a small friendly mostly-musical festival. Or so we thought!

Getting the requisite permission to do it all was relatively easy given our standing in the Community at that time. For a start the manager of the Bangalow Bowling Club was a man called Laurie Schultz. I had had to approach him prior to the first Fowlers Lane Festival we ran in 1976 because he was the local police sergeant at the time. That's one of the things you do if you run festivals.

So now, because we had won each other's respect out of those

former dealings, he was able to introduce me on the right level to the local police chief and made it easy for me to get his blessing for this project. Furthermore because of the massive exposure of our high budget bi-centennial film clip, *'Keep Sailing On'* on local TV prior to this time, shanto had become a well-loved figure right across the board. She was so well known as to be constantly approached in places like supermarkets by people with nice thigns to say about her, the song and the clip. This popularity extended to members of the A&I committee and particularly to the woman who booked the showgrounds, whom I will call June.

Hune seemed to have that strange dynastic sort of power you find in country towns that goes back a long way and is never challenged. Anyway, she loved Shanto and our whole plan and we soon had written permission to run a three day event in January of the following year. So, in true hippy fashion we held a meeting! About 20 or so people turned up, agreed it would be a great idea and went on their way. We didn't hear from any of them again except one abrasive American guy who had gone overseas the week after the meeting and who came back to Oz about two months later expecting to tune in to a hippy-like festival happening.

But bu then we were well ensconced in all sorts of stuff and we had no room for him or his belligerent attitude, but let me get back to the first meeting and its aftermath. At that meeting was a guy I'll call Duncan. He had been one of the organisersof a famous local festival a few years earlier and had a reputation as a festival expert among other things. We had been involving him in our North Coast Music Awards (now Dolphin Awards) project and this festival idea had been spawned from that.

Anyway he suggested that the hippy way was not the way to go and that we should form a private promotion company and put the Festival on as a company project, and we agreed. There were to be six directors. Shanto and me, Duncan and his partner at the time, Joan, our studio partner and co-founder of all this, John (Darmin) Cameron and a local Chartered Accountant who had the business name 'Great Events' registered, which we were going to use for our corporate identity.

It couldn't fail!

One of Duncan's first Public Relations jobs was to land Shanto and me in a photo with him, arms outstretched to designate BIG, on the front page of popular regional paper the Echo, under the main headline 'Major Festival Planned for Bangalow!' Alarm bells were probably already sounding on both sides of the busy Bangalow highway.

We designed posters, and Duncan began producing mountains of printed stuff on his Apple Mac. We also started running regular 'Bangalow Dreaming' nights with a circle of local artists, wannabe Festival helpers and contributors. They were high-quality high-spirit nights and were a great indication of what our festival might have become.

Duncan and Joan began running meetings with Bangalow people to establish what he called 'accountability'. They also began turning up out of the blue at various church services in Bangalow, a shallow ploy that was to be justifiably interpreted negatively by lots of locals as the plot developed.

We had used the words 'circle magic' on a poster to describe the wondrous nights we were having at our dreamings, and to impart the knowledge we had that putting people in large circles at Festivals and such never fails to produce results that have no other appropriate description than 'magic'. We were referring to music, children, love and laughter. You will see how wildly this was twisted and perverted into something totally imaginary and inappropriate as we continue.

At one of these meetings Duncan mentioned our circles and apparently used the word Goddess once or twice, a word we often use in this area to describe the mother nature idea, or indeed women themselves! Unbeknownst to him, at this particular meeting sat a woman who was later to be the instrument of God, the Angel of divine justice who would succeed in banishing us all from Bangalow, like Archangel Michael turning Lucifer and his minions out of Paradise. The Christian Bitch from Hell!

She jumped on the words 'circle' and 'Goddess' like a dog on a bone, and didn't let go until the whole thing was on National media and we were driven back to the hills where we belong. This was coupled with staunch opposition from two other local couples, the Dildos and the Mangos!.

Barry Mango had apparently been involved in the applications for successful grants involved with heritage listing and restoration of the A&I Hall and seemed, to put it mildly, to have gained a proprietor-like interest in the building, if not the whole town. He vowed publicly that he would never let the Festival happen and wrote letters to the Echo accusing us amongst other things of stealing the name Bangalow for our own purposes, like it was Coca-Cola or Woodstock or some other famous name.

I wrote a very sarcastic article in reply, which apparently incensed many of the old conservatives who so far, had been sitting back watching the whole show from a distance. At the next 'accountability' meeting Batty Dildo announced that the local 'Country Women's Association', famous for their quilts apparently, had withdrawn their support for the whole shebang. I flippantly remarked that the Festival would probably survive without a few local little old ladies, and if looks could kill...I had obviously misread my audience.

Then the Bitch from Hell launched her attack. Instantly the town was divided into Anglicans and Catholics on one side showing support for the whole thing (right down to providing venues in their halls and even in the acoustically amazing Catholic Church), and on the other side the other five Churches, all different Protestant denominations, glued together by the amazing, dare I say Demonic, hatred and energy of this fundamentalist born-again creature from Hades!

Duncan jousted with her and Mango and would not stop 'his process' even when officially told to do so by the majority of us other directors. The media started to pick up on accusations of witchcraft, satanic ceremonies, and drugs, of course. Mango wrote in the paper that we were planning the whole thing 'at the height of the drug season' (marijuana) and inferred that we were doing so advisedly and with obvious intent of capitalising on trade in drugs.

Again I retorted in the papers that he was way out of whack by four or five months and that January was the peak of the off season, when plants in the ground had not even begun to head up, and when traditionally there was never much quality smoke around the traps. Some of the more conservative Bangalow locals publicly mused at my great knowledge of the illicit local product when all I was saying was elementary botany.

The Bitch from Hell, liaising directly with god and deciding the time was right, played her ace card and called the fatal meeting that was to end the whole affair. It was supposed to be a public meeting held to decide by show of hands whether the Festival would be allowed to proceed or not. I had a bad feeling about our PR when I got a phone call that morning from the ABC radio in Melbourne. I was sitting in the sun on

Mook '99

the front steps under the banana palms at Cooper's Shoot, the blue Pacific stretching out before me, when the phone rang. I sat where I was and leaned over and picked up the handset.

"This is the ABC News division here in Melbourne. Is this Mook Hanley?"
"Yes!"
"Do you mind answering a few questions and allowing us to broadcast your replies?"
"No, not at all?"
"Okay here goes! Hope you don' t mind me asking, but I have to really!"
"What' s that?"
"Do you really eat babies?"
"* * * *"

Shanto had been busy making cakes for the usual number of people who would turn up to these meetings. She would normally sell tea and munchies in the kitchen annex as an added fundraising activity. However that evening, when we arrived at the hall we were not really surprised to find the hall already packed to capacity with zealous local Christians, gathered around the holy Bitch who sat clutching her bible and muttering in tongues to herself. During the proceedings to follow, she would occasionally rise up like a rabid dog and, holding her bible aloft, either shut her eyes or point at Duncan accusingly, all the while frothing, babbling and shouting curses and incantations in some animal tongue – and all this was supposedly something religious and somehow connected with Jesus!

Where do these people get off? Witnessing a fait accompli way before the vote was taken, I opened the proceedings in tears, telling them all of plans we had for 'Midsummer Night's Dream' in the park, choirs in the church, children's pantomimes with puppets, music performances and workshops, choirs and percussion, a bamboo village, hi-tech sustainable energy/ appropriate technology village with domes, yurts and other amazing low cost buildings with solar, wind and water power supplies, and I named some of the exciting singers and acts that we were compiling for the event.

The noisy angry crowd buzzed and booed and gave me no space at all. I sat down defeated, then left early, unable to take any more mass stupidity. I never wanted to hear the fucking word Bangalow again. Or Duncan, Mango, Dildo; the list went on. The cameras whirred as Duncan and the Bitch locked horns, no pun intended.

National TV was to tell of our defeat, showing footage of the Bitch attacking Duncan, and him disarming her dramatically by seizing her bible, holding it aloft and ordering her to be seated. They freeze-framed bald-headed Duncan, only whites of eyes showing and mockingly holding up the bible like a toreador after a successful pass with the bull. This was the national image they chose to represent our side of the battle.

The next morning Shanto and I went for our usual morning walk south along Cooper's Shoot. Down the road apiece we saw an old local farmer collecting his mail or newspaper, and as is the custom hereabouts, we waved to him. He called out across the road:
"I was at the meeting last night! I'm afraid I didn't vote for you!"
"You don't live in Bangalow! What were you doing there?"
He was ashamed of himself.
"They got us all in buses. Picked us up from all over the district."
I was pissed off.
"Well thanks for doing us out of a job neighbour!"
He turned and retreated muttering:
"It was the Geea. We had to stop the Geea!"

To this day we'll never really know what the fuck he was talking about. They all talk in tongues! We think it was a reference to Gaia, a Greek word for Mother Earth, and a much preferred and used word in this area.

In the wake of her massive public victory over evil in the district,

the Bitch published a brochure warning people that the local New Age population and their practices were Satanic and should be stamped out. She pointed the finger at words like Aquarian and Spiritual and condemned practices like yoga, t'ai chi, meditation, astrology, permaculture even. There was a whole page of stuff she was out to get, but fortunately we haven't heard or seen her since. They've probably got her on ice for an apocalyptic global purge! She's good! Whupped our hippy arses!

Then after our eight months of hard work, frustration and outright battle for existence, we received a letter from the A&I Committee which said:
"At its meeting held August 1991, the Bangalow Park Trust Committee of Management rescinded its motion to allow your co-operative use of the Bangalow Park for January 92. The committee is in the opinion that the Festival as originally proposed by your letter of February 91 is not of the same format or function as is apparently now proposed. Accordingly the committee withdraws its consent to use the Bangalow Park forthwith. No further correspondence will be entered into regarding this matter.'"

They have since gone on to organize a Country and Western day now and then, the odd rodeo and an annual soapbox derby. Most of the old quasi-Christian bussed-in farmers have died or sub-divided and moved to retirement places on the coast north and south of here. Their holdings have been sliced up and converted to yuppie farms and housing estates, and a suburban sprawl is beginning to grow close around the town. Restoration and heritage listing continues in the main street, and the highway has been diverted a mile away, leaving a peaceful, pretty country town near Byron Bay with the best Festival site in the district.

And like the return of the Goddess, the North Coast Women's Festival was held successfully despite appalling weather conditions in March 1999 in guess what town! And a bigger, better one is planned for next year!

Up in the hills outside of Nimbin is the farm where film-makers, Jeni Kendall and Paul Tait live. It was a real buzz visiting them. It's a great house, full of wood beams and light, in a fabulous location. Right up in the forest depths, very lush and green. The only downside is its popularity with the mozzies! I had to sit out on the verandah liberally covering all my exposed parts with tea-tree oil. Mook and Shanto had accompanied me, and this was a re-gathering of tribe members. Hugs and kisses, guitars and the singing of old and new songs out front of their splendid home. Mook was in fine fettle, introducing Paul and Jeni to some songs which the film-making couple were considering using for a new film sound-track.

Originally out of Sydney, Paul and Jeni are early Nimbin settlers. And from that perspective were able to use their considerable documentary film-making skills to make the three part film, *Nearly Normal Nimbin* which was shown on prime time SBS TV. That film told pretty much the whole story from the Aquarius festival in '73, through the establishment of Tuntable Falls Community, the poets, musos and artists (including Mook and Shanto), environmental protests, the drugs, Mardi Grass Festival, the children of the dream, the police raids, right up to the stresses, excesses, glories, successes and failures of the Rainbow area: Australia's premier social experiment.

Since about the time of making the Nimbin film, Jeni and Paul have started out on a new, pioneering path. What follows, in their own words, is the story of:

Northern New South Wales in 1977 it was like an eaten out golf course. There was a story about the farmer who had owned it – that if he saw a blade of grass through his binoculars he would send his wife out with 17 cows to eat it down! As well, the original forest had been cut and pushed into crude charcoal pits by the front gate. The charcoal produced helped to run the local bus on gas during the Second World War. So it was when we walked onto our farm with no farming experience at all. Every morning we looked out the door and saw thirty five years work. It was so daunting that we mostly worked off the farm until a few years ago. But we did a few things right in that time...we took all the cows off, slashed the whole farm twice a year and planted thousands of trees. Three years ago we finally felt the land looked ready to cultivate.

We loved the idea of bushfoods after talking with Peter Hardwick who helped pioneer bushfoods into public consciousness. Peter did a consultancy report for us. It had lots of science and suggestions about species and expected yields and prices, but not much about layout of the plantation, spacing, design, future weed control considerations or basic practical information. We didn't know enough to ask. In retrospect, after making design mistakes, we now realise how important that detail really is in the initial consultancy report or planning stages. You need a strong overall plan when setting up an orchard, and if you don't think it through you can create years of unnecessary damage control.

Jeni and Paul

Our bushfood plantation

Jeni Kendall and Paul Tait

When we bought our 150 acre farm outside of Nimbin in

We would really suggest to people wanting to start a bushfood venture from scratch to consider the following:

1. Understand why you want to cultivate bio-dynamically and organically. Appreciate, enjoy, utilise the philosophy behind the system. It's not a dogma but a way of working with the cosmos.
2. What starting and running a commercial orchard venture may mean to the rest of your life.
3. What infrastructure is required for your venture.
4. Completing a business plan that looks at expenses and labour and what returns you may receive. When the end product finally arrives on the tree, are you going to value add and create products and markets, pool products like the Avocado Marketing Group, or just sell the produce to others? Will you have reliable supply? Are you aware of quality requirements, picking and handling procedures, strict health requirements?
5. Having a consultancy report done for your orchard planning. Ask yourself what you want and need from this report. Good to go and see what others have already done.
6. Are you a member of an association like the BFGA (Bio-dynamic Farmers and Gardening Association) and ARBIA (Australian Rainforest Bushfood Industry Association) that can give you assistance, teaching, direction , inspiration and ideas.

OK, so back to our orchard and our experience in cultivation. Firstly we wanted to grow bushfoods bio-dynamically. We feel Australia internationally has a 'Green and Clean' reputation. The necessity to keep the production of bushfoods organic seemed essential because of their very nature as wild and undomesticated foods. We were already practising bio-dynamics in our large house gardens and so it felt right to continue the principals and standards Into our 6 acre orchard. We were already members of BFGA but also joined ARBIA, which was newly formed to help nurture the bushfoods'

industry. We renewed our white-anted shed and gave it a concrete floor and put in an additional dam. Site selection is very important. Give thought to soil fertility, drainage, aspect, shelter, frost, access, and possible erosion from high rainfall From living here for 20 years we felt very positive about the site we chose and had good infrastructure like road access, clean water, phone, power, bio-dynamic stirring and spraying equipment, a tractor with blade, slasher and rippers, a Toyota 4 Wheel drive with trayback and...strong arms, lots of energy and enthusiasm.

We got our consultancy report and decided that lemon myrtle, aniseed myrtle, Davidson plum, domgo pepper, would be the major species. We would also try small numbers of other bushfoods on a trial basis to see what might be good in the future and to help biodiversity. We were advised that it is better to select 4/5 major species and focus on them. You need to do a good job on these few species before moving on to others. We decided to base the orchard on largely aromatic leaf trees that could be picked over long periods and would also be highly flexible in their enduse with excellent potential for use as essential oils, flavouring/condiments as well as perfumery, aromatherapy, skin-care and antiseptics. Also the aromatic leaf is less difficult to harvest, store and dry compared to the more perishable fruits. The report suggested to block plant these mixed species in stages, so as to have the opportunity to deal with the potential for unexpected production problems as we gathered experience with the trees. The rows would also allow ride-on mower maintenance between rows and farm tractor access on block perimeters to minimise soil compacting and maximise the productive utilisation of the site. The Davidson plum trees would go into a semi-shade area where we would plant wattles for further protection. Additional fruit, nut and flower bushfoods would go into an edible windbreak providing an opportunity to trial grow different varieties for later consideration. We had soil analysis done and found that the carbon levels were high because of constant slashing and no grazing, but phosphate, calcium, copper, iron, zinc and manganese were all low. We have a clayloam topsoil and clay base.

Firstly we used bio-dynamic preparation 500 on our intended

plantation. Then a bulldozer deep-ripped about 6 kilometres down the middle of the intended rows. We then put a ton of lime and 12 tonnes blue metal dust into the rips. It was autumn 95 and a good time to plant lupines over the area of the rips and help fix nitrogen and start the soil breathing. Before they flowered we cut them down. In summer we followed this with field or cow peas. We started to pick up our bushfood trees which had been specially selected and ordered well in advance from several nurseries. We could then see what performed well in our conditions so that when we were ready to expand to our next stage, we could go with that particular species from that nursery. We also selected some seed stock and some clonal stock. It is very important to get sound technical advice on species selection. Even the right species with poor genetic qualities will not be commercially viable. We would pick the plants up from the nursery late afternoon to try and avoid heat distress on the way home. Most of the stock was sunhardened, so we continued to look after them in full sun in our makeshift home nursery. Plants like the Davidson plum need sun harden-ing very slowly and are easy to kill, especially when young. It is taking us often six months or more to move them through the nursery without distress.

As the cow peas were dying off at the end of summer we started to dig the holes for the trees, putting a handful of gypsum and chicken manure into the holes. We also found a company called Nutri-Tech Solutions who analyse soil and make up fully organic blended treatments specific to your needs. Our soil was rated between adequate and good, and they suggested blends to Improve the soil which we would like to do but time and money have slowed us down in this direc-tion to date. Terry Foreman in an excellent workshop gave great advice in cautioning the overuse of fertilisers. Work out what you need and then use about a quarter. Better to use a little more often, than overuse in one application. Look at additional fertilisers as a medicine rather than something repeated regularly. David Williams also made the point that it may take years to find the optimum conditions for bushfoods. He said,

"...if these native plants are pushed by using rich compost they may become open to aphid or scale attack Try making your compost less rich by using leaf mould from native bushes and mulch from your own bushes, more related to their own type."

Finally with the help of two or three experienced people we planted the first stage of the bushfoods just before the wet season started in '96. We ended up digging long rows by hand and making mounds where the trees were planted. We planted the trees with the downward facing leaves facing north so the trunks would have less chance of getting sunburned. We mulched and tree guarded each tree to protect them from our adored wallabies. We drank champagne and felt very pleased with ourselves and then covered the rows with white clover.

Since then we have moved into Stage Two and planted out 500 more lemon myrtles and more Davidson plums, aniseed myrtles and Atherton almonds. We learnt a lot in Stage One that we didn't repeat next time around. Our major problem has been kikuyu. We should have cleared it off the site before we even started and then put a border around the whole orchard – perhaps lemongrass, pigeon pea, and pinto peanut. The deep ripping allowed the kikuyu to have a nice deep place right under the trees to live. We thought we'd got it out of the rows before planting but who has ever really done that!! Molasses 50% mixed with water and sprayed on the runners is meant to be good – it has worked for friends, but not for us, mainly because the wallabies just love the sweetened grass. So now, first we try and get it out of the row – then mow, as close as the mower will cut, brushcut right into the top half an inch of the soil to get the runners – then early morning when there is dew, bring out the fire dragon and the gas bottle and burn along the brushcut edges as soon as the kikuyu shows its head again. This is the best we've been able to come up with. Now we are finding that the kikuyu is retreating in favour of the compessum grass, a grass very similar to kikuyu in appear-ance but without the ability to grow In the dark like kikuyu. Also some of our local native grasses that have always grown in the semi-shaded areas are venturing onto the cooler sides of the tea tree mulch around the bushes. We've become a bit obsessed with this grass control, so when we started finding couch grass in patches we jump on it like a man and woman possessed!

We have kept up the clover on the rows, but initially made the mistake of allowing seed to fall too close to the trees. This just gives the wallabies an excuse to stand right on the mound and against the trees to eat and if they are startled, they are just as likely to jump through the bush and break it off. We have lost a few this way. Another point with the clover, thickly planted close to the drip zone is that it very efficiently takes water from the trees. Originally we bagged all the trees, not knowing if the wallabies would eat them, but they don't touch them – presumably as the oil makes them unpleasant. In the Stage One area, about 600 trees will now need to be put under weedmat to get control. Stage Two is beautiful, protected by thick tea tree mulch. Again Terry Foreman in his workshop said it was good to give plants a break at some stage in the year from being constantly mulched. He said that if plants are constantly mulched it makes the soil relate too much to the water world. Soil needs that exposure to relate to fire, air, earth and water. We are still inspired from his grasp and profound understanding of bio-dynamic farming and feel very positive about keeping on with the preparations 500 and 501 and fish emulsion separately. We would also in our case like to try the BD 508 preparation with silica. We have just last week made our first pot of Davidson plum jam (delicious!!) and sold our first 4 kilos of aniseed myrtle. Soil fertility wants to happen and it is good for that to happen over 3 to 5 years of slowly building up the nitrogen. Growing things well, just needs proper involvement, good intent and a fair dose of intuition. As the Irish say, *"the answer lies in the soil my son"*.

After Mook put out some words about the *Alternative Australia* project in the *Rainboweb* internet zine, I received a number of communications. Here's one that has more than a hint of weird wonderment built into it! I contacted Gary John Gray, the author, who sent it into me and together we updated with bits and pieces from his website and 'new' news.

Big Bong Peace Pipe Project
Gary John Gray

"There are many possible futures This is just a happier version than others!"

Friends, nomads and citizens of the wwworld, a moment of your time, I would like to set the record, well, if not straight, then at least, definitively bent, about the past, present and future of the Big Bong Peace Pipe Project.

You may, or may not, have heard about the mildly successful underground novel The Big Bong Theory – the book about the movie about the construction of a symbol to world peace – nor about the strategic campaign to commit a blatant act of wwworld peace by the erection of a fully functional 240 foot – 85 Metre HIGH Peace Pipe, if you haven't, it's because the decision was taken in 1995 to abandon the main stream publishing and movie industries in order to concentrate on the world wide web.

No web have U ever been,
   and no web have U ever seen,
web zone quite like this one.

As you will see from the webscheme-A-zoid on the next page, the BBt PPP web zone is a highly evolved structure of inter linked info-tainment nodules, there is a reading room (the electronic book section) a chat room where 'co-conspirators' can mingle and most importantly the web cam windows where you can watch the construction of the 'symbol to wwworld peace'. There are even instructions on how to build a scale model so that you can 'smoke the pipe of peace' where ever you are on earth. (herbs not included)

The basic story line of the novel and the web zone is; construct the most audacious statue yet conceived,' gather all the world's leaders together, or people who look like them, and then lock them inside the Peace Pipe until they are all become friends, thereby causing world peace to be 'seen to have happened.' Image, as the pop pundits say, is everything.

YOU ARE HERE
VV
V

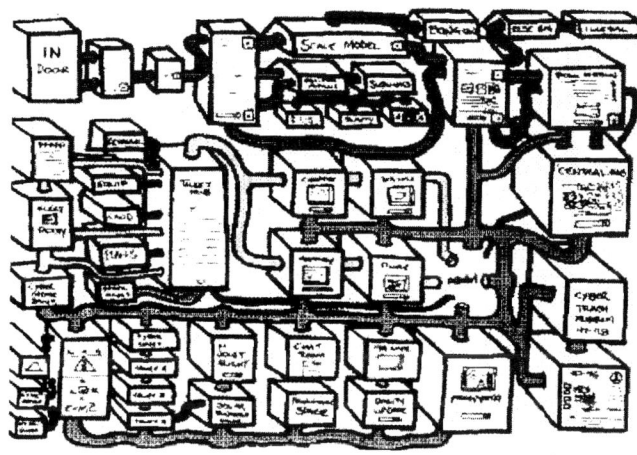

The Statue is a gigantic STEEL Cylinder, equivalent in size to a twenty floor building, the entire inside of the Big Bong will evolve into the Marijuana 'Hall of Fame' and the largest Pot Art Gallery on Earth. There are no stairs, rather ascending and descending spiral ramps that you will be able to walk along and groove on the Art as you breathe the air of green freedom. The Statue is simultaneously a Symbol to World Peace, a Pop Art Icon, a Tourist Attraction, a Concert Venue, a Movie Set, a Commercial Hemp Incinerator and an Internet Content Provider. It is the most audacious statue yet envisaged and

possibly the most exciting peace initiative currently under way anywhere on earth. The immediate area surrounding the Big Bong will be an internationally declared World Peace Zone and Hemp Theme Park, open to all the citizens of the world regardless of their smoking convictions.

Theoretically the Big Bong should be able fast track along the path already trod by Walt Disney. Walt started with a cartoon of a mouse, I started with a book about a Bong. Walt built a magic kingdom in Reality based on a fictional world of his own unique creation and vision, I want to create a magic kingdom in Reality based on a work of fiction, a Cannabis-based society. And yeah I know I'm talking about Utopia, but so was Walt. In his reality it took an awful long time to convince enough people that there was any point to build Disneyland in the first place, for some strange reason nobody believed that any one would come to visit a fairy tale castle built for a cartoon mouse...

Ummm, surely compared to Walt's concept, the Big Bong would seem to be a no brainer as far as attracting an audience goes? The amount of enthusiasm for this project amongst 'just' the back packer sub culture is awesome, they would all love to help build the symbol as part of their Australian experience, the fact that their friends and family back home will be able to see them 'On the Internet' is perceived as Too Cool.

Once all of the various infrastructure is in place then the lighting ceremony/finale scene can take place. Think 'Woodstock and then add lighting a Gigantic Bong to the mental image, need I say more? I'm sure I don't have to point out the obvious fact that more people will want to turn up at the concert than can possibly turn up, but don't worry, if you are unable to be there in person you will be able to hear and see the concert live on the WWW, you may even want to co-ordinate your own Peace Pipe Party for your friends in your arbitrary geographical reality.

In conclusion, I hope the preceding information has cleared up any misconceptions about the BBt-PPP Virtual Reality that you may, or may not have held, and/or, hopefully, has tweaked your enthusiasm gland sufficiently for you to visit the Peace Pipe Project next time you go online.

www.gasgroup.com/peacepipeproject

Peace and see you else web,
Gary John Gray.

LATE BREAKING NEWS: October 1999.
rebelart (which is me) is relieved to finally announce to us (which is all of we who are part of the BBt-PPP) that it has clinched a deal on a road side performance space.

An empty area beside a road rarely travelled, an empty space upon which to create the cyber movie set, inside the rim of the caldera of the extinct volcano that you will find at the eastern most edge of the great south land.

The Peace Zone is a blank canvas upon which to create, an empty parcel of land that is not connected (yet) to mains power or the telephone grid, it is truly in the cyber wilderness. To many people it may seem bizarre, trying to start a computer based concept inside the rim of the caldera of an extinct volcano, but of course, from our pppoint of view, it is the very fact that the Peace Zone is inside the rim of the caldera of an extinct volcano that makes this exact location so attractive, and anyway, this ppproject has always been about the creation of something new, something thing that you can't get any where or any web else, not to mention the Highly important factor that extinct volcano's are easy to find and hard to miss, being as they are, 'mountain sized.'

A tribal elder

Peter Cock is one of the 'names' that populates the myths and legends of alternative Australia. Indeed, he wrote the original book of that title back in 1979. It was subtitled communities for the future? and recounted the birth and development of alternative communities in Australia and links with both intentional communities and alternative culture on the world stage. I'd already read a fair bit about him from his contribution about life at Moora Moora in Bill Metcalf's *From Utopian dreaming to Communal reality*. In that book, Peter described himself as "an alternative seeker." I had also had an enjoyable conversation with him on the internet and obtained a copy of Alternative Australia.

Peter, like Bill Metcalf, is one of the Australian tribal elders of the alternative community scene. And, even more than Bill, he was personally involved in the hippy end of the 70s counter cultural scene. His 1979 book provided a good Cook's tour around the early hippy settlements at Barran Falls near Kuranda and the Cedar Bay beach settlement north of Daintree. Peter described them as "crash pads" and told how it was the media that had confusingly described them as "communes" and "hippy communities." Both remain icons of the Australian alternative movement, but their reality was more sordid, with glassy eyed hippies doped-out and destitute, scrounging handouts from new arrivals and anyone with a bit more energy. Now they are remembered, along with the early Nimbin festivals, through mushroom-enhanced, or rose-tinted spectacles, hindsight. In the 1979 *Alternative Australia*, Peter wrote of one, typical underground paper, *Mother Earth News*, that the editors, *"travelled around Australia visiting and interviewing alternative seekers for their magazine. They tended to hide the harsh, unpleasant drudgery of rural life, promoting the 'greener pastures on the other side' to youthful, alienated city dwellers."*

At a very personal level, Peter has been something of a human barometer of the alternative movement in Australia. He has shown determination, passion, sensitivity and obstinacy at different times and places. He has been dubbed as a 'leader of the alternative movement', 'inauthentic', 'observer', 'too academic', 'non-political', and from his own view "a bridge between the Corporate State and the alternatives movement." But, even more important, has been his move from observer and commentator on alternative lifestyles to committed member of Moora Moora, with all the conflicts and tensions that brings. After 21 years in the community (in Metcalf, 1995) Peter commented, *"Most importantly, coming up against my own limits helps me to listen to other voices. Life has humbled me and opened the door to larger guidance."* And, finally, *"If you should take the risk to venture into community, then be assured that you will learn more about yourself, about us and living with this planet than you ever dreamed possible. I have and I am thankful for the continuing Journey."*

ALTERNATIVE AUSTRALIA

Communities for the Future?

Peter Cock

Come and live a little with Peter in Moora Moora!

Community Building Pathways: stories from Moora Moora co-op.

Peter Cock

Alternative Australia is about rebuilding a culture of co-operation between people and the rest of the planet. Alternative Australians are building cutting edge realities that are a culture in waiting for the time and place for their role in transformation of the dominant paradigm: this transformation will surely come when the planet says 'enough is enough'. My part here is to tell stories of one community's experience of home building with the earth, sun and of working to make intergenerational partnerships for sustainability.

The first story begins four years after the beginning of the Moora Moora community which has been developing for 30 years. It is a time when the manifesto has been written, the land was found on top of Mt Toolebewong outside of Healesville in Victoria, and the planned layout of 6 clusters of 30 houses with a community centre was completed.

Developing connections between people and place

Moora Moora is in the midst of going through the uncertainty of gaining long term finance and seeking local government permission. We are struggling hard to find our feet. Will our divisions blow us apart? Will we take the risk and start building? What if long term finance doesn't come through or we are unable to persuade local government that we are not here today and gone tomorrow?

Our main asset is a shared vision, some beginning structures for decision making and a few resolutions to guide our development. We are often in conflict as we have few cultural foundations of community to trust in or to hold us. The advantage of this constraint has meant that we had to be on the land, in the place, to tune in and listen before we rushed around trying to remake the land in our own image. This time allowed for a creative dialectic between who we are and where we are that helped drive a pattern of community development suited to the mountainscape.

This first story is as much about building community relations as providing shelter. It is as much about building commitment to a place and learning to work with the materials nature provides of earth, sun, wind, rocks and trees. The experience taught us how to reconnect with nature by working with its locally expressed elements.

Co-operative building

With uncertainty as our dominant reality some of us committed to building. Like our community plans, our house design tended towards the grand. Of course mine had to be an autonomous house design, with the first Victorian designed solar centrally heated house with multi levels and angles that are never right. Sandra, my partner, was a life saver in her dogged determination to keep going. I suffered from my ideas being so far ahead of my hands. Thank god for the blindness and arrogance of youth. I had never built a house and have trouble hammering in a nail without bending. I was scared. Luckily I was Ok as a labourer and as an organiser of materials and help. House building involves so much to do and so many different domains of design and construction; from energy systems, landscaping, concrete pours, wood working to stone wall construction, hunting second hand materials, best deals and more. It always takes longer than your worst fears. Our home, which we dearly love, took seven years to complete. The sheer energy involved, the strain as well as delight means that it is no wonder most people get others to build their houses and spend their life time paying for it. Most owner-builders say that the key to success is to approach building your home as a life style, building as part of your everyday life.

A key to making the experience achievable and pleasurable was the community. Most of us knew something we could contribute to building but none of us knew it all. So we formed the first Moora Moora building group. Which was simply seven home builders agreeing to work together once a week building our houses. A roster was drawn up so that each week we rotated whose house we were working on. It was up to each home builder to organise the tasks and allocate the work force. We would meet for coffee in the morning and review what was to be done. Whose house it was provided lunch and drinks. We developed over time a system of credits and debits so that individuals were free to come or not without anyone feeling that they were missing out. We very quickly established who was good at what. As a group we found useful ways of employing each other and learnt to become comfortable with different levels of skill, standards of care and levels of courage to have a go.

It is amazing how mistakes can add character to buildings, or can be hidden and not matter. We each in our own way all wore a design or building cross. For some it was doing everything by hand, for others using stone work, for us it was building too complex a building, that would sustain our interest and pleasure for a life time – so far it has.

Our group consisted of seven members, three couples and a single mum. We were in the 25-35 age bracket. We worked together for over four years. Because of our success another building group was formed that worked together on another

day of the week. The group stopped when most of the work was done and our houses were liveable. After that, building co-operation was on a person to person, largely barter then paid basis.

This group provided the support structure to keep going and not to become overwhelmed. We all learned new skills through trial and error and were freed from having to do it all yourself. Even so, in our case, we also employed some outside labour.

After making houses liveable, there was then the slower development process. For example, houses were built usually in either formal discrete stages or informal ones which involved constructing a shell, then fitting it out with core living areas and then bedrooms. The final phase; the never to be completed finishing touches, is usually done much latter and often in tandem with updating.

We have used all kinds of ways of earth building, mud brick, rammed earth, rammed blocks and earth pour. The latter is a more recent use, as we have found it to be the most labour efficient and it can be used during all seasons. Twenty five houses later what we have created is a terrific variety of earth, timber and stone constructions. Some large and complex, others small and simple.

Developing renewable energy systems
All are passive solar designed and powered and built at less than half the cost of conventional buildings. As Moora Moora is not connected to the power grid, the developmental process also applied to energy systems. Houses often began with a few gas lights, one solar panel and then gradually upgraded the number of solar panels. We have tried a number of wind generators, which, but for one have been very troublesome. Even with six panels, our use of power is approximately one quarter of normal domestic use. With new invertors, more efficient and cheaper panels, solar power is much easier and more reliable than it was 30 years ago when we started to experiment.

There is nothing like helping to build your own house for it to engender an attachment as home. Those who have built stay longer than those who haven't. There is something special about walking around the property visiting houses you helped build. They are now part of me and me them; the land, community and self are joined in the process and celebrated in the end result. It is amazing what we can do when it is done together. Doing it all yourself asks too much. When self reliance is without community interdependence, then owner builders risk the paradox of losing their marriage/family while making their home.

Home building using local materials is one way of building community and love of place. Another, which only began two years ago, is through our co-operative cow, Sally.

Expanding community boundaries: Sally the co-operative cow

What matters isn't that we are self sufficient, nor that we build all of our own houses. If we are to become better carers of the planet and each other then we need to be engaged to some extent in taking care of our shelter and growing at least some of our own food. Doing this preferably in a co-operative context means that whatever we do helps us to relearn what it means to live with the earth and with each other.

In the early days we had two house cows which were difficult largely because we didn't know really what we were doing, but for a while we persisted because that is what you do when you are into self sufficiency. Soon we gave up. This time we were better organised. That is we said we will not start a cow co-operative unless there are at least six shareholders committed to milking once a week.

Peter at home milking our cow

Members were circulated with plans. As there was not sufficient interest we invited and secured expressions of interest from neighbours across the road. Since then Sally, a Friesian/Ayrshire cross, on her third calf, has been purchased. She and us are well settled into our patterns. We have back up milkers, and a built in community market for milk which is also made into cheese and yoghurt.

This cow has been a vehicle for building connections between clusters and between the co-operative and our neighbours. Sally has helped us to become more of one community sharing a mountain top. She has provided a stimulus for neighbours to work together on common projects and for the mountain top community to explore establishing a land care group.

Sally has also been a bridge to make connections to place and seasons. For those of us who commute to the city she provides an opportunity for an intimate relationship with another species and its particular quieting, reflective qualities.

Balancing formal structures with informal: our café

At the same time as Sally was settling in so too was our new café and food co-operative. Every Saturday morning members, residents and neighbours gather to collect their paper, bread and other co-op food purchases. Most of those who come either have a coffee or order a lunch. This provides the reason to sit around and chat with whoever is there. Conversation varies from the need for rain, films, children and their ways, the football and who has moved up the tennis ladder to the gossip of the week.

Moora Moora café

It is run on a cost plus small profit for the manager, or if she needs a break, whoever runs it for that day. The café is housed in a building that started life as a garage, then a flat, a school and a games room. Colourfully painted and adorned with members art works, the café provides an informal meeting place that helps to balance formal meetings.

Building intergenerational connections
The challenging journey we are now embarked upon in Moora Moora is building intergenerational bridges. This involves seeing the present in the context of looking forwards and backwards with equal intention. The trouble is that we have been socialised to not only believe in the power and autonomy of the individual, but to interact increasingly only with peers. To build a new paradigm society involves rebuilding intergeneration connections. Our migrant population has trouble seeing people and their contribution, who are a mere generation away, let alone being able to honour our ancestors and the spirit of all those who have gone before us. We all know the tendency if one generation does x for the next to do y, which the marketeers feed on to support the fashion industry.

When we began we were the young braves of the 70s, 30 years on we have been working to bring into the community a 90s version. If we are not able to attract the next wave of young bloods then we are doomed to a slow dying out with the first generation. When we began there was a clean slate. We didn't have the support of being part of a community with a history, it was all intentional, had to be designed, decided and gradually evolved. Now that this exists, it means that the next generations have this as a support. Established community culture and polices, however, can easily be seen as an oppression of initiative and freedom; the very feelings that helped to provoke the west's flight from the bonds of community.

I remember clearly a passionate conversation with one of our new braves who was railing against the co-operative owning beef animals to eat. I said words to the effect that the challenge we face, if we are to be in partnership, is for you to listen to the past and for me to be open to the future. The new young bloods struggle to be open to the older people and their lessons from the past. For me it is a challenge because it is more difficult the older I become to remain open to change and to trust that there are other ways of doing things, that while different it can still be in the community interest. After so long it is a challenge to allow space for each to make their own particular contribution, to shift from being an old warrior to honouring my love of place and community that calls me to be open rather than defensive of past achievements or taken for granted community/cultural practices.

Conflict between generations is inevitable given our current cultural milieu. Conflict is powerful and needs to be handled with care. Conflict can be a tremendous energy for creativity and innovation or alternatively risks division and smouldering and finally often explosive 'war'. Communities, like the ecology, can be slowly eaten away by the development of a gossip culture that means everyone discusses everybody else but rarely do they directly with the person concerned. Gradually the thread of truth is lost and when the community meets over coffee or a meeting the gossip baggage is piled high before anyone has spoken. If not managed effectively this can destroy a community, as it has a number of clusters over the years. It is how we deal with conflict that determines whether it is creative or destructive.

The issue isn't which side is correct, but rather the importance of benefit of doubt, of giving an open hearing and asking that there may well be another, even legitimate, view. When small groups of like-minded generations meet informally, their commonality of viewpoints is almost inevitably reinforced. In order for that not to result in the creation of a divide, communication across the differences is as important as mutual supporters. Once a 'right' position is adopted within a small group, for the larger group it can be the beginnings of division.

The experience of Moora Moora is that even if a mediator is used, it is difficult to resolve conflict once it has exploded. This is especially so if others have stoked the fires by supporting one side or the other, rather than helping to deal directly with an issue by being as a supporter of both and the need to resolve it. Here lies the co-operative interest. What happens when it is unresolved is that people eventually leave and the co-operative has to rebuild. The co-operative is robust, but rebuilding is a process that takes a lot of time and effort, and friends become casualties. You can only rebuild so many times.

A Moora Moora house

If we are to work effectively with difference and inevitable conflicts, acceptance of difference is a vital step. However, for there to be a community there has to be limits to tolerance such as our commitment that bans dogs, cats and agrees not to connect to the power grid. These things in common help to define what being part of a community such as Moora Moora means – they provide the common ground within which it is then possible to work together with differences.

It is a challenge to build a culture that confronts and transcends destructive gossiping. Practice of the principle of 'listen only, listen once' is not an easy habit to adopt. It is easier to join with another in judgement of a third party than, after listening once, encourage her/him to talk with the other directly.

Experiencing the phases of community development are the stuff of life. Regenerating experiences of community is one of the key challenges if we are to relearn how to be part of the earth and to live within its bounty. Rebuilding our connections with the earth are deeply interwoven with rediscovering our intergenerational interdependency.

These snippets from the Moora Moora stories illustrate that the processes of community development can be facilitated by co-operative engagement with provision of basic needs for food and shelter.

Introducing the Metamorphic Ritual Theatre

"We live in a time of cultural diversity, and yet global unification."

Orryelle Bascule/Defenestrate

Actually, if you've seen them they need no introduction. Internationally, they belong to the anarchistic performing territory which has embraced Welfare State, the Mutoid Waste Company, Archaos – all the groups who involve their audience as performers in the full-on, having-it action.

I'd wanted to include an Australian alternative performing arts group, something unusual, unique. The answer came surfing in from Graham St John, who e-mailed me, saying:
"I'd highly recommend Orryelle Defenestrate as a contributor for your book. He's probably one of Australia's foremost artists on the edge, responsible for Labyrinth installations at ConFest, founder of Metamorphic Ritual Theatre Company and dabbler in untold weirdness. He's also most loquacious."

Coincidentally, I'd just seen the *Going Tribal* video which included clips of Orryelle and Mutation Parlour, which gave me a clue or three as to where he's coming from. Then Orryelle did the nice thing and said he'd like to be involved.

The Mutation Parlour was originally a physical place, a bodyarts studio. Now it's the name of a band-come-amorphous-musical-collective. There is also the virtual Mutation Parlour, a website with a dazzling array of w-rite-ings, spell-ings, art, performance

records and other endeavours: http://www.crossroads.wild.net.au

Enough said, here he is: Orryelle Defenestrate. Join him as he removes a few of his myriad masks:

Photo© Sophia

Orryelle with batwing ear-wigs '98

The Metamorphic Ritual Theatre Group began in 1994. Often we will take the audience (individually or in groups) through a physical landscape as part of their journey; but even when we work within a one-room theatre we aim to offer the audience as well as performers the potential for at least one level of per-sonal metamorphosis via our ritual theatre. Our 'plays' are occasionally fully scripted but usually develop from a basic premise, concept or plot which is workshopped and developed by the group, individual performers devising their own (flexible) lines and move-ments within this context, with feedback and suggestion from the others involved. Sometimes sections of the plays, often towards the end, are left open to spontane-ous chaotic elements once the 'stage has been set' by the more structured sections.

The Labyrinth
Our Labyrinths are interactive spaces in which initiates meet different mythological and mytho-illogical characters in differ-ent atmospheric environments as they wind their way through the maze, spiralling into the centre where the night culminates in a final ritual performance before they are 'reborn' from this womb back into the rest of the festival.

At ConFest '95
The first Labyrinth, at DTE ConFest Easter '95, was basically a traditional Labyrinth weaving, using no electricity or modern technology. Webs were woven with wool and string into the

Central webs
1st Labyrinth
Easter
Confest '95

high and low ropes which formed the paths, becoming progressively denser and more textured towards the centre. The layout of this Labyrinth (designed by Orryelle, Bex and Ra'en) basically consisted of a spinning chamber which one would arrive in upon entrance, four spirals into the centre, and five elemental paths which connected these two main areas.

Ancient myths from various different cultures (Greek, Norse, Celtic, Australian, Aboriginal, Mayan) were woven together to form the essence of the performance/initiation cycles. Initiates entered through the labia-like gateway, formed from an old forked tree inverted, and came into the Spinning chamber, where they met Clotho – the maiden, the spinner, first of the Three Fates, the Moerae. Sitting at her spinning-wheel, spinning the threads of destiny, she requested they spin the Wheel of Fate. By doing so, they selected one of four elemental paths through the Labyrinth, as determined by where the torch on the wheel landed in relation to the elemental pentacle beneath it. They then set off on their journey, bearing the threads given them by the Spinner.

The elemental paths – fire, earth, air and water – were random mazes through the woods, designed by those individuals or groups who wove them. Sculpture, imagery and characters appropriate to each element occupied these paths and confronted initiates on their journeys.

Each path ultimately led to one of the four inner spirals.

Arachne crawled about in this web, above people's heads. When they reached the centre she calmly greeted them as Lachesis – the mother, the weaver, second of the Three Fates – and wove in their etheric threads.

Then initiates confronted the Minotaur, representing the beast within, people's shadows or primal selves. He symbolically killed them, often with an embrace, at which point Death, Atropos – the cutter, the crone, last of the three Fates – appeared. With their threads cut, initiates were sent (by Hermes – messenger, guide and psychopomp of the Labyrinth) down the spirit path (5th arm of the elemental pentacle) which led like a vaginal passage straight from the centre, back through the spinning chamber and out the labia gateway, to be reborn into the rest of the festival.

Each night's cycle ended with the death of the Minotaur. An initiate would be chosen as Theseus, the hero. Upon entrance the spinner, who was also Ariadne, would give him a sword and the Golden Thread, which he was to unwind on his journey through the Labyrinth. When he reached the centre to face the Minotaur, the Three Fates would there converge forming an eight-limbed (six arms, two legs) triple-headed kama-kali spider formation.

The battle ended with Theseus lopping off the Minotaur's head (a costume appendage above the player's actual head), after which he would then be crowned the new Horned God by Ariadne.

The opening of our first Labyrinth was a chaotic affair. We had many more people than expected and it very rapidly got out of control...it was a learning experience...the subsequent performances and installations developed from this tumultuous beginning.

After several days of intensive de-construction/cleaning up we vowed we'd never do it again, but two years later found ourselves discussing ways we could expand upon and enhance the original concept.

ConFest '97: 2nd Labyrinth
The second Labyrinth, held at the Down To Earth Confest Easter '97, was an even more spectacular and intricate event.

We received more funding from D.T.E., who remembered our earlier achievement, and we had a stronger core group committed to the realization of the project. We used modern technology to develop the same basic mythological/magical premises as used in our first Labyrinth (including a conglomeration between the Metamorphic RitualTheatre group and others, with Mutoid Waste Co, Dweller on the Threshold and Clan Analogue etc.).

Baphomet 2nd Labyrinth

The main constructional difference was the inclusion of DTE's large geodesic dome in the centre. The web-like structure of its metal framework fitted well within the spirals, and it provided an arena for performance. Initiates were admitted into the dome one at a time by gatekeepers on either side of it. After facing the Minotaur, Death's gentle touch led them into the mirror chamber...(initiates) ascended the spiral staircase which was the axis mundi of the dome. This represented the journey to 'Caer Arianhrod', the spiral castle of Celtic mythology where you go when you die.

Emerging on top of the dome, initiates would then climb a rope ladder down to the Netherworld, a kind of 'cosmic waiting room' between incarnations. There they would remain until eventually Theseus arrived in the dome, provoking the final performance. Electric/electronic soundscapes backstage, gradually increased in volume and intensity, until a full musical set accompanied the final battle...when the Minotaur died, the generator was switched off causing all lights and sound to degenerate into blackness and silence. Seven different acoustic chakra tones (chanted by the entire cast and crew) ascended the musical scale as the Minotaur ascended the seven steps of the spiral staircase, climaxed by a red flare shot off into the heavens with his spirit.

Then Atropos cut the threads surrounding the Netherworld, releasing everyone down the spirit path to be reborn. The vagina for this second Labyrinth was a long fully-enclosing red stretchy fabric tunnel. This second Labyrinth contained a Mutation Parlour at the Crossroads of all the elemental paths...initiates could be physically and psychically mutated as a part of their journey, if game to receive the 'doorstamp' which was a branding.

The major plot difference of this second Labyrinth was that on the last performance night (of three), a woman played Theseus. When she reached the centre and slayed the Minotaur, she became the new hermaphroditic Horned God/Goddess/Demon/Demoness of the PandaemonAeon: Baphomet!

This all happened around midnight going into April Fool's Day '97, and initiated the transition into an all-night de-construction doof party in the Labyrinth.

The Third Labyrinth at Earthcore 99 launched the Labyrinth CD, which translates the concepts into various atmospheric soundscapes, so the listener may experience aurally the initiatory

Three Fates at 3rd Labyrinth

journey through the Labyrinth. It is a combination of weird electronica and old-world instrumentation, recorded ritually to evoke the various atmospheres of the Labyrinth; The Labyrinth CD can be ordered for $15 (Aust) from: Orryelle, PO Box 2149, Fitzroy B.C., Vict.3065, Australia (Make cheques or money orders payable to Geoff Day), or via http://www.crossroads.wild.net.au/lab.htm

The third Labyrinth layered Egyptian mythology and

Qabbalistic symbolism into the panglobal tapestry, and each minotaur represented a different aeon according to the Pentagrammaton formula. The final cycle presented the merging (rather than slaying as previously) of Horus and Maat to form the hermaphrodite of the Pandaemonaeon.

Mutation manifesto:

Our bodies are toys to be played with. Humans are unique on this planet in their zest for transformation. Humans, have always been into transforming themselves and/or their environment.

Photo © Ben Last

Bird-masks of Maat on the Tree of Life – Pentagrammaton '98

There are transformations of the self which are more permanent – such physical changes as scarification, tattooing and body alterations. Irrefutable changes such as these are likely to affect the consciousness of those who undergo them. In modern western society there is a huge drive towards mass conformity. In reaction many of those who differ from the norm do so to the extreme. Those who do not wish to be identified with the imbecilic conforming masses make an effort to individualise their appearance as much as possible.

Over the decades there have been many different subcultural styles. In the nineties these are all being mixed and merged and mismatched into new mutated forms. The modern mutant draws from many eras, places, cultures and subcultures, bending and blending them together, distorting and contorting

them into the future.

Tattooing is an ages-old art form that is finally being recognised as such. Modern western tattooists are at last breaking away from the confines of 'pop' art, cartoon imagery and realism, now incorporating tribal designs from many cultures. Some tattooists are beginning to take body form into account...moving beyond mere surface drawing and into the realms of painting and even sculpture. Reclaiming the tribal heritage is a major aspect of the modern tattoo.

We are not so bound to the forms we were born with as it may at first seem – our bodies are toys to be played with. The possibilities are endless. Stagnation is our enemy.

Mutation manifesto Part 2 – Mutation and Technology:

Since I wrote Part One of the Mutation Manifesto, the potential for mutation of the human species has increased rapidly. Advances in computers, prosthetics, robotics and genetics have begun to blur the boundaries between human and machine. Body artists such as Orlan and Stelarc have experimented with using new technologies as tools for physical transformation, offering social comment on future directions via performance art. Orlan's operations, performed theatrically yet very real, demonstrate an extremity of physical mutation via plastic surgery. Perhaps ultimately her message is that physical form is becoming less relevant, that it is becoming mere putty for modern technologies to knead and model?

Stelarc's cybernetic extra arm, operated by far-off minds via the internet, demonstrated the frightening potential of virtual/actual interactions. He claims that the human form is becoming obsolete – we are merely data in the information age.

Theories abound as to future of the human species and our relationship with cyberspace. It is being suggested that humans will eventually be able to 'download' themselves into cyberspace, to become freeform in realms of information; able to be 'uploaded' back into robots or other forms.

Fantastic alternatives and enhancers may be manifested, surely, but simultaneously these should remind us of the sacredness of the flesh, and of the Earth. Let us use technology for transformation and even escapism, but not to the exclusion of our outer biosphere.

My own mutations have been primarily organic in nature. By suturing on parts of animals, such as snakeskins to the arms and eagle-wings into the shoulder blades, I re-connect with my bestial nature, while also aligning myself with the spirit of the animal integrated and its magical powers. For me, physical mutation is a glorious celebration of the malleability of the physical form.

Let us use our technology to enhance and complement our physical environment and our physical selves, but not abandon them to it. *Organica Cyberia Hybridica!*

Global Chakra Workings:
The first in a series of Global Chakra Workings organized by Orryelle and the Order ov ChAos was performed on the October (Samhain) full moon at Mt Shasta, California USA, considered by many to be the Muladhara or base chakra of Gaia, the Earth. This Tenstar Weaving (see http://www.crossroads.wild.net.au/base.htm) laid the foundations for the 13-Tribe Weaving near Uluru (Ayers Rock) – Gaia's Manipura/ Solar Plexus chakra in mid-2000, a spectacular ritual which is to be a part of the mobile convoy interna-tional festival in Central Australia May-Oct 2000 – 'Earthdream 2000', organized by Mutoid Waste Com-pany.

By the time this book is out the Svadisthana working will have also occurred, at Lake Titicaca in South America. Such group chakra workings (not all physical weavings) will be performed at each of Gaia's seven chakra points, the initiates' chakric activations being microcos-mic resonances with Gaia's own rising kundalini, the awaken-ing Rainbow Serpent of Australian Aboriginal mythology (whom the Aborigines say rises at the end of time), called by

the Norse the Midgard Serpent (who also rises at 'Ragnarok' – the 'end of the world') by the Greeks Ouroboros and by the Babylonians' Tiamat ('serpent of chaos who sleeps at the bottom of the ocean of time'). Thus all mythologies coalesce towards the year 2012, by which time the kundalini of the collective consciousness should be sufficiently awakening to bring about the paradigm shift (the end of time/ the world as we know it) predicted by the Mayans with their 'return of Quetzalcoatl' (the 'Feathered Serpent', an obvious kundalini/ caduceus metaphor) and Terence McKenna's 'Timewave Zero' software which maps out time spirals according to the ancient Chinese IChing oracle. Activating group kundalini at each of Gaia's chakras via these weavings, progressively towards 2012, would help to resonate with the intense awakening of these Great Rainbow and Feathered Serpents, the Ida and Pingala of Gaia's kundalini.

Visitors from all over the world will converge on central Australia in 2000. I intend to hold workshops on the chakra tones for the months of festivities leading up to the weaving, so

Chakra Weaving – Pentagrammaton '98

that many can contribute their voices and energy into this spectacular symbolic union of all peoples.

The Thirteenth Tribe Weaving will be a balancing ceremony between sun, moon and earth. It shall begin in the afternoon, with the sun beating down on the twelve initiates as they are woven together by the Thir-teenth in the centre, connected by their own solar plexus (manipura) chakras to each other and the Kuxan Suum (Mayan word for the solar umbilical cord).

The Weaver connects the twelve initiates to represent the union of the Twelve Tribes or source races of humanity (which exist in Hopi prophecies, as well as Jewish and other ancient traditions) to form the Thirteenth, the emerging multi-cultural global tribe. The twelve-pointed star thus formed also suggests the traditional solar 12-month zodiac. The piercings through

Cast and Crew, 3rd Labyrinth, Easter Earthcore '99

the chest by which the initiates are to be woven together are reminiscent of the Indian sundance ceremony. (The Mayans, I may add, achieved trance to 'see the vision-serpent' by passing barbed ropes through their tongues and penises. Piercing as a form of gnosis is an ancient tradition.)

Then at dusk (the 'even-ing' between dark and light, sun and moon) the weaver hirself is woven in, as the 13th Tribe is symbolically formed. As the moon rises she moves out to become the thirteenth point in the star-web, which then represents: the lunar zodiac of which Arachne is the Thirteenth sign; the 13-baktun time-map of the Mayans, the Thirteenth point of which represents the final cycle from 1992 to 2012 – the Solar Age (glyph: AHAU); and the global unity of all peoples and cultures as the Thirteenth Tribe.

More about this project can be found at
http://www.crossroads.wild.net.au/lib13.htm

The above text and all photographs not marked otherwise are copyright ã 1999 **Orryelle Defenestrate.**

Whilst ferreting around for information on alternative publications in Australia I met up with Pip Wilson, founder of the alternative media, Rainbow Archives, at the Mitchell Library in Sydney. He has been kind enough to provide a very personal description of his own involvement in producing some of Australia's best loved alternative magazines, including *Maggie's Farm*. At about the same time, I heard about Susan Forde's research based from the School of Film, Media and Cultural Studies at Griffiths University. I'd already met with Bill Metcalf, who also works at Griffiths, and through him I tracked down Susan, who has provided the following summary of the development of Australia's alternative news media. It's a bit more academic than many of the other pieces, but no less important for that!

From Battlers to Big Issues: News coverage in the Australian alternative press industry, 1914-1999
Susan Forde

The alternative press in Australia has formed a vital part of the newspaper industry for more than a century, but it is often considered the 'poor cousin' of the mainstream dailies and their associated publications. But there is much evidence that the history of the alternative press is as romantic and rich as that claimed by its mainstream counterparts – publications such as *Direct Action* and *The Worker* captured the halcyon days of the great strikes and the anti-conscription movement in the early 20th century in great detail. Similarly, the counter-culture or underground publications of the 1960s and 1970s such as *Oz* magazine and *The Battler* recorded the social revolutions and change of this important period in our history. Richard Walsh's *Nation Review* and later Max Suich's *Independent Monthly* built on the reputation of earlier publications, and for some time enjoyed large readerships and financial success. This article is based on university research I undertook recently. My aim is to provide an historical overview of the Australian independent and alternative press industry, from the working-class publications of the early 1900s, through to contemporary alternative news publications such as *The Republican, Sydney City Hub, Green Left Weekly* and *The Big Issue Australia*. I've also made an evaluation of their role in the development of journalism in Australia.

The publications that fulfil the definition of 'alternative' or 'independent' cover a broad range – from alternative lifestyle magazines such as *Grassroots*, to surfing publications of the 60s such as *Scrounge*, through to the radical left publications, *Socialist Worker* and *The Battler*. Generally, there is too much to cover in one study, so it was out of necessity that I limited my research into Australia's alternative press to those publications that were providing news and information, rather than publications presenting only alternative lifestyles, new age magazines and so on. I generally selected publications to examine based on the following:

- · … they were not owned by major chain
- · … they cover general news and social issues
- · … they come out at least six times a year
- · … they are not affiliated to any of the major political parties
- · … and they are not niche publications dealing with specialist issues only such as environment magazines, feminist publications, surfing magazines, alternative music magazines and so on.

I want to give a general overview of the scope of the industry through Australia's history, as well as briefly looking at the contemporary state of it. This article examines the alternative press in three major blocks, primarily chronological: the working class press era, the underground press era, and the contemporary era. Literature on the non-mainstream press in Australia is very thin, and indeed many of our publications have not experienced the success of their counterparts in the United States and to a lesser extent Britain. This is usually attributed to issues of large distances for publications to be distributed, a widely dispersed population, restrictive defamation and libel laws and essentially monopoly control of distribution in Australia.

The working-class press

Historian Verity Bergmann identifies *The Radical*, established in 1887, as Australia's first regular socialist newspaper (1985: 35), while Edgar Ross claims Australia boasts the first trade union-owned daily paper in the world, the *Barrier Daily Truth*, which was established in 1898 (1982: 26). The Aboriginal print media was even further advanced than the radical working-class press, with the emergence of the first Aboriginal newspaper, a weekly newsletter called the *Flinders Island Weekly Chronicle* as early as 1836 (Rose, 1996).

A group which played an extremely important role in the workers' movement and which contributed greatly to the growth and popularity of the working-class press of the time, was the movement led by the Industrial Workers of the World (IWW) during World War I. Publications such as *Direct Action*, *Solidarity* and the Australian Workers' Union newspaper *The Worker* challenged the stereotypes of this anti-capitalist, anti-war group which were presented in the mainstream media at the height of the IWW's popularity and influence.

From the beginning, there was a clear difference between the mainstream publications and the alternative or independent publications. While the latter were openly advocatory, the mainstream was claiming objectivity. Compare, for example, the following two paragraphs written after war was declared by Britain. The first was printed in the mainstream *Bulletin* magazine – clearly in support of the war – the other in the IWW's *Direct Action*, which had opposed working class involvement in the war:

"For Britain! Good old Britain!
Where our fathers first drew breath,
We'll fight like true Australians,
Facing danger, wounds or death.
With Britain's other gallant sons
We're going hand in hand;
Our War-cry 'Good old Britain', boys,
Our own dear motherland."
Frank Johnstone, 'Sons of Australia', *Bulletin* magazine (in Turner, 1969: 3).

"Let those who own Australia do the fighting. Put the wealthiest in the front ranks; the middle class next; follow these with politicians, lawyers, sky pilots and judges. Answer the declaration of war with the call for a GENERAL STRIKE."
Tom Barker in *Direct Action* (in Turner, 1969: 3).

And the famous TO ARMS!! poster, also by *Direct Action's* Tom Barker:

"TO ARMS!!
Capitalists, Parsons, Politicians,
Landlords, Newspaper Editors, and
Other Stay-at Home Patriots.
YOUR COUNTRY NEEDS YOU IN THE TRENCHES!
WORKERS,
FOLLOW YOUR MASTERS!! "

At its peak in 1917, *Direct Action's* circulation stood at about 15,000 copies per week (Armstrong, 1990: 67). This compares with the current circulation of around 6,000 for *Green Left Weekly*, and 1,500 for the International Socialist Organisation's *Socialist Worker*.

In 1917, the Federal Government ordered the withdrawal of *Direct Action* from the postal service because it had acted against the national interest by opposing the war effort. In late 1917, the presses of Direct Action were seized by police, and the newspaper banned from publication, after the IWW (which had changed its name to the Workers' Defence and Release Committee) was declared an illegal organisation (Turner, 1969: 86).

The Australian Workers' Union's, *Worker*, was achieving similar success *to Direct Action*, principally on the back of its strong anti-conscription campaign. It experienced similar problems with the government – editor Boote was convicted for failing to submit articles on the war to the censor (Walker, 1976: 253). It can be safely said that such publications had a greater impact on the politicians of the time than contemporary socialist publications – Boote was invited to sit on a three-member board of editors to advise the censor on war issues in 1918, but declined the offer (Walker, 1976: 254).

The heightened influence of these publications is most likely due to the strength of the workers' movement at the time, reflected in the strong circulations enjoyed by the radical newspapers. The Australian Workers' Union membership, for example, increased from 19,000 in 1905 to 61,500 in 1914 (Walker, 1976: 138).

In addition to these city-based publications, provincial towns supported their own anti-establishment publications, mainly associated with left-wing and socialist groups – the

Maryborough Alert, the *Gympie Truth*, and the *Charters Towers New Eagle* were just some examples of late 19th century Queensland alternative papers (Bergmann, 1985: 181).

The end of the anti-conscription movement signalled the end of a strong period for radical newspapers, although some continued into the 1920s and 1930s. In 1923 the newly formed Communist Party of Australia launched its own newspaper, the *Workers' Weekly*, which experienced a particularly strong period during the 1930s due to popular dissatisfaction with the economic downturn and massive unemployment of the depression (O'Lincoln, 1985).

The early radical press in Australia had a strong mobilising function, continually encouraging readers to agitate, demonstrate, and motivate fellow workers. This is a theme that follows through to the contemporary era.

While the alternative press industry in the early 20th century was dominated by the working-class/socialist/labour political press, the industry in the 1960s and 1970s took on a new face. Emerging after the conservative Menzies era of the 1940s and 1950s, the 'underground' or 'counter-culture' press represented a important stage in the development of an alternative press industry. Like their counterparts in Britain and the United States, their aim was to challenge and shock conservative moral and social values.

One of the best-known Australian alternative publications was *Oz* magazine, established by three Sydney university graduates, Richard Neville, Richard Walsh and Martin Sharp, in the early 1960s. The *Sydney Oz* magazine, which had a peak circulation of 40,000 in the mid-1960s, was most well-known for the trial and conviction of its three editors on obscenity charges. Oz was preceded by several independent publications which really set the ground work for the boom in the alternative press in the 1970s. In 1958, *Sydney Morning Herald* financial editor Tom Fitzgerald established *Nation*, a fortnightly opinion publication dealing with issues of major national and international significance.

From 1958 until its closure in 1972 (when it merged with *Sunday Review* to become *Nation Review* – see below), *Nation* gave voice to a number of writers who later became major players on the AuStreetralian political and journalistic scene – Mungo MacCallum (snr), Geoffrey Sawer, Bob Ellis, Manning Clark, Max Harris, Robert Hughes, Brian Johns, Sylvia Lawson, and Max Suich among others.

Fitzgerald was spurred to establish *Nation* after the closure of two independent publications in the 1950s, Allan Fraser's *Observer*, and Harold Levien's *Voice*. Fitzgerald's personal opposition to the White Australia policy, and his belief that Australia needed to position itself more in the Asian region, rather than continually aligning with Britain, formed the editorial basis of the early editions. Throughout the time *Nation* was published, Fitzgerald was offered financial support by both the Fairfax and Packer publishing houses, but Fitzgerald refused offers in the interests of maintaining his publication's independence. He retained his position as Financial Editor on the *Sydney Morning Herald* throughout most of his time at *Nation*.

He finally accepted an offer from millionaire Gordon Barton to buy out *Nation's* masthead and list of subscribers. Nation had actually made way for the new publications to flourish, and introduced a new type of mainstream/alternative publication to the Australian media landscape. The 1980s saw the emergence of several new publications in the tradition of *Nation*.

A number of alternative mastheads dominated the Australian scene throughout the 1970s. *Source* magazine, *Revolution*, and *High Times* were four major publications with varying levels of success. Also *The Digger, The Works, Scrounge*, and *Connection* had varying levels of success in appealing to a politically aware readership eager to challenge social mores and values.

The well-publicised but unsuccessful, *The Living Daylights* (*TLD*), was established in 1973 in an attempt to topple *The Digger* as the major counter culture publication in Australia. *TLD* was edited by Richard Neville after his return from the success of London *Oz* magazine. *The Living Daylights* was published by the parent company of the *Nation Review* which also owned the *Sunday Observer* newspaper (which folded in the early 1970s. *The Living Daylights* operated for one year, and lost thousands, Cock says, *"partly because its glossy hip manner was not popular amongst many radical participants"* (1977: 5).

An interesting addition to the industry in 1975 was the *National Citizen*, launched on the wave of the Whitlam dismissal. Established by unionists and media workers unhappy with the mainstream press, the *National Citizen's* aim was to be a *"permanent radical weekly representing labour politics and alternative journalism"* (Fitzgerald, 1977: 11). It openly supported the Labor party, with theories about the Whitlam dismissal occupying a large section of its content. *The National Citizen* only lasted three editions, all within a two-week period in December 1975, but during that time distributed about 450,000 copies throughout Australia (Fitzgerald, 1977: 12).

The land rights movement also established its own publication, *Identity*, in 1971. It was the latest in a long line of indigenous publications which had emerged since the first *Flinders Island Chronicle* in 1836 (Rose, 1996). The Aboriginal publications of the 1960s and 1970s, which also included the more 'militant' *Korrier* and *Black Action* (Rose, 1996: 68) were tied to a specific political cause, but their emergence was clearly due in part to the increasing profile of new political movements such as land rights, environmentalism and feminism during this counter-culture era.

Alternative publications of the era which were tied to a specific political cause included the anarchist *Troll*, and the Trotskyist *Direct Action*, *Militant, Australasian Apartacist,* and *Workers News*. The International Socialists published *The Battler*, and pro-leftist publications such as the *Independent Australian, Eureka* and *Peoples Independence Voice* also developed. The 1970s also saw the development of *Arena,* now also offering the bi-monthly *Arena* Magazine, and also Australian *Left Review* and *Intervention*. During this time the old *Direct Action* masthead was reborn and eventually used by the Resistance socialist group. It has now evolved, with many changes, to become *Green Left Weekly*.

Perhaps one of the biggest success stories in alternative journalism to come out of the 1970s was *Nation Review*, published by millionaire Gordon Barton who also owned the *Sunday Observer. Nation Review* was launched soon after the failure of Pete Steedman's *Broadside*, a left-wing publication published by the Syme group which also owned the *Melbourne Age*. Most of the *Nation Review's* writers and the cartoonist (Leunig) had originally worked on *Broadside*.

Described by a former worker as a *"millionaire-owned 'left-wing' newspaper"* (Wilson, in Walsh, 1993: 22), *Nation Review* published weekly for almost 10 years, in its final moments as a monthly. *Nation Review* established itself as a left-of-centre weekly which had the potential to attract a large mainstream-ish readership. In 1971, the newspaper's circulation stabilised at 41,000, with an estimated readership of 149,000 (Walsh, 1993: 162).

By the time *Nation Review* folded in 1981, most of the Australian 'counter culture' publications which had emerged from the socially radical days of the 1960s and 1970s had also died. O'Lincoln identified a general dissipation of political activity towards the end of the 1970s, which in part explains the disappearance of many titles. Perhaps *Nation Review's* success can be attributed to the significant political changes which occurred in Australia during the 1970s, particularly the election of the first Labor government in 33 years, its subsequent dismissal and the Vietnam War. *Nation Review* openly supported the politics of the Labor party rather than more conservative policies which were advocated by the Fairfax dailies and some of the Murdoch tabloids. *Nation Review* shifted headquarters from Melbourne to Sydney in 1975, and Barton sold the publication in 1978. It closed in 1981.

The mainstream-alternatives of the 1980s
In the year following *Nation Review's* closure, a new independent magazine appeared on the scene. *Australian Society*, operating with the scant resources of the Australian Society Publishing Company, was launched on the premise of providing serious social comment to Australian audiences. Editor Peter Temple's first editorial read (1982: 1):

"Starting a new magazine is a risky business. It is even riskier than usual when the magazine doesn't intend to pay its bills by providing an attractive ambience for shampoo, refrigerator or deodorant advertisements. 'Australian Society' is taking the gamble that there are enough Australians interested in the workings of their society to support a serious social issues magazine."

Australian Society took a more traditional approach to non-mainstream journalism. Again, *Australian Society* was able to boast high-profile contributors such as Barry Jones, David Bowman, Ronald Henderson, Humphrey McQueen and Brian Toohey. The publication endeavoured to provide an editorial alternative to the increasingly concentrated Australian press, but was unable to continue on its meagre budget.

In 1992, it evolved into and was relaunched as the monthly *Modern Times*. On the wave of the recession and falling advertising levels, *Modern Times* was absorbed by the social justice Jesuit publication, *Eureka Street* (see below) six months after it was launched. Despite these financial failures, *Australian Society* and later *Modern Times* continued to provide an independent voice on Australian political and social issues for more than a decade.

Max Suich, contributor to *Nation*, and later editor of the *National Times* and chief editorial executive for Fairfax, launched the glossy Independent Monthly in July 1989. In some ways, Suich appears to have been in a similar situation to Tom Fitzgerald when he began *Nation* – a respected Fairfax editor who perceived a need for a new journal of opinion.

However, unlike Fitzgerald, Suich accepted Fairfax's offer for financial assistance with his new venture, and The *Independent Monthly* was launched in July 1989 jointly published by Marinya Media (media holding company of John B. Fairfax and family) and Max and Jennie Suich (*Independent Monthly*, 1989: 3). The *Independent Monthly* continued to publish for seven years, although in 1993 it revitalised presentation and content to some extent, downsized to an A4 glossy magazine and was renamed *The Independent*.

By the time of its closure in July 1996, *The Independent* was the last surviving independent magazine emerging from the 1980s. It had demonstrated, as had *Australian Society* and *Nation*, that there was a middle ground between the mainstream and the alternative press industries. Most of the personnel involved in publications such as *Nation, Nation Review, Australian Society, Modern Times* and *Independent Monthly* had their backgrounds in the mainstream press of the era. Indeed, some of the independent publications enabled contributors to forge a career in the mainstream, based on their popularity as columnists for the independents.

The *Republican Weekly* is a later, although less successful, attempt at this mainstream/alternative middle ground. The unique nature of these publications provides a rich field for further research.

The contemporary alternative and independent publications scene in Australia is hugely diverse, and, like both the British and American industries, carries material of varying standards. Contemporary alternative publications are a little harder to define than those appearing during the counter-culture days, as there is no clear 'alternative' lifestyle to which all are uniformly attached.

As discussed previously, specialist publications and fanzines were not included in this overview as they do not offer alternative news. There was, however, one category of specialist publications included, as their audience is quite broad and news-oriented. The indigenous press was included because it covered major political issues also making headlines in the daily press – native title, reconciliation, ATSIC, social justice, the 'stolen generation', Pauline Hanson, and so on. The stories run by indigenous publications offered a truly alternative perspective on events that were reported daily by the mainstream media. Otherwise, the search for Australia's contemporary alternative press consisted mainly of general political publications, the left-wing press, the right-wing press, and independent publications which contained political commentary.

Generally, the alternative and independent press industry of the late-1990s varies from the low-key, 20-page A5 publication *The Stirrer*, published by the Universalist Association of New South Wales, to the glossy social justice magazine *Eureka Street* and through to the commercially successful political comment and arts newspaper *Adelaide Review*. In between these publications is a myriad of socialist, anti-feminist, humanist and general political publications which greatly vary in style, length and quality.

Left-wing alternative press

In general, the left-wing press is reasonably strong in the current alternative press industry. Publications such as *Arena* magazine, *Green Left Weekly, The Guardian, Neighbourhood News, Peace 2000, Socialist Worker*, and *The Stirrer* continue to publish left-of-centre, social justice oriented news. Within this group the range is enormous – *Socialist Worker*, for example, is a publication of the International Socialists' Organisation and advocates socialist revolution rather than reform of the existing structure, whereas publications like *Peace 2000* have a more specialist and reformist focus on nuclear disarmament, anti-uranium mining and other related issues.

The Libertarian Workers' group produces a weekly A4 newsletter, *The Anarchist Age Weekly*, and compiles the material in this for a tabloid 36-page monthly publication, *The Anarchist Age Monthly*. The monthly also includes new articles which have not been printed in the weekly – both publications offer an anarchist perspective on recent social issues and generally discuss problems with the existing political structure.

The 'soft left' social justice press

Other independent publications which present general social justice perspectives and which also categorise themselves as left-leaning or 'progressive' are the *Sydney City Hub*, published by US independent newsweekly publisher Laurence Gibbons, *Impact* magazine which is published by the Australian Council of Social Security, and *The Republican*, the newest major edition to the Australian alternative press which published weekly news and politics until its sudden closure in August 1997. *Eureka Street*, a product of Jesuit Publications, provides in-depth coverage and features on current affairs and social issues and boasts high-profile staff such as editor Morag Fraser, and regularly attracts contributors who otherwise write for mainstream newspapers.

Softer left-ish publications with a youth-oriented theme include *The Big Issue Australia,* a publication produced to raise money

for homeless and disadvantaged people. *The Big Issue* is modelled on the British weekly newspaper equivalent and includes feature articles on current issues such as cuts to legal aid funding, economic rationalism and also covers a reasonable amount of youth-oriented news. Similarly, *Nu Wave* newspaper, produced in the Queensland Sunshine Coast town of Noosa, provides a perspective on youth and welfare issues and is produced by a youth collective which is partially funded by the Noosa Shire Council. *X-Press Magazine*, produced in Perth, offers a similar mix of alternative music and politics. It is a music street magazine and is the one of the few in Australia to also offer political commentary to its mainly young readers.

A Brisbane publication, The *Weekend Independent*, is produced monthly by staff and students from the University of Queensland's Department of Journalism and offers hard news as well as political analysis, features and investigative journalism. As it is produced as part of a journalism course (as was the now-defunct *SNOOP*), the focus is strongly on covering a broad range of political and social issues, coupled with the softer news areas of arts and sport. The *Weekend Independent* was renamed The *Queensland Independent* in March 1998, and is now distributed in newsagencies throughout the state.

'Independent' conservative magazines
Throughout the course of my research, it became evident that some sections of industry were not comfortable with the term 'alternative'. In particular, most journalists and editors from conservative publications preferred the term 'independent press', perhaps because of the traditional association between 'alternative' and 'left-wing' or 'counter-culture'. These publications are therefore included under the heading 'independent' publications which is their preferred term. *Quadrant*, a conservative comment magazine (formerly edited by historian Robert Manne and now edited by columnist P.P. McGuiness) fits within this category, although there was much debate about *Quadrant's* shift to the political centre under Manne's editorship (*Radio National*, 20/11/97). Manne resigned from *Quadrant* after years of disagreement with members of the *Quadrant* board, with one former editor claiming Manne had shifted *Quadrant's* focus from a magazine which questioned the 'great Australian consensus' to one which supported the 'boring consensus' (Peter Coleman, on *Radio National*, 20/11/97). Nevertheless, *Quadran*t can still be considered a steady right-of-centre comment magazine with some liberal influences.

Adelaide Review is a political comment and arts publication edited by John Howard's former speech writer Christopher Pearson. Despite Pearson's personal conservative politics, *Adelaide Review* regularly contains articles from political commentators such as Don Dunstan and David Bowman, both of whom advocate a more liberal approach to most political and social issues. A firm right-of-centre publication is *In The National Interest*, irregularly published in Maryborough, Queensland by an individual previously linked to the Confederate Action Party, and now involved with Pauline Hanson's One Nation party. Since my research began, *In The National Interest* has changed its name to *Wake Up Australia*, and has become linked closely with Pauline Hanson's One Nation. *The People's Equality Network* is a small publication produced in Melbourne which has a strong anti-feminist stance and seeks to correct what it sees as a conspiracy by government and the mainstream press to distort research and statistics relating to gender issues in Australia. *News Weekly* is another publication from the right-wing of the independent press industry, offering news and opinion from the perspective of Freedom Publishing Company, an arm of the National Civic Council. It includes comment on international issues as well as national affairs, unemployment issues and arts reviews.

Indigenous publications
The indigenous press has a reasonably strong presence also, although only two publications, *Koori Mail* and *Land Rights Queensland*, were included in my study. *Land Rights Queens-*

land offers a monthly round-up of indigenous news and politics, particularly covering the major issues (mainly land-related) which have appeared in the mainstream news agenda. *Land Rights Queensland* also establishes its own agenda with community profiles and a small number of soft cultural stories. It includes specialist columns from indigenous leaders, politicians and academics as well as hard news copy contributed by journalists. *Koori Mail* provides a slightly less political perspective on indigenous issues, with a focus on positive cultural and 'role model' stories. The fortnightly *Koori Mail* also includes general political news but perhaps from a slightly more conservative viewpoint than *Land Rights*. There are several other indigenous publications – the Northern Territory's *Land Rights News* and the Kimberley Land Council's *Kimberley News* – but all indigenous publications could not be covered in this study. The chosen two were selected because they offered slightly contrasting viewpoints from within the general indigenous' perspective.

Internationally focused alternative papers

There are several publications in the contemporary alternative press landscape which I have placed in this general 'international' category. This indicates they are publications with a special interest in Third World, development, aid or global issues such as environmentalism, wars and so on. *UNITY*, published by the United Nations Association of Australia and edited by a veteran mainstream editor and manager offers independent news and comment on aid, social justice, indigenous and developmental issues. In a recent funding cutback, *UNITY* was downsized from a 16-page A4 magazine to a small newsletter distributed to members of the UNAA only. In 1999, it was produced as an email magazine, sent to a list of limited subscribers. The email version, which is sent in Rich Text Format, provides an excellent rundown of human rights issues in Australia and around the world. *New Internationalist* is another international publication although it is not produced exclusively in Australia – it has an Australian-based editor who contributes and co-ordinates copy for each edition. There are also editorial bases for the publication in the United Kingdom

and Canada. It focuses principally on Third World issues, poverty and inequality and often contains special features on recent issues such as new technology and its impact in the Third World.

Miscellaneous

There are several publications from the alternative industry which are not easily categorised. *NEXUS New Times*, produced in Queensland, is a bi-monthly magazine which includes information on recent international political events, environmental disasters and advances in medicine and science. It is distributed internationally and targeted to a mixed new age, UFO, and conspiracy theory readership. It has much in common with Victoria's *New Dawn* publication, which offers similar conspiracy theory information mixed with political features, science and UFO-type stories.

One Brisbane publication which is also difficult to categorise, except as a sharp satirical comment newspaper, is Brisbane's *The Bug*, which is produced by former mainstream journalists and varied helpers. *The Bug* is published irregularly, and generally includes satirical comment on recent political events with a critical (left-ish) perspective. Along with *The Bug*, the alternative press scene's most recent addition is the political satire magazine *The Chaser*, produced by Chaser Publishing P/L in Sydney.

Conclusion

The roots of many contemporary alternative publications, in Australia as elsewhere, can be found in the radical working-class press of the late 19th and early 20th century, and in the underground culture of the late-1960s era. There is also evidence that the Australian alternative press is about to experience a resurgence – the mainstream media is experiencing a decrease in the number of outlets and there is general public dissatisfaction with the reportage of the mainstream media (Fibich, 1995: 18). Furthermore, Davis reports that over the past 50 years per capita newspaper circulation has fallen 75 percent (1997, 230), which surely indicates a solid rejection of the mainstream press's way of delivering news. At the same time, the alternative press industry in the United States has experienced huge growth over the last decade, to the point that mainstream dailies are now launching their own alternative newsweeklies in an attempt to corner part of the market (Avis, 1992; Association of Alternative Newsweeklies Directory 1995).

The contemporary Australian alternative press industry is extremely diverse, and supports some highly professional, and some less than adequate, publications. It is comprised of, among others, political publications in the tradition of the early working-class press, but also boasts the new 'alternatives' – independently owned publications competing commercially with the mainstream, and offering a community-oriented, unobjective type of journalism (Forde, 1997). Overall, the industry is continuing to provide a true alternative to the mainstream version of current events. Trends overseas would indicate they will continue to do this, on an increasing scale, in the coming decade.

REFERENCES

Armstrong, M, 1990, 'The Industrial Workers of the World in Australia', Socialist Review, 2, 65-83.

Association of Alternative Newsweeklies, 1998, National Directory, at http://aan.org/aboutaan/mission.html

Association of Alternative Newsweeklies, 1998, Advertising, at http://aan.org/advertising/alt.advertising.html

Association of Alternative Newsweeklies, 1995, National Directory, AAN, Phoenix.

Association of Alternative Newsweeklies, 1995, Fact Sheet, AAN, Phoenix.

Avis, E, 1992, 'Hip weeklies are hot!', The Quill, 80(1), 11-15.

Cock, P.H, 1977, 'Australia's alternative media', Media Information Australia, 6, 4-9.

Comedia, 1984, 'The alternative press: The development of underdevelopment', Media Culture & Society, 6(2), 95-102.

Cryle, D, 1995, 'Whither the print media?', Metro Magazine, 99, 21-24.

Curran, J, 1978, 'Capitalism and control of the press, 1800-1975', in Mass Communication and Society, ed Curran, Gurevitch and Wooollacott, Edward Arnold, London.

Curran, J, 1978a, 'The press as an agency of social control: An historical perspective', in Newspaper History from the Seventeenth Century to the Present Day, ed Boyce, Curran

and Wingate, Constable, London.

Davis, M, 1997, Gangland: Cultural Elites and the New Generationalism, Allen & Unwin, Sydney.

Fibich, L (1995). "Under siege", American Journalism Review, September: 16-23.

Fitzgerald, D, 1977, 'A Labor paper dies: The choking of the National Citizen', Media Information Australia, 5, 11-16.

Forde, S, 1997, 'A descriptive look at the public role of the Australian independent and alternative press', AsiaPacific Media Educator, 3: 118-130.

Fountain, N, 1988, Underground: The London Alternative Press, 1966-74, Routledge, London.

Glessing, R.J, 1970, The Underground Press in America, Indiana University Press, Bloomington.

Hyams, E (1963). The New Statesman: The History of the First Fity Years, 1913-1963, Longman, London.

Johnson, M, 1971, The New Journalism: The Underground Press, the Artists of Nonfiction, and Changes in the Established Media, University Press of Kansas, Kansas.

Kornbluh, J (1964). Rebel Voices, University of Michigan Press, Michigan.

McAuliffe, K.M, 1978, The Great American Newspaper: The Rise and Fall of the Village Voice, Charles Scribner's Sons, New York.

Nelson, E, 1989, The British Counter-Culture, 1966-73: A Study of the Neville, R, 1995, Hippie Hippie Shake, Heinemann, Melbourne.

O'Lincoln, T, 1993, Years of Rage: Social Conflicts in the Fraser Era, Bookmarks, Melbourne.

Perry, P.F, 1977, 'Alternative magazines and the growth of the counter culture', Media Information Australia, 6, 10-13.

Rose, M, 1996, ed For the Record: 160 Years of Aboriginal Print Journalism, Allen & Unwin, Sydney.

Ross, E, 1982, Of Storm and Struggle: Pages from Labour History, Alternative Publishing Co-operative for New Age Publishers, Sydney.

Turner, I, 1969, Sydney's Burning, Alpha Books, Sydney.

Walker, R, 1980, Yesterday's News: A History of the newspaper Press in New South Wales from 1920 to 1945, Sydney University Press, Sydney.

Walker, R, 1976, The Newspaper Press in New South Wales, 1803-1920, Sydney University Press, Sydney.

Walsh, R, 1993, Ferretabilia: Life and Times of Nation Review, University of Queensland Press, Brisbane.

I used to work on *Maggie's Farm:* Prescribed reading for the sub-clinically prophetic

Pip Wilson

It was the late 1970s and northern New South Wales was the scene for by far the largest communitarian movement to take place in Australia, before or since. Many thousands of new settlers with a broad spectrum of counter-hegemonic ideas were settling in a band of mostly fertile, climatically appealing land between Elands, near Taree, and the towns of the 'Rainbow Region' – the far-northern NSW towns like Mullumbimby, Murwillumbah and Lismore.

Bellingen is situated approximately in the middle of that strip. It might be a geographical reason that made 'Bello' sit somewhere between Sydney and the far north coast in ideological terms as well. Bellingen has long been alternative, but never what the dominant paradigmists would call *"too way out"*. The full counter-cultural melting pot is there, but her energy has always been somewhat more stable than, say Nimbin's. This is not a criticism of either magic town: merely an observation of one wayfarer who has tasted both. Usually when the fair valley of the Bellinger River was full of jugglers, magi, divine lunatics and really far out change agents, when the air was filled with the lamentations of the sub-clinically prophetic, they were on the hippie trail to the Rainbow Region. When heroin hit the counter culture, Bellingen got socked in the chin while Nimbin was mangled badly about the head and guts. Bello is a bit more middle path. The anarchists wear red and grey.

When Australians think 'alternative', they think Nimbin. But Bellingen, more modest cosmic lady, is also a crucial node of the movement. Bello is green and warm and humid, and you can watch the trees and vegies grow taller before lunch. By 1979, hundreds – thousands – of the tribe had moved into the shire. It was obvious to your humble writer that communication between the tribespeople of the valley, and further afield, was crucial but not happening. The big cities of the day had talkback radio amongst the magazines of consumer capitalism by now, but out in the bush, and among the starry-eyed and mostly young refugees and change agents going bush, there was nothing but the telephone.

So here's how I saw it: here we were slap bang in the middle of the most important social leavening to happen in Australia's history. Here we were geographically in the thick of it. We were in the best country in the world, in the best climatic zone, at an optimum mileage from Babylon (halfway between Sydney and Brisbane), with the best soils, with some of the country's most creative and idealistic people. And we had no magazine of our own?! Bullshit!

There had been counter-culture magazines in the Eastern States. Some concentrated on organics, some pontificated on left politics, some on this, some on that. Invariably they were completely a reflection of the biases and insights of the owners and editors. There was nothing very broad and deep in vision. In the final analysis, capital had to dictate what the masses read.

What we needed, and I was amazed some cooler, more 'ideologically sound' (1970s for PC) bloke or Ms or collective hadn't already birthed it, was a magazine for all the valleys. The north coast was buzzing! God, every time you looked out the pub window into the main street of Bello, you saw a half-busted vehicle pull up, loaded like Jed Clampett's truck with two or more hairy adults, a bunch of kids, op-shop furniture, batik wallhangings, bamboo flutes, mung bean sprouters and a mud map. Above-mentioned hairy adults would get out of said vehicle, stretch their backs, scratch their crutches, break wind and head towards the real estate agency where they asked to see the cheapest bit of mountain goat country in the valley.

Generally the agent would draw another mud map for the hippies and send them on their way to some old Macdonald who had a lower fifty he'd been trying to sell for $5,000 ever since dairying went broke after Britain entered the Common Market. The hippies would offer him $10 grand, the deal would be sealed and, after picking his jaw up off the floor, old Macdonald would get on the steam telephone and tell Farmer Brown next door what these lunatic hippies were paying. (That's how broke dairy country started spiralling to become rich middle classville, but that's another story.)

The valley was filling up fast, and the same story was being repeated all up the coast in towns like Federal, Nimbin, Byron, Mur'bah, Burringbar, Dorrigo and on and on. The newcomers were full of dreams and zany ideas, but they had no journal. It had to be.

And what it had to be, was a publication – monthly would be best – in which the readers were the contributors. Certainly, the editorial freeks would have a big say, but not the only say. So the principle had to be, what the readers send in, we will publish. The meme (not in your dictionary? Try the Web) I coined for this traditional alternative concept was 'Participation Press'. A magazine would be born in which the front office was the PO Box.

Now all we needed was a magazine. First things first: let's work out the reality later; what would be fun at this point would be to think up a name. With another young dreamer named David Lamond, who I'm ashamed to say I and others sort of edged out of proceedings after a while (and I don't remember why, and I haven't seen him in two decades to apologise), I dreamed up potential names for a new kind of magazine. Something with a twinge of irony suited my early post-modern nature, though I did not yet know how a pomo thought. *Yellow Delaney*? *The Runcible Spoon*? *The Herald-Sun*? Bobby Zimmerman aka Dylan, at least a decade earlier, had been booed at the Newport Folk Festival when he sang *Maggie's Farm* with (gasp!) *electric* guitar backing. With that song on that day he created the genre of folk-rock.

Maggie's Farm, the song, was taken by the counter culture as a prophecy on the state of the USA and one man's decision to opt out of the reckless status quo. *"I ain't gonna work on Maggie's farm no more"* was the mantra. I rattled off a hundred possible titles and fellow Dylanologist Lamond and I agreed it had to be *Maggie's Farm*. If Maggie's represented the system, the irony would be that we, rebels against the system, who were starting farms and a new system,

should look at what we were creating, and drop out of it where it went wrong. The name we chose was intended to pull itself down.

Robyn Meehan was editor of *Catchment*, a periodically inspired 24-page tabloid magazine that operated out of the Bellingen Community Centre and was tied up with a government institution called the Community Youth Support Scheme. I had fifty bucks or so and wanted to start *Maggie's Farm*. She was a smart editor and knew all the local talent. And she was on good terms with the printer. I needed help. Robyn and I caught fire when we discussed the potential for *Maggie's Farm*. It turned out that our synergy was able to get the mag going, with a flavour unlike anything before or since. A mad, unique mag was Maggie.

We had a similar analysis of the big picture, but different, and a similar dream, but different, and some kind of respect for each other that enabled it to happen. We got 30 days credit with the Hobson family press in town. I chucked in a bunch of contributions I had picked up around the north coast. (I had done a tour with David and a few bucks' worth of A5 pamphlets announcing that a new magazine was going to come out, which we dumped at health food shops, hippie stores, communes and sleepovers all around the Rainbow Region.) Robyn chucked in some *Catchment* holdovers. We got onto local photographers, writers, journos and anyone freaky enough and creative enough to help out.

No one wanted to know about it. But we got out Number 1 on September 1, 1979, two weeks after the big Terania Creek (near Nimbin) rainforest protest had got underway. The hippies of the north were now nightly news around the country, and hundreds of rainbow army volunteers were rocking up at Terania with the obligatory half-busted car, bunch of kids, batik wallhangings and so on and so on. A couple of friends, including Mikla the photographer (who some years later started the highly successful Wildlife Information and Rescue Service – WIRES) made it up to Terania and flogged mags around the camp. The protestors loved it, and many people took copies back to their different tribes in the valleys and urban communes around the eastern states. We only printed a thousand, but we sold every damn one right fast.

Now every creative person in Bello, and further afield, wanted to help. Human nature I guess. Artists started arting, photographers photographing, poets poeting. Some people just wanted to type or sell or join the production sleep/drink/smokeouts that became quite the scene to be seen in for the next 20 monthly ishoos, at which point I left to collapse and another Bello team emerged from the core to keep it going. Each month a troupe of Maggicians camped out in some house – a three-sided shack with kerosene lights, a pioneer cottage in Armidale, a suburban apartment in Sydney. One night in the bush a zephyr came through and scattered our little bits of paper through the scrub and we had to retrieve them all by lamp and matchlight. Once in Armidale a willy-willy (whirlwind) came through our garden layout session and carried next ishoo high across the fields.

We chose a theme each time and announced it for the next ish: Religion. Paranoia. Cities. The readers (now there were thousands because we sold 4,500 and each one was handed around amongst many), from all over Australia once we got national distribution through every newsagency, responded to our dream with poems, cartoons, photos, journalism, partly baked ideas, wonderful innovations on the tabloid canvas. We got contributions from punks and professors, freeks and bureaucrats. The original concept of a northern tribal paper was quickly transcended, as we modified our elitism and realised that the people's press was really for the people. We even published stuff we thought was shite, and stuff we disagreed with.

A fox can outrun a pack of hounds, and we were able to get radical ideas from the street and the heart of the readership long before they filtered into mainstream society. We were early with material on the rise of Islamic fundamentalism, permaculture, multiple occupancy, loopholes in the child pornography laws of our state, eco-feminism, deep ecology, new communalism, problems with rural resettlement, critiques of alternative culture.

We couldn't afford typesetting, so Peter Middleton used to type up the copy with two fingers on a borrowed antediluvian typewriter. It was 12-point and too big for the necessary squeeze of our large contributors' file, so we drove three hours to Armidale where we reduce-photocopied Peter's galleys to about 9 point. We hand-drew the headlines because we had no

money for Letraset, despite a healthy ad revenue. We doodled in the margins and we stayed up night after night, quite heavily medicated, sticking it all down on grids.

We couldn't afford a wax machine so we used schoolkids' paste. Not one of us had a clue what we were doing, which seemed to appeal to our readers. On page one of Issue One we had said that we were interested in new ideas of quality, not those decided for us by the Rupert Moloch-style machines of media. This was not, we affirmed, an excuse for not being slick and glossy, but a manifesto of our hope that real media can help people become more real. A piece of shite, we reasoned, if published, could itself be part of the massage: the shite-writer would see their work in print and possibly lift their game by being published next to non-shite. Of course, it was an experiment and we don't know how well we lived up to our ideals.

Naturally, sleepless nights, poverty and self-medication led to serious burnout even for a young man, and the reins had to be handed over. The Bello team kept a quarterly version going for a while, until that petered out too and Paul White of the Blue Mountains tribe near Sydney took *Maggie's Farm* under his wing. Paul's raison d'être was not the same, and Maggie was no longer a participation press gal, but an alternative magazine she was (with Paul's emphasis on ufolgy, psychedelia and Fortean material), and all in all *Maggie's Farm* lived for nine years, not a bad stint for any alternative magazine, and not bad for a mag conceived with a bank of $50.

So that's the true story of *Maggie's Farm*, kiddies, at least as old Uncle Pip remembers it. Of course, memory was one of those things that got a little bent in them days, just like the magazine industry. Of course, we made not one dent in the nature of media in the world. The situation is much worse than it was then as far as centralisation of print goes, but there's one old hippie that likes to delude himself that all that burnout was worth the stone we threw into the pond. Who knows where the ripples will end? Thank you Maggie.

When I met up with Pip Wilson of 'Rainbow Archives' fame, it was at his apartment near Sydney's Coogee beach. A small dinner party was in progress and I grabbed the opportunity to talk about alternative publishing and media with Pip, in between refills of wine and mouthfuls of food. It was only at the end of the evening that Stephen Abell's name cropped up. *"He's your man,"* Pip told me, *"...ran a really successful radio station some years back when we were both part of the Bellingen community."* That was the community north of Sydney on the NSW coast, where Pip had started *Maggie's Farm* magazine in the 70s.

I phoned Stephen and he agreed to share part of his story in this book. So, imagine yourself back in 1985 and living in a 'divided' community. The new settlers, dubbed 'hippies' and 'alternates', are barely tolerated by the original community members, who had seen their own livelihood based on dairy farming and logging dwindle to almost nothing. Stephen takes up the story, which was first published in *Simply Living* magazine.

2BBB-FM, Bellingen's community radio
Stephen Marc Abell, founder and manager 1978-85

I knew it was possible to wrest a broadcasting licence from the Australian government because I had seen it done first-hand. But in my newly adopted community of Bellingen on the New South Wales north coast, most sensible people thought I was crazy; only the dreamers kept telling me what a good idea it was. When I approached many of the local establishment's community leaders, they would nod their heads with approval as I painted for them the scenario of our own community radio station. But that was all – lip service. I rarely got any more support from them.

What I was up against was the stock shock reaction: *"What, hippie radio?!"* It was imperative to keep the image of the proposed radio station as clean as possible. Whenever I approached someone of influence for support or addressed one of the community group's meetings, I always wore a necktie to complement one of my 'radio costumes'. Press releases were always carefully worded. They had to sound as

if progress were being made, but not so much as to cause alarm among our antagonists, who were no doubt hoping that the whole scheme would fizzle.

The Bellingen establishment was reticent, wary and mostly bewildered. Why would anyone put so much time into a project without any capital rewards to be won? I'm sure most people saw the potential benefits for the community as a whole when I had the opportunity to explain the project to them personally. But some wondered whether I was merely trying to make a job for myself at public expense. Naturally the old-timers were suspicious. Who the hell was this Yank from out of the blue telling us his radio station would cure all of the community's ills? What would he know about the place, our lives, what we need?

It's therefore not surprising that most of our early support came from newcomers to the area. They had come from places where FM-radio was already operating. They missed the entertainment and information that couldn't reach them in this little country town. All we had here was one commercial top-40 station and the Australian Broadcasting Commission's Radio 3, both of which could barely reach us from 100 kilometres away. At night, or during a thunderstorm, forget it. Several local luminaries did come along to our first meeting called about September 1978 to elect a steering committee, two months after the project began. They had the vision to see what the community radio station could do to foster tolerance and understanding within the community; they had the courage to publicly stand up and be counted among us. Patricia Oakman, then shire president, was there and helped us with letters of support to the government's licensing authorities. Norm Braithwaite, descended from original settlers in the area, occasional shire councillor, and member of numerous community organisations, attended. Mary Anderson, librarian and shire councillor was there, too. In all about 15 attended that original meeting and threw in $10 each to boot, so that we could join the Public Broadcasting Association of Australia and send me to its national convention. A short time later a formal public meeting was called and 50 enthusiastic people showed up – a great showing for a small country town. Community Radio Bellinger (meaning 'clear water' in the local Aboriginal language) was up and away!

What was so important about having a community radio station anyway? The most obvious factor was simply entertainment. A lot of us missed the good music that can be heard in the cities – quality jazz, classical, folk, blues, rock, country and western, ethnic. Another reason was local news and information, with the opportunity to broadcast extended interviews with local people about local issues. Emergency communications in times of our numerous floods and bush fires would be invaluable.

But there were other more subtle and perhaps more important reasons, too. Some of us saw the potential for a neutral meeting ground where people from all sections of the community could listen to one another from the safety of their homes. Voices of good sense and goodwill would reach the ears of people they wouldn't ordinarily come into contact with. People's lives would take on new meaning. They could listen to and produce wonderful radio programs. The young and the unemployed would have something to throw their talents into, thereby contributing to community life and maintaining self-respect. The young and the unemployed would gain valuable work experience which could help them to later obtain employment. The radio station would provide creative outlets for the many retired people who have flocked to this area. In short, we envisaged this non-profit, volunteer-run community radio station as the panacea for every imaginable social, personal, or spiritual ill. 'Radio Healing – no job too big or too small'.

We recognised that to provide all this abundance we needed to have some idea of what people actually wanted to hear. So we conducted our first survey. The response was encouraging, and it came from all sorts of people. They wanted to hear music of every description; they wanted to hear news of what was going on around them. Yes, they would help make programs and, yes, they would subscribe. I spoke to as many people as possible to get their ideas: the Chamber of Commerce, the Country Women's Association, Rotary, the bowling club, Lions, the high school principals, the editors of the local newspapers, the clergymen, and lots of others.

Every bit of information, encouraging or scathing, had to be considered because, after all, in such a small place with such a small population base, we needed damn near everyone's support in order to get the operation off the ground and to keep it healthy. We ran three test transmissions up until the time we finally went on air on 9 September 1983. These tests were chiefly designed to give everyone a sampling of what they could expect once we began transmissions on a permanent basis. For the public, they heard all kinds of great music; our on-air and support teams tested the realities of live microphones. Over 100 people telephoned the showroom of Foster's motor garage in the centre of town which served as our studios for the first test just to say how terrific the show

Australia's first mudbrick radio station

was. Exhilaration is the only word I can think of to describe what I was feeling. We could drive all over town and up the valleys and there we were – for a few days at least – blasting out on the radio, on air, live!

Alas, government bureaucracy shared little of our enthusiasm. After all, there were scores of communities all around Australia trying to do the same thing we were with equal fervour. The bureaucrats were often sympathetic, but the big wheels of government turn slowly and issue only one or two or maybe half-a-dozen public broadcasting licences each year. Between test transmissions it was a job maintaining public interest in the project. I ran radio production training workshops, and we staged dinners, dances and raffles to raise money. We recorded the local church choir to produce Christmas cassettes for them. Press releases came out whenever we could justify saying something. We also kept busy countering what our detractors were saying about us. When the federal minister for communications came to speak with potential public and private broadcasting groups on the New South Wales north coast, there was an unannounced delegation who also met with the minister of five conservative Bellingen residents opposing our application. One letter to the local newspaper signed 'Square Eyes' queried: *"...Am I expected to turn off my television to listen to (shire) council business being bandied about unnecessarily?..."*

All we could do was try to shrug it off, keep smiling, and go about our business. I can only guess what frightened a few people was the idea of a free voice, beyond their political or financial control, belonging to 'outsiders' they didn't know or understand. They had set up their apple carts over years or generations, and they didn't want them upset.

After four years the Australian Broadcasting Tribunal granted us a licence. It took another year to get on air after that, our most difficult year yet. We had to train volunteers in broadcasting skills, devise station procedures and management systems, organise committees, begin programs, contact businesses about sponsorship, *plus* build the world's first mud brick radio station using 120 volunteers with only $18,000 for materials, half of which went into the concrete foundations. Thank goodness for a federal job creation scheme grant which provided three workers to finish off the studios.

It was a miracle that we did it, and let me assure you it was one hell of an ordeal. The joy of it was all those dedicated people who turned out for it, including a goodly number from the established community. Local lighting manufacturers, Planet Products, kicked off our Founding Patron drive with $1,000; one of our board members (who is old family and a retired shire councillor) gave us the block of land for less than

his development costs; and the big money came from a woman who thought the town needed a community radio station to break down the 'us and them' syndrome. Clover, aged 60, lives in a caravan on a commune with no money in the bank. She received an inheritance from her suffragette grandmother and handed it over for the construction of our studios – simply a case of altruism and putting her money where her mouth is.

After almost two years on air (written in 1985) we're settling into the social scheme of things quite nicely, thanks. A federal Community Employment Program (CEP) grant greatly helped us get started, but now we're completely volunteer-operated and there are about 100 of us. Our surveys showed that 65 per cent of those who can receive us listen to 2BBB-FM. All kinds of people are putting in programs. We've come to be acceptable, partially at least because we're usually so innocuous, but also because our programs are so good.

About the most gratifying moment in our history took place a year ago in the local RSL club when a record crowd of 500 or 600 people showed up for our Mastermind competition. Twenty-eight of the shire's organisations, like the Pony Club, Nursing Mothers' Association, CWA, Employment Co-op. Rugby League Club, Lions, and the bush fire brigade, competed for the $200 prize money. And each team brought their own cheering squad. No one expected the huge turnout, or the diversity of people, or being in the same room doing the same thing together with people they've never spoken to before. No one expected to share so much fun with so many from alien parts of the community. We got everyone together, and that is what we set out to do all those years ago.

Postscript
The above article was published in 1985 in the first issue of *Simply Living* edited by Pip Wilson. In September 1999, Radio 2BBB-FM celebrated its 16th anniversary. For years now it has broadcast 24 hours a day, seven days a week, on volunteer effort.

Way back then…

Just about all the books describing the alternative cultural scene in Australia take the Aquarius festival in Nimbin 1973 as their starting point. It was the Woodstock or Isle of Wght for Oz. Graeme Dunstan, one of co-organisers, wrote in the book, *The Way Out – Radical Alternatives in Australia* (Smith and Crossley, 1975):
"Nimbin is powerful magic. The word has entered the language of the land; it has become a reference point in its culture; it is a word which resonates with myth."

It wasn't the earliest festival, as Adrian Rawlins made clear in his book, *Festivals in Australia*. Really they date back to at least 1968 and the Orimbah festival. Adrian perceptively said that they were about people wanting to:
"celebrate and enjoy Australian creativity; to try to feel and understand what it meant to live now, instead of in some fixed cultural idea left over from the Second World War."

But Nimbin, the festival and the place, are the stuff of myths. The stories from that original 1973 festival organised by the Australian Union of Students do much to foster this hippy mythology. Take for instance the tale of Spaceman Bob, which John Jiggens re-told in *Rehearsals for the Apocalypse* (1983).
"He turned up in Mullum in the winter of 1972 with his strange story and his crazy ideas about spacemen. They were going to descend on the 7th of August at this place they had told Bob about: if you were prepared to fast and cleanse yourself, Bob would take you along to meet them and they would save the world."

Paul Joseph, who was to become one of the musical celebrities of the Aquarius festival, was one of the seventy people who joined Bob on the Wallacia Plateau to greet the spacemen.They didn't actually appear, but as John Jiggens recounts, *"Just before dawn Spaceman Bob and Paul went for a walk. 'I'm really upset,' said Bob, 'I feel like a fool. I've brought all of you here on a wild goose chase. Everyone must*

think I'm crazy." Paul listened. The night had been a great adventure. He had never been a fervent believer but he really enjoyed the night: sitting round the bonfire, singing, laughing; it had felt tribal, a white corroborree; the first meeting of the Mullumbimby tribe."

At the '73 festival, Paul Joseph produced some of his own magic in true Pied Piper fashion, with his festival song that thousands joined in singing for hours in a wandering band round the festival site. It was real communal music.

May the long time sun shine upon you
All love surround you
And the pure light within you
Guide your way home

And then there was Frank Knight who became the Messiah for the Nimbin festival crowd. Wearing a gumboot on his head he was proclaimed as the crowd's spiritual leader, in a sublime parody of the Divine Light Mission. Instead of Hare Krishna, the Dingo Pack, street theatre group from Melbourne, sang Frank, the 'Perfect Gumboot's'praises, with:
Hare Gumboot
Hare Nimbin
Hare Meat Pie
Hare Cynicism
Hare Rubber
Hare Dunlop
Hare Dollar
Hare Bad Vibes
Hare Hippies
Hare Counter Culture
(or something like that!)

Johnny Allen was another of the festival organisers. He said, of that time, *"In a Revolution there are no spectators – only participants. And the prevailing mood was of participation. Aquarian Age children of the dream, sneering, cop-hating revolutionaries, spacemen, Jesus Christs...all were prepared to make an art out of the very act of living."*

The spirit of Nimbin, for many, outlived the festival. A lot of participants stayed on in the Rainbow Region after the festival. Others joined them. Experiments in communal living, rituals, spirituality, a tribal culture and drugs became central to what the very name 'Nimbin' meant in the national psyche. Peter Cock said in his book *Alternative Australia, "The sense of (an alternative) movement was not seen by the general public until the AUS Nimbin festival."* (1979)

After 1973, many more festivals took place across Australia, including the Confests organised by the Down to Earth organisation (see Graham St John's contribution which follows the next one by Janice Newton). There was even the Alternative Australia gathering in Canberra, 1976, promoted by Jim Cairns, who had recently been Australia's Deputy Prime Minister. There are few prominent politicians in any country in the world who spent as much time campaigning for alternative social experiments. Like many at the time and since, Jim Cairns viewed his involvement with what he called the 'New Society' as opting in, not opting out. He urged people to *"create new living experiences, in community groups of many kinds – local, ethnic, women, co-operatives, workers, learning and growth centres, neighborhood houses, refuges and so* on." And on an earlier occasion proclaimed,
"People belong to the earth, not the earth to people."
(both quoted in Ormonde, 1981)

For a nicely personal view of the 'meaning' of Nimbin, here are some illuminating recollections from Janice Newton, who now works at the University of Ballarat.

Cultures and generations –images of the Nimbin 10 year anniversary festival 1983
Janice Newton

Prelude: the dreams
Rural Victorian Secondary School, 1973. Stockings and pink mini skirt. Whilst others of my generation shed the refinements of civilisation and join the Aquarius Festival at Nimbin, here I am clad in the 'teaching wardrobe' I have inherited from my sister who is now heading for India on the backpacker trail. Years pass and the legend of Nimbin grows. Stories filter back of friends who have visited and experienced, and changed. For a strong political activist friend from university, Nimbin is a site for transition from one Asian philosophy to another. He becomes a Buddhist monk. I still dream of visiting, even staying. Nimbin has lodged somewhere in my imagination.

An opportunity
Fieldwork in Papua New Guinea, a short stint at University of Queensland teaching anthropology. I'm closer now. The 10 year anniversary festival is on and I am still mumbling my subterranean litany about going to Nimbin. My landlady/friend opens a door. Her son is going with friends and perhaps I might join them. I am 33 and I join for the journey an artist, writer and potter, all in their twenties.

The trip
We share cars and travel in tandem, stopping for breaks together. The other car picks up a young Japanese tourist. He is fresh faced, very neat and has good quality back-packing gear (and a tent, which could be useful!). By the end of our journey my co-travellers have invited him to Nimbin. I cringe at the thought of the culture shock he will experience and mentally I distance myself from any responsibility for his imminent discomfort.

The arrival
Nimbin township, like every Australian town, but also like none other. We mention something to the young man selling us our festival tickets about Nimbin origins and Spaceman Bob. He is young and smooth. 'Don't ask me, I was in short pants when that happened!' We retreat to our own generational shells. We are bussed to the festival site, drive past the open showers and

I begin to sweat. We have some links with the tent from North Queensland and we hope they have come prepared with food and cooking equipment. We haven't. We walk through the upper levels and hear a voice cry out. Our Japanese friend is being welcomed by a nude Japanese woman reclined in front of her tent. I inwardly gasp – but he is cool and pleased that he has found a compatriot.

The festival

The next days are a blur of sensory experience as each of our travelling group follows individual journeys. The writer is totally energised, bursting with new potentialities after a morning with a men's consciousness-raising group. The healing level seems to centre the spirit of the festival – spontaneous eruptions of drumming from neighbouring tents, swaying and chanting from a spiritual group while primal screams cut the still Nimbin air from the adjacent grassy hill. A disabled youth writhes in pleasure during his sensory oil massage. I am struck by the confluence of nudity and asexuality. I am still doing mental gymnastics about whether I can deal with my own nudity, whether like the Emperor with new clothes, I can wear a mud suit like a mask and pretend I am clothed. Our Japanese friend has flung off his scouting gear and is running naked and liberated with a band of laughing, mudbaked savages. They run through the different levels of the festival, crossing paths with the committed woman and children marching for peace. There is a tribal theme: Indian teepees, Aboriginal birthing and rituals. A couple recognise my Papua New Guinean string bag and I talk of my village experience. They are with a large group of friends who are trying to model their camp on a tribal village. Strict sexual division of labour. Men's and women's business. I develop my eye contact skills as she is heavily pregnant and stark naked and he wears a banana leaf thong. Amidst the ludic abandon of many adult festival-goers, the serious and motivated children of Nimbin move unfazed through the crowds, selling their Nimbin Newsletter, which was produced at primary school. Later I find myself walking next to a young ten year old boy heading for the idyllic water pool at the lowest level of the tiered festival site, a grotto for nymphs and spirits, where nudity prevailed. I make friendly conversation, as I am prone to do.

'Going for a swim then are you?'

'Yeah'

'Got your bathers?' (Oops, major faux pas here – everyone in the water was nude. What a stupid thing to say to a child of Nimbin! I tense myself, awaiting a sarcastic retort.)

'Yep.'

I retreat to the clothed ones, the permanents and environmentalists of the upper level. I 'do some anthropology', grilling my bushwalk guide, a 'permanent'. I learn of surfie to greenie pathways, shared kitchens, serial monogamy, limited self-sufficiency and havens for single mothers. In time my creative friends are ready to leave. As we depart our Japanese friend waves goodbye – he looks like he may stay forever. Nimbin Anniversary Festival: a multitude of spiritualities, political commitments and sensory experiences have interweaved, crossed paths, made way for each-other. Generations and cultures, cultures and generations.

Very early on in my preparations for the *Alternative Australia* book I was introduced to Graham at La Trobe University. We swapped writings; he gave me chapters from his thesis material on Down to Earth and the ConFests – I gave him copies of my books written with new Travellers and DiYers from the UK, Europe and beyond. The electronic conversation has continued. He's just finished his PhD and I'm putting the final touches to this (not so) little item. Over to Graham and his rap about the cohorts of ConFest-goers.

ConFest: Edge Central and the Feraliens
Graham St John

At 25, I lunged at the opportunity to make the journey to ConFest with friends over New Year 1993/94. Tales of exotica and high adventure had been conveyed by early explorers. While I was intrigued, nothing prepared me for what I was to experience that summer – random acts of kindness, gestures of refusal and pure unpredictability, almost every waking hour for five days. I was thrown into new 'territory', exploring a lifeworld which I had not been privileged to in my youth, but to which I had steadily gravitated. The shock of difference was inspirational, the effect of the ludic otherness encountered comparable to that of a circus on a child-novice. Like the mesmerised child, I desired to run off and join the circus.

For five years from April 1994 I undertook a comprehensive research project on

Fire walk frenzy

ConFest and its host organisation, Down to Earth, for a PhD in anthropology. I have attended the last 13 or 14 events in succession. The wide ranging ruminations that follow are a product of this ethnography of edge central.

In 1976, three years after Nimbin's famed Aquarius Festival, a diverse host of the disenchanted converged upon the banks of the Cotter River in the ACT to celebrate what they called

Body art

'ConFest' (a conference and a festival). Responding to former deputy PM and anti-Vietnam war crusader Dr Jim Cairns' call for 'A New Society', many of those who organised, facilitated and participated in this event later formed the Victorian Down to Earth Co-operative Society (registered in 1979). DTE had been part of a nationwide network of 'families' or branches which, following Cotter and up until the early 1980s, saw themselves united as ADTEN (the Australian Down To Earth Network). A watershed in Australian counterculture, the first Down to Earth festivals, particularly Cotter, provided thousands of participants with the opportunity to explore the possibilities and celebrate the lived experience of alternative culture. Twenty Four years on (32 events experienced by well over 100,000 people), ConFest – the most significant, and now, biannual, co-operative event in the calendar of Australia's alternate tribes – continues to be facilitated by the Melbourne based DTE.

The formative years of the DTE movement were characteristically optimistic. In an early ConFest handbook objectives were stated thus:

"DTE is a community of persons seeking new values and directions having questioned or in the process of questioning the goals, impact and directions of the existing alienating and dehumanising capitalistic society...A main aim of DTE is to assist in the development of a viable alternative society: a new

society...DTE – nationally and locally – consists of people dedicated to helping the cultural preparation and consciousness raising for a truly alternative society, free from alienation, oppression, exploitation and inequality." (Berri Handbook 1979)

Alas, the 'new society' never arrived. Such charters proved difficult to accomplish in the absence of strong political commitment, and ADTEN collapsed as a result of internal conflicts, financial mismanagement, wasted 'energy' and resources, the tyranny of distance, the attraction of the 'permanent festival' of Nimbin, and numerous communal experiments in permaculture and hamlets there and elsewhere around the country.

Though ConFest did not herald 'the new society' originally anticipated, it has not failed to stimulate lasting social change. Though *the* revolutionary transformation imagined by legions of contemporaries in a host of guises was not realised in the early years, many minor *revolutions* were, and have been since. Over the last twenty four years, together with untold behavioural modifications, a multitude of communities, therapies, gatherings and tribes have come into existence, or have been regenerated, as a result of ConFest. The 'new society' never arrived but many new 'societies' did. And they have continued to emerge as a result of the DTE ConFest becoming a multi-dimensional experiment in alternative living, a biannual process where dominant versions of 'the truth' are challenged and subverted, and a marginal centre where diverse alternate lifestyles are sought and discovered.

Over the years, as a co-

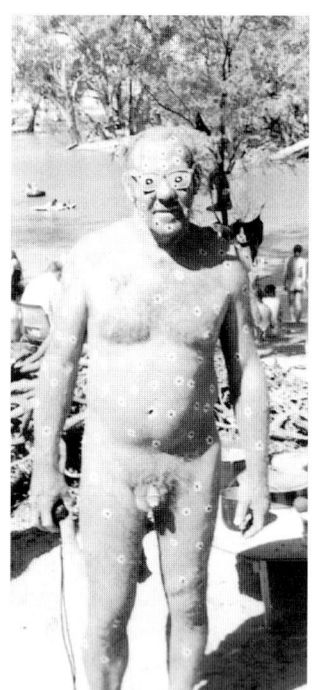

Blue Man

operative, DTE became an unstable, internally riven, yet enduring neo-tribe, now custodian to Australia's marginal centre. ConFest has become the principal preoccupation of DTE, an organisation not driven by master narratives, political manifestos, or religious doctrines. Members (around 1,500) possess an enormous variety of skills and come from diverse backgrounds: the trades, the arts, sciences, health and well-being, education, engineering. This not-for-profit co-operative has no paid positions yet is responsible for laying the groundwork and reproducing the infrastructure for temporary organic communities twice a year.

Widely referred to as 'the ConFest Spirit', a distinct community ethos has gradually coalesced over the course of ConFest's evolution. This inclusive ethic of selfless service, co-operation and tolerance distinguishes ConFest from most other festivals I've been to. The experience relies upon the input of every participant, upon people taking responsibility together. All are encouraged to contribute their skills, labour and art to the unfolding and upkeep of the community. As a result, each event explodes spontaneously into shapes and patterns unforeseen, a spontaneity making ConFest an extraordinarily unpredictable counterscape, an inimitable temporary autonomous zone. Though ConFests possess familiar landmarks and conventional features, every event is characterised by a fresh derangement of the familiar, a touch of chaos, a kind of magic.

ConFest is a gathering of the radical neo-tribes, an alternate kaleidoscope. Over the years it has accommodated diverse lifeworlds and youth subcultures conveying the *à la mode* ideas and practices of a multiplicity of contemporaneous movements: communitarianism, green, alternative technology-energy, women's, men's, queer, healing-arts, alternative spirituality. A host of enablers, co-ops, clans and alternative cults converge hawking a cornucopia of therapies, spiritualities, carnalities, ideologies. Such diversity is refracted through the network of on-site centres known as villages – weird and wonderful sub-zones of pleasure, politics and pantomime (e.g. Healing, Art, Pt'chang Peacekeepers, Forest, Queer Presence, Kids, Food Not Bombs, Spirituality, Tek Know, Rainbow, Magic Forest, Labyrinth, Spiral, CIDA, Sculpture, HEMP, Wolfgang's Palace, Where the Wild Things Are, Circus, Laceweb, Earth Sharing and the Solar Stage).

The villages are the principal staging areas for workshops. ConFest's workshop system is extraordinary. There are blackboard walls whereupon anybody can notify fellow participants of their wish to give a workshop, funshop, discussion group, forum, whatever, on just about anything at any time throughout the event. Information and skills are exchanged via a vast subterranean switchboard connecting militants and mystics, revolters and refugees, maoists and musos, rastas and radicals who bed down together in the most fantastic neighbourhood ever imagined – a miasmic confusion of students and teachers, artists and activists, accountants and anarchists, ferals and professionals and professional ferals, wizards and wankers, ravers and ranters, pixies, pagans, seers, queers, pre-apocalyptic goths and blissed-out prophecists, hip new agers and aging hippies, chai tea, tai chi, tipi dwellers, bank tellers, fractal converts, covert perverts, perverse extroverts, I Ching throwers, dope growers, 6 a.m. conch-horn blowers, vivacious belly dancers and tranced-out neuromancers, Jung devotees, deep ecologies, itinerant psychonauts with disputed methodologies, druidic triads, dynamic duos, hypnotic drum solos, sadhus, wanderers, warriors, wimmin and...yobos. Here reside the hard core, the soft centred, the tuned in, the turned out, the mixed up, the put down, the fucked off, the passengers and the voyeurs – the whole movie! The place is a DiY community drop-in-centre for the excommunicated, expatriate, ex-army, extreme! Is ConFest at the headwaters of an ecotopia, a utopia, a heterotopia, a dystopia? Or something else? Well...it depends on your perspective.

Multifarious marginalia circulate under the greater marquee of ConFest. Browsing the latest authentica ConFesters sample esoteric accessories, folk-theologies, funky fringe therapies, chic modes of enlightenment and fashionable words of wisdom. They champion the principles of a proposed new: 'Age', 'Jerusalem', 'cosmos', politic, 'tribe', 'spirit', ethic, 'consciousness', 'millennium'. Traversing this counterscape they: build internal resources via massage, Reiki, past-life regression therapy, shamanic journeying, firewalking and tantra; access new spiritual dimensions in the form of Wicca rites, full moon and wild women ceremonies, Celtic mythology, psychedelic spirituality; experience ritual-theatre, fringe-art and all night Trance Dance parties; advance environmental awareness and activist commitments; download information on permaculture, drug reform, forest management, veganism etc.

Tribal drumming

Patrons of this chaos theme park converge in moments of abandonment. The Fire Circle has served as a particularly potent focal point for the collective release of energy. At dusk this space metamorphoses into a mischievous nocturnal playground where the boundary between performer and spectator is fluid or non-existent – a spontaneous combustion of youth, colour, sound and spirit. At Tocumwal, Easter 1993, following an invocation of the original inhabitants of the area (the Yorta-Yorta), hundreds gathered to perform a fire walk under the full moon. Dancers, many naked with mud, ochre and paint-based body-murals and facial designs, gestured frenetically to the accompaniment of tumultuous orchestras. On this, as with most evenings, the air dense with dust and the ringing of bells dangling from a thousand limbs, necks and foreheads, and with the roar of firesticks overhead, there occurred one rapturous Dionysian cacophony in which the fire remained a central element.

From out of nowhere, orchestras of the weird appear in possession of a bizarre spectrum of instruments. Converging in the Fire Circle, around camp fires and at other locations like the chai tent or market centre, accompanied by shrieking crowds, they generate an infectious frenzy. I've 'gone off' in the midst of an eruption of djembe, double ended talking drums, pounding congas, doumbek and chekere, together with steel pan, cow bells, clapping sticks, xylophone, rainmakers (carved hollow wooden tubes filled with beads), 44 gallon drums, frying pans, cooking pots and anything loud when beaten. I've been mesmerised by a spectrum of wind instruments (flute, saxo-

The Mud Pit

phone, tuba, horns, bagpipe, didjeridu), and an equally impressive range of vocals, from tonal chant to rebirthing scream. I've joined the ranks of primal voguers, temporary exhibitionists and delirious circumambulants in the inner ring of the Fire Circle on New Year's Eve!

The Tek Know enclave has been a centre of pulsating rhythm. There, techno-shaman manifest a digitally enhanced aural sculpture, summoning the ambient, psy-trance or ethnodelic edges of techno music to potentiate a temporary Trance Dance community. At Moama 96/97, Tek Know attracted over 2,000 trance *habitués* over New Year's Eve. After dark, they were guided in by both the hypnotic throb and the fluoro fabrics lining the ground and trees on the approach. The village had a main doof and two chill spaces. Elders and young alike, some aglow on entactogenics like ecstasy, confronted with an

assemblage consisting of music, strobe lights, fractal slides, disco balls, Mutoid Waste Co. fire sculptures and industrial art installations, went maniacal.

Neon-crusties ascribed to the most sartorially insane body-rigs. They were adorned in folk-jewellery, hyper-fluoro wigs, layered leggings and big trousers fashioned from the most ridiculously juxtaposed fabrics. Some perfected androgyny – queering their bodies. Others sucked pacifiers and toted fluffy totems. Others still, wore bad-taste artefacts, like scout uniforms, or displayed insurgent t-shirt slogans such as 'ungovernable entity'. Deploying a manifestly retrograde style, a great many trance-*bricoleurs* lusted for an ironic panoply of past youth cultures – engendering a hippy/punk hybridisation.

As a key Tek Know installation, a large twelve hour clock was suspended from the top centre of a high scaffold tower from which an enormous Aboriginal land rights flag was also draped. The flag featured a smiley face (symbolising rave culture) on its sun. Near midnight, the rhythm became wilder as throngs of fluoro mace jugglers and fire-stick twirlers quickened their movements at the base of the scaffold, and two men swirled ignited catherine wheels at opposite ends of the tower. At this point, Mutoid Robin approached with flame-thrower in hand. Robin intended to set the clock alight to signify the termination of the old year, a feat achieved at midnight. Yet, when a couple of propane balloons backfired an unanticipated conflagration illuminated the amazed faces of the teeming trance enthusiasts as the flag itself went up in flames.

A potentially disastrous incident was ultimately understood to signify an alliance since the conflagration, an example of 'total fucking anarchy...it actually destroyed between us the last vestige of separation that may exist between the whites and the Koories'. I guess this kind of interpretation is understand-able since the Tek Know trance-floor is ultimately a realm of self-abandonment, a corporeal-estate fomenting the dissolu-tion of difference, a ritual of disappearance into the body – one's own, and that of others. In this temporary trance-community, I united with co-dancers to form a Fluoro-Rainbow Tribe: 'all colours, all races, all as one'.

At each ConFest there tends to develop a strong affinity

between those participating in a host of communions: between those dancing (trance or otherwise), volunteering, sharing in feasts, beach potlatches, firewalking, nocturnal coalitions and erotic symposia. The Art village has been one of ConFest's most popular temporary erogenous zones. Situated on the bank of a billabong, a mud pit ('primal ooze'), body painting, evening fluoro parties, 'the fridge' (a giant Coolgardie safe for people), a sauna, a kid's water slide and a steam tent are customary.

Entering the mud pit *en masse*, covered with what one nine year old girl called 'special mud', novices willingly submit to the permitted subversion of instilled rules of cleanliness and sterilisation. Here, the undisciplined body is celebrated in a grotesque degradation to the material level of earth and flesh. Like liminaries, they are melted down to a generalised, anonymous *prima materia* – lumps of human clay ready to be moulded anew.

With the mud dry, many have their bodies painted, often receiving distinctive full-body skin murals. To be decorated with water based or fluorescent paints, or even ochre, in a combination of styles and colours on any anatomical location – engenders an almost infinite array of possibilities in refiguring and recomposing one's experience of their body. For instance, the ConFester who had his body covered in mud, didjeridu painted in a black, yellow and red pattern (the colours of the Aboriginal land rights flag), and penis decorated in matching hues, presented a curious sight at Tocumwal. The clay plastered primitives and ochered chameleons mingle and dance, spilling out into the festival, wandering around all day in such temporary body modifications, such chthonic uniforms.

And they may spill out into the market where itinerant vendors trade in goods and services palatable to the teeming 'beautiful people': handicrafts, candles, crystals, incense, hemp products, cheesecloth garments, recycled fabrics, herbs, oils etc. Here, one can locate numerologists, aromatherapists, tarot, palm, rune and aura readers, or buy tribal staffs, rainmakers, medicine sticks, roo-bone amulets, Feng Shui meditation products, a range of percussive instruments and didjeridus. Food and drink sales are strictly vegetarian, wholemeal and non-alcoholic – meat, animal derived and disposable products are condemned, and inorganically produced foodstuffs are disfavoured. Bio-dynamic juices, like wheatgrass, are popular, as are 'solar powered smoothies' (at the Sun Cafe) and chai tea (in the chai tent – a familiar meeting place). The converted 'bus with the lot' of the bohemian Vege Out Cafe and the Earth Oven bakery are also favourite venues. Some stalls, like those operated by the Goongerah Environment Centre (GECO), Friends of the Earth, Ananda Marga and the Dzogchen Community, are operated for the benefit of not-for-profit, ethical and community organisations. At Moama, New Year 96/97, the market centre featured the ConFest Prayer Wheel. Upon writing their 'good feelings, prayers and wishes for the planet, us and the New Year', market patrons were invited to slip their wishes into the makeshift cylindrical device and give it a spin.

At ConFest, healing and ecological awareness are persistent, related messages. The common strand connecting many workshops is the complex relationship between person and planet, between Self-growth and Earth consciousness. Being healthy and being green are intimately related. Many workshop themes thus communicate a 'heal thy self, thy planet' ethos (also the theme of Walwa 90/91). Over the years ConFest has been a significant site for the manifold expression of a pressing self-globe relationship, one that is characterised by both a profound sense of interdependence and an ethical self-commitment. Acting 'locally' to benefit the planet, has for many begun with the locality of one's own self (the growth of one's mind, body and spirit). For others, personal anticonsumption and sustainable production strategies, such as using renewable energy sources, have become desirable.

A 'local' tactic developing into a subcultural career is the eco-radical project of *going feral*. A process indicating detachment from a state of domesticity, the parent *culture*, and identification with the *natural* environment, *ferality* is a biographical transition undertaken by thousands of young Australians, a contemporary rite of passage indicating reconciliation with indigenous ecology and peoples. During the nineties, ConFest has not only been a rendezvous point for the new semi-nomadic tribes celebrating and defending natural and cultural heritage, but is a safe space for expatriates of the dominant culture to stray from the paths, to go feral.

Indeed, ConFest is an open-staged ritual-theatre of the *feraliens*. Fire dancers, dreadlocked, multi-pierced psy-trance maidens and tribal drummers adorned with *feralia* – feathers, birds' feet, skulls and umbilical-cord necklaces – evoke defiance, wildness, otherness, freedom. Spectacular aesthetes, on a diet of tofu and tahini, belonging to anarchist eco-tribes, committed to direct actions, oozing eco-spirituality, these antipodean *terra*-ists represent an attractive subcultural career for youth disenchanted with their separation from the natural world, with the mass-consumerist mentality of the parent culture.

Workshops endorse eco-consciousness, as numerous activist organisations and ideologues seek support for green philosophical, political and/or spiritual agendas: deep ecology, eco-feminism, intentional community, alternative technology, permaculture, animal liberation, vegetarianism. Various villages have been sites for the dissemination of ecological awareness and activist issues. The agendas of activist tribes like FOE, GECO and OREN (the Otway Ranges Environment Network), HEMP (Help End Marijuana Prohibition), the Great Walk Network (whose motto was 'less consumption – more joy'), and individuals like human-sculpture activist Benny Zable (whose 'Greedozer and Company' sign reads 'work consume, be silent, die – I rely on your apathy') and Nelumbo (a workshop holder who claims 'we're all barracking for nature'), all provide evidence of a robust eco-radicalism.

ConFest is a recruitment centre for a growing Earth army. It has been a rallying point for campaigns such as protests at the WMC uranium mine at Roxby Downs SA in 1983/84 and 1997, the Errinundra forest blockade in 1984 and the protest at ERA's Jabiluka uranium mine in 1998. At Moama 96/97, activists from GECO and other eco-tribes initiated the Forest village which has functioned as a fund raiser and rallying node for native logging blockades mountted at Goolengook in East Gippsland. As such a recruitment centre, the event has served to fuirther the growth which bequeaths the disenchanted with an understanding of their kinship with the natural world and a defensible place in the natural scheme of things.

ConFest is today a pilgrimage centre at the margins of Australian culture, a matrix of pure possibility. It is where the perennial quest for release and diversion (festive play) collides with new awareness (conference workshops). It is a site where the pleasurable excesses of carnival coincide with the serious business of resisting the parent culture. It is where party meets protest. It is thus a multi-dimensional catalyst for change, a

Fire Dancer

Benny Zable – human sculpture activism

counterscape where spontaneity and immediacy have few parallels in the experiences of its participants, and where exposure to new frontiers of thought and behaviour foments multiple transformations.

ConFests aren't the only focus of alternate arts by any means. Oz is a big, big place and most events and tribal meetings take place at the local level. My days in the Rainbow Region included meeting Nuro, Mook and Shanto's daughter. I was impressed. Here was a real life Child of the Albion. A daughter of the Hippy Dream. She's all of that and more; an accomplished artist; a member of the Bahloo tribe and a powerful, sparky, sparkly individual making her own personal waves through life along with her friends. Having spent an evening with her, I was especially keen that she shared some of her life – the forest doofs and a bit more – with you in this book. Here it is. Enjoy.

A Night In The Life Of A Life In The Night
by Nuro Oliver

Alternative Techno Culture of the Far North Coast, NSW, Australia

CAFE: 1PM Friday
"two soy lattes please."
"coming right up."
"thanks...so what was I saying?"
"you were telling me about the doof to-night."
"oh yeah, I overheard someone here yesterday...they said it's going to be on...up at the crossroads in Upper Main Arm."
"cool, that's an excellent spot, do you know who's putting it on?"
"Si and the Byron crew, they seem to know what they're doing."
"yeah I like their music usually, should be good then?"
"yeah I'm hyped...tell anyone cool you know"
"OK I will."
"I was thinking of asking Ben if he's going, maybe get a lift with him. If he's got room are you up for it?"
"FUCK yeah!!!"

HOUSE: 10.30PM Friday
techno pumping and 3 girls getting ready. Trying clothes on, bindis glitter...jumping around, dancing, screaming and carrying on...packing bags: fruit, chewy, water, chupachups, tobacco/dope, $$, other clothes, condoms. swimmers, sarong, waterproof jacket...the motto is 'be prepared...for EVERY-THING!!'

"beepbeep".
"hey, our lift's here...LET'S GO."

KOMBI: 11PM Friday ...soft techno playing
"hello girls...ready?"
"ready as we'll ever be!"
"hi Ben!"
"I take it you've all used the loo as we've a long trip ahead of us?"
"let's get this show on the road!!!"
"get comfy...will someone roll a joint?"

ROADSIDE: 11:27 PM Friday
crickets and frogs chirp in the background...an owl hoots nearby...the kombi engine idles slowly...the lights pick out the trees beside the road...
"hurry up...we wanna get there!"
"yeah, yeah...a girl's gotta piss!"
"can you hear anything out there?"
"only birds and...oh...the boogie man!"
"well get back in and let's GO!!!"

KOMBI: 11:43PM Friday
forest on both sides of the road...silence...broken only by the kombi engine and us...
"where the fuck are we?"
"it all looks the same out there!"
"where's the map?"
"fuck the map...just keep driving!"
"oh yeah sure...we'll just end up in the middle of nowhere!"
"I remember it said something about taking a right at Manns Road..."
"we haven't got there yet!"
"gosh I've lived here all my life and all these roads look the same to me!!"

"just shut up everyone.I need to concentrate."
"there I see it…it's even got a fluro arrow on the sign post."
"cool we're almost there!!!"

as the kombi chugs along the primitive bush track, the deep resonating sounds of the bass can be heard booming against the backdrop of the mountains. The excitement grows in the kombi as everyone gets closer to the start of the real journey…the techno experience.

SOMEWHERE IN THE BUSH: 11:55PM
we know we've arrived by the neverending line-up of cars haphazardly parked on the side of the track.
"this looks like a good parking spot."
"yep we're here."
"fucken at last…man I was about to fall asleep."
"quick, hurry up and get out…my legs got pins and needles."
"ooh I need to do a wee so bad!"
The noisy engine stops…the kombi door slides open with a crash….the beat is everywhere…the night air is wall to wall techno…

I instantly get a rush through my body…happens every time…I love it…I am so excited knowing that a full-fledged party is going on 50 metres away and I am so close…any minute now and I'll be dancing.

"don't turn the lights off till we get all our stuff out."
"somebody grab my bag!!"
"who's got a torch?"
"bloody dark out here!!"
"no shit…has everyone got their provisions?"
"is anyone bringing water?"
"let's leave the fruit here so it doesn't get squashed."
"LET'S GET THIS PARTY STARTED!!!"

BUSHTRACK: 12:00 AM Saturday
darkness…someone up the front has the torch and is leading the way down the treacherous path…as usual I'm lagging behind and having trouble balancing my load and tripping over things…

flashes of light through the forest…the music's getting stronger…people heading back to their cars on a

mission…appearing unexpectedly out of the dark…getting close…glimpses of people dancing in a fluro world…we are HERE!!!

DOOF/PARTY: 12:05 AM Saturday
"let's find a spot to stash our stuff."
"did someone bring a blanket to put down?"
"was there anyone with brains enough to bring some toilet paper?"
"me as usual…don't I think of everything?"
"over here…this looks cool…under this tree will do."

we pile our belongings around the base of a giant ghost gum whose white iridescent bark reflects the swirling, flashing lights like a screen…trippy…let's go cruising…

DANCEFLOOR: 12:10AM Saturday
I'm in a logged-out clearing which is lit by a number of lasers and strobes randomly flashing-creating a chaotic attack on the visual level…while four huge speaker stacks at the corners of the clearing mercilessly pound the aural and vibrational realms with super-sonic surround sound…what a blast!!!

what I see down on the lowest level is a sea of people rhythmically moving in tune with the soundscape; the bass and kickdrum whack me in the stomach…as I look up I see the backdrop of fluro reflecting tree trunks and at that level in the music is an orchestra of sounds…chords and rhythms floating in and out…I look up higher into a myriad of fluro banners and branches…and the next sound level is one of samples, the messages they've decided we have to hear…the grabs and the loops that take you further on the journey…I look right up beyond the silhouettes of giant treetops into a circle of stars that match the alien bleeps at the top level of the music…sonic frequencies…scratches, patches, snatches of intergalactic code…that transport you to those stars…and hopefully back again…

after taking everything in and slowly digesting it…as it is a mega blast of energy to absorb, I wander around and check the scene…a bunch of dreaded ferals toking on a joint…two fluro freaks tripping each other out with some wacky dance steps…someone curled up next to the fire…some deros sitting in a ditch drinking cheap cask wine…whizzing stripes fly by as some groover pulls funky dancesteps…fire-twirlers creating flaming vortices to an awestruck crowd…a group of friends…

"hey there!!"
"having a good night?"
"pumping party don'tcha reckon."
"I just got here…but yeah."
"have you seen Sarah…she's been looking for you."
"she said that she's got something you would like."
"cool, where is she?"
"I saw her over near the fire."

FIRE: 12:20 Saturday

"this is the shit sis…pure Alice in wonderland style…you'll love it!!"
"have you tried it?"
"I dropped a tab about an hour ago…just starting to peak"
"and how is it?"
"find out for yourself…here…have a nice trip!!"

I'm sitting here once again in the middle of the forest…by a huge fire…warming my toes …drinking chai…and sharing a spliff…waiting for wonderland…fuck I love this life…

"hi Noobs, how ya doin'?"
"woah…who's that? Hey Dylan…how's your night?"
"yeah excellent…my ecky's just starting to kick in."
"pretty good setup…do you know this DJ?"
"he's some English dude…meant to be pretty good."
"the DJ line-up looks filth tonight…hay this track sounds wicked…gotta go dance…see ya later!"

DANCEFLOOR: 12:30AM Saturday

I go for a dancefloor adventure…dodging spastic dancers and 6 foot tall neanderthal hippies…zipping in and out of the crowd…finding a good spot near a stack of speakers, I start getting in the groove of things…I think this acid's starting to kick in…I spy a freaked out friend of mine off in the corner…I come up from behind him and grab him…

"FUCK…Who's that?"

"it's me…sorry to freak ya!"

Jed looks like something out of a cyber comic strip…dark dreads down to his waist, with beads and bones and an assortment of bits hanging off his head…two tripped eyes look out at me from a scruffy bearded face…

"oh hey…it's you…scared me for a minute…I'm tripping off my nut!"
"yeah I will be too any second…got some stuff off Sarah."
"that's what I'm on, she's always got good LSD…you're in for a ride!!"
"your outfit tonight looks pretty OUT there…ET style."
"yeah…I gotta give the morons something to look at!"

intertwined around his dreads is a weird gasmask looking head piece that seems to have lasers placed in the eyeholes…woah…and slung around him is a lasergun of sorts…I point to it and he brings it up to my face and presses a few buttons…over the pounding music I can vaguely hear a whirring and bleeping that's coming from his contraption…as well as a sequence of flashes and lasers…I can tell this is another of his way out inventions…I give Jed two thumbs up and keep on moving…

I'm starting to feel quite out of it…and can't seem to wipe the grin off my face. As I dance around I feel my body loosening up and feel the need to stretch…I go off to the side of the dancefloor and bend over to touch my toes…this feels good…I look up to see my friend Deedrah looking at me…laughing…

"what are you losing it over?"
"you…just looks funny."
"you'll look funny in a minute….do you wanna help me stretch?"
"I'll swap ya!"

this is what we do for each other at parties…limber up…we know it looks strange…but the dancefloor is our playground…and fuck it!!…we'll play…the stretching seems to make us loosen up and spastic out to the music…which is the reason we're here…TO DANCE…dancing is the way I clean the stains from my soul…

I notice a shift in the music...I look to the DJ booth and see that one of my favourite DJ's has just come on...he seems to always be in tune with the crowd and play exactly what we want to hear...I get excited and let out a "WHOOP!!"....the DJ is mixing the end of one track into a new one and everyone is seemingly hanging onto every beat where will he take us?...the new song takes over and is building layer upon layer of intricate noise...dipping up and down...in and out and around...crescendo-ing up into oblivion.

I look around me...into a mass of ecstatic faces...as the song moves into another climax I hear screams and cries from the crowd...the DJ is taking us on a merciless journey...no turning back...the music seems to be twisting and contorting our bodies into movements thought impossible ...this is what we love...at this moment in time we are one...with the music...and with each other...a unified sea of trance consciousness...no thought...only sweet movement...unadulterated and pure...this is what it's all about...FREEDOM....

"this is going off the richter!!"
"fucken wicked shit...this is on

the level alright!!"
"I'm so glad I came."
"me too!!"

BASECAMP: 3:00AM Saturday

"hey Allycat"
"hello baby...I haven't seen you in ages. Are you having a good one?"
"can't you tell ? I haven't been able to wipe this grin off my face all night. Just had the best dancing session before...haven't had one so good in about 6 months!!"
"really that good? I must admit I was enjoying myself...everyone was digging it."
"understatement of the year. Did you take any drugs?"
"yeah I had half an ecstasy tab and some speed."
"how's it going?"
"I wasn't feeling so good...then I had a spew and I feel really good now. I started rushing so hard that I had to come and sit down...chill out a bit."
"that marathon dance took it out of me...do you want a cup of chai?"
"that's exactly what I need...ta!"

CHAI STALL: 3:15AM Saturday

"two chai's please...and...um...a bit of that choccy cake...hang on...is there anything else in it?"
"nope...but we have some gunja balls and some guarana slice if you're interested?"
"nah...just a pure sugar hit thanks!"

It's interesting to think that here we are, a bunch of a hundred or so people gathered together...in the middle of the forest...dancing around on an old logged out clearing...celebrating nature, life and each other...and most of us are off our fucking faces...I mean the ratio of these parties that I've been to totally straight compared to drugged out is embarrassingly low...this culture can't seem to get enough substance abuse...I see it as partly an endurance thing – last out the night...but it's more than that ...enhancing the combined senses of music, visuals and movement...it seems that this and drugs make for a new sense...an ultimate trance state...a tribal energy...a sense of belonging...of culture...

EVERYTHING SEEMS SO CLEAR...AS THE NIGHT SKY as a fractal appears and disappears into the cosmos...in front of my eyes...a fluro banner emulates a 3-D effect...am I in another world? No I'm in this world, but it's different...quieter...distant...I can see the bigger picture...

"HAY!!! Are you alright?"
"yeah, yeah...I'm fine...just tripping hard...think I need to go piss."
"don't get lost...okay!"

BUSHTRACK: 4:00 AM Saturday
oh my god...everything is so black...thank heavens for the moon or I wouldn't be able to see anything...I'm soooo busting...here looks like a good spot...DAMN...I forgot the toilet paper...oh well drip dry...

DANCEFLOOR: 4:20 AM Saturday
another dance marathon coming up...I need this...I was losing it a bit back there...we have the sunrise to come...the stars are out...promises to be a glorious new day....

"where you been? I haven't seen you much tonight...are you having a good time?"
"yeah full on as usual...I've just been cruisin...how about you?"
"geez...you couldn't get me off the dancefloor even if I wanted to...the music's been awesome...you look like you need a cuddle?"
"that'd be nice."
"mmmm"

SAME PLACE: 6:00 AM'ish Saturday
"this is heaven!!! The sun's coming up, the music's cranking, I'm surrounded by my favourite friends and everyone's going OFF!?!?"
"yeah life doesn't get much better than that"
"YEEHA!!!!!"

I salute the sun...the new day...the rising of the golden orb...warm me...remind me that every day is a new beginning...a fresh start...I look around and a sparkling world winks back...the mist has risen and the dew lines every leaf...it is always strange to finally see where you have been all night...everything is sharper, crystallised in time...off in the distance mountains can be made out...outlining the horizon...

back on the dancefloor the music hits a new note...brighter...fresher...more melodic...in time with the rising day...Everyone seems to pick up on the shift, and hit the dancefloor with a vengeance...as with the surroundings, the people are now visible...the freaks have come out to play in the sunshine...

someone brings out fruit...we ravish nature's gifts and feel the sustenance...

after this last burst of energy the party disassembles...swimming...eating...chillums a smokin'...little packs of peoples disperse into the new day...a day of recovery...of sleeping...or...seediness...assimilating the night's journey...

and until the next doof...travel safe...and peace be with you...

John Seed – deep ecologist, earth patriot and new man of the trees

"The most important thing we can do is to hear within ourselves the sounds of the Earth crying."
Thich Nhat Hanh

"Because when we do that then our compassion is out there, we're out there with all of the rest it, we feel that interconnection, but also we then begin to be in a position to be able to do something about it. Without that pain there's not enough motivation. Our ideas aren't enough motivation to do anything." **John Seed.**

Before venturing from Brit to Oz, I had already heard about John and many of his buddies. I'd visited a couple of his associated web sites and even bought a copy of his book, *Thinking like a mountain: towards a Council of All Beings,* written with Joanna Macy, Pat Fleming and Arne Naess. We've only been e-mail correspondents, yet I feel I know him quite well. I like him for his energy, optimism and enthusiasm. He's definitely still out there, doing it. And he's a friend of Mook and Shanto's, sharing a history back to the Terania Creek blockade in 1979.

Listen to the resonance of the words he sent me from the Giblett forest, Western Australia – one of the last and most glorious old growth rainforests.

"Sitting by the campfire at the protest/witness camp here at Giblett forest in the SW of WA. Guitar and didge drift over from the other fire. I guess there were 20 of us camped here last night, a motley crew of young ferals and old hippies and Chris Lee up on his platform thirty metres above us perched halfway up a massive Karri tree, his seventh night up there. We were waiting for CALM (the State Government's Department of Carnage and Land Massacre – alias Conservation and Land Management) to declare the area a TCA (Temporary Control Area) and try and move all the people out."

"They have a quaint habit in these parts called 'scrub rolling', where they send in dozers and anything else they have that weighs a few tonnes to flatten the undergrowth, to clear the way for the chainsaws through the deep undergrowth. Ancient cycads, she-oak, snotty gobbles, bulich, tea-trees, lucepogan, isepogan – crushed orange everywhere. It's so disgusting, such a majestic, huge forest, most of it trampled into dust to expose the big trees, and then 85 per cent of the volume of these turned into woodchips. What's more, the whole thing is heavily subsidised by the taxpayer – all the roads and port infrastructure and, in spite of the loggers' and chippers' vast profits, the workers get paid so little that they qualify for social security support to supplement their income."

So, let's learn a bit more from the man himself. The following words are John's. They've been pieced together from a number of sources, including interviews with Ram Dass, Samantha Trenoweth and James Bennett-Levy. If you want to hear more from this remarkable guy, check out the Rainforest Information Centre site – http://forests.org/ric/ There's also a nice section about John at the rainboweb site: http://rainboweb.com/janos.htm

Painting by Geoff Williams

Background
"It went I.B.M., L.S.D., meditation and community."

My own awakening started when I left my job as a systems engineer for IBM and I dropped out and was living on the land. I had no interest in ecology but then I found myself, just through circumstance, involved in the defence of a particular forest. Once I started to do that I also started to become intellectually interested in the subject, and then I discovered that this rainforest that I was defending was in fact the place where I had evolved for the last hundred and thirty million years, and therefore it wasn't in the least surprising that it was able to get inside me and affect me so powerfully and use me in this way. Terania Creek, in 1979, involved a couple of hundred hippies staging what was, as far as I know, the first direct nonviolent action in defence of the rainforests anywhere in the world.

I had a very powerful spiritual experience of the environment through Terania Creek, the Franklin River, the Daintree and all those direct actions. Each of those things gradually transformed my life, until I finally surrendered to the earth. Now, I find myself asking for guidance and direction and energy and wisdom from the earth, knowing that I am part of the earth, knowing that I'm a cell in the body of the earth. I just go back to the forest, lie down on the forest floor, cover myself in leaves, imagine an umbilical chord going from my belly deep down into the earth and pray for nourishment, wisdom and guidance. There I find energy and an ability to act, to inspire other people, to think, write, dream, make films and do all of these things.

It took a number of years, countless demonstrations, press conferences, leaflets, and many people willing to sit in front of bulldozers and go to jail. But eventually 70 percent of the people of New South Wales came to agree with us, and the government established a series of national parks. To protect the remaining rainforests we formed an organization, the Rainforest Information Centre (RIC).

In response to our success, however, Australian logging companies began to look offshore, and in 1983, community representatives from the Solomon Islands contacted RIC for aid in resisting the same logging companies we had fought, as well as Malaysian and Japanese companies. In the years that followed RIC volunteers provided technical, financial, and political support to defend forests and communities in the South Pacific, Asia, South America, and Russia. In 1984 I was invited by Earth First! to the U.S.

More recently, in India

Meanwhile, all the psychological aches and pains, which had mysteriously vanished when my Earth service was all-consuming, now returned... So I returned to India in 1995 searching for some resolution to the spiritual crisis that had begun for me a few years earlier. In Lucknow I spent a month attending satsang with the 86-year-old Advaita teacher Poonjaji. I received a blessing from Papaji, which rekindled the flame inside me which had been wavering and doubtful.

Nearly 10 years before, in 1987, I had received a letter from Apeetha Aruna Giri, an Australian nun residing in the Sri Ramana Ashram at the foot of Arunachala. Could we please help her to reclothe the sacred mountain? I asked, John Button, permaculture designer, if he would consider a tree planting project in the deserts of Tamil Nadu. John and his partner, Heather Bache, have worked as volunteers organizing the rehabilitation of Arunachala. The space between the inner and outer walls of the vast 23-acre temple complex has been transformed from a wasteland into the largest tree nursery in the south of India. Hundreds of people have received environmental education, and a 12-acre patch of semidesert was donated to the project and transformed into a lush demonstration of permaculture and the miraculous recuperative powers of the Earth.

It doesn't really matter what symbols we use: Shiva, Gaia, Buddha, God. What we need now is for the followers of all faiths to turn their allegiance to the Earth. What matters is that we refuse to be drawn to one or the other of the great polarities: spirit and Earth. We must neither reduce everything to spirit, from where it appears that the material world is some kind of illusion, nor reduce everything to the material, so it looks as if spiritual seekers are abdicating responsibility to care for the creation.

Deep Ecology – a defintion

To me it refers to the biocentric as opposed to the human-centered approach to things. It means rather than seeing the world as a pyramid with human beings on the top, we see the world as a web and the humans as just one strand in that web. So it's the kind of deep questioning, using the intellectual science of ecology as almost a spiritual truth, to allow those truths to become personal.

Deep Ecology – philosophy, intuition and action

There's this idea that all our intelligence is in our thinking and that this is betrayed by feelings, that we need to be objective about things and not get emotional. We're unconscious of the fact that we survived for thousands of millions of years before thinking came along, which must have taken extraordinary intelligence. I came from my mother's womb and she came from her mother's womb and it goes back through womb after womb until wombs were invented. Before that, reptilian eggs and before that, spores. At every step of the way, each ances-tor of mine and yours had to somehow survive long enough to reproduce before being consumed. At every step along the way, millions died without being able to do that. How many eggs does a fish have? Well, we had a zillion fish ancestors, one after the other, and every one of those had millions of eggs, of which two or three survived. At each generation, our ancestor was one of those. There's incredible intelligence in that, yet it had no thinking associated with it at all. It was feeling, intuition, instinct.

At the moment, we can't smell anything except our own stench. We can't hear anything except our own thoughts and our own voices. We've forgotten that anything else speaks. The world is reduced to human beings and resources. It's a horrible idea but, when we let go of that, we can once again harmonise with the incredible choir of the myriad beings of nature and that is what has the longevity, that is the thing that potentially lives forever

Never lose hope

I've steeped myself in the prophecies of doom from the scientists – the number of species becoming extinct every day, what's happening to the atmosphere, the intractability of nuclear waste. I've soaked up all this stuff. On the one hand, I realise, there is no way that the environment movement is going to get us out of that. If all of the efforts of all the well meaning people were multiplied a thousandfold, it wouldn't get us out of that. It's so huge and the momentum is so fast. On the other hand, my ancestors survived ice ages, my ancestors learned how to walk the land after being fish, my ancestors went from being inorganic to being organic. When you identify with all that, there's this fantastic pedigree, this unbroken record of survival and success and it becomes difficult to completely lose hope, even in the face of what seems like a hopeless situation.

I had been steeped in the philosophy of Deep Ecology, but I felt that it wasn't enough just to think these things. I felt that, unless we could move from having ecological ideas to having an ecological identity, it wouldn't change our behaviour.

Council of All Beings

Working with the Buddhist activist Joanna Macy, we developed a ritual to address our contemporary situation. The Council of All Beings, as we called it, began with mourning for what has been lost, the acknowledgement of rage and anger. Using guided visualization, movement, and dance, we re-experienced our entire evolutionary journey. We made masks to represent our animal allies and give voice to these voiceless ones, invoking the powers and knowledge of these other lifetimes to guide us in appropriate actions and empower us in our lives.

The first thing we do in our rituals is a sharing of what our intention is, and how we see things. Then you suddenly find yourself together with a group of people who love this Earth and have the intention to heal the Earth and to heal our separation from the Earth. After that, almost anything that you do becomes a vehicle, so it can be as corny as you like. Everyone can go and hug a tree for half an hour. Most people haven't ever hugged a tree for half an hour, and maybe even if you just go off and do it by yourself, it might work for you. But if you're with a group of people and you do this and then you come back together in a circle again and share your experiences, you'll find that half of those people have had some very, very profound experience during that time. Or you can put your face really close to the ground and take a one hundred inch exploration of a little piece of earth, with your nose right on the ground and just inching forward. Explore a hundred inches of ground over half an hour and then get together with the group and discuss what you've discovered. To spend a day together just doing anything at all which is bringing us into contact with nature and looking at these things, every single person in that group will undergo some shift, some transformation.

Ceremonies and rituals

Ritual touches us at a deeper place than our intellect. We resonate with it.

I believe that loss of the ceremonies and rituals that acknowledge and nurture our interconnectedness with nature is a large part of the problem. We modern humans are the only culture as far as I've been able to find out who have ever attempted to live without these ceremonies and rituals as an integral part of our societies. The people who place great importance upon such rituals and ceremonies are people who live in very, very close connection with nature, hunter-gatherer societies for instance, where people are immersed, imbedded in nature all of the time.

I'm thinking in particular of some dances and ceremonies that I saw among the Hopi Indians on those mesas a couple of years ago. I was particularly interested in them because they seemed so like the Council of All Beings, where a hundred dancers were dressed from top to toe with different animal features, animal masks and feathers and all kinds of things. And I realized then that these people think this was the oldest continuously inhabited village in the Western hemisphere had been performing these ceremonies

and rituals without break for thousands and thousands of years. So this isn't a process that you complete. It's not as though, "Well, we are alienated therefore we need these therapies and then we'll be okay." It's more like being okay is to realize that these ceremonies have to have a space in our lives. It's not something that we're ever finished with. So I'm thinking of that and the Penan in Sarawak who are the last nomadic hunter-gatherers in Southeast Asia, who also speak for the other voices of nature just to make sure that everyone remembers those voices.

What sort of miracle?

So, what kind of a miracle do we need? Well, it would be a very simple one, really. All that it would need would be for human beings to wake up one day different than they were the day before and realizing that this is the end unless we make these changes, and then deciding to make the change. That doesn't seem like a very likely thing to happen, but on the other hand the whole road that we've travelled is so littered with miracles that it's only our strange kind of modern psyche that refuses to see it. I mean the miracle of being descended from a fish that chose to leave the

John Seed address protesters at the Daintree Blockade, Cape Tribulation, 1986

water and walk on the land – anyone with a pedigree like that, you can't lose hope.

A better metaphor (of what life is and what the Earth is) I think was described by Lovelock, the British scientist who popularized the Gaia hypothesis, when he said that what we're doing to the Amazon is as if the brain were to decide that it was the most important organ in the body and it started to mine the liver for some benefits that it might get from it. Once we realize the connection, we realize deeply that we can't do that any longer because we know that it can't be in the interest of the brain to mine the liver or in the interest of a leaf to destroy the tree on which it's growing.

How I act

I feel that my own journey is one where I continually make that surrender to the larger picture whenever I am at any kind of a crossroads – then I look at it and I make that surrender and I don't need to know that. My own sense is that the earth is undoubtedly alive, the earth is undoubtedly intelligent, much more intelligent than me, and in fact my intelligence is only the tiniest fragment of the intelligence of the Earth. I'm just a leaf growing on this tree. And so it's safe for me to just surrender and allow the sap to come from the tree and move me where it will. So I don't know and in a way I don't need to know.

When I look back over the last year for instance, I'd say I spent about half my time doing workshops, spiritual-psychological workshops, which is also fundraising because all of the money from these workshops goes back into the rainforest, and as more and more people become interested in this that part of it grows. And about half of my time is spent on political action including large projects to protect rainforests in Papua New Guinea and the Solomon Islands and Ecuador that I'm involved in and supporting, and on direct action like chaining myself by the neck underneath a vehicle to prevent it from moving into the forest. And I don't know how I budget that time – I just do what I feel like doing.

The Amazonian butterfly philosophy

Ram Dass: I experience you as becoming an *instrument for the earth*. You're a pseudopod that comes out of the Earth and speaks for it. You speak for the trees, you speak for Gaia, and you're kind of surrendering, not even intentionally, and I can feel how that transformation might have occurred in you. Can you talk about the change in your self consciousness as you become more and more surrendered into that intuitive way of expressing the needs of the Earth to be heard?

Well, once I understand intellectually that my relationship to the Earth is that of a leaf to a tree, the needs of the tree have priority over the needs of the leaf. The tree can exist without the leaf but the leaf can't exist without the tree. New leaves can come, you know. So once I know that intellectually and then once I discover the tools for taking that knowledge and allowing it to sink more deeply into my being to that place where my values are made, where my intuitive moment-to-moment decisions are made, and I practise those things, then I feel like I start to partake of the nature of everything else, which is just total ordinariness. It's not as though there's anything special about this way of being: I think about a certain species of butterfly that I saw on a television program in the Amazon where one flock which flies together is made up of two different colored individuals, I think black and orange. And when they land on a stalk of grass, the black ones all land to make a perfect circle and the orange ones form these petals around it disguising themselves as a flower that fools their predator. Now the black ones didn't decide, hey I'm a black one, I'm going to go in the center. They just did what they wanted to do, they just did what they did. And I'm made out of the same material as those butterflies. I'm related to them, you know, I've been around here since exactly the same time that they've been around here and we're all made out of the same aboriginal substance.

For a long time, because of this big bulge here [touching forehead], I forgot a lot of that, and I have this propensity to forget. The butterfly never, never forgets who it is and what it wants, but I can easily forget. Therefore for me to spend my weekends acknowledging and searching for and finding and loving my rootedness in the Earth and accepting my dependency on the Earth, accepting that I'm not an independent spiritual being but that my spiritual being grows out of a complex and exquisite biology, then I just become an ordinary miraculous butterfly-like creature.

Sustainability in Papua New Guinea

In the Pacific, in New Guinea and the Solomon Islands, in Vanuatu, where the people do have land rights, the decisions about the fate of the forests are much less in the hands of governments than in the hands of communities who've traditionally owned the lands. The only way to protect the forest in the end is to offer those people some alternative economic development that doesn't require the destruction of the forest. You can't expect them, having no economic life whatsoever, to take a lofty view of these things. They don't want to see the forest logged but they see themselves as having no alternative. The problem is that they don't have the skills or the kind of infrastructure that allows them economic development. So one of the things that we noticed was that there was a small portable sawmill called the 'Walkabout', that was being manufactured in Papua New Guinea. There were about 300 of them around the country, and wherever these sawmills were the logging companies couldn't get a contract because all of a sudden the people found that the trees had value for them. So the first thing we did was an ecological audit of existing walkabout saw-mills and we discovered, as we'd suspected, that the worst of them was an order of magnitude better for the forest than the best of the large logging companies, mainly because the sawmills require no bulldozers and heavy machinery. Compacting the soil is even more damaging than the removal of the trees.

The Rainbow Bus, 1986

We found an area to intervene using these sawmills. This was in Morobe Province in Papua New Guinea where a large logging company was about to sign a contract with the Zia tribe. This company had moved its way along that stretch of coast clear-cutting its way along, and it was so confident of getting this contract for about 250,000 acres that it had already built a wharf and a fuel dump, and it was a matter of weeks before the contract was finished and signed. We came in and offered the people a choice, saying if we could provide them with three of these small sawmills, one for each of the villages in that community, and a management plan to go with them so that they could rotate around through a small section of forest in a sustainable way, and also a guaranteed market for the sawn timber, would they agree to spurn the advances of the logging company which they did. So four months later, we now are handing over those sawmills this week. The Australian High Commissioner, I believe, is over there as part of that ceremony. The people are getting 200 times as much for each

tree they saw as they would have got for the logs from the logging company, and although in the short term they're not getting as much of a windfall in 1991, they can see that this is going to go on sustainably. Each sawmill only cuts seven acres a year, and we believe that on a 50 year rotation they'll be able to go back to the first side again and keep logging. So that's 350 acres per sawmill for three sawmills out of the 250,000 acres that were at threat from the logging company. So we feel like this is now a model and we're looking for other places where we can use the sawmill in this way, and also other modes of sustainable develop- ment that we can provide using Australian aid, and other funding sources.

Modern life and a cowboy story

I often travel by plane and I use all of this fuel. And the only thing that helps me in this is a metaphor from an archetypal cowboy movie from my childhood. All the cowboys were asleep and the fire's gone out and the clouds come over and there's a bolt of lightning and all the cattle start stampeding towards the cliff. The cowboys jump on their horses and they don't ride in the opposite direction, they ride straight towards the cliff, and they ride even faster than the cattle. Now their aim is not to go over the cliff, but they realize that it's only by keeping pace with the whole thing that they're going to be in a position to lean on that herd and turn them around before they reach the edge. So I use a computer and I know the chips were cleaned using CFCUs, but there is no harmless way to live these days, really. Or if there is, way out in the woods somewhere, it seems pretty irrelevant to me. I'm prepared to get my hands dirty with sawmills and airplanes and anything at all, but I'm also, I believe, prepared to let go of them like that as soon as...they'll wither away after the revolution, that's all I can say.

"I try to avoid hope. It's just a subtle form of suffering, you know. I'm just 'Be Here Now'." **Ram Dass, San Rafael, 1999**

Amongst the many books I bought during my travels around Oz was Ted Trainer's *Saving the Environment*. I found it to be full of sensible, down-to-earth if you will, commonsense. 'Here', I thought, is an academic who is actually out there on the front line doing something to bring about change.

Back in the UK I contacted Ted, and in the following pages he shares some of his knowledge, ideas and personal anecdotes of adapting to, and living, the 'Simpler Way'.

How to save the planet
Ted Trainer

I know how to save the planet. Lots of us do now. And it would be so easy – if only we could get the mainstream to change to our Simpler Way.

Firstly I want to sketch some key aspects of the global situation in order to argue for the form that a sustainable society must take, and then I want to claim that my experience of living in simpler ways leaves me with no doubt that humans could indeed easily live in sustainable settlements with a higher quality of life than most people in rich countries have now. The problem of course is to get people in general to understand why The Simpler Way is necessary, and more importantly to see how satisfying it could be.

The situation.

For some thirty years an overwhelmingly convincing 'limits to growth' case has been accumulating, to the effect that the affluent industrial way of life we have in countries like Australia is grossly unsustainable. Our rates of production and consumption and environmental impact are far too high to be kept up for long and in any case all the world's people could never rise to them. We can have them only because we are taking most of the world's resource wealth. The rich world per capita resource consumption is 15 to 20 times the level for the poorest half of the world's people. We get 86 per cent of world income while the poorest one fifth get only 1.3 per cent.

If the 11 billion people we are likely to have on earth soon after 2070, were to have Australia's present per capita resource use, world production would have to be 10 times what it is now. If we tried to rise to that level, estimated potentially recoverable

resources of all fossil fuels, and one third of the minerals would be exhausted by about 2040. (Trainer, 1995a, 1998).

Using a technique called 'footprint' analysis, Wachernagel and Rees, (1995) have shown that it takes at least 4.5 hectares of productive land to provide food, water, energy and settlement area to one person in a rich country. If 11 billion people were to live as we do in Sydney, the area of productive land required would be about eight times all the productive land on the planet. Our society is not somewhat unsustainable; it is far beyond sustainability.

The global environmental problem is similarly explained in terms of there being far too much producing and consuming going on. For example, the atmospheric scientists have told us that if we are to stop the carbon concentration in the atmosphere getting any worse we must cut the input rate by 60-80 per cent. If we were to cut it by 60 per cent and share the remaining energy between 11 billion people, each of us would have to get by on under 6 per cent of the volume we use now. Most people have no idea of these magnitudes, i.e., of the fact that we are far beyond sustainable levels of resource use and the environmental impact.

These and other lines of argument in support of the general 'limits to growth' analysis show that there is no possibility of all people rising to anywhere near the levels of production and consumption we now take for granted in rich countries like Australia.

To this we must add the absurdly impossible implications of the never-questioned commitment to economic growth. The argument above is that present levels of production and consumption are grossly unsustainable, but the supreme goal in all countries is to constantly increase them, without any limit in sight. Nothing is more important than raising 'living standards' and the Gross Domestic Product.

Let's assume that Australia averages 3 per cent annual economic growth until 2070, and that all the people in the world then will have risen to the same 'living standards' by 2070. The total amount of economic output in the world would then be 110 times what it is today! Yet, hardly any politicians, economists or journalists seem to see any problem with this.

It is not plausible to assume that technical advance. Recycling, the development of renewable energy sources or growth of the service sector will enable us to extend the affluent-industrial consumer society to all. (Trainer, 1995a.) The above figures and multiples are far too big for that.

Possibly the most disturbing problems being caused by the commitment to perceived affluence and growth are the deprivation and underdevelopment of the Third World. We in rich countries are receiving 80 per cent of the world's resource output and consuming resources at 15-20 times the per capita rate of the poorest half of the world's people. The global economy allows market forces to determine how resources are distributed and what is developed. The inevitable result is that the poor majority gets very little of the world's resource output, and the development that takes place in the Third World does little more than put their land and resources into producing exports to enrich corporations and First World shoppers. Conventional economic development is best regarded as a form of plunder. (Chussudowsky, 1997, Goldsmith, 1997, Trainer, 1995a, 1995b.)

We should therefore not be surprised that according to the UN's 1996 Human Development Report, the poorest one-third of the world's people are now actually getting poorer each year. Clearly the global economy is massively unjust. Its mechanisms deprive the majority to provide us with our high rates of consumption. Satisfactory development for the Third World is impossible unless the rich countries stop hogging the resources and stop imposing the conventional free market development model on the Third World. Gandhi summed up the situation long ago with the statement, *"The rich must live more simply so that the poor may simply live."*

Globalisation is rapidly worsening all these problems, because it is increasing the freedom of access of the big banks and corporations to the world's resources. Polarisation, inequality and social breakdown are accelerating and all the evidence seems to show that the experienced 'quality of life' in the rich countries is falling.

The solution.
From these findings about the nature of the problem we can begin to see the basic form that a sustainable and just society must take. There must be:
a) much simpler, less affluent lifestyles;
b) highly self-sufficient local economies;
c) much co-operation and participation, and
d) a quite different economy, one not driven by market forces and the profit motive and one in which there is no growth at all. (My book, *The Conserver Society* (1995a), summarises what many are saying in these areas.) The key concept is the development of settlements in which local people take control of the local production of most of the goods and services they need, with relatively little importing and exporting from small regions.

Some of the other elements in the sustainable society would include permaculture design principles such as dense, 'edible landscapes', all through our suburbs; local production of most food, furniture, crockery etc.; decentralisation, so most people can get to work on a bicycle; substantial craft production; few big firms; local working bees and committees; development of local commons as sources of materials, amenity and free, communal food sources; neighbourhood workshops, ponds, windmills etc.; the digging up of many city roads; localised town banks (maybe based on Credit Union principles); local currencies, exchange and barter including LETS; and town and suburb self government – and a greatly reduced need to work for money – perhaps only one day a week!

We cannot achieve a sustainable society without developing an almost totally new economy. It would have to be one in which there could be an important role for small private firms and for market forces, but in which these are under social control. The basic production, development and distribution decisions would have to be made collectively. It would not be an economy driven by market forces and profit. There would be few if any transnational corporations and banks. There would have to be no growth at all. There would also be many free goods, more giving and sharing, and much economic activity that does not involve money or markets, and far less work and production than there is now. Administratively, there would only be a small state, because most economic and political activity would be taking place within local communities.

The crucial point here is that these are not preferences or options among many others. This is the 'general form' a sustainable society must take whether we like it or not! We cannot solve the big global problems facing us unless in rich and poor countries we move to settlements, lifestyles and economies of this general form, i.e., to The Simpler Way.

The transition.
Consumer society, including its intellectual elites as well as its mindless shoppers, has shown a stunning capacity to ignore all this. After 40 years of personally trying to raise concern, I believe that we in the 'limits to growth' team, have made almost no impression on the blind obsession with affluence and growth. I no longer think there is much point in telling them that this society is unsustainable. I now focus on a different strategy.

Whether or not the transition will take place will depend entirely on whether or not those of us who understand the situation work hard enough to establish many convincing illustrative examples of alternative settlements. Our best hope is that as consumer society increasingly fails to provide for people they will be able to see around them settlements in which many people are living with a high 'quality of life', in sustainable and just ways. (The detail and the dangers in this strategy are discussed in my book, *What Is To Be Done – Now?*, to be published late 1999)

So far, our team has performed badly at this task. We have had an alternative society movement for some 40 years now, but it has not made a satisfactory effort to get the mainstream to understand its significance. The recent emergence of the Global Ecovillage Network could increase our effectiveness, (although unfortunately many initiatives within this movement put insufficient emphasis on the need for simple lifestyles,

local economic self-sufficiency, communal activity or the need to scrap capitalism.) Nevertheless the intentional community movement (described in this book by Bill Metcalf, Peter Cock and others) and Deep Ecology (outlined by John Seed in the last section) are making extremely important contributions to the pioneering of sustainable ways.

It needs to be stressed however that the arena where the most important work is to be done is not in setting up intentional communities. It is working out how to transform existing towns and city suburbs into more self-sufficient local economies.

The relevance of my lifestyle.
At first encounter with these arguments, many people react with horror, under the quite mistaken impression that in order to save the planet they are being asked to accept extreme reduction in 'living standards', and therefore great hardship and deprivation, and the loss of just about everything that makes life worthwhile. Yes, we probably will have to cut the GDP, incomes and 'living standards' by 90 per cent or more. But what is not understood is that we can do all this while actually increasing the 'quality of life'. How do I know? Because, like many others, I live close to The Simpler Way and I know from my direct experience how easy it would be for all to have a very satisfying existence without consuming many resources and without damaging the environment.

There are two factors here. The first is the willingness to live simply in one's personal or domestic situation, i.e., without buying much more than one needs for comfort, hygiene and convenience. This is just a matter of being content with what is sufficient for comfort, hygiene, convenience etc. For example, you can build a perfectly adequate house for less than $15,000.

The much more important factor is designing settlements that enable us to live well without consuming much, and without huge transport and infrastructure costs. Most, and probably all, our food, should come from within a few kilometres of where we live, and could easily do so if we developed settlements which included much home gardening, community gardening, local market gardening and 'edible landscapes' stacked with bush-tucker, fruit and nut trees in the parks and on local commons. If we did this the need for trucks, packaging and storage would be greatly reduced, and therefore we would not use much energy in food supply. Similarly, if work places were decentralised there would be much less need for cars to get us to work. If neighbourhoods were landscaped as leisure rich we would need to use far fewer resources in travelling for leisure. My homestead is leisure rich and enables me to work and produce food and other things without travelling, so I can see how easily we could all do these sorts of things – if our settlements and economies were restructured. Most people can't change to these ways immediately because they are trapped in circumstances which oblige them to go on travelling and consuming. Changing our settlements and systems is the main task.

In many ways I live like a Third World peasant. My clothes are comically ragged. I spend almost nothing other than on basic necessities. I cut my own fire wood and collect my own drinking water off the roof. My poultry pens and sheds and tanks are home made. I mostly use hand tools. I collect scrap materials for use in the workshop. I have built a house and windmills and waterwheels. One of my favourite activities is digging mud, extending the ornamental lakes and canals while getting earth to build more sheds and animal houses. Another hobby is sewing up old socks and jumpers to keep them going.

Why do I do these things? Firstly because I understand that we have to do things like this in order to cut resource use and to save the planet. But the main reason I do them is because they are things I enjoy doing. There are huge satisfactions in living simply and self-sufficiently. In fact these are the satisfactions that life is primarily about for people who live The Simpler Way. I cut fire wood and grow beans not just to be warm and fed, but because I get many rewards from doing these things. These are not just means to an end. Thus, the alternative way can make most work into a source of enjoyment, especially when it is done in a co-operative community working bee. Yet work for most people in consumer society is not a source of life satisfaction. The Buddhists sum up some of these themes well with the saying, *"Poor in means, but rich in ends."*

One of the most important rewards in The Simpler Way is the sense of self-sufficiency. I can grow beans, fix a tap, cut glass, repair a windmill, make things – I can keep my household in pretty good shape. I am not highly dependent. I am a Jack of all trades. Another source of satisfaction is the fact that so many daily activities involve creativity. You are always designing things, planning and constructing, often simple functional things like a better gate latch, but often ornaments, paths, gardens, pergolas etc. There is much scope for integrating 'art' with 'work'. (In fact, I don't do any work; it's all better described as productive play.)

Possibly the most important source of satisfaction is knowing that you are not part of the problem any more. I find it disturbing to go to the supermarket, or drive in a car, or travel, because I know I'm using up scarce resources and participating in a way of life that causes catastrophic global problems. By living more simply I reduce my footprint on the planet.

There are other profound sources of satisfaction that I do not have access to on my homestead, but which I would experience in a sustainable settlement. One of these is community. To work with friends, to share surpluses and experiences, to give and to receive, to participate in local celebrations and festivals, to be embedded in relations of emotional gratitude and debt, to feel bound to the place and its people, to know that concern and support are there if you need them and to be able to give these to others, to be proud of the community you have contributed to building – these are some of the most important sources of real wealth one can have access to.

Another source of satisfaction is being known and respected and valued as a good citizen. You can't buy a reputation like, *"Fred is always helpful. He came over during the storm when we had to fix the roof. He will always lend you his equipment. He's the one to ask how to fix wooden toys, and how to graft fruit trees. He's done a great job as chair of the orchard committee."* Status in this sort of community would be derived from contributions and from long interpersonal experience, not from acquisition of wealth or appearances.

And another source of satisfaction which is totally denied to us in consumer society is the experience of government. In a sustainable settlement we would all be involved in the committees, town meetings, referenda and most importantly the informal day to day discussion of public issues which determined what the best decisions were for the running and the development of our locality.

Most of these activities and processes are self-reinforcing. If we can only get people to experience the satisfactions that can come from being in a working bee doing something important for our neighbourhood, or helping to make important decisions about the development of our area, or from participating in a gift economy, then they are likely to want to go on doing those things, because they are enjoyable.

In a sane society where simple but sufficient living standards were accepted, life would cease being predominantly about producing and consuming. We would quickly and easily produce all we need (using automated factories where they make sense) and then be able to put most of our time into things that really matter, such as community building, personal development, restoring the environment, creating beautiful landscapes in which to live, celebrations and spiritual activities – and taking it easy. At present, we work about two to three times too hard! The Simpler Way makes these resources and dollar – cheap sources of life satisfaction abundantly available to all.

Again I can see all this, from my own experience. I am not theorising about what might be. I have experienced most of these things so I know it would be easy and satisfying to organise and run a sustainable society – if most people could be helped to understand that it is not about making big sacri-fices to do without all the things they like buying, but that it is about substituting other sources of satisfaction for the paltry, uncertain and unsustainable rewards consumer society offers.

So, it is extremely important that we establish more very impressive alternative communities and make them visible to the mainstream, so that people can see that The Simpler Way offers them a high quality of life while greatly reducing resource and environmental costs. This is the crucial responsibility of the alternative lifestyle and intentional communities movements.

Governments, corporations, and officials will not, indeed cannot, build a sustainable world order. It can only grow from the spread of sustainable settlements. These can only be initiated by people like us who understand that the consumer way must be scrapped and who know from our own experience that The Simpler Way is not only the sustainable way, but also the way that promises the highest quality of life for all.

Chussudowsky, M., (1997), The Globalisation of Poverty, London, Zed Books.
Goldsmith, E., (l997), 'Development as colonialism', in J. Mander and E. Goldsmith, eds., The Case Against the Global Economy.
Metcalf, B., (1995), From Utopian Dreaming to Communal Reality, Sydney, University of N.S.W. Press.
Trainer, F. E. (T.), (1995a), The Conserver Society; Alternatives for Sustainability, London, Zed Books.
Trainer, F. E.,(T.), (1995b), Towards a Sustainable Economy, Sydney, Envirobooks.
Trainer, F. E. (T.), (1998), Saving The Environment; What It Will take, Sydney, University of N.S.W. Press.
Trainer, F. E. (T.), What Is To Be Done – Now? (In Press.)
Wachernagle, N., and W. R. Rees, (1996), Our Ecological Footprint, Philadelphia, New Society.

It's time to meet your favourite PLC – the Pagan Love Cult!

I couldn't help but wonder, when confronted with the Web site for this lot – is it a bird, is it a plane, is it a band, or is it a sublime plot to overturn the world as we know it? The answer is out there somewhere. I'm certain. And perhaps, just maybe, Neil Pike and his musos, admitted weirdos and psychotics might hold some of the right cards.

Their web site is a miniature, but up-to-date version of the all singing, moving, interactive CD Rom which Neil was kind enough to send me. The CD Rom enables you to meet the band, sing along with their songs, learn more about their philosophy, join in a forest blockade and visit the beards of the century! Really. And that's not half of it. Certainly worth a visit to the web site and then you can make up your own mind whether to join the PLC or buy the CD. As Neil and the guys say,
"CULT is what you make it. Usually a weirdo spiritual or occult group, with bizarre and sometimes distasteful beliefs and practices. Sound good?"

The PLC can be found at http://www.nimbin.net/plc

Here are some of their ideas on life, your bodies, what you do with them, and what you could be doing with the Mother ship:

Pagan beliefs and practices are varied and geographically diverse.
The most common thread is
and awareness of nature
and humanity's place therein.

A major tool for reaching this awareness has always been the direct sensory and psychological experience

of the inter-connectedness of all life on the planet.

The ritualized use of psychoactive substances, trance-based participation and appreciation of music, art and dance, and prolonged and dynamically charging sexual practices have always been the keys...
sex, drugs and rock 'n' roll if you will...

Sex

In the 60s, researchers discovered that the average western male reached sexual climax within one and a half minutes. Hopefully we've increased that average somewhat over the last 30 years. Nevertheless, for the vast majority of humans sexual release is little more than a 'momentary sneeze'. Yet within easy reach of most people lies one of the oldest *spiritual* paths and practices.

Throughout history many mystics and occult travellers have stressed the power of sex. It is the primal energy and is common to all life. Sexual ecstasy is the closest many people come to any kind of transcendent experience, and when sex is prolonged for a reasonable length of time a very powerful, energising and enlightening consciousness change occurs. Put in laymen's terms, if you can delay orgasm for as long as possible, you get really high.

Many techniques have been developed over the centuries to assist this process, and many philosophies have sprung up to explain, harness and direct the resultant energy. Traditional Eastern 'Tantra' for instance advocates a complete abstinence from orgasm. European Cabbalistic Magick on the other hand, suggests using the point of orgasm as a kind of launching pad for all manner of spiritual, emotional and psychic energies. Whatever.

Find the techniques that work best for you, and look for the common ground amongst all teachings (therein lies the most

likely source of truth).

Three of the most popular methods of fostering **sacred sex** are...

Controlled breathing. Our breath is an essential key to our whole metabolism. By slowing and deepening our breath rate, our whole physical and emotional bodies become conscious and relaxed, and as a result a greater awareness and control becomes possible. Try it.

Focussed attention – Most people have the concentration span of a Coke commercial, the slightest distraction and they're off and running. A fairly high degree of focus is required to REALLY get high, so various tricks have always been used. In the past Mantra (or the continuous repetition of a certain phrase or prayer) has been employed to keep the mind's eye focussed. Unfortunately, most contemporary, cynical humans find this a bit fey. For this reason, the Pagan Love Cult recommends instead the use of appropriate music, lighting, colour, incense, environment and of course...

Drugs – Probably the most recurrent 'secret teaching' throughout history has been that sex plus drugs (within a ritualized environment) equals enlightenment (or as close as the average punter is likely to get). Patriarchal, monotheistic religious governments have never taken too kindly to this teaching. Its practitioners tend to be more centred, more free-thinking and a lot less controllable than most. Troublemakers, one and all. As a result, the philosophy of conscious, intelligent drug-use and guilt-less sex has remained underground and persecuted to this day. Despite this, drugs remain one of the most effective means of attaining the psychological and physical perspective where sacred sex is the only possible outcome. The Pagan

Love Cult particularly **recommends** marijuana and (given the right preparations, set and setting) a moderate dose of LSD or mushrooms.

More on drugs
Drugs and drug use are amongst the most contentious issues in our time. The 20th century has been a century of prohibition and yet most humans use one drug or another. The Pagan Love Cult believes that models for intelligent drug use are drugs needed. We say, *"Just say KNOW"*.

In tribal cultures, drugs are usually regarded as spiritual tools, aids to majick, initiation and a greater understanding of humanity's place in the world. At puberty, most pre-industrial cultures put their youth through a series of rites and initiations, often involving a major and naturally occurring psychedelic – most often mushrooms or one of the Tryptamines (DMT etc...). Not only does this give the young person an awareness of their traditions and place within nature and society, but as a first experience of drugs and altered states it spiritualises the substance used and creates a healthy non-abusive relationship with it. In the west we give 'em a six-pack and send 'em out to the car-park. Any wonder so many people within our society have 'drug problems'.

The Pagan Love Cult inc believes that psychedelics and marijuana are sacramental, and we call upon the long and

THE BIRTH OF DRUG EDUCATION
PREHISTORIC ROCK CARVING OF STONE AGE DRUG ABUSERS.
THIS IS WHAT YOU'LL LOOK LIKE, KIDS, IF YOU DON'T SAY "NO" TO MAGIC MUSHROOMS!

undeniable history of tribal and pagan use of these substances to support us.

Marijuana has had a strong relationship with humanity that is as old as civilization itself. Its use as an essential fibre crop is well documented. As a drug it has many aspects...medicinal, sacramental and recreational. The most dangerous thing about pot is that it's such a functional drug that you'll wind up smoking it all the time. For the last 60 years, users in the West have been harassed and persecuted, yet marijuana has become more and more popular.

Grow your own...
The real beauty of pot is that it's an organic, easily grown plant substance. Any fool with access to soil, sun, seeds and water (and enough nerve to risk a jail sentence) can keep themselves well-stoned.

Although smoking anything is bad for your lungs, the quantity of pot consumed by most smokers is well below cancer-producing levels, and the benefits (in our opinion) far outweigh the costs.

Marijuana is an excellent recreational drug, but its sacred and ritual use is not to be ignored. Try smoking a big fat joint and then doing some yoga or meditation, or if you really want to get high, oral sex on cannabis is one of the oldest spiritual exercises on (or off) the planet. But watch out for the boys in blue!

The Sacred Use Of Marijuana
This predates written history and has played a prominent role in the religions and civilizations of Asia, the Middle East, Europe and Africa. A pot-stoned head space is really not that far removed from the detached, blissed-out satori of many a dedicated meditator. Cannabis can transform any act into a ritualized, spiritual one (chop wood, carry water, chop wood, carry water). On the sensory level, marijuana readily lends itself to the stillness, focus and body awareness necessary for Tantra (see our Sex section).

This tradition continues today among diverse African tribes, certain Hindu sects, Muslim fakirs and Sufis, Rastafarians, as well as modern Occultists and Pagans (not to mention hippies etc.). Given the nature of the marijuana high and its world-wide distribution as a fibre plant, pot (along with psychedelic mushrooms) would seem to be a very likely source of many of humanity's original spiritual impulses and experiences.

LSD dosage
LSD is unique in its potency. All psychoactive substances known prior to it were measured in hundreds or thousands of a gram. Acid is measured in MILLIONTHS of a gram (mics).

When Sandoz were first manufacturing LSD it was distributed in l00 mic ampoules. Initially, this was considered a standard dose. It soon became apparent however that there is a threshold dose at which the psychedelic effects take a very definite turn for the intense.

By the mid 50s psychiatric opinion was divided into three camps, well two really. The first regarded LSD as a 'psychotomimetic' or psychosis-mimicking agent. In laymen's terms they felt that acid sent you madder than ten frothing dogs, and as such was a dangerous and very powerful chemical. Coincidentally enough, all of the American research done with this frame of reference was funded by either the CIA or US Army Intelligence. Both of these groups were extremely interested in the brain control potential of LSD.

The other school of thought suggested that acid was one of the most important chemicals yet discovered, an incredible tool for psycho-therapy and self-exploration. Two different types of therapy were in use.

Psycholitic therapy used from 50 to 150 mic doses, ideal for personal recollection and self examination. Psychedelic therapy began at about 250 mics and kept going, The results of this kind of therapy were much more intense and dramatic, often resulting in almost text-book mystical experiences and major life-change. In the mid 60s when acid was made illegal, a standard street dose was about 250 mics. Unfortunately, government-generated hysteria, and a poor general understanding of the rules of set and setting, resulted in many flip-outs. The media picked up on this and exaggerated it, creating a massive disinformation loop which LSD is only just emerging from now.

Set and Setting

In the early 60s, when LSD was still legal, researchers continually stressed the importance of what they called 'set and setting'.

'Set' referred to the expectations, mood, psychological disposition and general head space of the tripper.'Setting' is what it says – the physical and vibrational environment in which the trip takes place, including the 'set' of anybody else present.

Researchers found that when appropriate attention was paid to these two factors, 'bad trips' were virtually unheard of, and any negative feelings that arose in the tripper could be easily faced and resolved.

Relaxing, spacious music, a comfortable and attractive environment and sympathetic and sensitive company are the basic ground rules here, particularly when dealing with a psychedelic-sized dose. With the banning of LSD, these basic and fairly obvious prerequisites were largely ignored or forgotten, resulting in a dramatic upswing in the number of 'freak-outs' and acid casualties.

By the late 70s, the underground acid chemists generally had reduced the strength of their dosages to an average of about 100 mics...a psycholytic dose. As a result many people were able to enjoy a mild acid experience, without worrying about losing control, and soon acid became a rather popular party drug. Whilst this resulted in a lot less bummers, the sacramental nature of LSD has been largely forgotten. Indeed, there are now many self-styled 'trippers' who have never had a full-blown psychedelic experience.

Just recently (late-90s), some psychedelic strength (200+ mic) acid tabs have begun to appear. Whilst this is greatly welcomed by all the old hands, it must be stressed that adequate attention should be given to set and setting. Otherwise we're in danger of raising another crop of acid burn-outs.

The Pagan Love Cult believes that LSD is a wonderful and powerful sacrament, but we stress the importance of dosage considerations and set and setting. An average tab is fine for going to a dance party on. But if it's a strong one, think seriously about staying at home in a relatively secure and controlled environment. We guarantee that the light show will be just as impressive.

Gaia

Our Earth creates a single, holistic bio-sphere, complete and perfect within itself. All life here is interconnected and interdependent. Bacteria within the soil of an ancient forest create the perfect conditions for the strong and healthy growth, which in turn creates an abundance of leaf mulch and moisture and just the right conditions for bacteria which creates the perfect conditions for just such forest.

The same is true on every other level of life on this planet. Everything is connected. All life is part of the same huge web, and if one tiny strand is plucked or broken the repercussions are felt throughout. Modern conservationists and many Pagans have chosen to personify this global web of life as Gaia or Mother Earth. Whether we take this literally or not remains largely a matter of personal belief, but we are fierce in the protection of our Mother.

It became more and more obvious as the 20th century drew to a close that the one thing on this planet that's out of harmony with the bigger picture is the human race. Our arrogance and greed has turned paradise into a prison yard. The problem being that most humans are completely unaware of their connection to, and interdependence with, the rest of the planet.

Given the ego-dissolving qualities of the major psychedelics, it seems obvious that a good strong trip in the heart of a pristine forest should engender a direct experiential understanding of the Earth and our place within nature. It's very hard to maintain an uncaring attitude towards the planet after such an experience.

The Pagan Love Cult inc after considerable research has found that this is so...plant-based DMT seems to be the preferred substance. With its long tribal usage and short duration, it has consistently turned people on to their essential place on the Earth...just what the planet needs at the moment!

Aboriginality in Art

I am fascinated by Aboriginal art forms. In their diversity, they reflect much of the cultural and spiritual history of the Australian nation. They are also significant in showing how its original indigenous people, the Aborigines, are now attempting to make sense of Aboriginality. Ultimately, perhaps these art forms will prove to be the most important element in a real 'reconciliation'.

As I mentioned at the beginning of this book, I was student of Australasian social and economic history at the end of the 1960s. It seems both a long time ago, yet very recent. I mention it here because, even at degree level, the books we used for our studies gave an almost entirely European or white Australian perspective to the history and culture of the continent. Take for instance Russell Ward's 1965 book, *Australia*. There are just three references to Australia's original people; their ethnic status not even accorded capitalisation:

"One difficulty that Australian pioneers – unlike those of North America, South America, and New Zealand – did not have to contend with was a warlike native race...Nasty, brutish, and short though their lives were in many ways, no aboriginal tribe ever seems to have conceived the notion of exterminating or enslaving another, or of stealing its collective property or territory."

However, some Aboriginal resistance to the European occupation did take place. Particularly notable were the Eora guerilla attacks led by Pemulwuy in the period 1790-1802, which ended with his killing and beheading by bounty hunters.

Thankfully, the intervening years have offered opportunities

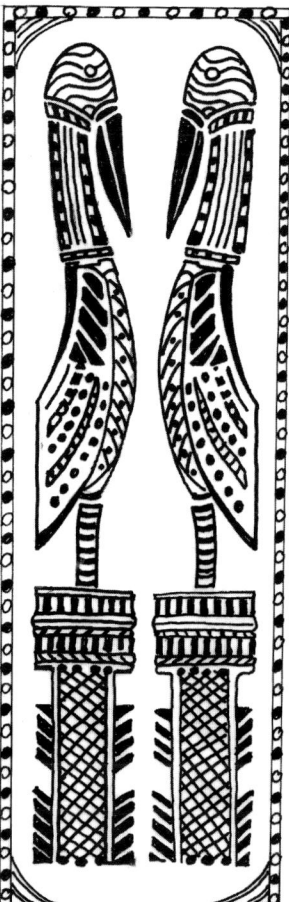

for Aborigines to begin to rediscover, celebrate and share their own culture, in which art and its essential relationship with the land and nature, is central. But it is a long and painful process. I think that Aboriginal dancer, Josie Lawford, gets close to diagnosing the problem in *A short field of poppies*. She says:

"I'd like to change the white Australian way of thinking, to say to them that we have got a culture here that is truly alive, you can learn so may things from us. You gave us education, you've given us so many things, it's time you started looking at us from the inside, instead of the surface, like people being drunk and no-hopers. Because that is not the reality." (in McCord and Anasoussiou, 1992)

Obviously this in stark contrast to the more stereotypical description of Aborigines by Howard Jacobson included in *In the Land of Oz* (1987):

"...sociable by instinct and rendered idle by design, they lolled about, sometimes badly drunk, but mainly engaging in half-hearted and self-conscious mischief – calling out, laughing, pushing one another, like the street urchins they have become."

Sadly, the latter description is sometimes true, and more obviously needs to be done to increase Aboriginal self-esteem, and white Australian acceptance of current and future generations of Aboriginal people as an important facet of Australian identity. Unfortunately, there are still many pockets of resistance to change, to which the rise of Pauline Hanson and the One Nation party bore evidence. Remember, it was Pauline who said she drew the line *"when told I must pay and continue paying for something that happened over 200 years ago."* In my own travels I was shocked to see the framed news cuttings on the wall by the bar in Scotty's Tavern in Alice Springs. These celebrated Keith Edmund's official report on the last execution in Northern Territory – the hanging of Jerry Roci and John Novotny, who were apprehended near Mount

Isa, after *"popular cab driver George Grantham was murdered by these men who then stole his taxi."*

Aspects of Aboriginal art

It has taken most of the last thirty years for the Art world to recognise the richness and variety of Aboriginal art forms. Historically, Aboriginal art was viewed as 'primitive' and as such it was displayed in museums rather than art galleries. Twentieth century white Australian art alternately followed European traditions and produced a large cache of stylised paintings of the outback and the bush by artists such as Tom Roberts, Frederick McCubbin, Arthur Streeton, Charles Conder and others. Collectively, this loose group became known as the Heidelberg School, named after Streeton's weatherboard house in the Yarra River valley near Heidelberg. The twentieth century 'modern' white Australian art movement continued this tradition of mythologising Australia's landscape and its people. In particular, Sydney Nolan's series of paintings of Ned Kelly appealed to the nation's love of anti-authoritarian rebels. Meanwhile, the art output of Aboriginal artists has been inextricably bound up in the federal and state policies relating to Australia's indigenous people.

The Arrernte landscapes

By the late 1930s, one group of Aboriginal artists located to west of Alice Springs, based at the Lutheran mission at Hermannsburg, began to gain acceptance for their stylised landscape paintings. Their most famous artist was Albert Namitjira, who had received some tuition from Rex Battarbee. *Haasts Bluff,* one of Albert's early paintings, was the first Aboriginal work to be purchased by an art gallery (South Australia) as opposed to a museum. Albert, his sons, and the Pareroultja brothers provided the artistic base for a steady output of watercolour desert scenes from Australia's Red Centre. Despite being introduced to Queen Elizabeth when she visited Canberra in 1954, Albert's fame and relative wealth only brought him and his family more problems. By this time Albert felt that Battarbee and others were exploiting his talent. Albert could still not buy a house in Alice Springs, because as

an Aboriginal he was not allowed in the town after dark; and following Aboriginal custom, he had to share his wealth with nearly 600 Arrernte at the Hermannsburg mission; and the income tax department was pursuing him for tax on his earnings, despite being denied citizenship. A further twist of ill-fate granted him and Rubina, his wife, citizenship in 1957. This meant that he would be allowed a house in Alice, but his sons were still wards of the state and could not live with him. Despondent, Albert started drinking heavily, and he was charged with supplying drink to members of his clan which was illegal. Despite protests and an appeal, he spent two months out of a six month sentence in jail. He never fully recovered and died of a heart attack in August 1959 soon after his release.

The local economy of Alice Springs and the surrounding area of the Northern Territory is now heavily reliant on the tourist industry. The landscapes of the Arrernte are still popular, and to some extent the art establishment jury is still undecided whether the paintings are fine art, popular art or tourist art. They also pose cultural problems, since they are seen by some as assimilationist – only proving that Aboriginal artists can successfully paint in a largely European style.

Personally, I like them and think

that their colours and style do present a distinctive Aboriginal vision. I even own a couple from the early 60s that I bought from a friend of mine, Craig Sullivan, who was touring with the Sydney Opera Company in Alice in 1964, and received them as a gift from the governor of the town's prison! The one reproduced on the previous page is by Edwin Pareroultja.

Traditional art forms

Much traditional Aboriginal art was, and is, produced as part of ritual life. It links the life of Aborigines with the sacred, the totems of clan and the spirits who created the land in the Dreamtime. The symbolic nature of much of the art is often impenetrable for non-Aboriginal people. Individuals, their clans and the separate nations perceive the world in terms of maps. But these maps are not simple topographical representations; instead they embody the ancient dreamings of the spirits who inhabit each place, and the meanings are intertwined with complex patterns and stories of journeys made. In this book I can only make a few observations to celebrate Aboriginal cultural diversity. If you want to get more information on the subject, I'd suggest you seek out Howard Morphy's recent book, *Aboriginal Art* (1998) and Burnum Burnum's *A Travellers' guide to Aboriginal Australia* (1988) as a useful starting place.

As I've said, there is no simple dividing line between ritual and art. Ceremonial grounds, often called 'boras' were marked out with two concentric sets of rings on the ground, linked together with a path. Other complicated geometric patterns have been inscribed on rocks and in caves, often alongside representations of people, spirit beings, animals, birds and insects. There are many famous sites, including:

· The Kimberley Wandjina rock paintings include representations of people which bear an uncanny resemblance to extra-terrestrials.

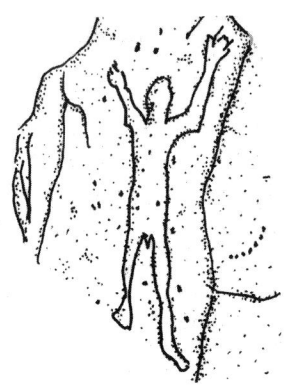

· The Eora artists of the Sydney region, from Broken Bay to Gibbon Point, produced rock carvings which include images of huge animals, spirit beings: Baiiame and Daramulun, the arrival of the Europeans in ships and much more.

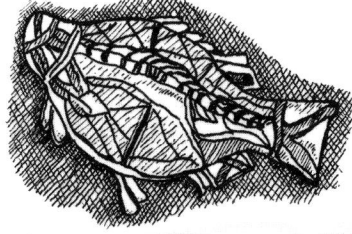

· The x-ray paintings of Arnhem land depict people, goannas, turtles, kangaroos and other animals and birds and include representations of bones and internal anatomy.

· The toas of the Lake Eyre region are wooden, painted signposts which also incorporate Dreamtime significance.

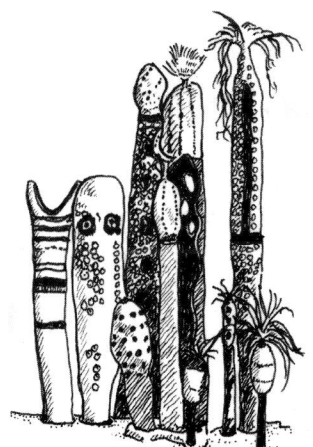

There's so much more as well. Body painting and scarification were elements of initiation rites and ceremonies and continue to feature in the traditional assemblies called corroborees. Shields and hunting weapons such as broad swords, spear throwers and boomerangs, and pitchi containers, baskets, ornaments and didgeridos were frequently decorated with complex, symbolic patterns, dreamings, and animal totems, all executed in a range of techniques which have been incorporated into the more recent phenomena: the Western Desert acrylic dot paintings.

The Papunya artists

The overlap between the secret and ceremonial art of the Aborigines has spilled over both into art and craft production and the fine-art world in a big way from the 1970s to the present day. Geoffrey Bardon, an art teacher at Papunya school in central Australia, was one of the first people to encourage the local Aboriginal community to commit their sacred and non-sacred designs onto a variety of surfaces, including walls, bark, board and even linoleum. The styles of art and design are

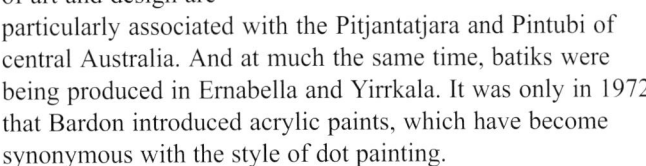

particularly associated with the Pitjantatjara and Pintubi of central Australia. And at much the same time, batiks were being produced in Ernabella and Yirrkala. It was only in 1972 that Bardon introduced acrylic paints, which have become synonymous with the style of dot painting.

Certainly, the complex dot paintings by artists such as Kaapa Mbitjana Tjampitjinpa and Johnny Warrangula Tjupurrula captured the western imagination, and Aboriginal artist collectives throughout central Australia and beyond started to adopt the style. Within the dot style acrylics, male and female artists often painted gender-specific images, appropriate to their clan positions, dreamings and social roles. For the art world, as well as the lucrative tourist market, these dot paintings seemed to present an authentic indigenous art form with which to identify the Aborigines of Australia. More importantly, the reception of the paintings possiblly represented a move amongst the white societies of Australia and the world towards a genuine respect for Aboriginal art and culture. The aesthetic appeal of the dot paintings, especially of complex dreamings and ancestral beings, moved the art away the ethnographic museum and as Morphy (1998) says, it was:

"intended to educate Europeans about the relationship between art and land."

New directions

Sacred tribal art, the Arrernte watercolours and the mythological mapping of the acrylic dot paintings all continue to be produced, but they have also provided stepping stones towards the more eclectic, and possibly more personal art forms, of new artists in the 1990s. Emily Kame Kngwarreye only started painting in her seventies and died when she was 86 – she was one of the artists to break through the artistic boundaries. Her work was quickly lauded by the art world as 'abstract impressionism', not always recognisable as 'Aboriginal'. It took some of the key elements: the dots, lines and cross hatching of the acrylics, and transformed them into looser, wilder forms. As with a number of family and clan collectives, some of her work was actually executed by her 'pupils' and signed by her. And like Albert Namatjira, she had little personal use for her new found wealth, continuing to live out of doors for most of the time,

and distributing her income to up 80 relatives.

There has also been an increasing involvement by Aboriginal artists in using art forms as a form of social protest. It has been a period of increasing self-confidence, with Aborigines in different areas of Australia celebrating their own local culture under names of their own choosing, such as the Kooris in the south-east and Murris of south Queensland and northern New South Wales. In 1988, the bi-centenary of European colonisation of Australia, was remembered by many Aborigines as the 'Year of Mourning'. In the National Gallery in Canberra, the Ramingining

Aboriginal artists built the Aboriginal Memorial, which now stands in entrance hall. It is a powerful and uncompromising statement, consisting of 200 carved and decorated hollow log coffins – one for each year of European colonisation.

Robert Campbell junior and Harry J Wedge are just two of the new generation of artists producing brightly coloured social indictments of white tyranny. *Death in Custody* (1987) and the *Aboriginal Embassy* (1986) from Campbell, and Wedge's *No Respect* (1992) build on some aspects of traditional Aboriginal art, but they are also at the cutting edge of Aboriginality as it enters the third (western) millennium. Dreamtime has a far longer history.

Intro on collectives... Surfing through a variety of Australian radical sites, I was much taken with those of Anarres Books (www. anarres.org.au) and the personal one for Takver (www.users.bigpond.com/Takver/) There, I found that Annares was the anarchist planet, and Takver, a character from an Ursula Le Guinn novel, *The Dispossessed.* As in the book, Takver in Melbourne says he identifies with *"ordinary people who strive for fulfilment in their lives with honesty, integrity and social conscience".* Can't be bad. From the web sites I also learnt lots about the history of collective action, the labour movement, feminism and radical politics. Finally, I did the web handshake thing with Takver and found out that he is John Englart, grandson of one of Australia's famous wharfies, Ted Englart, who organised some of the most passionate and bitter dock strikes in the country.

Like me, John uses his sport as a way of making a statement. I've been a keen cross country runner and particularly enjoyed my involvement with Dave Kelf (the Dungbeetle) and friends in Devon, organising, and participating in the mega-mud and beach event known as the Grizzly. Not so much a race – more a way of life – or near death experience! We even claim a certain Buddhist intent underlying the event. John uses his cycling as a focus for fund raising and consciousness raising.

John describes himself in the following terms: *"John Englart has been a member of collectives since 1974, including being a founding member of the Jura Books Collective in Sydney in 1977, the*

Black Rose Anarchist Bookshop Collective in 1982, and Anarres Books Collective since 1992 which he is still a member of.

As well as the anarchist movement, John has maintained a long interest in campaigning against uranium mining, and has had some activist involvement with Friends of the Earth and Greenpeace. He was involved in anti-uranium civil disobedience on the wharves in Sydney in 1977, and at Roxby Downs in 1984. He has been active in the union movement, including solidarity support of the MUA in 1998.

As a dedicated cyclist, John has participated and organised several bike rides, including Rides against Uranium from Sydney to Canberra, and Broken Hill to Roxby Downs. John continues to ride his bicycle, commuting to work each day.

Currently John is living in an anarchist housing collective called Bread and Roses, located in the inner city of Melbourne. The community is purchasing the house based upon a collective ownership agreement, and a form of income sharing."

Here is John's contribution, which includes short, italicised illustrations from his own life, which nicely personalise his description of collective life. This, in turn, is followed by Helen Lee's account of day-to-day life in the Bread and Roses collective as a co-parent.

Cyclists' camp, Roxby Downs, 1983

Collectives, radical politics and feminist issues

John Englart

"We front up to the facts and determine to live our lives deliberately, or not at all."
Henry David Thoreau.

Thoreau went off to live alone in the woods of Concord, to observe life around him and make deliberate choices based upon those observations and facts. He is perhaps best remembered for his essay, *On the Duty of Civil Disobedience*. An essay which greatly influenced the development of Tolstoy's ideas on Nonviolence and Ghandi's philosophy of Satyagraha (non-violent resistance). *On the Duty of Civil Disobedience* is a closely reasoned essay on the power of the state, and why it becomes necessary for individuals to resist the power of the state.

The message arising from Thoreau's writings, is the need for individuals to take responsibility for their actions, and not to delegate that responsibility elsewhere. We must learn to live deliberately, if we are to live authentic lives as free people.

My commitment to an authentic life has necessitated involvement in social and personal change groups over the past 25 years. It has involved a commitment to working within small collectives as a strategy for social change. In this contribution I have tried to give suggestions and examples from my own experience of working in small groups, and some of the pitfalls to try and avoid. I draw upon my experience in the Jura Books Collective, Black Rose Anarchist Bookshop Collective, Anarres Books Collective, Bread and Roses Community, plus numerous temporary small groups and campaigns.

What are the reasons for working or living collectively?

- Power and responsibility can be shared using a co-operative and directly democratic model of organisation.
- More efficient, and environmentally friendly, use of resources.
- More efficient use of individual skills, abilities, time, money and energy.
- Opportunity for personal growth in a supportive environment including:
  - developing confidence and assertiveness among all members;
  - developing effective conflict resolution and problem solving skills;
  - challenging oppressive and exploitative social behaviour.
- Sharing the (material and non-material) wealth equitably.
- The shared joy and pain of working cooperatively in a community.

Collectives are a method of organisation for sharing power more equally between the members. Power can derive from:

- access to information
- ownership of knowledge or resources (wealth)
- physical strength
- articulateness
- the ability to motivate others
- life experience
- special skills or abilities
- position in a hierarchy (gender, class, race, age, etc.)
- and much more.

Everybody possesses some power based upon our abilities and relationship to others and we can change power relationships by learning skills, modifying behaviour, or changing the structures that mediate our relationships.

For example, a very articulate person can exercise more power in a meeting than a person who is shy or inarticulate. By introducing a structure like consensus decision making, we give as much potential power to the shy person as the articulate member. It then becomes in the interest of both members to develop communication practices, including changing behaviours, so that decisions can be made more effectively and quickly.

How can we change the exercise of power in society?

There are huge imbalances of power in society, and this power imbalance is used to dominate, exploit and oppress those with less power. Men oppress women, old oppress young, the wealthy oppress the poor, rich nations oppress poor nations, and so on.

Collectives can work to empower those who are oppressed, and give them an opportunity for developing skills to overcome power imbalance between individuals. As part of a collective, individuals have greater strength in challenging institutional power and oppression.

What we have to overcome in Western thought is the legacy of thousands of years of conditioning that hierarchy and domination are necessary for the functioning of society. Domination and competition is instilled in each of us from birth, through social conditioning by parents, sexual repression, educational indoctrination and conditioning, and our own experiences at work or play. None of us are entirely immune from this conditioning because of its predominance in the social relationships in the hierarchical society we live in.

What we are not told about is the important tendency for mutual aid and cooperation in maintaining society. That it is social cooperation that produces the wealth of society, despite the inefficiencies of a hierarchy imposed on social organisation.

If you have ever been in an industrial dispute in which the workers decide to 'work to rule', you realise the importance of social cooperation in ensuring hierarchical organisations function normally. When that social co-operation is withdrawn, hierarchy cannot function efficiently.

How do we empower ourselves and eliminate hierarchy and domination?

Changing the values of society, from competition and hierarchy to cooperation and personal responsibility, can be effective only if we work on the personal and social levels together.

In our culture we need to re emphasise the tradition of personal power. We need to build a sense of local community control and solidarity, to empower individuals as part of a social community using decentralised and directly democratic forms of organisation.

We can do this through taking direct action in changing our values and lives. On a personal level, this involves questioning our own values, assumptions, conditioning and fears. Changing ourselves cannot entirely be effected on an individual level because the values are contained in social relationships, how we relate to one another and see ourselves as part of a wider context.

On the social level, changing the way we relate to each other and to the natural world involves commitment and responsibility. We need to learn to be open and honest with each other, to take responsibility for the consequences of our actions, and to be committed to changing ourselves through confronting and working through fears and conditioning together.

It is in the small group, where this can be done supportively and effectively. Individuals can gain support from each other in their attempts to act differently; to break with social roles assigned to them. The size and structure of small groups provides an alternative model of social organisation for society.

Darren and Jello from the Dead Kennedy's with the Black Rose Collective members September '83

An anti-mass model based on cooperation and shared personal power.

Why is an anti-mass perspective important ?
Mass organisation is hierarchical organisation in which the organisers tell other people what to do. A mass perspective revolves around a few people manipulating many people based on the lowest common denominator. In a mass society, we are all numbers to be used, consumers to be sold to, workers to be ripped off, people to be manipulated by the corporate media, politicians and various power elites.

Mass movements, political parties, and corporations have an interest in maintaining mass society, as it provides the leadership of these organisations with power and influence. To challenge mass society with a mass movement only maintains the status quo of domination and hierarchy. Mass movements cannot effectively change the nature of power relationships. The size and structures of mass organisation reproduce the power relationships of hierarchy and domination. Mass movements are essentially reactive in nature – and conservative in form.

Small group organisation is 'anti-mass'; diametrically opposed to mass organisation. Anti-mass is about people determining their own needs and cooperating together to achieve those needs. It is a proactive style of organisation. An anti-mass perspective is about building a diverse decentralist movement, working on a human interaction size scale able to be comprehended and used by all. A movement of small groups engaged in positive social change and direct action. Each group will have its own focus, its own agenda, and will be active in its own right. Self-determination and autonomy are important principles of the anti-mass philosophy.

The purpose of collectives can vary to meet short term goals or more longer term objectives; from consciousness raising groups to groups providing a basic structure for an alternative economy, culture and spirituality.

Where several groups need to work together, coordinating and federative structures can be established which are responsible to, and respect, the autonomy of the individual collectives and individuals involved.

Working in collectives

The small group can create free space where each individual can question submission and obedience to authority, sex role conditioning, and power relationships. It provides an opportunity for individuals to analyse power and domination from shared experiences, and to develop new skills, new behaviour, non-hierarchical and non-exploitative lifestyles. The small group can empower the individual members in free space – a temporary autonomous zone.

Small size of the group gives the opportunity for adopting new values based on personal power, but does not guarantee these values will be adopted. Hierarchical organisation can just as easily function in a small group, either through formal or informal structures. Where you find hierarchy in human organisation, you are likely to find a form of domination.

How much structure?

All groups of people have structure, both open and hidden. Structure in small groups determines how information flows and how power is shared. The extent of structure necessary for sharing power in a small group will depend upon the purpose the group sets itself, and the size of the group. For example, a consciousness raising group may need very little formal structure to engage its purpose, while a collective focused on an ongoing project – such as a newspaper, bookshop, running a refuge, radio program, cafe, etc. – will need much more explicit structure to coordinate activity.

The dangers of too little or too much structure

One of the major dangers for collectives is determining the right amount of structure to have.

To not introduce some explicit structure into the functioning of a group can result in an elite forming, or one dominant person, and the small group will become a 'tyranny of structurelessness'. This is the absence of explicit structures for sharing power enabling one or more individuals to exercise power over the group. This process is described by Jo Freeman in an essay called *The Tyranny of Structurelessness*, first published in the context of the feminist movement in 1970.

There is a danger in having too much structure in a group, in which some members, through their knowledge of structure,

have power over other members who may lack this knowledge. A form of bureaucratic power (or domination) is the result.

Formal structure should have a functional reason for existence and the reason behind and how to use the structure should be understood by all individuals in the group.

What sort of structures?

Structures should not be seen as fixed and immutable. They should be flexible and responsive to the needs of the group and individual members. The introduction, use, modification, and discarding of explicit structures should be under the control of the group. Democratic structuring within a collective could include any or all of the following basic structures plus others which the group may formulate for its own particular needs:

1. Defined decision making process.
2. Regular Meetings.
3. Defined joining and training procedure for new people.
4. Defining a level of commitment for working in the group.
5. Delegation of specific responsibility.
6. Rotation of all tasks.
7. Regular social events.
8. Rosters for tasks to be undertaken.
9. Evaluations and Clearness Meetings.

Decision making structure

The options for democratic decision making revolve around either a majority system (voting) or consensus decision making. Some collectives use a combination of these systems to suit particular needs. Quite often in a small group most decisions will be made using an informal consensual approach. Majority voting is also sometimes used as a backup method if consensus fails.

A common mistake small groups sometimes make when they start is in not formulating how they make decisions, and what method to use in what circumstances. This can exacerbate other disputes further on, when the group has no agreed method of resolving conflict.

One of the collectives I was in paid lip service to using consensus, but in reality had no agreed decision making method. Often, when conflicts arose, the decision was made by voting. When a major conflict over organisational practices surfaced, the collective found it had two factions with no agreed method of decision making. The collective was eventually dissolved, and two new collectives started with a division of the resources of the old collective.

Consensus decision making

The method most effective for sharing power when used by small groups is consensus. Consensus decision making is not always an easy process and can sometimes involve a lot of energy, time, and commitment to each other. However, this method of decision making encourages the participation of all members in formulating all decisions which builds group cohesion and trust. It also tends to make for better quality decisions.

Using consensus, group members learn to practice values of cooperation and respect, to share power and learn skills which foster better communication and relationships on both interpersonal and community levels. Consensus demands that members of the group be more caring, responsible and fair with each other.

There may be times when a consensus decision cannot be reached, or is being obstructed by one or two people. In highly committed collectives, these instances do not occur frequently. When they do occur, the group must assess how important the decision is, how strongly the members feel about a majority or minority decision being implemented, and if some agreement can be reached with individual members non participation in the implementation of a decision.

If consensus cannot be reached on many different issues, after all alternatives have been exhausted, this may mean the goals of the group and individuals need to be reassessed. If this is

the case, fundamental disagreements may be present and the group may need to disband or members leave the group.

For consensus to work well you need:

1. A certain amount of basic agreement on fundamental attitudes and issues.
2. All members to communicate their ideas and feelings clearly.
3. A non dogmatic and flexible approach to new ideas.
4. Patience in listening.
5. To attempt to understand the truth of others.
6. The courage to speak your own idea of the truth as you see it.

Regular meetings enable all individuals to participate in the sharing of information, distribution of authority, the sharing of responsibility, and the exercise of power and decision making involved in the group activity. Meetings do not guarantee that power will be shared. Elite groups and people with strong personalities may be present. Personal politics, sex roles and power relationships need to be acknowledged and discussed, and sometimes confronted and changed by the individual and group.

Once the power dynamics in the group and in the meeting are out in the open, structures and techniques to regulate and share power can be formulated. These techniques may include giving some type of emphasis to the less assertive people in the group.

Several formal roles or functions can be delegated to individuals for the efficient functioning of a meeting. These roles ideally should rotate among all members to share the skills and responsibility in the group. Sometimes these roles may be handled by the group as a whole rather than delegated to an individual. These formal roles may include: facilitator, minutes keeper, timekeeper, vibes watcher.

Other Structures:

Membership definition and joining procedure

Working out a membership definition ahead of time, can save time and eliminate a possible issue of contention during disputes. Groups with an unclear membership definition are open to manipulation by other organisations. A clear joining procedure provides a space for clarification by the prospective member and the group of expectations and needs.

There is a vast disparity in skills and abilities which individuals can bring to a group. These are often environmentally and socially determined by sexual identity, race, age, education, gender, or class background. These differences all need to be taken into account in a person's participation in a small group.

Defining a commitment level for individuals joining a collective makes clear how much is expected in terms of time, money, and energy. Defining the goals and the purpose of the group is equally important in clarifying what new members are committing themselves to. Not everyone will be interested in participating in the group's activity, or will have the commitment demanded by the group for sharing power and responsibility of the project.

Delegation of tasks

The delegation of specific responsibility to individuals within the group builds individual confidence in the exercise of power on behalf of the group. Individuals can be congratulated on tasks which have been undertaken successfully, or criticised for poor decision making or work. Criticism needs to be positive and should take into account an individual's ability and skill level.

Rotation of tasks

To ensure that power, information and skills are shared, ideally all tasks should be rotated among the group. Rotating tasks at first glance seems inefficient, as each member has to learn every task. However, job rotation provides many advantages: such as the ability for one member to quickly take over another member's job in case of illness, injury or other emergency. Also, each individual has a better understanding of all the work and can make more informed decisions as part of the collective decision making process. Rotation of tasks can also relieve boredom, and gives everybody a chance to enjoy the interesting jobs.

Social events

Having social events as a collective can be an important activity. Most collectives will choose to celebrate socially at least a few important times: anniversaries of establishment, birthdays, events of importance to the members. Regular social events build our feeling of trust and community with each other and the friendship networks we are each a part of. They also allow us to enjoy the fun side of working together and participating in each others lives.

> *My household chooses to celebrate the equinoxes and solstices with feasts, to which we invite our close friends. May Day and International Women's Day are also celebrated. Birthdays are celebrated both as household rituals, and sometimes with a party.*

Enjoy the party. As the infamous feminist and anarchist, Emma Goldman, once said:
> *"If I can't dance, I don't want to be part of your revolution."*

Rosters

Rosters are a method of delegating responsibility for basic tasks to individuals. They can be used to ensure routine work is divided equally and fairly among all. Rosters are particularly useful for examining our socially conditioned roles, such as those roles based on gender, class or age.

> *One collective I was in utilised a voluntary cleaning roster, in which members volunteered their names beside tasks. The cleaning mostly got done, but most of the work was done by the female members. In comparison, most of the high status tasks were done by the men in the collective. The issue of rosters later became a part of a conflict over organisational practice.*

Rosters which all members participate in, can force members out of socially conditioned roles, and provide an opportunity to pick up new skills, and broaden our experience.

> *I have seen a number of male friends broaden their cooking skills through a roster for preparing a weekly public dinner. Similarly, women have been empowered by the opportunity to do jobs entailing initiative and responsibility.*

Evaluations and Clearness Meetings

Evaluating a meeting is an important learning process for the individuals and the group allowing reflection on our meeting process and interactions. Our meetings can be refined and made more efficient.

Sometimes it is helpful for groups to have a general evaluation of aims, goals, processes and directions. These meetings are sometimes termed Clearness Meetings as they can assist in clearing problems and seeing clearly into the future.

Conflict and problems:

Dealing with conflict

Conflict is bound to occur in a group of people and particularly during the decision making process. Conflict is natural and may be approached by the individuals and the group as a constructive or destructive process.

Conflicts can occur around issues, personalities, or values. Of the three, value conflicts are more difficult to resolve. Resolving differences in values entails much deeper enquiring into

Nicky, Helen, Greg, John, Daniel,
Jes, Erin, 1991

how each of our value systems are created. In some value centred conflicts we may have to agree to disagree, and work out procedures and ways of working around the different values.

When there is a conflict, the use of 'I Messages' can give valuable feedback of feelings, and can make criticism seem easier to hear. 'I Messages' are when the person making the criticism, owns their feelings.

Not all problems or conflicts need to be resolved immediately. Assess if a quick resolution is needed, or it can be discussed and worked through over several meetings. Or perhaps a temporary solution can be implemented while a more permanent solution is being discussed.

Dealing with emotions

As with conflict, emotions need to be accepted as a natural part of ourselves and our interactions with others. Communicating our feelings can help reduce tensions in group situations and build group trust.

Within meetings it is important that strong feelings be dealt with during the course of a meeting. It is important that members 'own' their feelings rather than blame the group or another individual for the way they are feeling. 'I Messages' are particularly useful in this regard.

> *My present household starts our weekly meeting with a 'Gripes and Good Things' session. Each of us explains to the group those actions, events or emotions which are bugging them and those which are positive and uplifting. This allows the group to understand where each of us is coming from emotionally during the meeting, so we can make suitable allowances in the interactions in our meeting.*

Gender Dynamics:

Old baggage from the past

We live in a society where male values and culture are dominant and have been dominant for thousands of years. It is a patriarchal society that oppresses women in many different ways. Even our languages are patricentric. Growing up in western society we have absorbed unconsciously much of the dominant patriarchal values.

So it is not surprising that we bring many patriarchal and anti-social values and gender stereotypes into our day to day lives and relationships.

In all mixed groups gender dynamics is an important issue, even if it is unacknowledged within the group. Within groups where it is considered irrelevant and not discussed, the following results:

· alienation of the women members,
· the women members leave, or
· the women remain subservient to the men in the group.

It is possible to let go of old baggage we bring with us into our relationships. Although it may take much effort and practice to do so. Some common problems and possible solutions of gender dynamics are discussed below.

Who speaks

Commonly in mixed gender groups, the male members will speak more often and longer than women. Why does this happen? Because of old baggage, a patricentric language, and gender roles. If this is a consistent pattern it indicates a gender problem, and thus a power problem within the group.

An easy way to find out who is speaking the most in your group, is for one member to keep a rough count in a meeting of who speaks, and how often they speak. If a speaking count is done consciously by a decision of the meeting, this may encourage a more even pattern of speakers.

The Black Rose Collective used Round Robins, in which every person would have a chance to say what they thought without fear of interruption, to ensure all contributed to the decisions. This was highly important as it served to involve those members who were reticent about contributing to discussions. In situations where two people were in conflict over an issue, a Round Robin, served to broaden the debate and turn a conflict between two people into a group conflict of ideas, which then became more readily resolvable.

And who is listened to

Communication is a two way process: speaking and listening. Just because there is a general equality in who is speaking, does not necessarily mean the decision will reflect that balance. In many instances women raise issues or problems for discussion and are ignored, or are not taken proper account of by the meeting.

In a collective meeting, a woman member made a suggestion, which was ignored by the male members. A little later one of the male members made a similar suggestion which was discussed and adopted by the meeting.

Listening to others is an important part of the communication process. While male members, as part of a masculine gender role, will tend to speak more, female members, as part of a feminine gender role, will tend to listen more actively. In a small group trying to share power equally between members it is important to challenge the speaking/listening gender roles - to empower all members in active listening and speaking.

Gender roles in the meeting process

As part of a female gender role, women are expected to be nurturing and supportive. To maintain the house, maintain the friendship networks, to nurse and give comfort when needed. On the other hand, a male gender role expects men to be initiating, assertive, task orientated.

Within the context of a meeting these gender roles can translate into the men being focussed on task issues, 'on getting the job done', rather than how it is done. Women often take on a more invisible, but no less important, role of maintaining the process and cohesion of the group – of making sure all are involved in the decision.

Within a group with approximately equal numbers of men and women, the women complained about doing too much group maintenance. As the men did not appear to listen to their complaints, the women decided to stop doing any maintenance functions, including informal facilitation, in the group's meetings.

The meetings soon became frustrating for the men, and decisions took far longer to decide and implement.

Often it is informal facilitation by women which resolves problems of the group. Facilitation and group maintenance functions should be shared by all in the group.

Sexual dynamics

In any group in which people work together, building trust and feelings for one another, there is a tendency for people to become involved sexually. Sexual relationships within a group can affect the degree of sharing of information and power within the group. This can give rise to hidden agendas, never properly acknowledged by the group. This can lead to conflicts which are unsolvable on a superficial level, and may result in members leaving, or even to the break up of the group.

It is important to be aware that our sexuality can affect the dynamics of working collectively. Once this is realised, a choice can be made by the group on how to take into account the sexual dynamics of power. The foremost problem is overcoming the fear of discussing honestly something as personal as sexual relationships and how it affects the way we work and live together.

Over commitment

Collectives and small groups can demand much time, energy and resources. If you over extend yourself, you damage your own performance, risk individual burnout, and let down your comrades by spreading yourself too thinly. Try to set a sustainable level of activity, and focus on working within that level of activity.

Too often have I seen friends make commitments to several tasks or projects, only to find they end up rushing around trying to do things at the last minute, or apologising at meetings for not completing assigned tasks, or doing work shoddily or with errors.

Conclusion

There are infinite ways to work together in a small group. The most important point is that the structure of the small group meets the needs of the individuals involved, and is chosen democratically by those involved. It may sound like a lot of

hard work, but much of it is fun and can be very rewarding.

Collectives offer us a model of decentralised, directly democratic, organisation. Traditional mass movements and political parties are mass organisations which perpetrate the inherent problems of society in the form of hierarchy and domination.

We need to organise ourselves as an anti-mass movement of collectives setting our own agenda, one of direct democracy and decentralisation. The means should be as important to us as the ends we seek. Working in collectives can enrich our everyday lives while providing a glimpse of a new world in the shell of the old.

Bibliography

This article is condensed from a longer essay titled *Using Structure in Collectives*, available from the Anarres Books Web Page at
www.anarres.org.au
For those of you who would like to follow up subjects raised, the following books have been instrumental in developing the ideas:

Building United Judgement: a handbook for Consensus Decision Making, Centre for Conflict Resolution
Democracy in Small Groups, John Gastil, New Society Publishers
Facilitator's Guide to Participatory Decision Making, Kaner et al, New Society Publishers
Preparing for Nonviolent Direct Action, Peace News
Dreaming the Dark: Magic, Sex & Politics, Starhawk, Beacon Press
Towards an Ecological Society. Murray Bookchin, Black Rose Books
Post Scarcity Anarchism. Murray Bookchin, Black Rose Books
The Tyranny of Structurelessness. Jo Freeman.
Anti-Mass - Methods of Organisation for collectives.

From John Englart we've learned quite a lot about the issues and theories involved in collective organisation and living. Helen Lee now fills in some of the mortar between the brickwork, giving us a picture of some of the realities of living in a small intentional community – the good and the bad.

Bread and Roses: a personal social change strategy.
Helen Lee

"There are people who are struggling to change conditions that they find intolerable, trying to find new lives...." Barbara Deming

We don't just decide to change our lives or change the world out of the blue; first there has to be a problem, a gap between our dreams, between what we want to happen and what is going on around us. After all why would we want to change, why would we want to put in all that work trying to change things, if everything was OK?

I became involved in action for social change not just out of an intellectual conviction that there were things wrong with our society, but also because I didn't like what was happening to me. I wanted my life to be different.

In the 1970s the women's movement generated the slogan 'the personal is political'. This statement highlights the importance of looking at our personal lives as well as broader social institutions when we are analysing society and our place in it. For women a focus on personal lives is particularly important for it is in these personal relationships and obligations, to children and family, that many of the difficulties women face are generated.

My own experience as a woman, as a mother and a carer, led me to a feminist viewpoint: in particular to the conclusion that nuclear families don't work well for women. This was fine as far as it went but I needed more than analysis. I wanted and needed to live my own life differently. It wasn't enough to bring about change sometime in the future. This is a personal story about changes in my life and how I've responded to the challenges of my roles as mother and carer but it is also a political tale, because in the end it is the choices that we all make in our day-to-day lives that shape the future.

In the late 1980s I found myself in a difficult and frustrating situation. Shortly before the birth of our first child my partner was diagnosed as having brain tumours. The next year was a sleepless blur of uncertainty and anxiety. A second child two years later was an act partly of defiance, relief that the tumours appeared not to be a terminal proposition and a naive belief that things couldn't get any worse. Caring for two pre-school children and providing support for my seriously disabled partner proved to be very difficult. It was lonely, stressful and sometimes frightening. At the time I often blamed myself for my difficulties; for finding it hard to cope with my partner's epileptic seizures and for being unable to keep the house clean and tidy as well as caring for my partner and children. In the end I decided that it wasn't just me – the situation was impossible. I started to look for alternatives.

My first response was to decide that I couldn't look after the children and support my partner. I took the kids and moved out. Being a single parent was easier but difficult economically. I faced the classic single parent's dilemma: to have lots of time with the kids and live in poverty on the pension, or to juggle employment, kids and housework. Living apart wasn't ideal in that it made it difficult for the kids to maintain their relationship with their father. After some negotiation we were able to organise for him to care for them one afternoon a week with the assistance of specific home help.

This situation was very different from the dreams my partner and I had shared initially. Feeling pretty sure that a more communal life style was what I wanted, I started talking endlessly about possibilities: with my friends, with acquaintances, with total strangers on buses. What had other people tried, what were the people around me interested in trying? It was in these circumstances that a friend suggested he would like to co-parent with me and with the children's biological father.

Co-parenting is a child-rearing practice that aims to share the responsibility for caring for children on the basis of commitment to the children rather than simply one's biological relationships to them. Unlike the nuclear family, there isn't necessarily any sexual relationship between the co-parents. In our society looking after children is closely linked to biological relationship and to gender roles. Ideally, co-parenting is about sharing the care of children without the constraints of traditional or sexist expectations.

I was interested in my friend's suggestion but initially we were all cautious. I was concerned about losing control over what happened to the children. Their biological father was concerned about being marginalised and our friend was worried about getting emotionally close to the children when he would have no legal right to long term involvement – we could deny him access. There was also concern about how the children would respond to a new parent and whether they would accept him on the same basis as the other parents.

After lots of discussion we decided that it was worth a try. We spent six months getting to know each other better and discussing our ideas and parenting practices before we made a firm commitment to co-parent. Our concerns about possible problems were resolved partly with experience and with growing trust in each other and partly by negotiating a basic agreement.

- All decisions would be made by consensus – all three of us must agree to any decision.

- All the adults had the same right to an ongoing relationship with the children.

- We would all contribute to the financial up keep of the children in proportion to income.

- Child care would be organised on a roster. This helped make it clear which adult was responsible for the kids at any specific time.

Names are always an interesting question. We resolved the question of which adult's surname the children would have by giving them their own separate surnames – a three part hyphenated surname seemed a bit much and we couldn't work out how to decide which adult's surname they would have! The children already called their parents by their first names so the question of whom to call mum or dad didn't arise.

We assumed that because, we thought, we had similar values and beliefs our parenting would be similar. This turned out to be incorrect. One of the major issues we have had to work through is accepting each other's different parenting styles and values and negotiating practices acceptable to all of us. The issues we debated often seem trivial and a bit silly, but they were usually in deadly earnest for the participants. One memorable disagreement was the great, 'the right way to hang up clothes on the washing line' debate, which is still a cause for discussion in the collective.

Our group was blessed with three people who know the right way to hang up clothes – unfortunately three different ways. While we all lived separately this wasn't an issue, but later on when we moved in together this difference caused a great deal of discussion. The people who knew the 'right' way to hang up clothes became quite distressed about people hanging up clothes the 'wrong' way. This spawned another even more heated philosophical debate about whether there is such a thing as a 'right' way to do anything. We have never resolved this debate. After a lot of shouting we had to accept that there were things, in particular clothes hanging, that we weren't going to agree about. We had to choose our priorities and focus on the things we did agree about. Our final decision was that where we can't agree we will try to agree to disagree. Living and parenting together takes a hell of a lot of live and let live.

Two other factors affected our co-parenting. One was the serious disabilities of one of the co-parents. This meant that we didn't simply divide the child care by three and share it equally. Instead we had to look at the capacity of each parent and organise around each parent's needs and abilities. This has meant that two of us do most of the day to day routine care and our disabled co-parent participates as his health permits. In a week in which he has had an epileptic seizure this may be as little as a good morning and a hug. What has been more difficult has been working out ways in which he can become involved when he feels able. The kids' routine and the roster haven't proved to be easily adaptable and sometimes seem to shut him out. We are still working on this.

Starting co-parenting when the children were already two and four years old meant we had to make some careful adjustments. All of us wanted to feel our way a bit and we couldn't expect the kids to accept such a major change suddenly. After a six month trial period of visits and of our friend living with each of the other parents temporarily, we established a routine where the children stayed about one day with one parent and three days each with the other two. This worked fine for a year except for the occasional hiccup when a needed piece of children's equipment, gumboots say, would be at the wrong house. This year of caring for the children, part time, independently, gave our new co-parent an important opportunity to establish his own relationship with the children.

The children were already used to living in shared housing, mixing with and being looked after by a number of adults. They welcomed another adult who was interested in them, prepared to read stories and play with them as well as doing more mundane child care tasks. They didn't appear to have any difficulty accepting another adult as a parent. We made a gradual transition and didn't hurry anything. I think this was important.

Towards the end of our first year of co-parenting, we began to discuss some form of communal living and shared housing. This was proposed partly because shifting the children from house to house required much careful organising and we felt living closer together would give us more flexibility. We also had concerns about whether our disabled co-parent would be able to continue living independently as he was having increasing health problems. Living together would also mean we would all be able to spend more time with the children. At this stage a mutual friend, who was also interested in communal housing, decided he was interested in joining us in establishing

a communal house (but not in co-parenting). After some discussion we formed a group we called the Bread and Roses Collective. We made long term plans to buy a house together.

The aim of buying a house collectively and living communally was to share our resources; to provide practical and emotional support for each other; to share the housework; and to care for the children and each other in ways that respected our individual abilities and situations. We wanted to implement with each other, now, our shared commitment to co-operative egalitarian social relationships

The entire collective, including our one non-co-parent, were not able to move in together until we found and bought a suitable (large enough) house in 1993 – but when my partner's health deteriorated in late 1990 the co-parents decided we had to move in together immediately.

Bread and Roses, 1993
Greg, Helen, Tony, John
Jesi   Erin

We found the first six months of living together difficult. The children took some time to get used to sharing the adults' time and attention. There was a lot to do learning how to live together and clarifying our expectations of one another. We all had to modify some of our habits. At times, it was a painful experience.

From the beginning of co-parenting we had worked to a roster and we continued this when we moved in together. Having a roster meant it was clear who was responsible and available to, the children. They quickly adapted to this. One of the first things our daughter learnt to read was the roster that said who was looking after her. It was stuck on the fridge for easy access.

For our group, living communally means our primary commitment is to each other rather than to a sexual partner. We divide the housework as equally as possible between us, taking into account different capacities and inclinations but not gender based expectations. Household expenses are shared between us proportional to income. Our household is our social and personal base, a place to come home to and share the frustrations and triumphs of our lives outside the household. We celebrate festivals together, holiday together and look to each other for support when faced with any difficulty.

To live communally we have had to acquire and improve many skills. Our group uses consensus decision making processes. Improving our skills in this area, as well as in conflict resolution, affirmation, political and social analysis and effective communication, has been important. We learnt early on, that avoiding conflict wasn't possible or effective. The most critical factor in working together has been learning to discuss and resolve conflict effectively.

Consciousness raising has been an important process. There is ongoing discussion and review of our practice and goals (this often happens at the kitchen sink as well as at our regular meetings). By sharing our experiences we gain insights and can support each other in personal change as well as in broader political activities; for example unionism and involvement in local transport action groups. It has been necessary for each of us to acquire skills we were ignorant of because of our gender. Other qualities we have found useful are: tolerance of difference, commitment, persistence, imagination and a sense of humour.

Our common understanding of what we are doing is that it is part of an anarchist tradition. Our community is an anarchist strategy whereby we take control of our own lives and build social structures that meet our different individual needs and are just and egalitarian. This shared philosophy has been important to our working together successfully. Equally important has been our commitment to each other. The love, affection and trust we have for each other have helped us weather the inevitable conflicts.

The positive side of the family is the support and affection its members can offer each other but often the price paid, especially by women, is very high. As one social theorist, Mark Poster, in his book, *Critical Theory of the of the Family*, (page 204) comments:

"Love, domesticity and empathetic child care are in themselves unobjectionable. When restricted to the contemporary family they work to undermine sociability and distort relationships within the family."

Our experience is that by living communally and co-parenting, we have been able to provide each other with support and affection, while avoiding some of the more objectionable aspects of the nuclear family – the isolation and the exploitation of women's work. The co-parents have now been living together communally since 1993 and co-parenting since 1990. The whole group moved in together in 1994. Our children are mostly healthy and happy. They have encountered some curiosity but no hassles about their unusual house situation. Our daughter, when she was nine, explained matter-of-factly that she had a 'real' father and 'another' father. Living communally means we can provide our disabled co-parent with the support he needs and he can maintain his relationship with the children. The household provides us all with a supportive and stable home.

Action for social change can take many forms. We can protest, we can try and persuade others to change, we can refuse to co-operate and we can take direct action against destructive and oppressive institutions and practices. All of these strategies focus on bringing about changes in the society we already have. This is important but, if we are to move towards our vision for the future, we need to start developing new ways of organising our lives now. We need to develop social structures and practices that are compatible with our vision and principles.

A new society, co-operative, egalitarian and democratic, cannot spring magically into place 'after the revolution' nor will it sneak up on us unawares. Effective social change towards an egalitarian and co-operative society requires us all to change the ways we live and work together, unless these change we risk continuing or replicating the same oppressive structures and practices. New ways of living and working together have to be imagined and practised. This can start now. By changing our lives we can take some first steps towards transforming society.

If we believe in democracy, in justice, equality and co-operation, then we must act to defend them. But if we only do this in our work places, where we study or in public debate, and neglect our own personal lives, then we lose. We risk losing not just our fight to achieve a just and co-operative society, we also lose the opportunity to transform our own lives, to achieve some of our dreams here and now.

A New Future

I leave behind
despair and regret
reject alienation
everything is possible
I open the door
with a brave heart
I choose to live
to laugh and light
fires of passion and anger
like the Phoenix I arise
my wingtips are charred
but I am free
with fear and joy
I soar on new wings
from these heights now
I can see
through times of change
I choose the vision
and create a new future.

Once again, via the Internet, I made contact with Leonie Bell. She and her partner, JP, are friends of Mook and Shanto. *"What do you want to hear about?"* Leonie asked. Not having met them, it was difficult to respond, so I just said, *"Get JP to tell the story of establishing the Clown Doctors."* He's done rather better than that, and there's plenty of smiles along the way!

Clown doctors, the Humour Foundation and Terania Park
JP Bell

Having just become a grandfather, it is a reflective period in my life. Being asked to contribute my life experiences to this book comes at a delightful time. I have always been a nomad, a strolling player, a wandering fool.

My childhood was transient. One night we sat down together as a family and counted up about 138 moves in 17 years. I went to 27 schools –20 primary and 7 secondary. Other people moved for obvious reasons, a job transfer for instance. Ours was spur of the moment – chaotic, unpredictable.

I joke in performance that I never dawdled home from school in case my parents had moved while I was out. We were very close – Pat, Jack and five kids. There would have been more kids but a dose of the mumps meant Dad was infertile for a few years. Then Mum had three boys in five years. We felt most at home in the car. Home is where the heart is. We were always leaving, always on the way somewhere. We loved it. There were scars though, deeper for some of us kids than others.

There were times I hated leaving a group of newly made friends, or having made it into the school football team and rushing home with the jumper, only to be told we were leaving at the end of the week. I couldn't face school the next day. Eventually I had to inform the headmaster that I was leaving. *"Nobody leaves this school,"* he said. He meant that children in the 50s stayed at the same school; nobody went anywhere.

My mother was a big influence. Always a stranger to neighbours, her children were her friends and confidantes. She always said she grew her friends. She is a bit of a beatnik. She writes poetry, loves books and conversation. My teenage friends loved her. You could smoke and drink and tell your own story – she prodded it out of you. I knew she was outrageous when I came home with my Form 2 report card, marked as a fail. She opened it up, scanned the low numbers, and told me it was not good enough. *"Have you got a pen?"* she asked. She changed the 3's to 8's. By the time she finished my future looked much brighter.

Armed with my report card, and newly confident, I was warmly welcomed by my new school. I passed comfortably into Form 4 two schools later. I was always the new boy. I wasn't big or mean so I joked and downed my way to acceptance. Eventually I attracted the attention of a drama teacher at Eltham High who encouraged me to become involved with the school play. I brought the house down. I knew the direction my life was to take.

I joined the local arts association and performed my first mime at a party, setting my course for the future. As a 17 year old I joined the New Theatre in Melbourne and went to Sydney for a National Workshop at Sydney New Theatre. Despite being robbed, I fell in love with Sydney and moved there the following year. I have always set my own course. My background gave me the skills to live in the cracks and be on the fringes. I wanted to study mime, and a wonderful Dutch couple – Wim and Mieke Burkunk – came into my life. Wim had studied with Etienne de Croux. From the many that auditioned for his Theatre Laboratory, Wim accepted three students. After a month, the other two left. I was 18 and Wim became my mentor. I was sad when, after six months, Wim was offered a job as a theatre director and returned to Holland. We still keep in touch.

It was an exciting time creatively. Performing at 'The Place' in Kings Cross one night, I met singer/poet, John Bear and this changed my life. A creative partnership was born. He was a Kiwi, a third generation stonemason, and an Olympic level wrestler. With his storytelling and my mime we created 'Deluvia', a hit on the folk circuit and other Sydney venues. Deluvia was a gentle, magical show where I interpreted John Bear's songs through gesture.

JP Bell

John Bear decided to go to the USA, after a visit home to New Zealand. An American friend invited him to spend a white Christmas in Connecticut. On the spur of the moment I decided to go too, much to the shock of my then girlfriend and now my wife, Leonie. Just a small problem...I could not get a passport because my conscription registration papers were lost. It looked as if my first overseas trip would be to Vietnam. A flurry of letter writing saved me from the next intake into the army, and I joined John Bear in New Zealand. We performed on a returning Greek immigrant ship, disembarking at Acapulco.

Many adventures later we arrived in New York, and settled in Andover, Connecticut. We performed on the east coast and the Americans loved our unique show. America seemed a bit of a time jump...Australia in 1972 was experiencing the emergence of the counter-culture, in America long-haired dope smokers actually had jobs!

Performing burnt out John Bear. He retreated to a Buddhist monastery and I joined a mime company in Toronto Canada, had the lead in a TV series, worked with a theatre company and performed my solo show. We teamed up again as Artists-in-Residence in Aspen Colorado. A fantastic experience in the Rocky Mountains – wealthy hippies, Trust Fund baby boomers, eccentrics, celebrities, coke dealers. Eventually we had to come down the mountain and venture back into the 'real' world.

John Bear stayed on in the US, and after performing in New York and Iceland, we arrived culture-shocked (and very soon broke!) in London. We found the classic bed-sit, I hired out ice-skates for 2 dreadful weeks while Leonie worked in two pubs. One night we went to a fringe performance of a group called 'Friends' Roadshow'. Nola Rae, a mime with the show, turned out to be an Australian. She was about to set up her own company, London Mime Theatre, and asked me to join.

We spent a year touring Europe, mostly Holland and Germany. Amsterdam had alternative venues such as the Shaffy Theatre, Melkweg and Paradiso – a dynamic, creative, eclectic blend of music, theatre, and food. It was a vibrant avant-garde scene with theatre companies from all over the world – Hauser Orkater, Carlos Traffic, Salt Lake City Mime Troupe, Friends' Roadshow. The Fools' Festival was born, and grew into one of Europe's major theatre festivals. These performers became my world-wide 'extended family'.

I was so busy...performing with London Mime Theatre, doing solo shows, and late night improvs. For a while I was perform-ing in a theatre with London Mime, hopping on a bicycle at interval to pop over to the cinema to do a quick 10 minutes before the feature, getting back to start the second half, then on to do a late night improvisation. Sometimes 30 people from various theatre companies were on stage improvising. Nights of laughter and lunacy!

Longing for the Land Down Under, we headed home on the 'hippie trail' through Turkey, Istanbul, Afghanistan, Nepal and India. We had missed the brief period of Labour Government, but the social changes lived on. In theatre, 'The New Wave' had a lasting impact. I'd been away while the collective of actors and writers at The Pram Factory in Melbourne,

celebrated and explored Australian themes for the first time. Alternative independent theatre was flourishing. I returned to Australia as The Last Laugh opened in Melbourne, and I worked in one of the early shows – Cannned Peaches and Tin Sailors. The next show was a circus – the tightrope above the dinner tables! – and Circus Oz was born.

Still, Australia did not have the network of theatres that were throughout Europe. Holland for example, had a theatre/library/bar complex in every town. I returned regularly to Europe for the summer festivals – especially The Festival of Fools. Friends from around the world started touring in Australia too.

We started the Living Room Theatre – a tiny shopfront venue in the inner-city of Sydney. Creating my own venue was a fantastic experience. I could prevail upon visiting friends from Europe and the USA to perform. It had a mime studio upstairs, so I also taught mime classes. It folded when we became parents – 3 a.m. finishes, and supporting a family and a theatre was too difficult. Writing and performing comedy for ABC TV children's shows and touring was enough!

Two elderly eccentric ladies, Joan and Betty Rainer, had approached me to tour schools with their company Australian Children's Theatre. Having been to so many schools as a child, the idea appealed to me. It provided the best touring circuit. I still tour schools some 23 years later.

I have many friends around this wide brown land – I have toured every part of it, from remote Aboriginal communities in central Australia to city festivals. I have a huge extended family! I love many parts of Australia, but none more than the Rainbow Region of northern NSW. I performed at the Lismore Folk Festival in 1977 and fell in love with the area. The coun-ter-culture was young, idealistic, naive and optimistic. The desire to create collective sustainable co-operative ventures appealed to me. The people I met inspired me, and some of them are now my closest friends.

My career has been full and varied with constant change – theatre, stand-up comedy, cabaret, television and film. I was ripe to be conscripted by the inspirational Dr Patch Adams. A huge man with long grey pigtails, a Dali moustache, weird pants and amazing cloaks, Patch is a doctor who is also a clown. I first met him in 1994, when the Gawler Foundation brought him to Australia. He touched a great desire in me to use humour for healing. This was right up my street – after years of performing comedy I knew laughter was the best medicine, and large doses needed to be administered. As a kid I had dreamed of being a doctor. I never imagined I would be a Clown Doctor!

Some months later, Andre Poulie from the Theodora Foundation in Switzerland arrived in Australia with my phone number. He wanted to set up Clown Doctors in Sydney. Similar programs were well-established in other countries. For one reason and another, funding did not eventuate. However, the seed was implanted. So with the help of my wonderful wife Leonie, and close friends Peter Barker and Dr Peter Spitzer, we formed The Humour Foundation, a non-profit organisation to promote the health benefits of humour.

The Clown Doctors started visiting sick and injured children in Sydney Childrens' Hospital in 1997. Myself, as Dr Bubba-Louey, Peter Spitzer (Dr Fruit-loop), Helen Quinlan (Dr Sniggles) and Justin Case (Dr Nut-case) were the first Clown Doctors. It was a great success, and I am proud that two years later we have 15 Clown Doctors at 4 host hospitals in 3 states – New South Wales, Queensland and Victoria. We aim to expand to every state.

Clown Doctors bring fun and laughter not only to the children in hospital, but also stressed families and staff. Using clown and improvisation skills, we waltz through the hospital, coming across kids, parents and hospital staff. Clown Doctors need to have not only excellent performing skills, but also be very sensitive, warm and caring. The atmosphere changes as soon as we enter the ward. Often, the more serious the situation, the bigger the laugh. We dilute the intensity of intensive care, help people to relax in emergency and distract children undergoing painful procedures.

Clown Doctors gently parody the hospital routine, helping children adapt to hospital life – hence the name Clown Doc-

tors. There are so many wonderful stories and small miracles. We call it 'open-heart surgery'. Every situation is so different, and we mostly interact on a one-to-one basis. We can often change a serious situation into fun and merriment. We might state the obvious with, *"Oh you don't look well, but you sure look beautiful."* I passed a 17 year old boy, man-sized in his school uniform, looking disconsolate amongst toddlers and babies, *"That boy's been here so long he's grown up!"* I said. He just beamed. I hit the button there!

This way of performance healing brings me great joy. Some days have wonderful cherished moments. There are sad situations, dismal scenarios and miracle recoveries. Hospitals never close. Here people constantly live in a world of expecting the unexpected. For some children, the hospital is their home for years.

We have strong corporate support and many individual donors. It has been one of my ideals to inspire the corporate sector into supporting social programs and contributing to the community. The Humour Foundation plans to develop workshops for doctors, nurses, parents and children using love, laughter and compassion in the great stumble forward. We already run workshops for the Clown Doctors, and speak to many community organisations.

I feel empowered now, and building up a head of steam. I bought 6 acres in The Rainbow Region 3 years ago with a desire to create an 'escape facility' – a fun camp for children of all ages to laugh, learn and play. Terania Park is at The Channon – 45 minutes from Byron Bay. It is nestled in the valley leading to Nightcap National Park. Currently it has cottages, caravans and camping facilities. My dream is to develop a multi-purpose site promoting the healing, artistic and environmental talents of the north coast. Local alternative design and technologies will feature – solar energy,

passive solar building design, composting and worm waste facilities, permaculture. A collection of nomadic structures – gypsy caravans, tee-pees, and yurts and the odd tree house over the creek – will provide accommodation.

Events will include music, theatre, dance, and movies under the stars. It will be available to the community as a gathering and celebration site. Residential workshops, and camps for kids are other possibilities. Camps for the siblings of kids with life threatening or chronic illnesses would give them a break and support. Workshops for health care workers would promote the health benefits of laughter for both self-care and patient care. It can be a retreat for healing – allowing people to express their grief and pain in a safe caring environment.

We want to
> Praise 'em all up
> Spin 'em all around
> Fill 'em full of hope
> And send 'em back to town

Being a wanderer myself, I suppose symbolically I am creating a safe haven for the nomads and wandering minstrels. This little place will promote a sharing of one's heart and a sense of community.

The Art of Protest

When making plans for the trip to Oz I was in touch with Lisa Macdonald at the Green Left organisation. She kindly gave me info about the *Protest! Environmental activism in NSW 1968-98* exhibition being held during my visit at the Police and Justice Museum in Sydney. And well worth a visit it was too! Caleb Williams, the curator, had made the staging of the exhibition into a highly personal task and I found its exhibits, video, background info, accompanying book and the chance to meet with Caleb really useful.

Bad laws and the police

The exhibition was impressively presented, with its eclectic mix of protestors' statements coupled together with police commentary running alongside. It seemed, when compared with the situation in the UK, and probably many other of the Australian states, that there has been much more consideration in NSW about the role of activism and protest in challenging bad or ineffective legislation. Direct action can mould popular and state and government opinion, and ultimately influence policies and legislation. Within that, there is also the question of policing 'protest'. The exhibition and the accompanying book tackled this thorny subject head on. Caleb Williams' wrote:

"At 'Operation Redgum' (1989) the commanding officer was keen to go beyond a confrontationalist, 'us and them' model of policing conflict. Strong emphasis was laid on peace-keeping, harm minimisation and the avoidance of harassment, intimidation and discouragement of protestors. All new police arrivals at the protest were given verbal instruction that their conduct was to be non-violent, non-provocative and 'fair to all sides', and that arrests were to be effected in a 'low-key and non-aggressive manner."

"Police that erred in their behaviour would be identified, removed and sent home. Negotiation and liaison with the encamped protestors was stressed and a 24 hour communication network set up. Police even accepted an

invitation to attend a peaceful resistance seminar run by the Wilderness society. Despite strong pressure from the timber industry and forestry commission for the protest to be broken up and moved on the police did not do this. Much strategic energy went towards defusing the very real possibility of outbreaks of violence by pro-logging groups, particularly during periods when logging-truck drivers were held up by blockades."

"(It) made a lasting impression on a number of activists who, nearly ten years later, recommended that the Northern Territory apply the same sort of 'enlightened' protest management techniques at Jabiluka."

At a landmark judgement in favour of North East Forest Alliance protestors and against the Forestry Commission in the NSW Land and Environment Court, Justice Hemmings concluded that the Commission, *"could not be trusted to comply with the law unless restrained."* This flew in the face of the traditional police role, as at Chaelundi Forset, near Dorrigo, where the police had, possibly unintentionally, helped the Commission to evade its responsibilities.

In New Zealand there already exists a sophisticated police-activist liaison network. A similar mechanism designed to reduce destructive confrontations is beginning to exist in some parts of Australia. Again quoting Caleb Williams, *"On 26 June 1998, a remarkable 'Forest Protest Protocol' was signed by P.J. Walsh, Commander of the Northern Region of the NSW Police and co-ordinators of the North East Forest*

Alliance. The protocol covered issues such as police-protestor liaison, police impartiality and the need to refrain from actions that could be construed as harassment...(it also allowed for) legally qualified protest monitors who would be identified by white t-shirts emblazoned with the word 'Legal Observer'. These individuals would be free to roam around the protest site and record 'evidence of misconduct by timber industry supporters, State Forest staff, police or any other person."*

This new found questioning of the infallibility of the law was even more in evidence at the 1998 Bateman Bay Aboriginal Land Rights case, where Justice McHugh summed up saying: *"Any realistic analysis of law, politics and society must recognise that not every law on the statute books continues to have the support of the majority of members of the community or always serves the public interest. Laws that once had almost universal support in a community may now be supported only by a vocal and powerful minority...There are sometimes very good reasons why the public interest of a society is best served by not attempting to enforce a particular law."*

Finally, one hopes there will be more tolerance and acceptance on non-violent direct action from the courts, politicians and the public. Following the Greenpeace demonstration where 17 activists placed solar panels on the roof of the Prime Minister's Sydney residence, as a protest against fossil fuels, Magistrate Mitchell stated:
"I accept that you were acting truthfully in terms of your own convictions and it is a mark of Australia's devotion to liberty that this sort of thing happens and is respected in our community...I guess Australian society would be a lot duller if

there weren't some people who were prepared to say what they think!"

The many examples of activism and protest

In conversations with the young and old activists across Australia I was struck by their great sense of pride; of achievement; of helping to make things better. Later in the book are examples of young protestors voicing their beliefs and telling their stories of the Giblett and Wattle campaigns in Western Australia and the establishment of the Lorax Group in Fremantle. We've already heard from John Seed, Ted Trainer and others about their involvement in activism. Still to come are tales from the Oms not Bombs sound crew who use parties to make their protests, and near the end of my collection, comes the work of the Earth Repair Foundation and environmental demonstators, Benny Zable and Alana Light.

Peace March, Mullumbimby, 1990

© John McCormick

In no way are these isolated actions. They are part of a historic tradition which belongs to individual states, Australia as a nation, and an increasingly global movement. To return very briefly to the actions which have taken place in Oz, and that have been chronicled, it's worth looking out for some of the following books:

I Protest! from Phil Thornton and journalistic colleagues, presents a general guide to taking part in, or organising effective action. It offers some quite useful info on dealing with the media and examples from various campaigns.

Green Fire offers Ian Cohen's blow-by-blow accounts of his own Green political evolution and involvement from Terania forest blockade through his 1986 exploits body-boarding the bow wave of a US nuclear warship in Sydney harbour, to life as a 'politician-protestor' member of the NSW Upper House for the Green Party.

The Coral Battleground recounts poet, Judith Wright's campaign to prevent sections of the Great Barrier Reef being exploited for industrial purpose. As Judith says, *"The Reef's fate is a microcosm of the fate of the planet."*

Toxic fish and sewer surfing is the book version of university researcher, Sharon Beder's University of Wollongong PhD concerning sewage, pollution and political cover-ups concerning Sydney's beaches.

The Battlers for Kelly's Bush is an account by thirteen women of the partnership they forged with the Builders' Labourers' Federation to bring about the First Green Ban, which prevented developers from building on a substantial area of open space by the Parramatta river, outside of Sydney.

The Way We Civilise is something of an academic landmark, offering an account of exactly what happened in terms of Aboriginal affairs in Queensland 1840-1988. But this is no boring historical account, but instead a fine example of 'investigative' historical research. A formidable critique of what Rosalind Kidd calls, 'the politics of deception'.

These are just a few of the stories from the 'edge'.

Tactics around the Globe

I'm writing this quite soon after the J18 (named after the June 18th date) *Carnival against Capitalism* protest has just occurred worldwide. In a mass world collaboration of protest and outrage, the NVDA (non violent direct action) movement managed to disable large sections of the international financial and business community for much of June 18th. The media mostly chose to selectively report some of the uglier events that occurred, rather than the central purpose of the action. Activists took to the streets to highlight the need for the G8 leaders to cancel the international debts of third world countries and adopt more sustainable environmental, social and economic policies. It's all a part of what Brent Hoare, in the *Protest* book, called *"the synergestic cyber-collaboration."*

Loose knit groups such as Earth First!, Critical Mass and Reclaim the Streets are products of the 1990s DiY culture.

Brent sums up this globalisation of the art of protest in an interesting way. He says:
"It's funny how things that go round, come around. It is no exaggeration to say that the modern direct action environment movement in the UK was spawned in large part due to the efforts of activists who'd participated in actions in Australia taking these experiences back to the UK with them. Now, here we are setting off (on the M2 and Olympic campaigns) inspired by the experience and achievements of communities on the other side of the world." (in Williams, 1998)

What happened was that a significant group of relatively well off and middle aged people in Sydney were completely energised after watching an edition of the *Undercurrents* alternative news video featuring the UK road/tree protests, compiled in Oxford, UK. Brent recalled that,
"...the transformative effect of the video on this living room full of respectable middle class citizens was incredible to behold. Resignation and scepticism was replaced with new resolve and determination."

Like in the native American legend of the Rainbow Warriors coming to defend the sacred lands, Brent hopes that the Tibetan prophesy of the 'Shambala Warriors' will come to pass. These are warriors who wear no uniform, and wield the twin swords of insight and compassion in balance, who will rise up and achieve victory in the face of environmental destruction. The actions of the 'few' have already had a profound influence on public opinion world-wide on road building; emissions and in the last year, genetically modified crops.

Jabiluka
"Jabiluka is definitely a test case...Kakadu is one of our most beautiful places. It's a World Heritage area. If a company can

mine there, then there's no place in Australia they can't mine." Eric Miller. Anti-uranium activist.

The very name 'Jabiluka' has become a powerful icon of protest and resistance both in Australia and anywhere else it is recognised in the international community. The area known as Jabiluka is surrounded by Kakadu National Park with its World Heritage listed wetlands (which serve as a source of traditional living for the Aboriginal owners). Politicians like to play the game of saying it's not actually *in* the national park, which led to protestors presenting hundreds of doughnuts to Parliament House as a symbol of outrage. Jabiluka is at the very heart of Kakadu.

Uranium was discovered there in 1971. Energy Resources of Australia (ERA) planned to develop a uranium mine and mill. This was opposed by many of the region's traditional Aboriginal owners (the Mirrar sacred site of Boywek-Almudj exists within the Jabiluka and Ranger mineral leases.) and by the national environment movement. However, the story of Jabiluka is an incredibly complex one, with many, many twists and turns. Nor is it over yet.

During the 1970s, Pan Continental investigated the extent of ore reserves, issuing an environmental impact statement (EIS) in 1979, and concluding a deal in 1982 to allow mining to occur with the Northern Land Council (using the provisions of the 1976 Aboriginal Land Rights Act). The Mirrar continue to assert that the deal was made under duress and by misinformation. Yvonne Margarula, the Senior Traditional Owner has said,
"My father was forced to sign the Ranger (uranium) agreement in 1975. Our people were given no choice in the Jabiluka agreement – and all Australians will lose if mining goes ahead in the Park."

Contrast that with the determination of the uranium mining industry
"There can be no compromise with the Aboriginal position; either it is treated as conclusive, or it is set aside...In the end, *we form the conclusion that their opposition should not be allowed to prevail."* (Ranger Uranium Environmental Inquiry)

The election of the federal Labour government in 1983 and creation of the 'three mines policy' suspended development at Jabiluka indefinitely. But, by 1992, Pan Con had sold its lease to ERA for $125 million. Uranium mining policy underwent a reversal with the election of the Howard Conservative/Liberal coalition government in 1996. A non-restrictive uranium mining policy was begun, and Senator Robert Hill, Environment Minister, recommended the Jabiluka project proceed. Senator Parer, Minister for Energy and Resources even kept a straight face when he announced to the world, *"Nuclear energy is environmentally a good idea since it doesn't contribute to global warming."*
Obviously his family fancy a nice Eastern European holiday in Chernobyl district!
With approximately 80 per cent of the worlds' uranium supplies sited in Australia, actual mines exist at Ranger in Northern Territory and Olympic Dam in Southern Australia; potential uranium mining sites across Australia include; Paterson Project, Kintyre, Turee Creek, Lake Way, Lake Maitland, Mulga rock, Angelo River, Manyingee and Yeelirrie in the Western Territories; Westmoreland, Valhalla, Bigriyi, Maureen, Ben Lomond and Barote Springs in the Northern Territories; and Beverley, Honeymoon and East Kalkaroo in the south.

A set back for the government's uranium mining came in 1998 when the UNESCO Mission report found that the Jabiluka mine posed serious threats to the cultural and natural values of the Kakadu World Heritage Area. In December that year, the World Heritage Committee accepted the UNESCO Mission Report and resolved the construction at Jabiluka cease until the Australian government could prove that the identified threats to Mirrar culture and country were avoided. And more recently the Federal Court has allowed Commonwealth environmental approval for the Jabiluka uranium mine to be challenged by the Mirrar people (June 1999).

The umbrella organisation, Jabiluka Action Group (JAG), alongside Gundjehmi Aboriginal Corporation – representing the Mirrar – organised a blockade camp in Kakadu in March 1998. Drawing national and international attention to mining in Kakadu. Arrests for trespass were made, including Yvonne Margarula, representing the Gundjehmi. Protestors successfully blockaded the only road into Jabiluka mineral lease for 6 weeks.

Policing policy at Jabiluka appears not to have followed the NSW lead. Police have been condemned as heavy handed and biased in favour of the mine. In an anonymous letter published in the *Northern Territory news* (quoted by Johnson in *Protest!)* a police spokesman described the protestors as, *"disgustingly filthy pseudo-terrorists."* And the courts have passed harsh sentences, reflecting the law in Northern Territory, where a first offence against property brings a mandatory 14 days in gaol. The two ploughshares activists, Treena Lenthall and Cairon O'Reilly disarmed an excavator on Nagasaki day (9/8/98), without the support of the official Jabiluka protest camp. Later both were charged with trespass and criminal damage, resulting in prison sentences.

To try and raise some of the complex issues surrounding Jabiluka and other protests, I've chosen to include a slightly abridged version of Rebecca's letter, drawn from her experience at the Jabiluka camp from April to August 1998. I think that it provides a fascinating personal insight into the problems of power/race, and the splintering of endorsed and non endorsed groups, that can arise whilst being involved in a campaign. I'm not sure how far all her individual criticisms are accurate, but the issues, conflicts and tensions ring true of protest action around the globe.

I'd hoped to also include Stella Kinsella's story as an (outside) journalist visiting Jabiluka camp, who told me of some of the problems that can be encountered within protest campaigns.

As she recounted, *"I arrived with camera equipment, journalism connections and no dreads. I was treated as a spy. It was an experience."* However, that was not be.

Jabiluka Blockade – An Open Letter from Rebecca

This is an open letter I have written as a result of my experiences of being a member of both the blockade and camp at Jabiluka, from April to August 1998. It was intended to be read out at a camp general meeting. It has also been disseminated as widely as possible outside of Jabiluka. It is not intended in any way to try and destroy the anti-Jabiluka campaign, simply to analyse problems that are apparent so that people are aware of them and hopefully act to change them. *rebecca.*

To All,

I am writing this letter to everyone concerned with the campaign currently happening to halt uranium mining on Aboriginal land at Jabiluka. I address this letter to all concerned as I feel sending it only to the people that I believe are undermining the camp would be pointless, as it is my belief that these same people would not pay attention to the points raised. Considering past and present experiences I have had with these people in leadership positions at camp, I have come to the conclusion that criticisms would be ignored or deemed irrelevant. It is extremely important in relation to the effectiveness of the campaign (blockade???) that people become aware about what is happening and for communication to be open and for debate to be encouraged and uncensored.

My reasons for becoming part of the anti-Jabiluka mine blockade were simple and direct: to join with others to stop the uranium mine being built and to aid the Mirrar people in their struggle for self-determination. On arrival at camp I was impressed by the shared responsibility and grass roots decision making that went on. It seemed that this was the best way to run the camp, with the people most affected by the decisions making them. The exception to this was shown in the way that blockade actions were planned and carried out – with a few leaders making all the decisions (in consultation with Gundjehmi, not with the participants!), and expecting people to put their 'life and liberty' on the line through blind trust.

The secrecy was always justified by people being told to put their egos aside and by participants being told they didn't need to know until the last minute, in case informers in camp got word and tipped off the police. Of course, the people planning the actions always put themselves in the elite position of never

Further lack of support for camp members is evidenced in the camp and JAG response to people stranded in Jabiluka – many people purchased return bus tickets which they can no longer use since the cessation of buses to and from Jabiluka. When I queried about this the leadership explained, and I

risking arrest or putting themselves where there would be potential for arrest, but never the inevitability. These people held/hold positions of power in camp as they were privileged to Gundjehmis' liaising with them and were expected not to pass on information given by Gundjehmi, e.g. being told logistical information such as the arrival of work-site equipment and keeping it secret while building a mass action around it. While this may seem acceptable on tactical grounds the logical outcome was a hierarchy that lost touch with its responsibility to the people who were risking arrest and charges.

Over time this leadership was forced to deal with the media collective which was beginning to become more of a priority with Gundjehmi, as they repositioned the campaign to appeal to middle Australia, and so all actions now needed to be media friendly i.e., non confrontational. The use of camp comrades as cannon fodder was one of the most outrageous aspects of camp policy. People were told at their induction that *"once you are arrested you are on your own"*. This left the arrested activists with little logistical or legal support, e.g. after mass arrests people had no means of getting back to camp (300km from Darwin). On a number of occasions the only reason the bus ended up going to Darwin to get people as they came out of prison was because another person and I would not let the matter drop. While in Darwin people found themselves without money (having been arrested on actions), without places to stay (billeting in Darwin was chaotic and inadequate at best), and without proper legal support.

quote, *"people got a good deal on the price of the tickets, even for one way"* – this reaction sort of misses the point! Not everybody up there has access to mummy and daddy's bank account to pay for a commercial bus back to their home!

The lack of solidarity shown to members of camp who put themselves on the front lines of actions, is typical of those in positions of leadership. Unfortunately, the Jabiluka blockade leadership exhibits traits that can be found in any political movement controlled by the white middle class with conservative direct action agendas. They seem to have found good bed fellows in the Gundjehmi Aboriginal Corporation too. Between the leaders at camp and Gundjehmi there seems to be no difference in their lack of respect and manipulation of the white rank and file. It has got to the stage where the conservatives running the green groups with the campaign (TWS/ACF/ECNT) have delivered the Jabiluka issue to the ALP.

These actions have alienated large numbers of activists from the whole campaign and will alienate many more, as they see themselves as being used by interest groups furthering their own individual agendas. At worst this tactic has burnt out a generation of activists who will be unlikely to put their trust into such an intense campaign again.

In order to put parts of this letter in context it is important to draw attention to what Gundjehmi Aboriginal Corporation actually is and their role in the campaign. Gundjehmi Aboriginal Corporation is a group set up to manage the affairs of the

Mirrar people. The issue of the Jabiluka campaign is not the only thing that these women have to deal with – their responsibility is to the Mirrar in all aspects of Mirrars' day to day life. It is no mean feat to keep such a troubled community functioning. While being determined and dedicated to the issue of Jabiluka, none of these women have any history of direct, grass roots activism. Jacqui Katona, the executive officer of Gundjehmi, has only the experience of working in well funded government projects.

While Jacqui's experience may be seen as an asset it hardly lays the ground work for working in a non-authoritarian, non-hierarchical, consensus based framework, which is the basis of camp structure as set out in the camp hand book. When I arrived at camp it was my understanding that Gundjehmi, or more specifically the Mirrar people, would have veto over actions on the grounds of 'cultural sensitivity'. This is not the way it turned out though – it has ended with Gundjehmi, and whichever interest group has their ear, dictating the entire strategy of camp, with no respect for those following their orders. This strategy, and its obvious consequences that have led to a lack of solidarity between working parties connected with the campaign, has not been revised in a positive direction, only a negative one. So, the present chaos of the national campaign is the direct result of such a policy (see attached 'endorsement form', faxed 20/6/98).

Gundjehmi, it must be stressed are only representatives of the Mirrar, not Mirrar themselves, and consequently the decisions that they make may not be the same as those the Mirrar would make themselves. While there are obvious problems in obtaining a decision of integrity from the Mirrar, e.g. major cultural differences and the daily pressures of poverty and alcoholism combined with a lack of experience in running an international campaign do make it difficult for the Mirrar to take an effective decision-making role in the blockade. Because of this, it's important to realise they're in a position ripe for exploitation to further other people's political agendas.

While it would seem logical that the Mirrar should have the right to control what happens within their own community lands, it must be acknowledged that we were invited to come and fight with the Mirrar, not for them. Fighting with somebody means that you do it together, not with one party dictating how everything will happen.

On August 9 1998, Treena Lenthal and Ciaron O'Rielly non-violently disarmed uranium mining equipment in the Jabiluka mine compound. They also spray-painted messages on the equipment and poured their blood over it to symbolise the devastating nature of uranium. Pictures of victims of nuclear weapons were also left at the site. They then sat in prayer so as to reflect on what they had done and to invite others to join in the disarmament process that they had begun. They did this action without camp approval, though security around the action demanded it to be this way. There is a camp policy of no property damage, though Gundjehmi did initially approve this action regardless of this policy. Approval was withdrawn for this action not because of camp policy and not because of cultural issues, but because Jacqui said that the timing was wrong – it was not the media image that we wanted to present at the moment. In Treena and Ciarons' letter: *"apologies good friends",* which was addressed to camp, they said *that "we respectfully beg to differ".*

After the action there was a press release circulated that stated it was a 'Ploughshares' action, not one done by the official Jabiluka protest camp (the Ploughshares' movement is involved in non-violent, direct action against war and the raw materials used in war). During the night of the action statements of intent and apologies to camp, along with the Ploughshares' media release were placed under the door of the media collective office and the Gundjehmi office.

These statements were then taken to camp and put on a notice board for all to read, however they were soon removed by persons unknown to me. This was the start of a smear campaign against these two activists. Tyrone Gibb, who was being held in Berrimah jail when Treena and Ciaron were arrested for this action was released soon after it. When Ty was released the media collective circulated a fax that stated that there were no more of our people in jail, thus denying the existence of Ciaron and Treena as political activists connected to the Jabiluka cause. From that point in time to now the camp has censored their cause out of existence – denying them their right to solidarity and support. At camp they have been labelled as racist, Christian fundamentalists (in another attempt to destroy the credibility of their actions and to alienate people that would otherwise offer support). These are low slanders to make against people who are unable to reply to them, and those who are making them need either their intelligence or their integrity questioned – perhaps both! It is statements such as this that seem to convince me even more that white guilt is guiding this issue (maybe the whole of the Jabiluka campaign!) – as if any action undertaken without Aboriginal approval is a racist act!

With all due respect, the Mirrar are not infallible, they did agree to this mine in the first place, albeit this was under extreme pressure from the government, the Northern Land Council and Pan Continental. If the Mirrar people had self determination and decent living standards at this early stage of events it would be likely that we would not be in the situation we are now all in. The damage done as a result of the colonisation of this country must be repaired, but blind obedience and syco-phancy are not the way to do it.

Another incident that highlights the authoritarian nature of Gundjehmi is the 'big stick' episode. As a result of ongoing, unresolved problems with camp and some ridiculous allegations, Carole and Christine from Gundjehmi came out to camp brandishing big sticks. A message came over the camp radio simply saying that people were to be in the meeting space in 20 minutes or they were no longer welcome at camp – no further explanation was given. People were then organised into a circle by James Wardell in a way that prepared us for the scolding to come! Carole and Christine stood beside their car (having driven into the middle of a car free camp) watching as this happened, and then they stepped into the circle and took charge. There were two things made clear at the beginning of this lecture: that children and their carers were not welcome and that if anybody felt that they had anything to say the best course of action for them was to get up, pack their bags and to leave camp for good.

There were a number of issues raised by these two women, the most significant being: that people were rumoured to be going to the compound at night and throwing rocks at the security guards (told to Gundjhemi by our friends the police); that people had been breaking or loosely interpreting the rules that had been laid out for camp; and that people were either idiots or racists because they drank at the local pubs – one owned by ERA, the other by the local pro-mine Aboriginal corporation (this coming from women who live in ERA houses).

It was constantly repeated that the people gathered had no right to say anything, even against the unfounded, highly dubious allegations of rock throwing. At some point two large sticks were taken from the car and thrown into the middle of the circle and we were told that this was how Aboriginal women dealt with problems they had with others (enough of a cultural experience for you?). People were then told that it was not known who was guilty of the accusations being levelled but they were challenged to come and take up one of the sticks.

Naturally there were no takers and so the tirade continued. There were various other threats made, one being that we were told that anybody going up on the lease at night had better look out because there would be Aboriginal (Mirrar?) people patrolling it and anybody caught would be 'dealt with' – something along the lines of a spearing was suggested. After this collective flagellation I saw many people who were very angry about being treated like this and promptly left camp for good, many others followed suit in the following week. One revealing comment I heard of many supporting the dressing down was, *"it's good to see white people put in their place by Aboriginal people".* This sort of sentiment only confirmed my growing fear that key elements of camp were cow-towing to Aboriginals out of a sense of white guilt.

All in all the camp and the campaign have made some tactical moves that have compromised the original aims of the blockade. From its well intentioned inception to its 'sellout' to the ALP and high profile green groups, the campaign has been unfortunate enough to follow the classic line of descent that many other environmental campaigns have taken, in that they abused and disrespected what at one time was their most valuable asset – the activists.

At the moment the 'blockade' as such doesn't exist – it is only there as a symbol of resistance while the 'important' people make their decisions in private and count the money that's being used/ misused? A recent story I heard about The Wilderness Society using Jabiluka funds to pay off a considerable debt on their shop in Newcastle does not inspire any confidence. The ALP will not be our saviours in the Jabiluka issue as they have already admitted that their hands are tied in respect to stopping the mine. The ALP has stated that it will only stop Jabiluka if no contracts have been signed and if no export licence has been granted – both these processes have already happened, there's signed contacts in abundance, and according to the ALP the cancelling of their validity is not an option.

I am aware of the potential controversy that this letter may stir up, however I feel strongly for the people involved in the Jabiluka campaign, both black and white, who have given time, energy and resources in the hope of stopping the mine. I see it as part of my responsibility to these people to air what I believe are fundamental problems in the running of the anti-Jabiluka campaign. I realise that for a lot of people this will be the first they have heard of such problems, and it is partly this lack of knowledge and flow of information about these issues that has prompted me to write this letter in the first place.

yours in solidarity
rebecca.

I can be contacted at chimpo_gimpo@hotmail.com

Letter from Gundjehmi to all Jabiluka Groups (here's a verbatim copy of a letter that Jacqui sent out to ALL JAG GROUPS, on the 20th of July, 1998, and expected a reply to, by the 24th. I have referred to it as the 'endorsement form' in my open letter)

FOR URGENT ATTENTION OF ALL JABILUKA GROUPS!

Dear friends,
The Gundjehmi Aboriginal corporation, the organisation established to represent the interests of the Mirrar, is in the process of undertaking a review of the structure of the Jabiluka campaign. Over the last year the campaign has been extraordinarily successful, with Jabiluka now firmly established as Australia's highest profile land rights, environment and anti-uranium struggle. A recent news poll has demonstrated that more than two-thirds of the Australian population is opposed to the construction of Jabiluka mine – a significant achievement in the current political climate.

The challenge facing all those involved in the campaign is to maintain and increase the current momentum up to and beyond the next federal election and the world heritage bureau visit. In addition, the Mirrar must maintain the ability to direct activities that impact on country, including aspects of the solidarity campaign. With this in mind, Gundjehmi Aboriginal corporation is planning to implement an 'endorsement' scheme for campaign groups and activities. Each regional or metropolitan centre will have an endorsed group(s) which has a direct line of communication with Gundjehmi Aboriginal corporation (or its delegates) and which operate with the endorsement of the traditional owners. Other (non-endorsed) groups desiring to work on the Jabiluka campaign will be asked to operate within endorsed groups.

Upon receiving endorsement, each group will be supplied with a written protocol for liaison with the Mirrar which will include a requirement to provide regular reports to Gundjehmi and to seek approval from Gundjehmi before undertaking activities which will impact upon the Mirrar. Ongoing endorsement will be subject to this protocol.

Unfortunately, we are operating on a very tight timeframe due to our impending fundraising and lobbying tour of Europe. Accordingly, Gundjehmi will require all groups who wish to gain endorsement to submit an application by close of business on Friday July 24. Applications should be forwarded on the attached form. Groups will be notified of their endorsement by Friday August 31.

We are proposing this initiative to develop a process which continues to acknowledge all elements of the campaign and ensures an effective and co-ordinated use of resources. I would like to reiterate how successful the campaign is progressing from the perspective of Gundjehmi and to congratulate the tens of thousands of people who have spent invaluable energy helping the Mirrar to protect country and break the nuclear fuel cycle.
yours in solidarity
Jacqui Katona.

APPLICATION FOR JABILUKA CAMPAIGN GUNDJEHMI ENDORSEMENT
(this form must be returned by Friday July 24. Late applications may be refused. Additional information may be attached to this form)

1. DESCRIPTION OF ORGANISATION. (include name, structure, membership, affiliation with other organisations, co-ordinators, resources, contact details etc.)
2. DESCRIPTION OF AREA COVERED. (include geographic & demographic)
3. GROUP ACHIEVEMENTS TO DATE. (actions, media, information distribution, fund raising, solidarity links. Please attach all copies of stickers, posters and other material currently in use.)
4. PLANNED FUTURE ACTIVITIES. (as above and participation in national working groups, timelines etc)
5. STATEMENT OF COMMITMENT TO ONGOING CONSULTATION WITH MIRRAR & RESPECT FOR MIRRAR DECISIONS ABOUT COUNTRY.

Doof On.....

Back in Brit, I've been very involved writing books and articles with members of the new Traveller and DiY scene. With their vans, tipis, bands, sound systems and other tat, they've brought some hard core anarchy into European life. While visiting Australia I was determined to make links with the nearest equivalent groups, 'cos after all, it's now a global nation – one tribe and many.

I'd already been in contact with Ray Castle in Sydney and previously looked at his fluoro-techno trance pages on the Web. Ray and I spent a happy couple of hours in a Newtown café in Sydney, chatting about the whole history of the rave, party and trance scene, countries we'd visited, and how doofs had developed in Australia. After the meet, Ray called it a *"memorable and vivyfying exchange"* and added, *"I felt a strong communality of 'new age' idealised and realised consciousness with you"*. It wasn't painful, and sounds good enough to me! Ray's contribution follows, offering his very personal reflections on the worlds of doofs, the Rainbow Region and more! Then comes tales from Pete and Faith Strong, who are part of the Oms Not Bombs collective.

The Sydney rave scene of the mid-nineties was dominated by the Vibe Tribe. This then splintered, sending what Pete calls *"fractal fractures through the concrete of the established Sydney dance scene"*, with Oms Not Bombs leading the way with protest doofs across the nation, while Organarchy concentrated on getting home grown tunes out on their own label. And alongside both, the Mutoid Waste Co, with its international tentacles, continue to breed their own techno events, and are among the main pilots for the hoped for Millennium 'Earth Dream' gathering in June 2000. Maybe readers of this book will be there (or, even been there)!

And if you aren't (or, weren't), then you'll enjoy the vicarious pleasures of Rak Razam's *Rainbow Dreaming* – a futuristic (but maybe not so fictional) trip into the cyberspaces of the Rave Olympics in 2011! Rak, like the Oms Not Bombs crew was networked into this book via Ray Castle. Then finally, it's back to the here and now of the 'EarthStomp' gathering with Denise Groves, a very fine Aboriginal lady, and her friend, Kelly Rowe. I met up with Denise through Sally Droosh, who I stayed with in Freo on the westcoast stage of my Oz adventures.

And, over to Pete and Faith Strong.

Oms Not Bombs
Pete and Faith Strong
The first time the name Oms Not Bombs was used was in 1995 where the crew in the beloved Ambi set off to Canberra to create a dance protest on the lawns of Parliament House, this was done two nights in a row until police interference saw the party relocate. Starting in Sydney, the collective put on several dances and secured a variety of sponsorship to make the Stop Jabiluka tour a possibility. We left Sydney in early July 98.

Oms Not Bombs – *"Dig the sounds not Uranium 98"*
Launching the Mobile sound system project
"It is a great feeling, we are a community on wheels, a mobile autonomous zone."

On the full moon of July 10th 98, Oms Not Bombs hit the road armed with a sound system, infodelic literature and videos and a crew of people active in Sydney's electronic music underground. The idea of a travelling sound system voyaging through the Australian outback has its roots in the aspirations of the Vibe Tribe, a community based party collective active in Sydney in the early to mid nineties. Since then the underground has grown and diversified. The Jabiluka issue was a catalyst to get the travelling sound system up and running quickly. Two parties in Sydney earlier that year raised the cash for the project along with a series of sponsorship. The campaign hotted up in Sydney, with a permanent tent embassy outside the office of the company responsible for the Jabiluka mine proposal, Energy Resources Australia, (ERA). While protest techno events went off in the middle of Sydney's central business district, the anti-uranium roadshow took to the road. Since leaving Sydney the tour has connected with many

liberationist groups across the land as well as putting on some amazing events and providing the soundtrack for various actions from Goolongook to Jabiluka.

Canberra
At the Aboriginal Tent Embassy in Canberra situated outside the old Parliament House we learnt of the increasing confidence of Australia's indigenous activists to attain justice and a treaty to offset the genocidal occupation of this land since 1788. The Jabiluka issue illustrates the ineffectiveness of land rights against the wishes of the multinational sector to gain maximum profits for the few as they ravage the earth. The blue and white Wollongong bus having received support from Greens and Democrats' representatives at the New Parliament House, cruised out of Canberra south in mid July.

Goolongook – Melbourne
The next stop after a three day mechanical breakdown were the forests of East Gippsland, where we assisted a blockade at Goolongook trying to save the last remnants of Victorian Old

Growth forest from mindless clearfell logging. Having arrived in Melbourne we raised money and energy for the tour by co-creating a huge night occupying three levels of Swinbourne University. The event called 'Oms Away' was a benefit for the Jabiluka action fund and the Oms Not Bombs Tour. The recovery was a full scale blockade of the One Nation Meeting at Hawthorn Town Hall just down the road. A couple of thousand people blockaded the building so that Pauline Hanson was unable to deliver her speech.

With the help of Melbourne welding wizards, Mutoid Waste Company, the bus was refurbished for the lengthy land crossing ahead. The fifth issue of *Sporadical* magazine active since the Vibe Tribe era, was released, containing stories, facts on uranium mining, cartoons and reviews. The zine has helped to disseminate information on the tour. Live electronic dance acts Serene Chaos and The Leyline Brothers (members of Organarchy sound system) as well as D,J's Ming D, Otaku, Chin Bindi, Morphism and Demtell have been programming the tracks at the events and spontaneous doofs.

Adelaide – Roxby

A Mad Hatters' tea party was staged on Hiroshima Day (August 6) inside the foyer of the Commonwealth Bank where Minister against the environment, Robert Hill has his office. Yellowcake and Magellan Creek tea was served, whilst men in white overalls carried a vat of toxic waste, accidentally spilling their load of vivid green slime. The Mad Hatters continued their picnic, suddenly convulsing and dropping to the floor one by one. This action made a 30 second spot on the evening news on channel 9 and 10.

Later the same morning the Oms Not Bombs set up a sound system outside the offices of Heathgate, an American conglomerate, opening two new uranium mines in South Australia. The Beverly and Honeymoon mine proposals plan to inflict the internationally banned (in USA and Europe) in-situ acid leaching process that threatens to poison the great artesian water supply of central Australia with DNA mutating radioactivity.

An awesome warehouse party occurred in town co-created with local crews raised the much needed petrol money for the long journey north. Heading north out of Adelaide with 'Earth Defender' graffiti on the side of the bus for a few days at the magical Wilpenna Pound in the Flinders Ranges. We explored a huge crater shaped formation, centre of the earth energy gridline 44 (connecting it with other power centres throughout the world; the Pyramids, Stonehenge, Machu Pichu etc). All along the journey we have been shooting footage, parts of which have been shown on the SBS's Alchemy show, other segments get shown through our video projector at events. A documentary of the tour will be edited together at a later date. Our website at omsnotbombs.cia.com.au contains stills from the digital camera as well as more detailed information on the tour. The site was written on the road thanks to Melbourne's Wd40 crew whose old skool ambulance joined the convoy in Melbourne. The vehicle equipped with a small 12 volt sound system added instant renegade party potential. As we headed up the seemingly endless desolate and surreal Stuart highway we stopped to protest against the expansion of the Roxby mine. Passing through Port Augusta we learnt of the vehicle movements where huge structures the width of the whole highway were to be transported. We set up a roadside protest as the mammoth structures came by receiving a mixed reaction from motorists waiting to be able to use the highway again.

The Red Heart

"If it isn't a tourist resort, it's a uranium mine – Aboriginal theft" – graffiti, Yulara, near Ayers Rock, Northern Territory.

By mid August we were at the heart of Australia, the majestic Uluru and Kata Tjuta rock temples were an experience many of the crew had looked forward to. Having been given the cold shoulder by the Yulara resort which refused to accommodate our entertainment package we set up camp just outside their strongly stated exclusion zone. More vehicles arrived from Sydney as we planned an event here. The centre of Australia at this time was like the Garden of Eden, recent rains had reactivated dormant seeds into a myriad of new green and multi-coloured growth. We put out a flyer, the resort were onto it immediately threatening to sack staff and evict tourists who dared to attend our party. A great night was had, however, with a few brave folk defying the ban, dancing in the red soil till dawn, the air seemed as alive with ancient Dreamtime energy as the land we were camped in.

Charged up with magical energy we headed off to Alice Springs. The Arid Land Environment centre helped us to spread the word on our 'Earth Boogie' dance event. A good turnout at the event on a clay pan on the edge of town ensured we had enough petrol to get the final leg to Darwin. A kind camel herdsman gave us a place to camp and helped us find the venue. Another night went well at a local warehouse, music studio called AV Sound. It was here that we spent a long session remixing a local artist's reggae tinged anti Jabiluka folk song. The breakbeat remix was aired on triple J the following week in Darwin. We continued up the highway passing the Devil's Marbles. The termite hills got bigger as the temperature hotted up. Past Mataranka springs, Florence falls and Katherine we finally came to rest at where the Stuart highway would go no more.

Darwin – Jabiluka

We finally hit Darwin after two months on the road spreading the anti-Jabiluka Vibe across the land. The day after we arrived we were involved in a theatrical action in support of the Mirrar people outside the Darwin court where senior traditional owner, Yvonne Margarula was up on trespass charges. Yvonne and others were protesting by walking on the bogus Energy Resources Australia lease when they got arrested. On arrival at the Jabiluka camp 250k east of Darwin we set up a camp in the hot shanty town village. The bus assisted actions supplying music and transportation, the anti-Jabiluka mine voice sam-

ples were activated over the various forms of funky beats. Protesters locked onto vehicles placed to stop equipment entering the mine. Tactical response police were extremely hostile. Doofs were held at the Jabiluka camp, and one night

saw Yvonne Margarula's brother turn up and perform a dance with didge player after which he delivered a heartfelt speech thanking the mob from down south for standing up with his sister. On two occasions ERA trucks ran amuck though the camp endangering people and then claiming that they were lost, which is the version of the story that the extremely right wing *Northern Territory Times* reported. In Darwin tensions were high after the ERA offices were firebombed by persons unknown. The police started harassing anyone who looked different and were associated with the blockade.

At a club night at a local hotel a brawl erupted at the end of an extremely successful and trouble free night. The security who resorted to violence at the first possible opportunity caused the brawl that saw people injured on both sides and the police cordon off the pub. Our reports to the police and paper fell on deaf ears, with the *Northern Territory Times* again coming up with a biased report of what happened. Protester numbers were increased with the Strong Country Celebrations at the end of September leading up to the very disappointing election result.

On the main day of action three hundred protesters massed at the lease gates wearing John Howard masks. The Peace bus on its second coming to Jabiluka arrived providing the techno soundtrack to the revolution of people power at the Jabiluka Mine gates, the bus having undergone the Sydney Graffiti Hall of Fame mobile sound system rebirth. Meanwhile arrests were made, compounded by everyone claiming that they were John Howard; the Mirrar delivered a speech and reports which attempted to get as much of the action into the media, a task that was difficult in the pre election week. Some protesters took the spontaneous action of driving a van through the gate erected by police to keep us out. They had to get out of the way quickly. This action was played upon by the media and did not go down well with the Gundjehmi Corporation who act as the buffer zone between the protest and the authorities. The group set up to support indigenous interests in the area had frustrated the blockade by mostly saying 'no' to direct action prior to the day of action. Much misunderstanding and conflict has occurred over the style of resistance employed to stop the mine. The inability of Labour, who promised to halt the mine, to topple the Liberals in the election was the last straw affecting morale on the Campaign. Soon after the camp was sadly closed for the wet season, with the Movement far from over. With two mobile sound system buses in town a huge action occurred back in Darwin at the wharves where they were Loading Yellow Cake Uranium

from the Ranger mine onto ships. Protesters were plucked out of the water and a huge spectacle created as police attempted to clear the way for the shipment.

Return Journey

The twin brightly coloured buses left Darwin in early October leaving the town a night to remember. We gathered in the central Darwin park playing music to the mixed mob that had gathered to see us off. The buses pulled off to leave, much to the happiness of local authorities. A Pied Piper style action followed, over a hundred people taking to the streets dancing around the loud techno float, numbers swelled as people came out of pubs and restaurants to join in, police came actually offering to find us a venue but we were off. We drove through

the night south from Darwin, but the Oms Not Bombs bus never made it, cooling problems led to our engine blowing a piston, the Oms crew jumped ship in the now overcrowded Peace bus while the Earth Defender Oms Not Bombs bus was loaded onto a trailer and carted back to Darwin for repairs. The Doof refugees were taken south through the vast interior past Mount Isa, a convoy following from other crew from Jabiluka returning to the East Coast. Spontaneous street parties were put on in Roma and Moloolonba on the East Coast.

Brisbane

We finally touched down in Brisbane to join in the ZZZ market Day Festivities. Market day went well in Brisbane, the Oms Not Bombs Infodelik Sound System and Organarchy playing blistering sets of unreleased dance groove punctuated with their unmistakable brand of issue based voice samples from the Jabiluka campaign and beyond. We put on a recovery at a warehouse in Fortitude Valley, then there was an Acidisco party put on by the Brizzy crew at the 'Che Bar', after which we put on the 'Technorganarchy' event. It only went for one hour before the Brisbane Police came to say turn it off because of a complaint. D.J Ming D was djaying when he was confronted by the three police. On demanding his name he initially refused questioning the reason for the request. In a flash they handcuffed and arrested him. I awoke to see Ming being dragged away from the control centre. I questioned them and then ended up insulting the police, still asking them why they had applied the cuffs on Ming in an extremely violent and painful way. I got the same treatment as did Tony, the peace bus driver. Our recovery party was annihilated by the Brisbane thug police who were obviously on a cultural intolerant trip. We knew of the reputation of these characters and had witnessed their blundering violence at the 1996 Market Day riots that they had caused. After being charged to appear back in Brisbane in early November the peace bus headed south to Byron Bay.

Byron Bay

There was a feeling of relief as we crossed into the friendly territory of northern New South Wales. We arrived in Byron to organise the Hills Doof that a local crew had promoted well. The party, the biggest of the Tour since Melbourne attracted about five hundred folk; the event went off with a hard floor system and a live stage area. The event raised some of the much needed funds to rescue the stranded Oms Not Bombs bus still stuck up in Darwin. It was a great party bringing together a diverse bunch of people, with an electric activist party vibe. In the morning rain finally stopped play at about 10.a.m.

The Peace bus is back in Sydney with some of the doof refugees from the stranded Earth defender still stuck in Darwin. The large green mobile doof tank created an area at the last Reclaim the Streets in Newtown. Reclaim the Streets was a great day, the police showing restraint at the event. The Peace bus pumped the tunes as did the four or five other P.A's and King Street went off all day at the rainy but totally vibey autonomous dance zone.

The Future
Stay tuned for more travelling sound system actions of the future as this culture grows and as we attempt to do something about the earth destroying activities of the greed motivated multinational operations across the country. (http://omsnotbombs.cia.com.au)

Earthdream 2000
Since the Mutoid Waste Co hatched the idea several years ago there has been talk about the Earthdream 2000 event in the middle of Australia in June 2000. Bringing a global travelling sound system lifestyle to this land, to join in this growing movement that has the potential to snowball as we demand the corporate earth raping sector change their behaviour to one that is in tune with the forces of nature. Outback Mad Max style anarcho techno sanity is a dream about to be realised, stay tuned...

Doof disco didges of the digerati
Ray Castle
From time immemorial the Aboriginal people of Australia have danced, sung and celebrated stories of the sacred land upon which they live. There is a strong correspondence between such ritualistic dance ceremonies and the nomadic lifestyle of the East/West hippie traveller cult, seeking neotribal techno transcendentalism with nature.

The dance space in trance-dance parties is a sacred space. It is a form of meditative, collective, spiritual worship. It is a reconnection with the elemental, primordial rhythms of organic, cosmic, life force. This sonic satori-state is heightened when people dance together in nature under the stars and experience the celestial shift of dark into light with sun rise.

At the core of Aboriginal culture are ceremonial song and dance rituals which are a communion with their ancestors, animate spirit guides and the totemic power of the landscape. There is a transmission of higher levels of knowledge through their song and dance, which is a direct conduit for the religious experience and unites them tribally. This 'knowledge' is central to the maintenance of their culture as well as to their relationship to the spirit power in the earth and cosmos, which is depicted in their 'Dream Time' iconographic earth, rock, body art and dance mythology. Outdoor techo dance party gatherings, celebrate an experiential celestial electro communion – a participation mystique – with the numinous oneness and interconnectivity of creation.

A lunar/solar journey from dark into light with the ascendance of dawn. Redemption and order out of chaos. A quantum quick step – accelerated consciousness – reconnecting with the instinctual cosmic realm and its eternal cycles of becoming. A psycho-spiritual healing. A rebirthing peak experience, where the separated self dissolves and morphs into a group-fusion. A dynamic meditation, synchronised rhythmystically, into a yin-yang, yantra-mantra. A cyberdelic social alchemy, that is shamanarchically ritualised into a non-hierarchical event. The underground, new-age, hippy traveller cult, with its exotic, escapist, cyborganic, aesthetic, has redefined the techno rave dance space as an autonomous – safe zone – sacred space, within which, to synergistically explore oneself through a transpersonal Dionysian drama of hypnostic beats, art, and nature. A shared tribedelic resonance is generated within an enviroteque elixir of groovology and symbolic art chain reacting a hyperspatial energy flux that allows the dancer to access psychedelic portals through veiled worlds

of heightened perception. In terms of modern capitalist society, both social sub groups feel marginalised, disenfranchised and estranged from fully participating in main stream consumer values. Tribedelic hippies, techno pagans and animistic Aborigines are more inclined to subscribe to a pantheistic spirituality, grounded in a cosmic apotheosis rather than the deification of money or God experienced via a patriarchal Church authority. By not successfully adapting and subscribing to fiscal paradigms of ownership and fully participating in commodity trading to derive a sense of identity, casts these sub cultures of society into the outsider role of dissenters and ontological anarchists. Indigenous native cultures are prone to varying degrees of dysfunctional maladjustment in adapting to capitalist concepts of economy and ownership. Various subgroups of modern society counter cultures intensely identify with the romantic ideals hinged around the pure, primal, omnipotence, experienced through living close to nature.

In Australia, those that drop out of suburbia to embrace a back-to-nature simple life style, are known as 'ferals'. They are perceived as having gone wild and taking on a post hippy tribedelic identity. There are many permutations within this 'freak' fringe dweller archetype. The most devout, live in rainbow rural counter culture zones like North NSW, the epicentre of which is the bubble zone hinterland triangle of Lismore, Mullumbimby and the fashionable new age chic beach town of Byron Bay.

The voluminous terrain of this ancient island continent is a geological cast off from early Africa. Its topography resonates a solid rock, rugged, individualism. An edge of the world nascent identity. There is copious space and tolerance for alternative counter culture experimentalism in this palatial fat country. The ferals are one such sub-clique of Oz counter culture, typically their appearance is their ethos: a tattered, thread torn, tattooed look, heavily pierced with jewellery, they don animal skins, bird wings and snake skeletons. There is a reverence for animistic belief systems, animal talismans, shamanism and gaian consciousness.

Another more urban-reptile sub species of this style genre reside in the inner Sydney, crusty counter culture suburb, Newtown. Their attitudinal insignia tends to be more politically gutsy, kooky and kitsch with elements of dark industrial, goth, punk attire as well as typically savage/tendril haircuts with lots of loud fluro highlights. There are even feral barbie dolls. Bush doofs (raves in nature) have become legendary down under, as the long dry summer climate and semi tropical zones favour outdoor adventure. The feral hippy frequency cults of the techno pagans are self sufficient with 4 wheel drives, trucks, buses, jeeps and generators. There are flotillas of teepee, chai shop, decorator and DJ crews, plus posses of video projectionists, drummers, jugglers, didgeridooo players, fire twirlers and whirlers. These psychedelic circuses manifest on moon cycles and solstices.

Most elements of the organisation are put together in a collective decision making process as well as fashion driven commercial promoter events. Every summer weekend you will find various versions of these doofs on the outskirts of the big cities, either in national parks, crown land or private property, and sometimes on the beach, if you are lucky. Dust frisking, doof disco, didges, whip the air with pranic pneumatic pulsations. Kangaroo kick drums punctuate the biosphere. Bodies gyrate a molecular experiential syzgism, syncopated to the insectoidal pulsations within the terra firma of timeless rock formations and termite hills. Reptiles and koala bears scurry from the sonic onslaught of the Bacchus beatz which bombard the biosphere of these Eleusinian electro benders, fuelled with psychotropic elixirs. These elemental, temporary, telecosmosis hyperspaces are a haven for tribedelic nomads, situationalists and urban ravers on the trail of the perpetually peaking party high. With the camaraderie of camping out in their station wagons, VW microbus vans and around open fires, they inhabit a shifting, electronic, dissident, soundscape, enviroteque, in the wilderness, where they psychonautically body surf through hyperspatial gyration force-fields, into techno transcendental trance-catharsis. Mind expanding frequencies and sensuous beats that facilitate a reconnection to a lost primordial innocence and child like playfulness. A kind of redemption experience. Underground freakquency fashion cults are like religious sects. Sonic techno sectarianism provide a reflective, empowering medium of values to articulate shared emotion, collective synchronistic consciousness within an individualised transpersonal digital aesthetic.

The tribedelic hippy romanticisms of technopaganism have transmuted 60s counterculture fashion and lifestyle into the electronic ecological aesthetic of late 90s cyberculture. Technologically totemic in a quest for the sacred in the computer chip, rave culture harnesses the revolutionary euphoric meta beat of the hard drive CPU. It spark plugs an accelerated amplification of cyberdelic, shared psychic resonances. A technogeist which exponentially spores a tek-gnosis-teleology. The computer has become an umbilical portal to the matrix for the universal mind. Cyborganica beckons the algorithmically reconfigured human species of the 2000 Aquarian epoch, into the realm of the digital chromosome. Precipitous to a mitosis of a self replicating spiritual machine. Neo-paganism and the nascent 'new age' entered 60s counterculture through a flirtation with Eastern mysticism occult-astrology, the tarot, witchcraft, magick, ethno shamanism, and re-emerged in 90s cyberdelica. The mystical mythical raptures of the 60s with its apocalyptic premonitions have been reinvigorated by those born in the 60s, who are now in their 30s and are taking control, as they propagate silicon driven spectral, hallucinogenic prophecies. The digerati, generation-x, cyber-tots from the 60s are commanding the software and designing the hardware today. They are manifesting an evolutionary destiny via integrated circuits as reflected by the radical conjunction between Uranus and Pluto in Virgo in the heavens at the time

of their birth in the 60s.

Their parents were oscillating to the reverberating revolutions of this time. This explains, in part, the vibrational parallel themes which have been promulgated by the psychedelic revivalism of the 90s, and the euphoric, techno transcendentalism upon us now, with Uranus and Neptune currently in Aquarius. Cyber hippies maintain that, unlike the 60s, they are not a drop out subculture, but want to bring about change to society by working within the system. It's now... 'Turn on. Plug in. Tweak out.' The dance culture credo pivots between a fashion geared around the sensory assault of drug-enhanced hedonism, through to the sanctimonious purification processes of healing circles and therapeutic group encounters.

Everyone is chasing spirit in one form or another; be it the ultimate dance track, visionary drug experience, lover, group meditation or perpetual peaking climatic sun rise experience. Techno pagans and new age digerati disciples are loosely associated with various human potential movements. The DJ can be faceless and functioning as a group catalyser at smaller parties with a circle of speakers installed amidst nature and mystical sculptural art decoration. Now that techno is becoming mainstream and the music industry is catching up to market it, the speakers and stage are reverting back to rock and roll heroism with the dancer now stereotypically becoming audience again, while facing a hierarchical show of big name celebrity DJ deck spinners. Visually and symbolically, techno acts and DJs are as dramatic as watching someone doing the ironing. Maverick multi media shamanarchists and green scientists know the real magic is in the test tube and the circuit board; but primarily, on the dance floor. The chewn chooser is really a drum skin tuner juggling bongos of other people's music, riding the groove clutch to perpetual never ending peaks of pleasurable ecstatic ecstasy.

Oz, a lizard culture of sun worshippers (skin cancer is endemic), languidly basks, slip, slop, slap, on oceanic expanses of coast, beach, bush, desert and rain forest. Most of its 16 million population live on the edges of its south eastern coasts. The border between North NSW and Queensland's Gold Coast is a bipolar contrasting embodiment of Aussie beach culture values. A tabloid from Surfers Paradise, in the heart of the Gold Coast tourist mecca, described the full moon bush-doof revellers across the border, as 'scrub druggies'. For back in the 60s, the hippies went as far north as they could, looking for nirvana in the sun, but dared go no further into the very staunchly conservative Queensland State. In extreme antithesis to the North NSW free wheeling, exotic counter culture, paradise, Surfers Paradise, one hour north, on the Gold Coast of Queensland is a vastly different reality. It is a fantasia playground for the bronzed, golden, 'beautiful people', packaged Asian tourists and silver-set retirees. Modelled on tropical Florida simulacra with 'Bay Watch' babe convertible fictions, it sports muscle beach beefcake posturing with endless dream home track housing development estates on canals festooned with luxury launches. It is a cheap Coca McDonald Vegas of tinsel veneer, clustered on manicured lawns, hollow-glazed with the mirage lure of an endless summer dream. The seductive fantasy of 'the good life,' under blue skies on palm lined boulevards. The hideous shallow pretentiousness of the Gold Coast's synthetic thin aesthetic mirage, is reflected in the environmentally disastrous down town, beach planning, which has crudely mimicked Hawaii-like high rise, with short sighted shonky speculative development. By mid afternoon the creeping shadows of these seaside, eyesore, condo towers of schlock, block the sun from Surfers Paradise's pristine main event and cherished natural asset: an endless white sand stretch of beach, that architraves the rolling deep blue waves of the South Pacific Ocean.

Byron Bay, across the border, the most eastern point of Oz, has no MacDonalds, stretch-mark limos or casinos. It's the dolphin loving front door of counter culture and green consciousness. Its biosphere reflects all that is alternative, new age and spiritual, except fundamentalist Christians who are big time, back across the border in the Queensland bible belt. Most residents here, walk bare footed, smoke dope and are vegetarian. They see their hallowed hermitage as impervious to the rigours of a straight, harsh, conformist, saturnalian, suburban society. Highly idealised by its hippy new age denizens, as a spiritual sanctuary, the Byron scene cultivates an air of enlightened chilled-outness. This is the haven for transneptunian rainbow bubble zone, escapists, inspirationalists and therapists. Natural living in an ecologically friendly environment is the code of conductivity which this international populace of disenfranchised bohemian visionaries, healers, dealers, travellers, artists and beach bums,

resound to. They have rejected a suburban consumer society, to hack out a dissident footing of – 'know worries mate' – in these spacious green pastures and glistening beaches of self becoming.

Nimbin, in the 60s and 70s, had been the epicentre of the hippy movement, but the free market rationalism of the current new age economy has centred the focus around the more boutiquey, upbeat trendy beach ambience of Byron Bay. These days its cafes and fashion shop fronts are geared for tourists who have come to consume the region's exotic, holistic, ambience. Many nouveau riche, on-line entrepreneurs, from Sydney, run businesses, and have holiday retreats there. But the feral social-security-dependent freaks and hippies take sanctuary in the rolling green hills and rainforest clad valleys which womb back inland toward Mullumbimby, Lismore and Nimbin. Here, you will find the inner sanctums of the crusty lunartek fringe that live in old farm houses, bush hide-aways, multiple occupancy communal households, as well as teepees, yurts, caravans, house trucks and tents. This rainbow zone is the most expensive rural real estate in Australia, which means most spend their entire dole, or solo parent payment, on rent; and typically grow a ganja cash crop for extras.

As the local cash flow is generally tight, bartering is common place. The more purist cognoscente of this rural fluro, mung beaner, underground scene, are ensconced in the hinterland hills and rainforest valleys stretching spaciously inland.

Mullumbimby and Lismore are where the locals shop as business is less high-profile than Byron, with its upwardly-mobile, whole earth polish. If you are a denizen of this 'love n light' triangle, you are an eco-organic purist, get around in a 4 wheel drive or VW microbus decorated with forest foliage, fluro stickers and feral talisman nick knacks; use shank's pony or just hitch hike. Many of the palatial bush retreat pads in the hills and rainforest are wired with solar power, some have swimming pools and their occupants compost with worm farms.

More and more are being rigged-out with midi studios and there are lots of multi media hackers to boot, plus there is a plethora of record labels, party crews, decorators, and DJs. Most things are done in between tugs on a bong, but the well-heeled and more internationally connected who are affiliated with the Bom Shanker Cult, and have done time in Goa, smoke chillums loaded with freshly crumbled charis from Manali, and do some psychedelic fashion business on the side, in Bali, on the return trip home. Some local shamans delve into ethno-pharmacological psychotropic horticulture practices and know the formulas and incantations to brew up DMT from the bark of local indigenous trees. After Terrence McKenna visited the area and held court at a 'Beyond The Brain' party, sitting around a candle toking on glass pipes became the vogue for many hardened psychedelic heads, after which there was no turning back. For many, such intense sanctimonious ritualistic experiences into hyperspatiality have made the standard issue, party acid trip, seem as leisurely as watching daytime TV.

Nimbin is tucked away further inland from Lismore and has fallen from grace somewhat, compared to its previous, lumi-nary revolutionary radiance in the 70s. The village now emits a listless vibe, with pockets of smack use creeping in. Belying the gaiety of its freaky, colourful painted, main street shop fronts, is a cul-de-sac moribund mood. There is a museum of original flower-power artefacts with displays of Aquarius summer-of-love memorabilia. It reveals a time warped era when the region was the shining light of counter culture and social experimentalism in Oz during the first wave of hippydom. If you are from out of town, you will fall prey to an overture from the locals, wanting to sell you dope. Compared to up-beat, Byron, with its chic savvy and transient-traveller

boom, Nimbin is languidly torpid, insular and time warped in a nostalgic kind of way.

After its first industries of logging, whaling and abattoir, Byron Bay became a surfer village and through the 80s and 90s rapidly incarnated into its present vivid, exotic, sophisticated, ecological aesthetic, reflective of its freaky earthy biosphere which serves up a smorgasbord of newage-isms. Rolling green hills curvaceously undulate into its sub tropical hinterland, which are now slowly regenerating rainforest after the rape of early settlement logging and erosion caused by cattle farming. During the summer season its backpacker and sublimely stylish hotels are maxed out with tourists. Those that have flocked to this Shangri-la on the edge of the nuclear free South Pacific are escapees or drop outs – depending on your point of view – from the big city centres and international hippy trail. They are seekers of a more natural, organic, relaxed lifestyle, removed from the din, stress and toxidity of the city. Everyone is either a healer, artist, macrobiotic gardener, or a dealer. The surfers who used to rule are now in the minority. The skin colour here is very white compared to the multi ethnicity of the big cities. This bubble zone with its succulent rainforest bush is a nexus magnet for burnt-out travellers on the Asian psych-edelic trail, needing an anchorage from the rigours of dispos-sessed vision-quests and pilgrimages on the global, thrillseeker, dharma-nirvana, trail.

This loose collective of survivalists, hippies, new age seekers and golden dawn facilitators see themselves as the rainbow serpent tribe in their own romanticised garden of Eden. This utopia of free-wheeling ideals is prone to the incestuous rankle of small community undercurrents, which at times becomes divisively bitchy with divergent values. Open relationships, splintered extended families, where children have a multitude of step parents are all part of the non-nuclear-family social experiment.

The bush doofs (techno parties in the nature)' and weekly flea markets, bring certain threads of this many layered counter culture collective together. Rurally scattered, chilled and detached, in their far flung hide-aways, it is a reclusive community of multi-nationalities. Though ironically, those born in Australia, are pretty much in the minority. This eccentric enclave, which at times takes on the motley appearance of an odd ball, freaks' ghetto, is dominated by ex-pat poms (the colloquialism for Brits down under). They have acquired an exotic dream ticket to an idyllic, far out place, in the sun, compared to the pathos of British counter culture high life, with its austere winters, meagre wilderness and stitched up politics, which leaves few escape routes, except India, which has now gone nuclear.

Rainbow Dreanming

Subject: Rave Olympics
Date: Tue, 20 June, 2011 17:43:34 +1000 (EST)
From: Rak Razam <shazaman@netspace.net.au>
To: It's a Wild Wild Wild Wild Wild Wild World<W6W@piratcnct.com>

We were about 50k's past Maree when we saw the first convoy of phreaks heading out to the Earthdream party, a motley, rainbow caravan of dust encrusted buses and camper vans, VW's and Bedfords, ferals, travellers and urban hedonists pirating the airwaves with digital mantras, blanketing the quiet earth along the Oodnadatta Track and generally funking shit up. The big vans and buses were crowned with giant inflatable objects like bananas and mangoes and blazoned with anti-uranium logos and activist stickers. We'd been getting reports on the CB radio for days, up and down the coast from every direction – these Psy-Trance Cowboys had been rustling the forgotten monuments of the 20th Century from quiet country towns and tying them to the roofs of their vehicles like scalps, plastic totems cannibalised from the Giant Ram, the Giant Koala, the Giant Pineapple, the Giant Homogenised Icons of White Middle Class Prosperity.

Now here they were, all in a row like floats in a post-Apocalyptic pagan love parade, cruising through the desert at high speed and kicking up a storm. Yessir, they were riding their groove boxes onto the high frontier, layered in bass and in search of a WAY COOL PLACE where everybody can DO Their Own Thing.
"Fuck me gently with ze chainsaw," Bridges said from the back of the van as we were overtaken by a double decker schoolbus with an inflatable Godzilla on the roof and a gaggle of stoned Germans hanging out the windows waving.
"Now there's something you don't see every day." She was right. I'd never seen Germans so friendly before. Something was definitely up. *"See if you can get a shot of them on the handy-cam,"* I shouted over the rattle of the van as we went over a pothole and everything lurched up into the air. We had a cache of the latest Ultra-Tech in the back to film the party – and the Gamez – and provide a continuous internet uplink for the rest of the world. This was the thirteenth Earthdream Desert Dreaming Festival and the prelude to next year's global

chakra cleansing ritual. Phine phreaks and klued in people of every shape and hue were gathering together, nomad tekno adventurers from all the 12 Trybes flowing into a rainbow mix snaking its way through the red earth. We'd bought the

latest Mitsubishi micro-camera contact lenses but the dust and the bumps along the Oonandatta Track wouldn't let me use either. The idea was to provide digital downloads over sensechips to the viewers at home – you would see, hear, smell, touch, and taste whatever the live reporter is sensing. At the moment it was some A-grade skunk we'd picked up 800k's back in Adelaide and a mild case of sunstroke from the glare. *"Got 'zem,"* Bridges pronounced in her singsong Israeli-American accent. *"Lovely establishing shot with ze buses elongating across ze horizon at dusk."* I suppose you want to know what she looks like. I would, and since we haven't got the equipment working properly yet, I'll have to describe everything for you.

My assistant, Bridges, is like somebody's sassy little sister gone the way of the urban disco feral. Enough piercings on her face to set off an airport metal detector. Dredds wax perfect, dyed blue and red and black. Big brown eyes layered in cheap Killer Loop imitation sunglasses. Handmade firestick and a bottle of Kerosene and Citronella by her side. Indian pants from Chakra or Ishkar. Black puffy jacket with a Chinese Dragon feng-shuing its way across the back. Dusty Monster Boots with six inch moulded plastic heels. She's also the best damn camera woman this side of the Nullarbor and can roll perfect joints while driving the van and mixing MP3's on the Diamondback decks at the same time. Not only that, but she's the only one who knows how to pilot the ultralight glider. I'm all legs when it comes to flying.

"Start narration, take one – Earthdream 2011." I'm recording on my built in throat mike that sends data pulses to our Apple Mac G12 laptop, auto remixes credits and soundtrack over the footage Bridges is shooting and transmits the final package via our satellite dish on the roof. We broadcast pirate

transmissions into the world datasphere and get a nice little pay per view package from inphomation junkies all over the place.

"Welcome to the Middle of Nowhere and another edition of 'It's a Wild Wild Wild Wild Wild Wild World'. I'm your host, Rak Razam, reporting live from Lake Eyre in South Australia, where the 12th annual RAVE OLYMPICS is getting into gear as part of the Earthdream Desert Dreaming Festival. Contestants are hightailing it through the sunburnt earth of the Australian Outback after a surreal Scavenger Hunt from coast to coast, bringing with them fabulous kitsch items of yesteryear as decor for the Gamez. As we pass the famous Mutoid Waste windmill flower sculpture, gateway to the desert circus, geodesic DOMEZ the colour of old Coca-Cola bottles litter the land-scape, filtering out UV light. The DOMEZ take advantage of the coolness of the earth to condense water from the atmosphere at night to grow plants and shade the soil during the day, thus encouraging further water collection. It's hoped that the retention of water by this means will eventually, by transpira-tion, create a changed local climate and encourage rainfall. Fluro-canvassed teepees are also going up with heraldic flags billowing in the wind like Tibetan prayers. Renegade soundsystems are banging out the latest Neo-tekno tunes from car stereos and speakers as revellers and the Raverati start shaking their juju and getting into the groovy."

I put the van on cruise control and let the automatic pilot system scan the terrain in full 3D topography. It carefully threads our way around the perimeter of the camping grounds, letting Bridges pan across and film everything as we go. A beautiful feral family with bones through their noses and clad in animal skins look up from their camp and smile as we pass. They've got a fire going in the heat of the day and are cooking what appears to be a giant turkey all stretched out and ginormous. It has to be one of the new genegineered ostriches that run wild in these parts. I nudge Bridges and she turns from filming a group of Swedes with blond angel dredds trailing down their backs to shoot the bird on the spit.

"The black and red and yellow sunned Aboriginal flag is flying proudly from the Keepers of Lake Eyre's Permanent Autono-mous Zone headquarters on the main track. The local Arabunna people welcome all travellers and revellers who

respect and revere the earth and thousands of people have turned out in what appears to be the biggest Earthdream festival yet. There's vans and buses and cars and tents all around, surrounded by tacky, giant inflatable totems that everyone has brought, like Easter island heads recycled for the Nu Skool Mythology. Colossal SCHWAA aliens and Smurfs, Gorillas and Koalas, papier mache Avatars of every description litter the desert like a feral Las Vegas – the perfect fluro Apocalypse.

As regular viewers already know, the RAVE OLYMPICS is a cross between extreme sports and an acid inspired dadaist tournament. Contestants have been battling it out in the middle of the desert since the inaugural contests in '00 designed to counterpoint the Spectacle of the mainstream Olympics, beleaguered by bribery and drug scandals and gross economic exploitation. Where the Greeks invented the Olympic Torch, the Ravers have the inevitable Olympic Scoobie – a giant joint over a metre long that's passed in relay from person to person in a long and mellow opening ceremony. When everyone's toked on the peace pipe and unable to move, the Gamez begin. Giant props have been cyberfitted from the old tv show, 'It's a Knockout' with trampolines and slides, giant barrels and fluro sackraces soundtracked with thumping industrial bush musik. Contemporary events include Sumosuit Wrestling, Doof Twister, Firetwirling, Drum-OFFS and the cream of the crop, Robo-Ostrich Racing. The only rules to the Gamez are that they have to be FUN."

Bridges zooms in on a helium filled blimp moulded in the shape of a golden frog with black swirls, the totem of the Psycoroborree crew in the Mini-Blimp Nerfjousting event. And cut. Perfect.
"What'd you think?"
"Just the right touch of crass," Bridges replies.

Subject: Rave Olympics
Date: Wed, 21st June, – 2011 12:00:05 +1000 (EST)
From: Rak Razam <shazaman@netspace.net.au>

To: It's a Wild Wild Wild Wild Wild Wild World<W6W@piratenet.com>

It was a dry wind and it crept across the desert at noon. It was a nice 28 degrees by the SONY palmpilot's built in thermostat. Winter in the Outback. Bridges and I have taken to the air for a better view of the proceedings. I have a tequila hangover from hell. Bridges looks perfect, as always, the curse of youth. Our ultralight is a converted golf green lawnmower with two seats and a built-in 16 horsepower engine. A pink and white striped parachute like those used in paragliding puffs out 'bove us for our wings. "Get a load of THAT," she says, pointing to a long flat stretch of desert north of the main camp. The Barrelfull of Monkeys Crew have rolled out the world's longest Twister set, over 100 metres of plastic Twister mats sewn together into a patchwork tapestry of red, yellow, green and blue dots. Like the dance till you drop contests in the 1930's, contestants are doofing on the spot while Twistering in the world's most bizarre endurance test. Human pretzels twisted into absurd contortions abound. I've got the Mitsubishi mini-cam contacts in over my bloodshot eyes and am recording streaming footage of the activity down below. Racers in spring loaded kangaroo boots bound across the flat desert terrain, bouncing a good three feet into the air.

To the north a crew of pale English travellers in sunhats are grappling with giant plastic marbles around a circle as big as a football field. From the air I can see there's no sense of strategy; the eight foot marbles are simply heaved by teams at other marbles that go ricocheting into one another and across the flat terrain. "Take her down for a closeup," I shout over the whine of the engine as we divebomb the players. Bose speakers embedded in the doors turn on and broadcast cheesy old movie soundtracks to cover the sound of the motor.
"Up. Down. Flying Around. Looping the Loop and Defying the Ground. They're ALL so frightfully keen... those magnificent men in, magnificent men in...magnificent men in their FLYYYIIIING MA-CHINES."
The English all look up and cheer as we pass over. A giant marble skittles across the desert from the opposing team like a tumbleweed and bowls them mercilessly to the ground. The clouds hang low and lazy, hugging the earth, the sky a deep blue like the colour of people's eyes in the movie Dune. Bridges lights a joint and pulls the ultralight up into the blue.

<Start narration>
"Day Two and it's the Winter Solstice here in the Southern Hemisphere. Thousands of tek-heds from all over the world have come together to dance the longest night and feel the pulse of the earth here near her heart chakra. Sunlight glints off solar panelled vans and buses and catches on the metal blades of miniature windmill generators fixed to the roofs. The earth is red and flat all around. The flies are ubiquitous and you swallow at least three a day unless you shut your mouth and open your eyes. Down below they're putting up the doof, tekno style. Mutoid Waste madman Robin Cook is testing the old giant fire blasters for the party tonight. They're four cyclical metal pillars arranged around the perimeter of the dirt dancefloor as an elemental anchor that let off belches of flame in perfect syncopation with the bass. The infamous Tekno Ostrich Races are all set up in a protective bioplex ring in the middle of the dancefloor, racing right under the giant fire towers. The genegineered birds stand about eight feet tall and look like mutant turkeys with attitude. They've got the graceful curved neck of the pink flamingo but are let down by legs as thick as wrestlers on Megasteroids. They remind me of a one night stand I'd rather forget." Cut.

Bridges elbows me in the ribs as the ultralight veers to the left over Lake Eyre. There's a crew of full on Israeli tek-heds dancing up a storm by the edge of the water. They're dressed in full body wetsuits laced with smart fabrics that automatically adjust body temperature and sweat. Their big Monster Boots are fully motorised piezio-electrical walking devices that use the kinetic energy of the walker to power the hardware – which in this case includes water pumps that send moisture and urine back up through micro filters, making it safe for redrinking.
"Zey are ze Calvin Kleins of the desert!" Bridges quips as we zoom in low over their heads.
"Hmmph. More like futro drug dealers."
"Zem bootz is made for dancing and that's just what zey'll do.One of these day zem bootz is gonna walk all over you. Bootz – start dancing!" she sings, tilting the ultralight to and fro.

"Are you stoned and flying again?"
"It's ze only way to travel," she retorts.
I take a deep toke (for the sensechip viewers at home, of course) and marvel at the desert terrain all around. We're sitting in a sea of blue that stretches out forever, red earth and thumping bass reverberating from below. With the telescopic enhancements built into the Mitsubishi lenses I can see the broad outline of the electric fence over 60ks to the west. Aerial schematics downloaded from a pirate satellite flow into the SONY palmpilot as well as full telemetry of the area. I'm back on-line:
"I can see that the Pangea Mining Company and their private security goons have the perimeter of the nuclear waste area, or the DUMP as it's come to be called, sealed up tighter than a nun's proverbial. The electric fence is twenty feet high and a concrete partition extends under the earth another ten feet. It stretches over 100 square kilometres and has to be one of the Seven Great Wonders of CorporateTerrorism. Undisclosed tones of radioactive sludge are buried here, deep in the Australian heart-land, shitting on the sacred spots and burning into Gaia's delicate biosphere."

Bridges gives me a look like I'm dangerously close to alienating our sponsors, but fuck it, a journalist has to have some integrity, right? And integrity's like virginity – you can only lose it once.
"New telemetry data's coming through, viewers. Switch to HYPERLINK mode for live satellite feeds in infrared and eye-spy frequencies for only $1.95. Satellite images show deep thermal activity in the Forbidden Zone around the DUMP. Looks like the Army's on manoeuvres again."
I cut the link and take another toke. The Military budget has blown through the roof since the Republic of Australia started fortifying the border from Indonesia and the flood of refugees.
"You know ze Vietcong used to play Nancy Sinatra tunes to ze G.I.'s in the field as a brainwashing technique. Ze same track over and over again for days, echoing out over the rice paddy fields and jungle till ze G.I.'s snapped and broke zeir cover."
"What a coincidence they're permanently patrolling the area around the DUMP."

"There's no such thing as coincidence," Bridges says, taking the joint back off me.

Subject: Rave Olympics
Date: Wed, 21st June, 2011 6:56:11 +1000 (EST)
From: Rak Razam <shazaman@netspace.net.au>
To: It's a Wild Wild Wild Wild Wild Wild World<W6W@piratenet.com>

"It's four minutes to race time and some ultra smooth electro disco funk is rippling out on a cloudless night. There's falling stars everywhere and outside the ring thousands of full on doofers are getting down and dirty to the beats. It's not quite a full moon, but state of the art laser and holography techniques have lit up the sky anyway with moving pixilated pictures. The giant, grainy baktun glyphs of a Mayan calendar turn lazily against the stars. Aboriginal Wandjina chalk men hundreds of feet high groove like albino stick figures to the sound of a thumping 4/4 Psy-Trance beat. Even the ghosts are dancing. Indian, Mayan, Aborigine, Hollywood – all the Old World kultures are represented in this swirling maelstrom. Fluro string webwork hangs over the main dirt dancefloor in sacred geo-metric patterns within patterns, fractaling inwards in a UV mandala. The patterns are like phosphene imprints on the eyes that allow viewers to find their own message and open up deeper connections. The DJ arena is in a Cone of Silence like bubble made of aerogel plastic to protect the decks from dust. The BPMs are tweaked to literally turn on the crowd with their hypertrybal vibrational frequencies.

Surreal and absurd tekno sculptures transformed from urban junk litter the landscape; gestalt car robots that rotate and move, Harmonic Generator Coils that light up like the inside of an electric light bulb but thousands of times as big and bright. When filmed at high speeds they melt into a glowing double helix reminiscent of strands of DNA. The tekno wizard himself, Robin Cooke, sits at his giant Fire Organ with a puckish grin on his face, playing the keyboard and creating musical flame. As the fire rips up the tubes the organ lets out sound as tongues of flame lick out. The tubes glow red and orange and then finally white hot from the heat and have to be left a while to cool. Further out from the centre, party shamen groove around four burning mechanical pillars crowning the dirt dancefloor in more flame. Black light projectors create hypnagogic patterns on the ground, flashing on and off in binary streams. It's like a Christian Fundamentalist's version of Hell crossed with a tekno-pagan explosion.

Thousands of people are stomping on the earth, dressed in rainbow skins and smiles. They've come in costume for a grande Masquerade and really funked themselves out. Cyber-crusties in the loudest SKINS known to humankind dance alongside mutated performers in ultralight exoskeletons. LCD threaded fabrics glitter and swirl animated GIF pictures across countless bodies – the crowd has become a canvas. My brain wants to shut down just looking at them. Oh, the wandering Sadhu fools, all of us in different head spaces all the time, billions of possible permutations fuelling the party, the look, the flavour, the KODAK MOMENTS."
<Pause transmission>

And that's only scratching the surface of it. Bridges is dressed in her Cyber-Sinderella outfit – black mesh tank top, evening gloves and veil with thin strips of silver polymer strapped strategically round her body like surgical gauze. She's datamining the crowd, interviewing a few choice jewels while I get ready for the race. I pull her away from a Maori warrior with full on tribal tattoos etched across his body and spilling up over his face. He smiles, revealing a set of metal teeth like the villain in Moonraker.
"CACTUS?" Bridges repeats with a sly grin.
"Of course. When in Rome and all that. A full blown power lunch with Mescalito is de rigeur for all desert journeys," I explain.
"The viewers at home expect only the finest experiences, Bridges," I chastise. The Cactus has been on the boil all through the day since dawn. It's viscous green-grey texture looks like snail roadkill mixed with bitter phlegm and the taste is even worse – if you can get it down. I did – barely, and the taste of Satan's ballsweat dogs my every breath.
"Just swallow this and chase it down with some lemonade," I say, handing her a two litre water bottle half filled with green cactus discharge and distilled juice.
"But you must be quick because I can already feel it coming on."
"Shame I've got no lemonade," she says and winks, chugging

down the juice. Her eyes ping open as a shudder visibly moves over her body.

"Oooh, zis is very, how you say, hot shit stuff!" She takes a big swig of tequila from her hip flask and starts to sway a little. *"C'mon, I've got a race to call and you've got some cheating to do. The fastest land mammals after the cheetah are waiting and you don't want to make an ostrich mad. Those beaks are deadly, y'know. "*

The OSTRICHES are all lined up and being groomed on the inside of the bioplex ring that separates the dancefloor from the race track. The big birds move like catwalk models, poised and taking delicate steps, bobbing their long necks up and down as they go. They've all got phutro names like a cross between racing dogs and Psy-Trance DJs:

> 1> Tron's Revenge
> 2> Frequency of Bliss
> 3> Tryptamine Meditation Ensemble
> 4> Ambient Head
> 5> Chakra Flowers in Spring
> 6> Oscillating Wavefront
> 7> Feral Cheryl
> 8> White Noise
> 9> Eden Hashish Centre

Human jockeys have been phased out to make way for hyperadvanced robo Furbies – modified versions of the robotic kidz toy that talks and moves and has a memory cache of 100GB. They look like hairy gremlins strapped in their miniature saddles, gripping the reins with tiny motorised hands. These lil' critters can be programmed to perform small chores around the home and some smartarse has modified them to ride the ostriches. They're remote controlled by contestants outside the ring, making it the perfect sport for lazy, drug addled ravers. Bridges and I have cooked up a little personality algorithm for our Robo-jockey based on 80's testosterone movies. Basically, it reprograms them to think like Rambo, Indiana Jones and the Terminator all rolled into one. It'll be the perfect denouement to the Rave Olympics, but part of me worries that it won't be long before they can do everything we used to, and on that day humankind will be obsolete, replaced by a Japanese Tamabloodygimmick. Fuck me, I'm getting maudlin.

The ostriches are doing the once round as their numbers are called and they're weighed in. *"Look closely at the ones that poop,"* I tell Bridges. *"They'll be lighter in the race and have an advantage over the rest of the flock."* As we watch, a few of the giant birds gingerly release their droppings as they walk along. A gorgeous transsexual done up as Madonna in her Sex phase comes and cleans it up with a little broom and shovel.
"Her tits are better zen mine," Bridges pouts as I drag her to the DJ booth where I'm calling the race from.

Everything's shimmering like the horizon at noon as the cactus comes on strong. Just looking at the names of the birds makes me feel like I'm tripping. Bridges is controlling her robo-jockey on ostrich number 7, Feral Cheryl.

We're filming on the handy-cam and cross linking with the Furbie throughout the race. *"Be a love and roll me a joint,"* I ask her as the fire organ belts out a fiery clarion call and it's all happening, hold onto your sanity, here we go...

"Okay, they're moving in and we're all ready for a start. They're at the post...ready...there's the light – and they're OFF! Tron's Revenge is away well followed by Ambient Head and White Noise, with Chakra Flowers in Spring on the inside track close behind. In fifth place is Eden Hashish Centre and Oscillating Wavefront, with Feral Cheryl and Frequency of Bliss three lengths back and Tryptamine Meditation Ensemble coming up the rear. Ambient Head has taken the lead by half a length from Tron's Revenge at the turn of the field as White Noise, Chakra Flowers in Spring and Oscillating Wavefront battle it out in the centre. Across the track is Eden Hashish Centre skittling past Feral Cheryl and Frequency of Bliss is back on the inside followed by Tryptamine Meditation Ensemble."

There's nothing finer than watching a flock of 8-foot-high, 350-pound flightless birds being piloted by small robot jockeys while on mescaline. Colours shift and swirl as angles distort and everything takes on a strange kind of surreal logic. Robin Cooke's going OFF on the fire organ, playing some thumping deep bass that's being picked up by radio receivers and broadcast over the local area. People are listening to the race and the doof as far away as Port Augusta. I tap into the Mitsubishi lenses for a second to see what the viewers at home are seeing and am bombarded with cyber edged speed line manga visuals breakbeating and slipping all over the place. Optic nerves pinch and zoom as the digital camera in the Furbies' eyes relay the race from a bird's eye view roadrunnering across the shimmering desert terrain, kicking up clouds of dust as they pass under the fire pillars on the edge of the dancefloor. Roadrunner the coyote's after you. Roadrunner. When he catches you you're through.

"Tron's Revenge is coming down the straight and behind him Chakra Flowers in Spring. Two lengths back is Ambient Head followed closely by White Noise and *LOOK OUT* here comes Frequency of Bliss up the side – she's zarting fre and fro and look out for the beak on that one, she's plenty mad today. And Oscillating Wave Front and Tryptamine Meditation Ensemble are fighting it out in the middle as they go round for the final lap. Eden Hashish Centre is trying to get up the side and two lengths away at the rear is Feral Cheryl, who seems to be having a bit of trouble with her rider. The Furbie is out of its saddle and it looks like...oh my God it's jumped onto the tail of Eden Hashish Centre and is clawing it's way towards the other jockey."

I chance a quick look at Bridges who has one eyebrow cocked and a grin bigger than Texas plastered across her face. The fire organ's squeeching and squelching out ultra low hertz sounds that travel up my spine and explode somewhere in the back of my head. The crowd is cheering wildly and dancing around the ring.

"And as they travel down the straight Chakra Flowers in Spring has taken the lead with 300 metres to go, with Tron's Revenge half a length behind and White Noise in third place. Getting a run on the inside is Frequency of Bliss in front by two thirds a length from Ambient Head and Oscillating Wave Front. Something's happening with the robo-Furbies as Feral Cheryl's rider

has knocked off Eden Hashish Centre's jockey and the bird's running wildly across the field. Oooh, look out, she's collided with Tryptamine Meditation Ensemble and both birds are down. The rogue Furbie is jumping birds and dispatching their riders to a fast death under monster ostrich feet. It's ruffling feathers and holding on for dear life to Oscillating Wavefront and the panicky bird is speeding forward, past Ambient Head and Frequency of Bliss, past White Noise and Tron's Revenge. The two Furbies are wrestling at the reins of Oscillating Wavefront and slamming the bird into Chakra Flowers in Spring. She's not happy about it and her beak is flying out and savagely pecking the unsaddled Furbie. Jesuspaghetti! he's loose and flying through the air. Chakra Flowers in Spring is going to hang on and win..."

What happened next is pure post modern psyber-haiku. It appears that at a certain frequency of sound transmitted over radio, precisely duplicated by the fire organ belching out it's flame music, Furbies explode. Who was to know? The lil' killer robot burst into flames and showered metal and fur all over the finish line, the other jockeys disintegrating in their saddles one by one like a string of firecrackers in the night.

Betcha glad you choose the REMOTE VIEWING option, huh viewers?

Subject: Rave Olympics
Date: Wed, 21st June, 2011 23:11:11 +1000 (EST)
From: Rak Razam <shazaman@netspace.net.au>
To: It's a Wild Wild Wild Wild Wild Wild World<W6W@piratenet.com>

"It's going OFF!!!" Bridges says, smiling and smiling and smiling.
"Ain't that the truth." We're tripping round the desert doof hanging onto the slender thread of sanity. Everything's raw and dusty like the party itself. We're 80ks from the nearest town and having the best damn time of anyone in a 1,000 square kilometre radius. We're building a Harmonic Wave Beacon, y'know. Orchestrating all the dancers into a whirling dervish of altered states of mind like the Sufis do. Turning on the chakra pathways up the spine through sight sound and dance. Building e DOOF. The Psy-Folk Funk Quartet are sampling in tambourines and Dylanesque whisky breakbeats to the

musical proceedings. We're grooving down by the central bonfire, surrounded by thousands of ravers, dancing. And dancing. And dancing.

I guess there's no other way to tell it but like it is, y'hear? *"For the sake of the viewers at home on your live satellite feed I'm switching to autopoetic lapis MODE. For only $2.95, you too can upload the sensory datafeed in full immersive VRscope,"* I babble, letting the lyrics melt into the transmission>

　　boom boom…booming right back AT CHA boom boom booming right back atcha! Right back right back right back atcha!
　　　　　　　boom
　　　　　　　　　　boom
atcha
　　　right back right back right back
　　　　　　atcha
　　　right
　　　right
　　　back
　　　back
　　　right back right back
　　　　　　　　right back
atcha

　　Boomin right back right back right back atcha. Everything smearing together – music and love and light – higher phreakquencies of vibrational NRG are bouncing building beaming right back atcha in the doof, boom booming boom booming

　　grooving red desert dust under feet beat boomin right back right back right back atcha, its all coming down, drowning in it, what finer place than right here in the middle of nowhere with Bridges and the Psy-Folk Funk Quartet cooing the light phunktastic, bouncing beatbox'd funking groovy red devils, smiles all around, splashing in the dust and there's all these kids in furs and skins going off, rolling around in big tractor inner tyres, and there's a big black bundle of dog padding alongside with a plastic boomerang in his jaws, just moseying along so fine if you please, and its all like a dream, like doof a vu, a frozen moment and I wonder if its all as simple as this,

as feeling good and dancing to a wicked bass and having the right people around you, all in the same head space, all in no-time>
　　　　　　right back atcha
　　　　　　　　　　and a booming
beatbox'd bass phades in and out and into another Old Skool track, white men turn up the treble, <boomin> black men turn up the bass <right back atcha>, turn up the treble, <boomin>, turn up the bass <right back atcha>. Rhythms and lyrics overlap and I smile the same smile that's flitting from face to face, blossoming through the crowd, becoming a Psy-Trance phase space.

Man, I'm TRIPPING.
Programming code is flooding the central processing centres of the brain, I'm MeLTinG>>>>> There's a Coca-Cola sky and everything's inverted like a Photoshop filter as the rainbow serpent rises through us. The beat goes off the scale as it boomboxes right back atcha and everyone's caught in a karmic feedback loop, rising and inverting, fractaling inwards. Boundaries shifting melting overlapping. Twister mats scattered across the sand as far as the eye can see, desert doofers phunking it up like there's no tomorrow...

And the drummers are drumming and the twirlers are twirling their firesticks in the early dawn light as the longest night comes to a close. People are juggling flaming bowling pins and grooving to the beat and the twirlers are going off into hyperdrive> double sticks crossing, lightsabring the air, the smell of citronella and magik quicksilvering through. Open mouths and smiles fall through the crowd like dominoes, a hard 4/4 Psy-Trance beat boomboxin bass through the earth and all the way up your spine, tingling kundalini. THE TWIRLERS SHALL TWIRL AND THE DRUMMERS SHALL DRUM and the DREAMERS shall dream. And the MUSIC MAKERS shall make music. And the Doozers dooze, always building. Moving, doing, never getting to the end. And the journeymen shed their skins and settle into the trip.

The Trybes are coming home, the rainbow serpent is rousing to the bass. Everybody's sparkling.

EarthStomp '99
by Kelly Rowe and Denise Groves
(photos by Killian)

Preface
I (Kelly)

met Denise at the Doof 'Syncro'. She was interested in putting on a party. I originate from the eastcoast, love to Doof, and I'm often wondering about the insanity of non-community: trancing tells me it is untrue. 'Syncro' was a Doof in central Perth organized primarily by John, an individual who later come on board the EarthStomp Committee.

I (Denise)

had just arrived back from the U.S. with the experience of 'Burning Man'. For me, many similarities exist between psychedelic/trance parties and the ways that we as indigenous peoples gather. Songs, stories, dance, rituals and ceremonial gatherings reinforce our spiritual relationship with the Dreaming, as well as our relationships and obligations to Country and each other. I felt it was very important that EarthStomp had an indigenous component as a recognition that we, the Aboriginal peoples – the first peoples, have been the custodians of Australia for over 50,000 years...I feel tribal gatherings are a great way to foster co-existence, and couldn't help but feel an overwhelming sense of pride and honour when the Wardani elders welcomed EarthStomp participants onto their land.

One Earth – One People – One Love
Within a week we were looking at inspirational photos from Burning Man. We were excited and started brainstorming to create a similar event here. Three weeks later there was a Doof on the beach in Fremantle and a Rough Ideas handout was given to various people. Martin, one of Fremantle's inaugural Doof organisers and more to the point, a psychedelic visuals' magician, was fresh from a trip to the eastcoast for 'Earthcore'.

I (Martin)

returned to Fremantle (Freo) from a musical study tour in Africa with a renewed feeling of my own community's tribalism. I found this sense of community in the psytrance/doof parties that were gathering in the east coast of Oz and now here in Freo. A techno-tradition I can feel as my own.

EarthStomp was my first Doof festival to organise. My role was Artistic direction and Video Production. I made and organised fluro banners, sculptures and a meme garden of hanging messages in the chill out. When we give ourselves time and space to really meet each other, then true social interaction takes place.

It was here too that Toby, who had recently returned from Europe, was recruited.

I (Toby)

discovered after the event that my role was Music Director and Stage Manager. Getting the DJ's together was easy because I have a bunch of talented friends who DJ and I wanted to give them a gig. But the gig itself was like a Baptism of Fire – everyone is under a lot of stress and it shows, you can't help but show it. Not sleeping for sixty hours.................I'll make sure I get at least one or two hours sleep at EarthStomp 2000. Being down there and knowing we were actually doing it.......it felt a little unreal, it was amazing, a combination of extreme pride and extreme humility.

Tribe of Gaia
Given the task of what we wanted to create, for efficiency, we kept the EarthStomp committee to eight members. However, many others worked to ensure the Idea happened – collectively we unified as the Tribe of Gaia. Tribe of Gaia is everyone who feels that they are predominately Gaian or global citizens. Their boundaries are defined by gravity and biosphere not illusions like nationhood or class.

The philosophy of EarthStomp
Perth Doofs have been happening for several years. A handful of dedicated individuals including Tipi Sam and Martin Phillips, have been active organizers. With the new millennium dawning, a couple of us were interested in creating something 'more than just a Doof'. We wanted to create a space, away from the overwhelming confusion of city life, a space which would enable a myriad of collective awakenings and unification of human consciousness to the wider interconnectedness of Gaia.

Although we were uncertain of what this meant we had a couple of themes in mind. One of them being the Earth herself. Environmental destruction is often the impetus for Earth causes today and this tends to set a framework of duality, a confrontationalist mood of right and wrong, political absolutes of correctness and badness. So: politically speaking, Earthstomp was not a cause, it was an offering, a purification.

Presuming fun and colour and freedom to be of a mind nutritious to the Earth, we began to create a party, a forum for any inhabitant to give an ecstatic homage to their planet, to participate in the multiplication of energy made possible by a large gathering of people. We wanted to celebrate the Earth in her present beauty, offer a right-now-happiness unspoiled by dark forecasts. Defending the Earth from the Powers That Be is a noble task. However: we wanted to express joy and hope before such a perennial battle comes to an end (no end).

Our Task
We wanted a Doof distinguished from what had gone before. Deciding to have an event run over three days (which might even be called a festival) set us in motion for this. Our framework was suddenly larger and we began to expand into other spheres not traditionally associated with a Doof. We could have stalls and healing tents, why not invite alternative living groups to promote themselves? Also: we had more scope to develop a carnivalesque atmosphere. We wanted a feeling of festivity and celebration, a space in which illusionary boundaries could be transcended. It had to be in the forest, a 'returning to the source' where a sense of wilderness and primal energy could be unleashed. We wanted people to come together, to be moved, to open their Hearts, to unify and strengthen the Tribe.

One of the key elements of EarthStomp was combining the Earth and Technology to create Beauty. This presupposes that technology can be used in the interests of the Earth. Sound is a potent force when it comes to igniting human energy fields, it has the ability to make you move. We utilized technology to syncronize Earth, Body, Mind, and Spirit. Hence: a dance, a

trance, a beautiful vibration for you the Earth. A Temporary Autonomous Zone on behalf of Her, our fears surrendered upon entry: WELCOME HOME.

Earthstomp was also motivated by an absence of community in the world. In a society dominated by fear and consequent alienation, we attempted to show how community is not only possible but natural. It's what we are before fear divides. And inter-related here is the wonder of Time. Separation, from the Earth and each other, causes a distinct lack of Time. If only I could find the time. Indeed. In the Oneness of Community, Time is abundant, there is time, for instance, to be a friend.

Fears and Uncertainties
Amid the whirlwind of excitement there were a number of worries. Money was an unnerving factor for much of the term of pre-production. How much do we actually need and whose got it? Six weeks prior to the event we were uncertain if EarthStomp was going to happen at all, given that apart from having no money, we had no venue. In the end, it was Rowan's faith and finance in the Idea that charged us thru.

But we don't have a venue?
We will have.
The Council want clauses 5.1(b) and 12.3(a) fulfilled?
I don't panic, I never panic.
Electrical cord?
Rowan made a four hundred kilometre plus round road trip (to be sure) for an estimation of the entrance gate location. He doesn't worry, he acts. Other worries included EarthStomp coinciding with the Fremantle Buskers' Festival, administrative difficulties with the local Shire about using twirling.

First Aid was also a dilemma: it was included in the well known hush of toilets, Council by-laws, and the howabouts of tarps, ropes, and car parking space. On what was perhaps the final meeting, the issue of first aid came out of the Void.
Marty: *"What about John? He's doing nursing...and he's a Doofer."*
Rowan: *"John who?"*

Marty: *"Doof John."*
Rowan: *"Tell him there's $200 in it."*
The only official casualty over the 48 hours was a person who was badly mosquito bitten. In between weekly meetings, phonecalls were made, faxes were sent, flea markets were scoured, and ideas were pushed and poked. Finally, we received a phone call from Tipi Sam who had been negotiating the possibility of an Aboriginal Sacred Site for a venue, now in the hands of a private owner. The phonecall was affirmative. The meeting exploded into applause and happy exhalations of relief. Then a lovely earnestness directed the remainder of the meeting.

Celebration
A full moon is perfect for a pagan festival. The Goddess (Nature), unleashes her passion and sensuality. A full moon is the peak of the Goddess's pleasure. To this, we celebrated with a festivity of colour and imagination, a party for the original mind in honour of the Great Mother. Easter = Eostre, she is the Goddess of fertility, a time blessed for new beginnings. EarthStomp: our birth into the new millennium.

The Wadarni People are custodians of Country vibrant with Beauty and Spirit – Indjidup. A nexus, created in the wake of the Dreaming, weaved in the path of the Waugal, the Rainbow Serpent. Indjidup is a respected place, a meeting place, a Dreaming place. In keeping with indigenous protocol the committee sought permission for EarthStomp's gathering.

EarthStomp
On the day: cars trooped in and entrants were handed a flyer at the gate:

You are now entering an Aboriginal Sacred Site. EARTHSTOMP is a celebrating the Earth, Freedom, and Colour. Talk to strangers, dance with your neighbour, eat good food. Indjidup Amphitheatre is a Vessel secluded from an inauthentic world. Express your Individuality. Will Pleasure. We are a community of Light minded individuals delighting in Diversity, Creativity and Difference. EarthStomp is a…Bang, a Rush, and a crescendo: never forget what you experience this

---

weekend and dedicate it to re-birthing Planet Earth. ENJOY.

1,000 people showed. The atmosphere was one of celebration and Light. Even today EarthStomp is remembered for the loving atmosphere it created. Visually, crowds of beautiful

people gathered as One. There was the distinct sensation that we were elsewhere. Forget reformation, we were already there: didjiridoos and drums, the vibrancy and colour of the psychedelic imagery, the wizardry of the DJ's, the chill out area, the wholesome foods, the massage tents, and simply, the incredible beauty of the site itself.

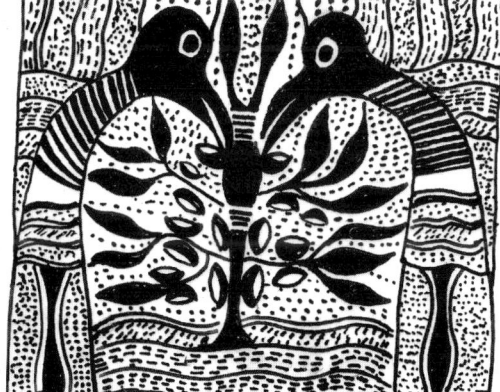

For information on EarthStomp 2000 and beyond, check out our website: www.earthstomp.au

On the forest frontline: *"We use our bodies to bring about change."*

Fremantle was 'home' for the last week of my Australian trip. I'd phoned an old British mate, Harry Blagg, who now works at the University of Western Australia, and he kindly invited me to encamp at his Freo home. Through his lady-friend, Sally Droosh, and some of my own mooching around in places like MP, Carmen Lawrence's office, I was able to meet up with active members of Western Australia's environmental campaigns. It was also the time that a number of these young ferals and activists were forming their own group: The Lorax. I went to the launch exhibition sited in the fashionable Claremont shopping mall. It is the mall which includes international fashion designer, Liz Davenport's elegant emporium. And Liz was giving her own personal backing to the group, having just been arrested herself for a spot of up-market tree protesting!

GALA OPENING
FRIDAY 5TH MARCH

Back in the UK and across Europe, the road protestors and eco-warriors have won many battles in the war to stop car culture trashing the Earth. I was pleased to have helped many of the front-line troops publish Kate Evan's remarkable account of the last ten years of the tree protests: *Copse*. What comes over most strongly in that book and in the next two contributions, is the heartfelt anguish that some young people feel at the environmental destruction that is taking place in the name of 'progress'. This is the real stuff of direct action protest.

Leith, who co-wrote the following account of the Giblett Forest campaign offered me a wonderful description of that Claremont evening launching The Lorax:

"Liz has genuinely seen the beauty in the ferals. It was a posh info evening in an equally posh centre, her store mixed up with ferals and ladies who lunch, all of whom had been professing their love for ferals! It was topped off by a message from God's Garbage, a full-on bikie gang who had been mentioned in a media beat-up the night before, saying they would join forces with loggers to beat us up. Instead they sent a message to say they wanted to see an end to the logging of old growth forests too! After we had drunk champers with the rich and famous we went into the car park and drank beer to recover – a very surreal night, but typical of our campaign here at the moment. It's great!!"

Performance of The Lorax at the opening of our space, March 99

After Chris and Leith's account of their own involvement in non-violent direct action comes Emma's description of the setting up of The Lorax organisation. And if anything in this book celebrates 'diversity', it is the groups of individuals such as The Lorax, which have brought together young ferals, retired environmentalists, and members of the Aboriginal community.

Love letter from the trees
Chris Lee and Leith Maddock

Background
Giblett is an area of State Forest greatly treasured by West Australians and was the site of Australia's longest continuous forest blockade in 1997. It stands about 15 km north-west of Pemberton in the South West of WA. made up of 1,600 ha of jarrah forest and 2,300 ha of karri/marri forest. Except for 50 ha clearfelled and illegally exported for woodchips in 1994, the forest is all old growth and full of very large old trees with numerous hollows for habitat. Much of the understorey is ancient she-oak groves which are mostly bulldozed and burnt as part of clearfelling operations. In 1994 Giblett was placed on the interim list of the Register of the National Estate for a wide range of conservation values, and this year Giblett was listed by the National Trust for its significant cultural and natural heritage value.

The beautiful old growth forest landscape around Pemberton and across the south-west is of immense significance and value. After 150 years of clearing and logging that landscape has been transformed. Half the pre-European area of karri forest and a third of the jarrah forest have been permanently cleared. Now only one per cent of WA is covered by tall forest. and of that one per cent less than one-fifth is in conservation reserves. Time is running out to protect the small amounts of old growth we have left. Giblett itself is an unlogged jewel of a forest in the heart of an almost totally logged area.

Local Pemberton residents have prepared a proposal for the Greater Beedelup National Park which would incorporate the existing 1,800 ha Beedelup National Park, Giblett forest and other adjoining old growth forests. There is a great deal of community support for this proposal but there is also a continued refusal by the department of Conservation and Land Management (CALM), the timber industry and Government to offer protection to Giblett. The recently signed regional forest agreement protected just 10 per cent of Giblett, strangely enough only the bits the timber industry did not want to log!

The Giblett Forest Rescue
After spending a couple of months in the Giblett logging coupes (sections of forest designated for logging) in 1994 and failing to stop the devastation, forest conservationists were outraged to hear from a Pemberton local in late April last year that scrub rolling had begun again. Logging contractors started work on Tuesday 29 April 1997 and the Western Australian Forest Alliance (WAFA) quickly organised a picnic in the coupe for the weekend to gather supporters together and decide what to do. Meanwhile in Margaret River a handful of people decided to take the initiative immediately and quickly designed and built a lightweight steel tree platform about the size of a single bed. The climbing gear needed to get the platform up a tree and the camping gear needed to make a small support camp underneath were hastily assembled and the Giblett Forest Rescue had begun. Little did any of us know we would still be there seven and a half months later, or that Giblett Forest would become an icon in terms of our old growth forest and a beacon of hope for many people who wish that these precious and endangered forests can be left to stand in their original glory.

We arrived at the forest on Saturday 3 May 1997 to find that in the four days Bunnings contractors had been working they had scrub rolled almost the whole coupe and begun felling trees in one corner. A huge old karri was chosen for the platform – it was a good choice, close to the landing but far enough into the coupe to prevent safe logging. Using a compound bow and fishing line we got a climbing rope over a limb about 30 metres off the ground. Wade, our reluctant climber, ('I'm too old for this caper') went up to make the fixing for the platform with steel cables and up went the tree platform. Supplies, stove, bedding, batteries and a mobile phone were hauled up and installed on the Sunday watched by a couple of bemused cops and a few dozen picnickers. Eventually in the afternoon it was time for Chris Lee, the first of many tree sitters, to go up. After a very quick tutorial on climbing he farewelled loved ones, said a prayer, and using a whole lot of gear he had never seen before, up he went!

This was the first time we had taken action in the forest in a proactive way and it felt good to be in charge of the situation rather than on the back foot trying to stop work minute by minute. Another huge first was the phone, which was central to our strategy. Gibleft is remote in a sparsely populated area, the density of the forest makes radio communication almost impossible and in the past this had been the cause of much frustration. The authorities were amazed that we were able to get the phone working, we had a special antenna made, and found that instead of watching us trying to attract the media into the forest (which is always hard unless there is blood to be seen) they heard us speaking our passion for the forest live on radio and TV direct from the treetops.

At the time we put the tree platform up we thought we might be able to hold our position for a couple of weeks. To Chris's amazement, and everyone else's, he stayed up there for five weeks watching in awe as the tiny camp grew into a small village whose population expanded on some weekends to two hundred people. This platform would be continuously occupied

for the next seven and a half months, and two others would also be installed nearby and occupied when numbers in the camp allowed. Over the long winter we were gifted with many donations which enabled us to maintain camp health and safety as well as the integrity of the forest we were camped in. A particularly prized item was the self composting toilet but our well equipped workshop with its own generator and welding equipment was also invaluable. So was the office caravan with the computer! A South West craftsman visited the camp and built us some bush furniture so strong and beautiful the Pemberton Museum asked for it to be donated to them when we left. It was a cold and wet winter in the forest and we worked hard to maintain the camp but our spirits were high in the knowledge that without our presence 460 ha of Giblett would have been clearfelled.

Building a non-violent community
Whichever aspect of the Giblett camp we look at we see the integrated philosophy of non-violence working in new and exciting ways. We took many lessons from the '94 blockade with us and were careful to establish a strong identity for the camp, working with established organisations in the campaign but being very clear that whilst we would listen carefully to their views we would make our own decisions and not be bound by, or dictated to by any other group. As a distinct new group we were able to apply the principles of non-violence to the campaign in a new and vital way, working at a grass roots level and totally maintaining our commitment to communication and conflict resolution within the group, with local people and in our dealings with the government and bureaucracies.

When new arrivals came to camp we ran non-violent action workshops, teaching the absolute importance of a non-violent approach in our dealings with each other and in all aspects of the work we were doing. However, while non-violence in itself can provide us with the skills needed to communicate respectfully with adversaries but it does not provide a spiritual base for building community across difference. Only love can do that. For this reason we tried to embody the spirit of *ahimsa* in the way we taught and lived our non-violent action. *Ahimsa* is the Sanskrit word from which English word non-violence is derived and it means more than simply the absence of violence – it is the active presence of an unconditional love and respect for the other, which can only disallow all forms of violence in thought, word or deed.

It is in this way that love was made the foundations and structure of the Giblett community. Not the gooey theoretical sort of love but the sort that is based so strongly in truth that it can appear almost brutal in its unconditional honesty. The sort that meant we could sit in a circle and discuss ways we could really love the people in uniforms and suits opposing us as opposed to just looking like we did (which would have been both dishonest and hypocritical). These feelings about truth and love were not things that were pushed onto the group by some noisy evangelical minority they came from just about everyone.

The camp was made up of mainly young people and they embraced the opportunity to experiment with a different lifestyle where passion, love and truth were the essential elements. It was as though these were the main elements missing in mainstream society and we were determined that they came before anything else at Giblett. Many people felt they could only stay if these were the guiding principles of the camp. An important way we found to express our passion, love and truth was in regular heart circles, where we could share our despair over what was happening as well as our visions and hope for the future. There is a sort of magic that happens when we take the time to listen to each other in this way, a magic that lets us see the beauty and the vulnerability in each other and allows love to be present. In camp we accepted everyone who wanted to be there and, of course, had at times to deal with all the problems present in mainstream society such as drugs, theft and anti-social behaviour. We found we could find solutions to these issues that enabled us to keep loving the person whilst not condoning the action. People who struggle in society are often the most sensitive and passionate and we wanted to find ways to work with that sensitivity and passion in our campaign. Love and compassion combined with

patience can allow huge changes to occur and we saw many individuals make massive personal changes once they realised we would not reject them.

Somehow, we want to get across the sheer power of Giblett – how it empowered and radicalised so many young people, how it shouted the need for social change from the treetops. There were no designated leaders, just a bunch of young people all learning to be leaders. This was not the soapbox standing, tub thumping shouting of rhetoric, this was a huge living experiment, a chaotic event strutting its stuff, warts and all, in public. From this we built a community, a place where we could trust and love each other as well enact our love of the world by working to protect this pristine bit of forest.

Non-violent direct action

The result of our commitment to non-violent direct action was that we gained a level of acceptance and respect in the local community we had never before experienced in the South West. Potentially violent situations with angry loggers and timber industry workers were always defused by the total commitment of forest rescuers to non-violence, and we became trusted in the community to stay true to those principles. We didn't deny the position of strength the tree sitters gave us but we didn't play on it either. Instead we used both the power of direct action and the raw power of the forest itself to help us to act as true warriors rather than just soldiers. We learnt to let insults and anger wash over us as we recognised the power of receiving these blows whilst feeling love and compassion for the perpetrator, empathising rather than arguing. It is impossible to shut out such love. Regardless of the words that come out of their mouths an opponent cannot help but be affected in his or her heart when faced with honesty, courage and love. Such is the state of our society, that these simple things have become extraordinary rather than the norm. Not only are they unusual but they are desired so deeply by all of us that it is difficult to resist when our heart is touched by them. This may sound idealistic but we know that it works because we proved it over and over again.

During the time we were in Giblett we weren't content to just blockade the forest – we took our energy and commitment for the forest out to the community in lots of ways, working closely with local and city-based forest groups. We tried hard to engage in dialogue over the future of our forests with CALM and with the Minister for the Environment, but made no headway. This was extremely frustrating because we knew that we had such a high level of public support for what we were doing.

We also carried out carefully prepared stop-work actions at the Bunnings Diamond Woodchip Mill and the woodchip loading facility at Bunbury Port to draw attention to the fact that our precious tall forests were being destroyed for the profits of a few. These direct actions were undertaken in a spirit of love, kindness and respect but were planned and executed in true warrior style. The planning was very thorough with particular attention paid to how the workers and authorities would be feeling as individuals when confronted

At a rally in Perth

with people locked onto trains and machinery and refusing to come off voluntarily. We always made sure we were in a strong position by having people locked on in inaccessible positions so that an end to the action would have to be negotiated rather than imposed. Being open, honest and communicative in these actions was essential. Once we were in position and the authorities arrived we told them exactly what we had done and provided police and industry liaison representatives to conduct negotiations on our groups behalf. From working in this way we were able to retain control over what was happening and ensure there were no violent confrontations for our adversaries or the media to feast upon.

The Giblett camp was closed in late December 1997, after the Minister for the Environment had assured us there would be no logging of Giblett until the Regional Forest Agreement was complete. We have maintained our commitment and our public support since then but we are afraid for Giblett. It was still on the logging list and we are prepared to go back there in strength at the first sign of logging.

Suffering

Non-violent direct action does require suffering, there is no way around that – especially at the sharp end of direct action. We use our bodies and our commitment to civil disobedience to bring about change. Our hard core protestors, who are often those the broader community struggles the most to unequivocally support because of the way they dress, are willing to surrender almost everything if it will help save Giblett, or any of the old growth forests we have left. Many of them are giving up their property, their vehicles, their licences, their money (including access to the dole) and even their employment to fight this battle. That is partly strategic – it is difficult to punish someone who has nothing – but it is also suffering. It usually takes the poor and disenfranchised in a society to act to change an injustice, and the Giblett Forest Rescue was no exception. Paolo Freire, the South American liberation philosopher, said that no-one understands oppression like the oppressed – perhaps this is why so many poor and unemployed young people responded to the call to save Giblett. They know that our society does not love and treasure the young, the poor and the unemployed. They also know we do not love and treasure these last stands of old growth forest enough to protect them. They see the beauty and the vulnerability of the forest because it is in them as well. When we trash the environment we trash their future. If Giblett falls we are sending a powerful message to these young activists, and everyone who works to save the forest, that future generations matter little next to desire for the mighty dollar.

The ongoing campaign

The spirit of Giblett lives on in the many people who visited the camp, and in the countless others who have been touched in some way by the forest campaign of the last couple of years. Since then there have been continuous blockades in the jarrah and karri forests, lots of stop work actions and subsequent arrests. We are clogging up the Manjimup

Court, a whole week has been set aside in October and again in November just to try forest activists when court usually sits for a few hours one day a week. We have had rallies all over the state, Bills debated in Parliament and taken up pages of the newspaper every day for months. On the down side we have had our forest camps attacked and burnt by loggers in balaclavas wielding axes, several firebombs thrown at one of our environment/activist centres and the usual escalation of anger and hatred towards us as it becomes apparent to the timber industry that their days in the old growth forest are numbered. We have stood strong in our non-violence, and keep working on a solution that will meet the needs of the forest for protection as well do something to ease the fear timber workers are experiencing as they realise their industry must undergo rapid change.

In the last year, the campaign has escalated beyond our wildest imagination, and we now enjoy the overwhelming support of the West Australian public. Ferals are fashionable in the leafy suburbs, which has been both surreal and powerful! The politicians are in paroxysms — the Government is on the run over the issue, with a major rift between the Coalition parties and a new Liberal (conservative) Party being set up called Liberals for the Forests — regrettably with all the same terrible policies, but with the exception of promising an imme-diate end to old growth logging. The government department responsible for logging the forests, as well as conserving them(!) is to be split. Overseas companies, such as Britain's Railtrack, are refusing to buy West Australian hardwoods because they are not logged sustainably. The stories go on and on. All in all it has been an extraordinary couple of years, and yet we still don't know exactly what forests will be saved, if any.

At the moment we are preparing for the renewal of logging in a pristine and glorious piece of forest called Wattle – we have spent more than a year there, we virtually know each tree and will not let them go easily. And if they do log it we will use our grief and anger to fuel our campaign even more. The terrible thing is that we only have to keep going for a few more years because then it will be all gone.....

Check out our website to keep up to date with what is happen-ing in the wild west:www.wafa.org.au

Emma and The Lorax

I went to the forest in 1997 for a weekend. Two years later, I'm still fully involved in the campaign to save our remaining old growth forests. There is a beautiful inevitability in many of our stories of how we first came to the forest. The threads run through us all and I believe without a shadow of a doubt, that there were greater forces at play than my whim for a few days off, that led me to the Giblett forest camp. I travelled right across this huge continent twice in one year, for no good reason that presented itself at the time, to arrive here.

In a time before I heeded my dreams, I was dreaming of these southwest forests. Coming from a farming and boarding school background, I found myself in a forest camp, which, had I looked before I leapt, I would never thought to be a place I'd ever call home. Two weeks after I arrived, I was sitting up a tree platform in the canopy of a karri forest. The theatre of camp was played out for me each day; geckos and birds became my confidantes; frogsong marked the dusk. All these things led me to a huge paradigm shift – I arrived at deep ecology without ever having heard of it. My experience of the tree sit allowed me to *experience* deep ecology. I had long considered the environmental predicament we have found ourselves in – sitting in the tree, this moved from my head to my heart. I had a sense of dissolving into earth systems – feeling my place in this earth and the consequence of my life in

Group pic at Swarbrick tingle forest

the outward ripples of my every choice. This was a radical shift.

The notion of self-responsibility is not one that comes easily to us. We grow up under systems of power that afford the few the authority and prestige to make decisions that do not serve the many. We are compelled from an early age to perpetuate this by competing for an illusive and illusory goal of happiness through material gain and social status. There is often a distance between our actions and their consequences. From flushing toilets to supermarkets, landfill to electric lights, we rarely pay or see the real cost of our choices. This disempowered state of affairs is a common experience for many of us. I think we have all recognised, in a sideways-glance-kind-of-way, that this is not the way forward. What to do with this knowledge when there is no real language or validation to face the necessary changes head-on?

The campaign for the south west old growth forests is huge in its scope and ambitious in the things we want to achieve. For some its about the trees, for some a particular forest, for some the downfall of government; for others its an opportunity to rebel, to 'fuck shit up '. For most, it's a million things all at once. The interesting part is integrating the myriad perspectives, agendas and worldviews into a cohesive campaign.

Non-violence is the thread that binds a lot of it together. The challenge of living the change we seek, allows many to extend their perspectives to consider that perhaps all these issues the world over, are symptoms of a greater malaise. In looking to the bigger picture, we find ourselves complicit in everything we seek to change. Non-violence asks that we look as much to change ourselves and to change the world. I make no apologies for advocating the philosophical as much as the strategic worth of non-violence. I want to be brave enough to look at how I am a part of the things I want to change. I want to break the cycle of violence, irresponsibility and disempowerment in my own life as in the rest of the world.

The commitment of this 30-year campaign to non-violence has seen this issue capture the hearts and minds of the whole state and beyond. We have reached and inspired the suburbs to action. A grassroots campaign based on the education and empowerment of people through community action has found itself on the front page, the TV and headlining as *the* election issue the government faces. This is exceedingly rare for a single green issue in the conservative heartland of W.A.

How many people believe they can change the world? How twisted has our notion of truth become, when you must dismiss my truth to assert your own? How, in these first days of the new millennium, with the huge issues we face, can we still be saying everything is **OK??** Someone *else* is looking after it!!

I see the cult of burnout, despair and cynicism to be the tragedy of activism. Somehow, the building of a community to support our actions and the work of empowering others to become involved, often runs a distant second to the urgent daily demands and chaos of being involved in a campaign. I am passionately committed to social change. This work has given me incredible experiences, skills and company I feel privileged to enjoy. It also threatens to destroy me sometimes through exhaustion, the enormity of it all and the sheer hard work that goes on, and on, and on.

My experience of this campaign has mostly been living in the forest. I have lived in forest camps where the dozers never arrived, when they came and flattened everything, and where they came after months of wait and got only a third of their logging plan through months of stopwork actions. It's one of the hardest things to fall in love with a bit of bush, only to see it unceremoniously clearfelled before your eyes.

I've always been struck by the great divide between the city and the forest. The campaign seemed largely to offer the blockades and an annual rally as the two main avenues of action. It was in Wattle forest, with our top camp right on the HWY, that we began to show the tourists and weekenders the desolation of a clearfell. The road buffer zone and tourist route does not prepare one for clearfell – perhaps nothing could. Walking 500 metres off the HWY to the clearfelled Wattle 1 coupe, the land is exposed to the elements and baked by the sun. The stunning absence of forest and the precise lines of roads and forest-edge provide a sharp relief to the tangled confusion of the coupe. The landings are piled high with the trees that used to create a closed canopy supporting an intense diversity of life. Whole trees, branches and twisted boughs are pushed into piles, ready for the burn.

Clearfill – the reality

It was out of these visits of up to 40 tourists daily, that the idea of **The Lorax** was first born. All these city based people, with city based lives, wanted in some way to do something; find out more; get active. The Perth based Conservation Council and Wilderness Society are flat out in their role as political lobbyists and interpreters of all the developments of the politics of the issue. We wanted to create a public interface, a grass roots action space and a real link to the forest camps in the city. It was with this rough mission, that we came to Fremantle to set up The Lorax.

The Lorax is a wonderful book by Dr Seuss. The wisdom of its nonsense appeals more to me each time I read it. The fundamental message of the book is that nothing is going to get better, *unless* we all make it so. The task of planting the seed and caring for its growth is placed firmly in yours and my

hands. This is perhaps the fundamental intention of this space.

Five months down the track, it's a good time to reflect. We've confounded many with our complete lack of budgets and faith in providence. A donation arrives the same day as the phone bill. People keep giving us things. In a strange twist, the yoga studio below us, thinks we're all a bunch of dole-bludging, dirty ferals who never worked a day in our lives. Interesting perspective from a yogi...

The Lorax is different every day. As much as we educate and empower the people of Perth, we also struggle with dilemmas of group dynamics, fluid leadership, chaos and the implications of those would-be anarchist activists who never understood the implicit responsibility in freedom. We're trying not to get bound by administration, trying to inspire more and more to action, and trying to effect change NOW. The forest issue is an urgent one, for only 9 per cent of our original forest (pre-European invasion) remains as old growth. There is the constant tension between the big picture – seeing how the hearts and minds of so many have been captured by this issue, and the change in all these peoples' lives – and the very harsh reality of the forest falling daily. We don't have the luxury of time for the change to occur slowly. 25 years of woodchipping has taken its toll.

This is a single green issue that has reached the suburbs, and inspired conventionally disparate aspects of society to stand together. In the face of all this, the government makes cosmetic concessions that perpetuate the conflict and pitch conservation against a potentially sustainable industry.

Perhaps with blind naivete, I believe that it can't be too much longer before we see some change in forest management in WA. Certainly, there's not too much time before we have nothing left to fight for. The deepest fear I hold, is that we may see the change in this issue, but not in others. The international 'community' would see a nuclear waste dump in the desert of WA.

The last day at Giblett forest camp – it was a real celebration, where even CALM and police were smiling

As I write this, the violence in East Timor is escalating following an overwhelming vote for independence. Even if the forest issue is resolved, what have we really achieved, if through this non-violent campaign, we saved the forests, and not inspired society to see the bigger picture? The forest provides a particularly tangible and familiar warning of issues we face as humanity. I can only hope that we take on responsibility for our actions and choices beyond the forest I love so much.

Graffiti in Freo

One that almost got away – Raja Ram

Before the next major section of this book, which focuses on a number of performance poets, some of whom are musicians, here's a bit of an interlude...

This was a meeting I had been looking forward to. Raja Ram is a man on a mission, eyes sparkling with light and delight. He wanted to tell me *everything*. Born Ron Rothfield, with a Russian mother and Scottish father, he grew up as part of an Australian Jewish family in the Melbourne of the forties and fifties.

"The moment I was born I wanted to leave. I wasn't unhappy – getting laid, sun, drink, sports cars –but I was deeply unsatisfied...it was New Year's Eve 1957 and I hopped on a ship and sailed to India and travelled through Europe. One year later found me in Ibiza and Spain, smoking dope."

Ron at about 23, in Yarra, near Melbourne in the early 60s

From then 'til now he's been a musical, spiritual and artistic traveller of the world. Classically trained in flute at the Melbourne Conservatory in the early 60s, his apprenticeship continued in New York with jazz master, Lennie Tristano.

Two years of practising and painting on the tiny Greek island of Aegina followed, and in 1968 he found himself in London with his own art shows. Notting Hill Gate, London, was to become his 'base' for the next 32 years, and it was where he met his Swami, who told him, *"You are Raja Ram. Become your name, it will give you a focus."* Some name. It means, quite literally, King-God!

And as Raja Ram, he advertised for others to join him in the band *Quintessence. "None of us were great musicians. But we communicated with each other."* Their enthusiasm and trippy bliss were infectious. Each show was one long improvisation, weaving mystical Indian threads and chants around the gently freaking-out audiences of would-be hippies. In the UK they had three top 50 albums, played 500 gigs between 1969 and 1972, and along with the likes of the Incredible String Band, Hawkwind, Caravan and Edgar Broughton, were a major part of the alternative music scene of that time. People either loved them and danced along with their eastern mysticism, or found them and their music, pre-packaged 'enlightenment'. But they were gentle hippies, and Raja even played a solo flute gig at London's celebrated Royal Albert Hall. I saw them at least four or five times. How should I know, exactly? It was all a part and parcel of the late-60s obligatory consciousness-raising trip!

Then and now

It's 1999, and I'm talking world techno and trance with Ray Castle in a suitably bohemian cafe in Sydney's Newtown area. I ask Ray who really knows what's going down in the dance scene? *"You've got to see Raja Ram,"* Ray tells me. And that's the link to this next bit...

Raja in Quintessence

It was on New Year's Eve 1988 that Raja Ram found himself partying in Goa. Connections were made. Raja began the process of reinventing himself in the world of dance-trance. *"Quintessence were jazz; improvisation; in touch with feminine energy. We asked, 'what's your being?', we invited people to invent their own religions...now is the same and different, the music is dance, is trance, is improvisation, its essence is repetitive and finding the notes opens the gates..."* From 1989 and into the future, Raja Ram has produced over 50 cd's, establishing Tip Records in 1995. He's still there playing flute, but with a new generation of perfectly recorded rhythm and sound bites. He says, *"...there are thousands around the world waiting to listen to the new music."*

On the lunchtime I met up with Raja in London, he was just back in from two weeks playing parties in Israel. In Oz, he's played a number of forest doofs and joined up with the likes of Ollie Wisdom's *Space Tribe* based in Mullumbimby. (www.spacetribe.com) Part of the attraction for Raja Ram, I suspect, is its 'undergroundness', its lack of inhibition, vitality and freedom. *"The cops hate it, the smilin', the drivin' into jungles, caves; it's not just a hippy revival..."* The use of 'natural substances' is also one of his pet subjects. He talks of shaman using 'ethnological indigenous drugs' for thousands

of years, and asks, *"how can natural things be against the law? There are 36 thousand natural things in the rainforests – these are substances which can be used pharmacologically to better ourselves. Our brain is our castle and our freedom."*

The next Tip Record parties are scheduled for the jungles and caves of Sao Paulo on the west coast of Brazil. As we talked, we listened to *Shpongle,* one of the trance albums he'd recorded with his sister company, Twisted Records. I've continued drift around to it back at home, and to other more up-beat recordings Raja has made recently such as the Ibiza

collection: *Trance de Eivissa.* The back cover blurb sounded oddly *quintessential, "...sparkling under a pagan vermillion sky where amongst acres of tattoos and trees world travellers, unravellers, shamans, laymans, the pierced, the freaks on peaks and the hip converge, zip through the night and into the dawn where the cool breeze of the ocean mingles with the warm glow of the chillums...under a zillion stars in a fantastic remote hideaway, these drug fuelled party epics will karmically cleanse and pump you up the celestial stairway to the gates of elixir!"*

Raja Ram hasn't forgotten about Australia. He told me, *"It was a great place to leave, but I keep going back. When I return I welcome the spirituality of the land – the vibe of the land."* So, Raja Ram finds himself learning new musical crafts and dodges from 22 and 23 year olds. He says he finds 'respect' for his experience. He's 59 years young, looking forwards: the next project, the next party, the next recording. He's just recording the 'Yeti', and that and 'Shpongle' are out on tour, perhaps at a cave or forest near you!

For more info about the music, or to contact Raja Ram: Tip Records (embracing the planet through sound), 92d Oxford Gardens, London W10 5UW. Tel/Fax: +44 (0) 20 8960 4880
Web: www.tip.com

The next piece forms a bridge into the substantial collection of contributions on performance poetry. 'Poetry' in Australia seems to span a wide range of word-forms. I've gone with that concept and included pieces which started life as songs as well as more conventional poems. Liz Hall-Downs touches on this theme in the following:

The alternative movement and the Australian literary scene – some personal reflections

Liz Hall-Downs

I was born in Melbourne in 1961. Unlike many in the 'alternative movement', my own entry into it was what, in Aussie terms, would be called 'arse-backwards'. A hard-working student from a stable but seriously dysfunctional middle-class family, very much the 'girl most likely to succeed' at the end of high school, I encountered a downturn in fortunes and prospects within five years which forever changed my view of the world and my own place in it.

Let me explain. At twenty I had completed two years of nursing training, had left to pursue a degree in the Arts, and saw myself in the next twenty years on a reasonably secure fast-track, nursing for money while I built a career as a writer. In 1980 there was still low unemployment and high job prospects. I had a strong work ethic, had never considered going on the dole, and my only real 'radicalism' lay in a desire to become as independent as possible from my family.

Although influenced culturally by the Baby Boomers, I wasn't looking to 'drop out'. It wasn't society, but my own devalued place within a patriarchal family structure that seemed the obvious thing to run from. Besides, I was only just starting high school when the first hippies went to Nimbin, and was too young to go to Sunbury. I never saw myself as a member of that generation. At that young age, the idea of participating in 'straight' society seemed to me to be thrilling and full of possibilities rather than oppressive.

The year I turned twenty was also the year I was diagnosed with Rheumatoid Arthritis, a condition that manifests in severe pain and inflammation as an out-of-control immune system seeks to destroy the body it inhabits. From this point I began to understand how easy it is to slip out of the mainstream and onto the fringes of society, how tenuous an individual's links to the status quo really are, and how difficult it is to jump back into that 'straight' world once one has been outside the system for any length of time.

I was unemployable, pensioned off. I needed something to do to give me some self-esteem, some sense of belonging. I became a poet. I'd been writing since childhood, but it was the discovery of the poetry reading scene that brought me out of the closet. (I learned that readings, heralding a fresh interest in orality, especially amongst the young, had begun burgeoning in the 1970's in response to few publishing opportunities for poets, slow editors who took up to a couple of years to get accepted work into print, and a literary establishment who balked at the audaciousness of what by now was being described as 'performance poetry' – an odd moniker, given that most of these 'performers' were still reading their texts onstage.)

Street Poetry venues abounded in Melbourne in the 1970's and '80's, as did readings in pubs. Though there was some crossover, these readings were of two distinct types. At the pub readings I met established poets whose work I'd admired, but was often disappointed by their behaviour. The pub readings were not easy places for young women to read at that time. Sexual harassment was rife, with the result that women were poorly represented. But it was at these readings that one met editors, publishers, movers and shakers. As I refused to tolerate this treatment, or to be excluded on the basis of my gender, and because much of my writing at this time dealt with sexual politics, I was often pilloried as a 'feminist bitch'. Ultimately, frustration with this situation produced the 'Bitchpoem', a piece which deals with these concerns and, annoyingly, has become a defining part of my public persona, despite the existence of superior work!

Street Poetry venues kept me writing and participating through these years, specifically Cafe Jammin in Middle Park. These cafe readings had a totally different vibe. As well as poets, there were hippies, oldies, rastafarians, musicians, dancers, single mothers and their kids. Some nights eighty percent of the audience would take their five minutes on the stage. It was exciting, vibrant, often amateurish, and wildly supportive. It was here that I learned to perform, to not bore the audience, to use a microphone, mix on stage, sing in public, gain confidence in my own material. Many others went through the same process. Street Poetry provided a real alternative to the pubs and the literary establishment. Its philosophical commitment to a community arts model made it inclusive rather than exclusive, it's idealism attracted free thinkers, and although a fair proportion of the work given away on the streets was not of a particularly high standard, it gave many beginning poets a start. Now established poets in the Melbourne scene who often read at Street Poetry venues in the '80's include Lauren Williams, Kerry Scuffins, Ken Smeaton, Myron Lysenko, Komninos, Lisa Jacobsen, Adrian Rawlins, and Pamela Sidney. When Gilli Smyth and Harry Williamson (Mother Gong) moved from England to Melbourne in the early 1980s, it was the Street Poets that appreciated them. (Conversely, I once saw them at a 'literary gathering' being told to 'get that synthesiser off the stage', as though musical backing was some form of sacrilege!) The rainbow region contingent (such as Nimbin's Silly Symphony and Gong's Daevid Allen) made regular forays down south, and the Melbourne-Mullumbimby connection was born. Groups of poets from Armidale also came to the venues. The connection with the alternative lifestyle movement was always very strong.

We did marvellous things in those years. A 'poets village' was a regular fixture at the Down-To-Earth festivals, offering 24 hour poetry to all comers and a ready-made audience for the first-timers. In 1986, we staged 'Poets for Peace' and showcased over fifty poet performers as well as bands, peace groups, and the obligatory open stage. We did countless gigs at fundraisers and gatherings for like-minded groups, and ran poetry stages at community festivals and fetes. Thom the World Poet, with no arts funding, ran around like a dynamo, convincing people to get involved, to share, to have fun with it all, to stop being so darned serious about their precious writing. Throughout the decade, we had strong links with

groups such as Friends of the Earth, Movement Against Uranium Mining, Down-To-Earth, the Unemployed Worker's Union, the permaculture movement, the Squatter's Union, Animal Liberation, and Ananda Marga.

By the time I left Melbourne for the rainbow region in 1991, changes had occurred. Some poets were starting to really 'perform' their work without the prop of a written text, the slam movement was beginning in America and regular slams sprung up at the Esplanade Hotel in St Kilda. The divide between the pub and cafe venues lessened, and more gender balance was achieved. Thom left Australia to take up residence in the USA. The name 'Street Poetry' still crops up at certain venues, but the movement as it was does not really exist now, except in people's memories.

On the North Coast, I met performance poets whose background was more in rock and roll than in writing. I performed with the Stand-Up Poets through 1993-4. This was an enjoyable period, but our shows brought up the inevitable discussion in the local press about 'performance' versus 'writing'. The difficulty is that a good performer can get away with a bad poem in an 'entertainment-oriented' context, while really excellent poets can be overlooked simply because they lack performance skills. My concerns about this issue led me to get involved with other groups in the area, such as 'POWEM' (Poet Women Mullumbimby), and the Pink Dot readings in Brunswick Heads, which provided a more attentive, listening environment. I also started teaching creative writing classes through Adult Education, encouraging my students to participate in local readings. Since 1994, I've been doing 'performance poetry' and music with my partner, Kim Downs, as *Fit of Passion'*. But because we are primarily writers, we continue to do more conventional readings and to publish poetry and fiction.

Now, after years of self-publishing, we've both landed contracts with a publisher in Victoria, a sign that if you hang in there for long enough, even the radicals on the fringes eventually become acceptable to the mainstream!

A few years ago, we moved over the border into Queensland, something we would never have considered doing in the 1980's. In those years a very conservative government and a corrupt and intolerant police force drove the non-conformists out of Brisbane. A whole generation of young people moved south, rather than put up with the continual harassment that their dreadlocks, tattoos, mohawks, nose rings, and preference for marijuana attracted. Since the Fitzgerald Inquiry into police corruption in 1989 exposed what was happening and precipitated the removal of the offenders from power, Brisbane's arts community has exploded. Inner-city areas such as West End and Fortitude Valley now have a creative, multicultural feel. The city council employs four full-time Arts Officers and the level of state government funding for arts projects in relation to population is higher than in Victoria or New South Wales. The poets

Liz and Kim

and writers here are a refreshing lot. They well remember the days when free speech or appearance were dangerous behaviours, and don't take the current climate for granted.

In the face of continuing illness and poverty through these years, the oral poetry movement has given me a sense of achievement, of involvement in a community. The friends I've made through these years have combined to form a network that has helped Kim and I to travel on very little money, providing gigs, PR, and accommodation throughout Australia and the USA. At the time of writing, researchers are making progress in treating my disease, and I'm hopeful my health will improve as access to these new treatments become available. Things are looking up! I love my life as a writer, and the occasional forays into performance help me to judge and refine my work. I wouldn't want to be anything else. Or, as we say here in Oz, *'I wouldn't be dead for quids'!*

Liz Hall-Downs

The Performance Poets

Australia has gained a justly proud international reputation for the quality and diversity of its performance poets. These are not recluses. These are women and men who are as 'in yer face' as many of the audiences for whom they do their words. As one reviewer wrote about the 'Writers of the Storm' group who, are well-represented here, *"This is not poetry to be savoured in wistful repose. This is stand up knock down stuff to split your sides in laughter or rage. Sexual politics, social politics, political politics; this is entertainment that jumps from page to stage, from comedic to the satiric to the deadly serious."*

Meeting David Hallett was an experience. One minute I'm sitting opposite this rather serious man, drinking coffee and explaining the nature of this book. The next minute David beckons me outside. *"You like Bob Dylan, Mook says…"* *"Yes, along with a lot of other musicians and bands,"* I replied. And, off he goes. His Bob Dylan full-on rant, right in *my* face! I could see (and feel) exactly why this guy had won the Poetry Olympics *twice*! He's also well known as mainman in the Stand Up Poets! and author of *War and Peaces.*

David Hallett in Nimbin

In Oz, the dividing line between poets and musos is so thin that sometimes you can't see it at all. Take Daevid Allen, for instance. Founder member of Soft Machine, front man of

Gong, he has had many personas: Bert Camembert, Virgin Dingo, Jah Am, or just Daevid the Alien! I was at university in Canterbury, England, in the late 1960s, and in some of the same seminar groups as wizard-hatted, mystical guitarist, Steve Hillage, who was then playing with Australian, Daevid, in Gong. Thirty years later, when I met Daevid over in Oz, it was a quiet, courteous, tea-sipping Alien who told me how he had seen himself much more as a poet in the last fifteen years, with his stand up performances in front of the Poetry Wall. But recently, Europe has beckoned the Daevid of Planet Gong back for successful tours. No mention of floating teapots whatsoever! He's also continued to be involved in performance with the likes of Thom the World Poet (more in a moment) and Mark Robson from Kangaroo Moon. In this collection, Daevid has provided a vitriol laced slice of his acerbic wit – dedicated to, and about, the ordinary Australian. Try pinning up a copy in your local bar!

Liz Hall-Downs and Kim Downs perform individually and collectively and get their pieces published in both Australia and America. *Fit of Passion* published by the Queensland Office of Arts is their most recent collection. I read Liz's *Bitchpoem* lying in my sleeping bag at Mook and Shanto's Bangalow dwelling. I immediately decided that it belonged in this book for its stridency, its acid humour and feminist attitude. It took me a while to make contact with Liz – actually through Doug Broad, whom I'd met in Brisbane's West End. (Doug's contribution on Mount Oak community appears near the beginning of this book).

Daevid Allen at the Poetry Wall

Liz and I swopped quite a few e-mails as we became acquainted. At first, Liz thought I wanted to use her work as a representation of the Rainbow Region scene. As she told me, *"(Bitchpoem emerged) from Melbourne's urban alternative culture. My own involvement with alternatives began with the Melbourne Street Poets (SP) throughout the 1980s, and extended to contact with groups such as Friends of the Earth, Ananda Marga and the peace movement. What made Street Poetry different was that it was a community-based, open-all-comers open stage, with no literary 'star system', but equality for all viewpoints and levels of skill. Many well-known performance poets in Oz came up through the Street Poets movement; it's arguable that many of these writers would not have surfaced in the mainstream without the early support provided by S.P."*
As we got to know one another, Liz became a valued 'networker', helping me to contact other contributors.

Kim Downs says of his work, *"I grew up in America. Some of my work reflects this. Most often I attempt to write serious pieces but usually I fail. My work is infested with whimsy. I haven't found a cure as yet."* Based on what I've seen of Kim's work I hope that he doesn't try too hard! I'm pleased it is here for you to enjoy.

Thom, the World Poet is probably the key figure in Australian's street poetry scene. That's very much the view of Daevid Allen and Liz Hall-Downs. Ken Smeaton, editor of *Nightclub Poetry,* described Thom as:
"Melbourne's best known poet. Creator of the STREET POETRY movement. A maestro motormouth. Can create epics on the spot about anything. Notorious distributor of STREET POEMS. Conqueror of Swanston Street. Colourful. Naughty. A brilliant UNSALEABLE STAR."

I've included some of his work in this section. Here's Thom's re-telling of the early days of the Melbourne scene.

Thom in full flow at Lismore, 1998

herstory of street poetry – potted poetry memories

The countercultural realities of Melbourne in the 70s and 80s: poetry was on the streets and we were part of it – handing out thousands of free sheets of anyone's poetry (at our own expense) for some 15 years – at first outside Princes Bridge Station from 5.30 a.m., then when the City Circle cut out pedestrian traffic – we moved to the Bourke Street Mall at lunchtimes (12 to 2 p.m.) handing out poetry for the sheer joy of it! Venues sprang up –too numerous to remember – but witnesses and participants will recall CAFE JAMMIN, the RAGLAN CAFE in North Melbourne – the OUTPOST INN (poetry hosted by Ken Smeaton) the BUTTERFLY and the TIGER readings at Carringbush Library in Richmond (with CARMEL BIRD), as well as LIVING ROOM THEATRE on Saturday nights in Bridge Road Richmond – these were full scale poetry and music professional productions featuring Daevid Allen from Gong in RETURN OF THE ALIEN, and Gilli Smyth in FITZROY STREET ANGELS – we handed out poetry at rock concerts and performed at festivals in POOR TOMS POETRY BAND – begun at the Rainbow Festival at Nimbin and generated at the original COMMUNE in North Melbourne, which, when closed by its founder, BOB (MUD) McMahon, spawned the NEW COMMUNE, VINCE and WENDYS in South Melbourne and THE SUNFLOWER in North Fitzroy. Poets such as Daevid Allen, set up the original CAFE JAMMIN which lasted 5 years, and was followed by COREYS – itself a poetry venue right up to 1997, mixed it with an OPEN STAGE which allowed POETS FOR PEACE to mix with the Nimbin poets down south – OPEN, LIVING, FREE were the keynotes for all STREET POETRY enterprises. STREET POETRY erupted in Adelaide, Tamworth (with DAN BYRNES), Sydney, and Armidale – but the epicentre was always Melbourne with its horrendous weather and indoor culture – poetry was, and is, perfect for interior meditations. Improvisations with music and dance were the norm and the basis of POOR TOM'S POETRY BAND which allowed anyone to play in the band and never practised, only performed. Evidence of STREET POETS exists in the EPHEMERALIA collection at the Victorian State Library, and in the individual memories of surviving poets – such as Liz Hall-Downs and Kenneth Grahame Smeaton, Gilli Smyth, Daevid Allen, and Anita Sinclair (who runs the WORKHOUSE THEATRE in Collingwood as of now). This is a chapter in the cultural life of Australia – a precursor to the present revival of verbal culture. Ask the survivors-they were there. Poetry lives!
THOM THE WORLD POET

"In times like these, it is helpful to remember that there have always been times like these."
Paul Harvey

Then there's the Mookster and Shanto, whose words resound through many pages of this collection. And here are a few more of them; words from some of their songs, which in themselves tell the lowdown and upbeat tales of alternative Australia, almost as well as the man himself. And it was through Mook that I first saw poems by David Heilpern (Walter is included here). David is now making a name for himself as a reforming magistrate. He and Steve Sorrensen (She took the stash) were members of the 'Writers of the Storm' group with Liz Hall-Downs.

Dennis Aubrey, the smartarse songwriter belongs in this category as well. His wry little observations are wonderful vignettes. Many years on from his debut on the streets of Sydney in 1972, Dennis is still determined *"not to go back to working for the man."* You might even catch up with him and the Graffiti Band at the Excelsior Hotel in Surry Hills, singing songs which he claims, *"write themselves."*

the ordinary australian

Daevid Allen 99

oh lawd save me
please save me lawd
it's sunday
& it's 1999

please....
save me from the ordinary australian

i don't see too many round here thank god
i thought i saw a couple in woolworths once
sometimes you see em on tv ads
there's a few up the road that try pretty hard
but not quite hard enough
do you mista tuckerbag?

i cant stand
ordinary australians

ordinary decent hardworking tax paying australians
honest decent red neck right wing money grovelling
earth flattening
sea poisoning
koorie hating
anti land rights
bigoted racist xenophobic
ordinary decent
hard working australians

ordinary decent hard working
culturally challenged
australians...
...can somebody
essentially
oil the rusty cringe?

but
doncha love em to death?
those ordinary decent
small time
insensitive. stupid. dim witted

arrogant. aggressive. lying bad tempered. shit centred
over paid. over fed. lazy spoilt brat
hard working tax paying australians
with their rational national excuses
for ripping the soul out of public rainforests
to make exquisite japanese wrapping paper
& then pocketing the yen snarling:
hands off my money
you thieving barstards
or i'll get you busted for smoking hope

oh baby
doncha love em wherever they are?
those ordinary decent hardworking battlers
mouths stuffed with
pavlovs pavlova
fingers stickin to the script of the hundredth monkey-sayin:
she'll be right &
no worries mate &
fuck you jack i'm ok

marching like packer-programmed lemmings
off cliffs into b grade soapies
resenting all excellence
mowing down the tall poppies without even knowing about
the opiate of the people

hey
get that barstard off the mike
get the fuckwit outa sight
just get him out.....

yeah right!
bring on the spin!
so i say fuck you too donald bradman
& sporting heroes of the fourth reich
you got the answer have ya?
just bring on the spin bowlers with their ugly mouths. & then:
bring on the
sports tonight
spin doctors
to spin us all out
till we're wrecked on
the recreational drugs

you prop up by prohibition
addicted to the romance of death by hard work
hard drink hard drugs
hard eyed with national pride
yeah
i'm an ozzie mate an my mates are too
so if you're not an ozzie
wot are ya?

to this i say:
australia
take yr mango flavoured condom off
you wont catch anything except a
not so flash reflection
of yourselfish
no
you wont catch anything you haven't got already
except the sad s'truth cobber-mate-bluey...
that there is no honest
decent hardworking australian

waaaaaaaaake up australia!
this is not your land
your castles made of sand
this place was never called australia
we ripped it off
& that's cool dude
that's something to fight for...ay?
so we can use it up
& burn it out
before the kids get a chance to taste it
& waste it
even more
yeah! we are people of
no country no nationality
no pride
simply worried world citizens
with bad taste in clothes &
bad breath in bed
(& that's why i aught to keep
my big mouth shut) she said

so come on
you ordinary decent

aussie battlers
do the only thing you do well
beat up the poet!
that'll show him won't it?

cum on ozie cum on
stick the boot in
while he's down

that's the way we grinners
win in sport
stick the boot in
even when he's history

that'll teach him
to tell the truth
in a free country

Bitchpoem
(or it's really quite a compliment)
Liz Hall-Downs

For five years my brother forgot my name:
"Do the dishes, bitch".
At seventeen I got straight A's:
"Unmarriageable bitch".
Equal rights in conversation?
"Loudmouthed bitch".
Intellectual argument?
"Smart-assed bitch".
Justifiable complaint?
"Troublemaking bitch".
Embrace the spiritual?
"Irrational bitch".
Cry when you're sad?
"Over-emotional bitch".
 Confront the past with therapy?
"Neurotic bitch".
Admit ignorance?
"Stupid bitch".
Say it's unfair?
"Complaining bitch".
Don't want 'looking after'?
"Ungrateful bitch".
A poem about a sleazebag?
"Man-hating bitch".
Pissed off at injustice?
"Aggressive bitch".
Get your hands off my breasts:
"Frigid bitch".
Sexual feelings?
"Bitch on heat".
Stand up to backstabber?
 "Nasty bitch".
Political power?
"Unfeminine bitch".

Tired of voluntary work?
"Selfish bitch".
Work hard for advancement?
"Competitive bitch".
Put on weight?
"Fat bitch".
Say no at the nightclub?
"Stuck-up bitch".
Don't dress like a lady?
"Ugly bitch".
Prefer the company of women?
"Lesbian bitch".
Write about women's lives?
"Feminist bitch".
My favourite coffee cup?
"Life's a bitch
and so
am I".

My Hippy Lover

Brendan Hanley and Julie Oliver

As I sat down one evening, in the old Rainbow Café
A sad-eyed hippy waitress, to me these words did say
"I see that you are a hippy, and not just a yobbo nong
Coz nobody but a hippy drinks his coffee from a bong!"

My lover was a hippy, there's none like him today
If you put hash-oil on it, he could smoke a bale of hay
He never shaved his whiskers from off his hippy hide
He'd grow 'em long and stash his bong and all his dope inside

My lover came to see me on a rainy Nimbin day
He breathed his bongy breath on me and blew my brains away
The coppers came from Lismore, to spill some hippy blood
My lover backed his kombi out and splattered them with mud

The cops all swore to bust him, by planting him with drugs
They giggled as they set him up, like little schoolboy thugs
They planted him with acid, they planted him with speed
They planted him with hash and smack and half a K of seeds

They filled his van with supergrass, his pockets all with pills
And followed him as he drove home to his cabin in the hills
They waited for an hour or two, then fired a warning shot
But when they busted in they found he'd dropped the bloody lot

His eyeballs they were pinholes, his brain cells were on fire
And as they watched he floated up, and drifted higher and higher
He floated out the window, and up the waterfall
And as the cops fired shots at him, he chundered on 'em all

He drifted over Nimbin, into the starry night
And somewhere near the Southern Cross, he disappeared from sight
And so I lost my lover, and sing this sad sad song
And here I wait till someone drinks his coffee from a bong!

Walter

David Heilpern

Hello my name is Walter, I'm a gentle new age fellow
I'm soft and sweet and kind, cuddly and mellow
I never raise my voice, or tell a sexist joke
I never go out drinking with the normal ocker blokes

I'm always very skinny with some hair upon my face
I'm a very useful person for my wife about the place
I smile when washing dishes, nappies, floors and windows too
I always say something useful – when I am spoken to

For me sex is not power, it is sharing warmth and love
I like to be underneath as well as up above
I never come too early, I never come too fast
If at all possible, I like to come...last

But when I go to sleep at night I have these awful dreams
Filled with hate and death and grime and lengthy gruesome screams
And I'm always strangling women, with strength and guts and glee
And I'm fighting off the bitches who are trying to kill me
And the fields they are thick with torn female limbs
And my old school mates are egging me on to win to win to win
We depart to a desert isle in a big old macho truck
Drink beer all day and every second word is 'fuck'

But my dream is interrupted by a mournful little whimper
And I get out of bed to nurse our child in dressing gown and slipper
I hold his face against the breast of my sleeping wife
And I wonder at the glory, of my new age gentle life

What do You Do?
Kim Downs

Whenever women ask me: "What do you do?"
I feel like I've been tossed a hand-grenade
– with the pin pulled –
and I have to toss it back,
before it explodes in my face,
peels back the skin from my life,
exposing nerve and ripping vein
until my very essence spurts and flows across the floor;
for all to examine, tread in – later –
wipe from their shoes
– or maybe – stir about a little
with the stick of their curiosity.
"What do you do?"
Such a loaded question from a woman.
Oh!
You mean, what is my status and probable income?
so you can determine what sub-culture I run with,
my likely views on abortion,
my sexual proclivities,
am I worth making?
or can I be dismissed as: "not a very good catch".
"What do you do?"
Well, I sleep, I eat, I consume, I excrete,
often, I read, I write, I laugh, I cry,
I'm prone to fart under the bedcovers.
If not watched carefully,
I might belch, scratch my balls, stare at your boobs,
and proposition you later in the parking lot!
This is how I feel whenever women ask me:
"What do you do?"
To be perfectly honest,
this is how I feel whenever anyone asks me:
"What do you do?"
So don't bloody ask me what I do!
(and I won't ask you.)

D2E
Thom the World Poet

He wears big badges like his eyes believe them
He lives in an op shop disposal store world
He drives a car bomb with the original rust
He lives in a communal household

He shops at the markets for fresh vegetables
He's never got money 'cause he's on the dole
And he gets around on his bicycle
And he lives in a communal household

He's learned how the Poor Box is supposed to work
He's been on the protest (police tore his shirt)
He's been photographed, fingerprinted, arrested and worse
He lives in a communal household

He subscribes to 3CR and Friends of the Earth
He goes to the Confest run by Down To Earth
He's all for dolphins, no uranium, and home birth
And he lives in a communal household

All his friends have money and they flaunt their style
He goes to the cafes when he needs to smile
His world is rich and deep and wise
And he lives in a communal household

('D2E' previously appeared in *Nightclub Poetry*, Edited by Ken
Smeaton, Street Poetry Lab, 1989.)

A Potted History of a Day in the Life

David Hallett

and it came to pass on the 8th moon
of the 72nd year of the 20th century
of the most published god,
that the conservative government
(that would not conserve)
fell,
and the house of Gough did rule .
the land of milk and wheat and sheep-dip,
and they did give the 'nyet' to the Viet war
and they did fly home on wings of petrol
their troubled sons from the
jungles of blood and herbicides
back to the bosom and the beer of their suburbs,
but for many
the bosom had withered on
the credit card of desire,
and the cake of ambition and career tasted of
toxin and carcinogen and boredom;
of a sudden did flow
from the river of the Aquarian jug
scouts and ambassadors of Dunstan
and Allen and Peter Stuyvesant,
who did come upon the village of Nimbin
in the valley of Mulgum
in the dark age of shattered trees and
slaughtered beef and banana spray
and inbred feudal lords,
and the scouts did call and trumpet through the land
of this company of rainbow power, of this
one alternative way

that coursed and curled their clan from the towns and the city-
smoke/
and they supp'd upon the sacred mushroom
and slept face-first in-the dung;
'twas a band of gypsies
playing in the rain
and they gave the seed unto each other

and they filed the government papers
and they moved in cars and vans and sandals
and barefoot and bare-breasted
upon the land,
some came running
gladly, or madly bent,
changing names and colours and gods
changing the guards
into grass castle kings and herbal flings, a free
flight of raining forest
a moondance of market days
a flood and fire and frost,
the cascade of sleep
the breasting of babies
over the hills
of the faraway tree;

and in the time they turned to find the
tweezers to tug the tick from the
tip of their dick
they had children, and children's children
that grew a coat of many colours about them
that waxed in the old wave of their
waning Aquarian waters
that washed and fed the child
that poured the life in the day
of a day in the life of Nimbin.

After Mook suggested that I get in touch with Dennis Aubrey, I did just that. Mook had described Dennis to me as *"one of Australia's foremost busker/songwriter/minstrel type people."* Like the other poets and songwriters in this book, Dennis tells stories from the worlds and lives he inhabits. Here's his rant. As Dennis said to me, *"isn't email an incredible communication culture?"* As in the rest of the poetry in this section, I've left his words pretty much as he presented them to me. It feels the right thing to do, somehow.

dennis aubrey – smartarse songwriter

i was at the original nimbin festival in 1973. i spent several months up there, but most of my time since then has been more of an urban existence. my story is mostly concerned with the history of the effort to make street music legal. in 1978 mook and shanto were doing it in sydney while i was doing it in adelaide with chris aronsten who now lives in lilian rock. i remained, pushing that issue after chris fled adelaide with warrants outstanding. by 1984 i had spent 40 days in adelaide jail.

since then i have been concerned with songwriting which addresses our life here in australia. and without trying too hard and sounding contrived, i try to sing in our own accent, as distinct from that typical vaguely american accent which most english and australian singers seem to use. [mook is an example of someone who can sing in our real voice].

as a street singer i met a lot of characters that needed to be celebrated or at least recognised, so i have songs like 'the bag lady's waltz' about dorothy who was always upstaging the buskers down on circular quay and all over sydney. at the time i was really struggling to make a living and her dancing would distract the attention of my audience. i enjoyed her character but many times i wished she'd go away so i could earn my next meal. after I didn't see her anymore i realised how much i missed her and wrote this song:

dorothy wears all her dresses at once and she rotates them all every couple of months
but she would never say she is poor cause the salvation army has always got more.
dance, dance, dorothy dance. i've got a guitar, but she hears

an orchestra
dance, dance, dorothy….dance and your spirit will be….freeeee!

and 'westpac girl' is about the culture shock between an alternate lifestyle person and a young woman working in a bank.

she's a westpac girl, she comes from new zealand
she lives in bondi, she's on her way to england
she's giving me the eye, but i've got a feein'
she'd be better off to try to find a westpac guy

me and my mate sing for a living
we stay up late and we sleep till eleven
we're both over thirty but we're not overweight
it's not that we're gay, it's that we're not quite straight

i have one about my six months of busking in new york in 1989. it addresses the feelings one has when one is away from their home country [i should say that i am not in any way a nationalist but i do think we should all be proud to represent our own little corner of the physical and/or psychic universe]. the punch line/title is inspired by the positioning of the international date line in the mid pacific. i often used to annoy the americans by pointing out that *"it's always tomorrow in sydney"*.

some of my songs fit into the realm of alternate psychological analysis like 'baggage'.

she's got the venus de milo smile,
she's got the beauty, the brains and the style
she would be perfect in every respect
a total goddess, except for the fact she's got baggage, a ton of baggage
she's got more baggage than the moscow circus on tour

he's got the biceps, he's got the pecs
he's a machine that was built for sex
and he's intelligent, he's as sharp as a tack
but what's on his mind, down the back he's got baggage, excess baggage
he's got more baggage than the army when they're going to war

*probably something that got passed on from grandfather to
father to son
he's got a complicated mind like a maze, you could get lost in
there for days and days.*

on a more positive note my libran view of universal truth which
is designed to be sceptic-proof goes like this

*anything is possible
feel free to dream
that is my gospel
that is what i believe
anything is possible
but nothing is guaranteed*

*you can not always get what you want
but you can get what you need
it's an infinite universe we're in
imagine the possibilities......*

*you can be anything you want to be
but you can only be what you are
you can go anywhere that you can see
use your imagination set yourself free
from the limitations of what you can not perceive
cause anything is possible but nothing is guaranteed*

i have in mind writing a song which is about what happened
when i was in america in 89. i finally got to see the grateful
dead. i had heard freaks saying *"there is nothing like a grateful
dead concert".* having experienced it, i can now say that
musically they are nothing special in my opinion, a little too
musically floppy and poorly defined for me. but the freak show
which follows them around is amazing. they [the deadheads,
not the band] adopted me as the court jester for the four cities
that i stayed on the tour, buffalo, new york, philadelphia and
washington d.c. they pull nearly a hundred thousand people a
night! one show in buffalo, four in new york, and two in philly
and d.c. about five thousand people followed them from city to
city on their summer tour. they camp in the parking lot of the
baseball stadium in kombis and buses. there is a thing that
happens whereby those who only have tickets for the stands
want to get onto the baseball pitch so that they can get to
where the real deadhead action is. about twenty or so

deadheads will get together and make a mass leap over the
fence. the security guys can only catch one or two and the
others get away. when i was in washington d.c. at the rfk
stadium a guy got done by the security guy. the security guy
[let's call him dwayne] was a big beefy football player making
some spare cash tackling dead heads as they came over the
fence. one guy [let's call him leaf] got tackled so hard by this
big boof that he ended up in hospital with a broken collar bone.
his girlfriend [let's call her sunflower] reacted by taking a
running leap at dwayne. not to punch him, as you might
expect, but to throw her arms and legs around him in a flying
embrace. she planted a big wet kiss on him and it took him a
good ten or fifteen seconds to disentangle himself from her
embrace. he then returned to his gig, standing tough, flexing
muscles and chewing gum. for a while anyway. after about an
hour he was seen to be acting in a very uncharacteristic
manner, eyes glazed and gazing, mouth open in an expression
of ongoing amazement, somewhat lacking in balance generally. no prizes for guessing the nature of sunflower's revenge.
so i have had in mind 'the ballad of dwayne and sunflower' or
'sunflower's revenge' or something like that.

She took the stash, man...
S.Sorrensen

She took the stash, man...
I couldn't believe it,
She took the stash...
She took it, I found the shovel on the ground,
The stash hole dug up and no stash to be found,
She musta took it when she split last night
I don't know why – oh yeah, I do – we had this fight...

"I can't do that!" she'd made me shout,
"If I go straight, I'll freak right out!'
"Well, you'll have to choose," she said, *"Between me and
the grass,*
Or you'll end up in jail, with the law up yer arse."

"Oh, come on," I said, *"You need a joint,*
Let's not argue, what's the point?
Sure, relationships are heavy, lovers can he thugs,
It's a scary scenario...that's why we got drugs."

She took the stash, man, not to mention my heart,
Now I'm getting quite stressed, I've ripped the house apart,
Looking for a roach or an old bong I could lick,
While she's probably on the coast – selling my stash on tick!

She won't divvy it up right, she'll probably give it away,
to some spacious young hippie who just wants to get laid,
She'll get totally out of it and then into it with this guy –
She'll get soooo friendly, she'll let him come inside!

She took the stash, man,
She coulda took the car...
She took the stash.
Oh God what a mess when love's like this,
No sex, no stash, no bucks for piss,
I'm sorry, I'll get married I'm that desperate,
To get my stash back and smoke the rest of it.

But if she comes back and the stash is all gone,
I'll pack up my glad bags, my scales and my bong,
And I'll say, *"Goodbye sweetheart, there's not much hope,*
That we could be happy without my dope..."

Don't go near the water baby daughter
Brendan Hanley and Julie Oliver

CHORUS
Don't go near the water baby daughter
Mind the stairs and see that you don't catch cold
Better go off to school
And learn to read like a useful tool
And enjoy your Coca Cola like you're told, like you're told
And enjoy your Coca Cola like you're told

Send you to a State School like your brother
Learn to be as grey as a uniform
Learn to fight and strive
And take your place in the nine to five
'Cause that's the only reason why you're born, you're a pawn
That's the only reason why you're born

Gotta learn to smoke tobacco like your sisters
Cigarettes cost higher every day
And you can see where your money goes
Watching all the armies grow
With the tax you pay as you smoke your life away
Hear me say
With the tax you pay as you smoke your life away

Chorus

Learn to drink Bacardi with your Smirnoff
Southern Comfort's heaven for your soul
Drink up every day
And watch your sweetness slippin' away
While you make your little body sick and old
It takes a hold
While you make your little body sick and old

See that you marry a doctor or a lawyer
Never seen one with a hungry look like me
And drive your Mercedes Benz
And swing at the bar with your trendy friends
Learning how to think from your magazines
Such bad scenes
Learning how to think from your magazines

Chorus

Keep away from all them bad musicians
And don't go bringin' no longhairs to the door
Dig them boys in suits
Looking like bowls of plastic fruit
While their daddies plan to send 'em off to war
It's what they're for
While their daddies plan to send 'em off to war

Chorus

Rainbow Rabbit
David Hallett

Merry-go-round the forest
dusty hippies wild-dreaming caravans
watching compost walls –
& the logging trucks roll
past flapping plastic windows –
beast turns turtle turns beast turns bored
in a heartbeat
changing channels
changing tyres in a mud grumble;
seed-planting a jungle bog
nit picking snakes & ticks
blowfly blow & helicopters sniffing drugs;
paradise birds startle
waving into sunset showers:
the last rainbow fades the mountain
& twilight crashes the valley –
fresh dripping terraces of flowers & greens breathe
into night.

The car breaks down/the town wakes up friday
driving drink & drugs:
forest wetbacks/rural debutantes/dogface & the hippie.
Farmer Smith & Black & Brown/storekeepers!
barefoot natives;
& the black cracking leathers of gypsy-junkies:
changing bandages & bandanas
changing small change into broken veins
all rubbing together in the front bar
& sing & hit the drum/fix the car & get out!
Back into the meanwhile...

Old gumboots of fried rice/boiled rice/veggies & rice
buckets of lentils/buckets of rain
roaring down the roof –
mould creeping 'cross the kitchen wall
mould & white ants through the old guitar,
& the slush of red roads
breaking hearts & cars,
fevering cabin families
trapped in strawberry fields forever
way down the wet gully of palms & gums –

& river below
an ocean of mist.

Hurrying through sleep into heat-glazing days
backwards into town/blowing dirt
creek-diving valley-interfacing visitors again &
the garden:
Somewhere between
in the mirror of deep green mountains
(& the children rabbit 'round us all
in bounds of spring heatwaving into summers & gone)
the art of just being lucky
of just being, man
of just
The art.

lessons my father taught me
Liz Hall-Downs

my old man always said
"if you can pour a good beer
and make a decent cup of tea
you'll be okay"

my mother taught me
how to cook, dust, clean, wash, iron
and anything else to do with
serving men. she said
it's the way to catch one.

the man she caught gave her
twenty bucks a week, enough,
he said, to feed and clothe
five children (and i know now
it's not enough, even allowing
for inflation)

but he could pick a horse
(twice a year)
and he could pour a beer
(at the expense of his career)
and he knew how to fight
for his life when in a corner
and he knew how to win the hearts
of women...and his daughter.

now
i pour beers that look like icecreams
and my tea is weak as bat's piss.

My Father
Thom the World Poet

My father's ghost still haunts me.
I exorcise him daily.
He the harsh tyrant of my youth,
the ceiling of my fears, the limits
of my loving. The backhand violence
no longer exists. When last seen, he
was a white and wizened wizard.
Age had brought no wisdom. Just lip cancer,
false teeth and baldness, and a deafness
to others speaking. He had shrivelled
like plastic on heat. A spider in
a frying pan. His pumped up body deflated.
Soggy as an old balloon.
His eyes had lost that spark that once
had diamond drilled me to test
my true metal, broken bitted obselete
machinery. The boss in him has resigned
controlling. Is now a servant of
its service. He was once center of existence
now just another lonely planet.
The heat that furnaced my growing
and shaped and formed my fears
is now a rust pile of pities,
swimming pool of tears.
It is not love, nor even respect,
but curious as an animal sniffs
a recent death, twitching though still
in skin, a reminder in him,
of my fragilities. One day I will be he
who mumbles more or less, and talks
to few with common sense, just picking
up my pension. He is my advance weather
warning of a cyclone coming, that will
test my bomb shelter heart in the
world wars of emotion. No bicycle
of growing in this wheel chair of age.
Just rusted eyes, lost chances, regrets
and forthcoming silences.
Nothing to respect in this stripping
of a process. No uniqueness.
Just a falling, like an old man's trousers.

Hiding nothing much, just salivating.
His mind's bat flips away
to chase a moon somewhere. He is empty
wickets in a wide green field.
The players all gone home, leaving him
mumbling of his childhood oppressive father,
and all the things he could not be.
Having to play head of the family.

('My Father' first appeared in *Made In Australia: Poems by Thom the World Poet*, 1998.)

Leave it in the ground!
Brendan Hanley and Julie Oliver

My name is Jonah the Whale
Out on the oceans I sail
Out where the wind and the waves say you've nothing to save
But yourself!
You're fouling the sea and the air
And you're laying the rainforest bare
And you buy and you sell
In your man-powered hell
But we all have a story to tell

Chorus
Don't spread Uranium 'round (Leave it in the ground!)
Don't cut the rainforest down!
Don't spread Uranium 'round (Leave it in the ground!)
Don't cut the animals down!
And for your freedom's sake
Don't let men take
The power to burn us all down
Leave it in the ground!
Leave it in the ground!
Leave it in the ground!

Turn all your minds to the land
Give Mother Nature a hand
Head for the country and run free and easy
And see how the New People stand

Throw all your shackles away
Live for the moment today
Get back to living
And loving and giving
And turning the opposite way

Chorus

Labels Of Babels
David Hallett

there's hippies & yuppies & greenies
and hippies & yuppies & greenies...
and hippies & yuppies & greenies & Kooris & junkies &.
drinkies,
there's smokers & tokers & dope-thieves & jokers & mopers!
there's ball-kickers & ball-hitters & ball-tearers with pit bull
terriers.

there's drummers & dancers & dip-sticks & dubbos
yobos & touros & musos & preggos & embryos,
journos & photos & lezzos & homo sapiens & hetero sapiens
...& never-for-their-lives gonna be sapiens!

there's stoned builders & mud-brickers & organic-effluent-
powered
plumbers 'n joiners, metal men & amazons...
and the goddess in the kitchen.

there's painters & poets (thank god!) & potters
and butchers-&-bakers-&-candle-stick-makers
cobblers-&-weavers-&-wood-turners-&-tailors,
mad hatters & mask-makers & face painters
and glass-bead-game shakers.

there's yogis & bubbas & babies & swamis
and shaman & she-men & sufis & surfers & skaters & bikers,
and feral & herbals & healers & dealers & wankers & yankies &
jappies
& gerries & frenchies &. pommies & mad Irish (to be sure/to be
sure)
to be shi'ite to be shiva to be shipwrecked!
to be washed-out/watered-down/unemployed/uninspired
to be youth (yuk!) to be a teenager (worse still),
and secondary/primary/infant/pre school/day care/after care
...careless carefree without-a-care!
to be unheard/unknown/just to be seen & smelt & past-on-the-
street...
a pedestrian a shopper a robber a dobber a copper a crim
a loiterer a waiter a talker a laser-tongued-lizard...
an outpatient a schizo a dipso a zombie a runaway,
to be a coffee stop/to be froth...

and farmers & grazers & graders & dozers,
horticos & aggros/to be a shooter...to be shot!

there's cyber punks & funkies & goblins & gothics & rastas &
rats,
day-trippers & night-trippers & trapped-in-their-trips
tripped-out trippy-trekkers & turned-on tantric tale-tellers,
divine-lighters & cloud-liners & takeaway diners...

there's ex-lawyers & ex-doctors & ex-priests
and ex-exes & just exes...
and ex-teachers & ex-dropouts & ex-krishnas
and we all await the ex-police commissioner.

in my village there are people just called X, & Y, & Y-not,
and Zoomer & Zero & Zara & Zorro & Tonto,
In Nimbin there are plenty of kids called:
Sun, Moon, Sky, Tree, River, Rainforest
and Marley & Charlie & Che & Chai & Ty
and Teabag & Tick & Flea & Fly...(I kid you not)...
and Fallow & Tallow & Taro & Yarrow & Zen,
and Tansy & Pansy & Ebony & Ivory & Barbie & Ken,
and Cheech & Chong & Beach & Thong & Bong (the list goes
on & on),
there's Felix & Phoenix & Hunter & Ryder & Blossom & Leaf &
Dove
and Raven & Haven & Heaven & Kevin & Melody & Harmony
and Tempest & Serena. & Storm & Norm, & Rosebud & Thorn.

there are young men who are so "tourf" 'cos they just can't
"enourf",
'cos they only get to surf...on 2 feet of concrete turf,
there are skateboard chasing yuppies & punks with pet
puppies,
with chains from their knees to their toes to their navel to their
nose
to their eyebrows to their foreskin to their tit!
(and it doesn't hurt a bit! except when they laugh! or try to take
a bath!)

there are the little-old-ladies who worry about the babies
being bitten by the crazies with HIV-rabies, & worst of
all...scabies!
the blue rinse, the plaited, the bald & the matted –

there are merchants & vendors & 20-minute money lenders,
there are pub crawlers & street brawlers & pall bearers & hall
carers;

there's DMR & RTA, DEA & CES, SS & CSO's,
there's DO's & plenty of OD's, there's MO's & Oms...
ordinance officers, ambulance officers, project officers
and case managers (on your case).

there's youth workers & needle workers & council workers
and street sweepers & toilet cleaners who used to be dreamers;
there are movie makers & cake-bakers/on-the-make takers &
crystal ball fakers
and didgeridoo wielding natty-dreadlocked-congo-bongo-
hippie-trippy-shakers!

there are narcs dressed as nuns dressed as surfies wearing
guns/
there are school boys dressed as home-boys who've run away
from home,
they got much-too-much attitude to live in a tipi or a dome
(thank you mum)...
they're tough & independent/they got speed they got no car/
they say "I'm an individual" (dressed as an american basket-
ball star)

slam-dunkin' & funky-junkin'/the writing's on the wall
but if the graffitti's bad for business hear the developer scream
the call:
call a meeting! call the media! call the public! fill the hall!
call the police! call the choppers! or watch my village rise &
fall...

to be lovers/to be leftovers/to be left-right-up-downers/
to be around & around & around & arounders,
weekend-workshoppers & co-dependent conference-hoppers/
mid-life crises for midwives with vices & shotgun divorces over
hemp & horses...
to be labels/to be bloody labelled!
to be glue-sniffers of stick-on-labels right here in cafes on the
streets of Babel...
on the road from Babel to Babylon to Bourke & back to
Nimbin.

Love came cautiously
S. Sorrensen

like, at first, I tried not to notice her
    she was lovely, loveable, loved
    everybody loved her
    I didn't want to notice her
    she was too lovely for me
    so I ordered vodka...in a long glass
    with ice.

love came cautiously,
like, sometimes when she looked at me
    her eye would linger,
    like sometimes her hand would
    when we touched, by chance,
    near the bar
    and I'd go all stiff
    and mumble something stupid
like,
"I really love...Bourbon"
and I'd order triples...
to show her my love.

but love came at a price,
like, now I sit with my guilt
    at an empty midnight table
    with another herbal tea and another elke-seltzer
    And Mr. Guilt, dressed in the tatters of my life
    runs his burning finger across my chest
    naming my sins.

You see, we spent the night!
    spent it like a dollar
    and bought tequila and gin
    and a carton of coopers... (red label)
    yeah, spent it like a dollar
    and bought a rain-cocooned night
    where Guilt had to wait,
    wet and snuffling,
    outside Reverend Spooner's Motel.

while inside the room,

> our universe shrank to an ashtray,
> car keys, an empty condom
> and ten empty bottles flaked out on the table...
> My cigarette slipped into my drambuie
> and in the blinding flash that followed,
> I saw her glorious face and listered my blips.
> The room spun
> as I reached for the chardonnay '96
> Her body, hot and naked, straddled my retina.
> A champagne cork blackened my eye
> and the bubbles nickled my toes.
>
> I wanted her
> I wanted to tell her of my love...
> I wanted to call her name...
> But my come wouldn't words out right –
> You see, I was so tissed I could hardly pork
> And all my dopes were hashed.

I'm Not Drunk
Thom the World Poet

It's just that moods are my morphine
Overloaded opium crack down break up
tune in freak out. I'm drunk on air and
water. What you say? My head drifts
away. Sails. Clouds. Flamingos. Elephant
stepping on the corridor, rolling on the
parking meter crushing down tin cars
falling like rain on my rusted roof skull.

No, I'm not drunk, really I can describe
the architecture of your last sadness, his
flesh, her thoughts, the perimeters and
maps of all you felt, the log book of
longing, the filtered flavours, the
games and guessing, the hidden
assumption between speech and sparked
silence. I know the distant dreaming
beats its drum on your eyes' windows.
I hear the grass murmuring resistance.
Crawl behind walls if you will but I am
doors with your hand opening. And the
lid of your head is a bird cage, opening.

It's not that I stand here like a statue
talking automatic, telling machines not
to oppress us. It's just that death is the last
person leaving the office and most have
already switched their lights out. I grab
you by your shoulder because I want you
to know this. It's not entertaining to
speak from the heart. But from that
small space grows all resistance.

And if my eyes seem pink umbrellas and
your skin a pointing pyramid and my
body a rain forest and my clothing a suit
of armour and my speech a weather
report, it's not that the rolling thunder
drums are beating war clouds, it's just
that the white feathers of purpose are
plucked from the cold body of desire and

every glass is full of air, and liquid is a
dream of passing state. Appearances are
no funeral.

I tell you mate, it's not that I'm drunk.
It's just that I'm not invisible yet.

('Im Not Drunk' previously appeared in *Nightclub Poetry*, Edited
by Ken Smeaton, Street Poetry Lab, 1989.)

Shaking the beauty myth
Liz Hall-Downs

there's a chemical spill in my brain / it happened today before i
found my face / in the melbourne underground railway / it begins
when i enter the station / i buy my ticket, pass the newsagent,
where british monarchy vies with pinup girls for my eyes / i walk
on, down to platform seven / behind me walks a sure-footed
man, who bought the pinup girls and is smiling / ahead i see the
back of a mannequin, swaying on stilettos, a thin sheaf of wheat,
a bunch of bones encased by skin / i imagine she'd be sailing if
a puff of wind blew in / she and i sit down to wait for the train/ the
man walks by, his footsteps even / he is reading the curves of
airbrushed women / i see the woman pull from her bag the latest
cosmopolitan / watch her face, I glance across the pages that
she's reading / the made-up models stare, glistening / i look at
the woman on the bench beside me / her face has lines of frown-
ing / they run down from her nose to the sides of her mouth /
they run down the way that sadness does / they run deep like the
lines on a hungry third world child / i guess this first world woman
must be on another diet /

the train comes and we stand / i watch her jutting calves as she
moves towards the carriage / i watch the man shove broken electric doors apart / i watch the woman enter, stooping under his
raised arm / watch the man survey the woman, up and down / on
the train the woman sits upright, as if recalling an etiquette les-
son / her mouth is tight and red and long lines furrow across her
brow / i watch the man sitting opposite, the way he glances up at
details, disembodiments / legs / feet / hands / eyes / the woman
fidgets / she opens her purse / she extracts a tissue and a bottle
of oil / she wipes off the eyes, the lips, the stare / then she stands,
rips off the tights, the split skirt, the liberty blouse / she rips off
her lacy brassiere *l* her breasts goosebump in the gush of cold
air, but she doesn't care / the man sits stock still and stares / the
woman slips off stilettos, picks them up and aims them down the
carriage – there! and there! / the woman stands on the seat in
her knickers / she sways her hips to her own inner rhythm / she

rips up her copy of *cosmopolitan* / the papers swirl like autumn leaves around her / the woman looks at the man watching her / she does not posture or pout like the women in his magazine / she pulls the hair from her scalp till she is bald and wild / the whites of her eyes flame red in the twilight / she is becoming before his eyes / witch, crone, wise woman / her spirit emerging, she is no longer downtrodden / she's breaking out of beautiful, the gaunt-faced body / she is big, and strong, brave and healthy / she splits the seams of her size ten / she's gargantua's sister, she's a-comin' to get ya

her legs stand strong as tree trunks, walk with unhampered stride / she's walking out now, spanning the cosmos / and from her huge body she squats and gives birth / to the fertile round goddess so dim in our memory / the way women used to be / pre glossy magazines and fashion pornography /

there's a chemical spill in my brain / it was slow and insidious and took thirty years to reach these toxic proportions / but now i can smell it, the stench and the flames / i get off the train / run home to the mirror / i see my real face / for the very first time /

"...the best are always busy ...the rest are watching tv."
Thom the World Poet

Back in 1986, author of *Republic of Women,* Merrill Findlay, shared a lunch with Thom. Out of this communion was born the *Why Document?* published by the Victorian Ministry for the Arts. In it, Merrill documented Thom giving his all on the **why** of poetry – *"a monologue in poet speak".*

Merrill, Thom and Liz Hall-Downs shared this document with me and it offers some powerful, insightful comments on language and how we live. Thom has been described as *"a do-it-yourself sort of person"* and he frequently helps make things happen for others, sometimes at his own expense. Merrill says her life is rich, fulfilling and extremely interesting – even though it doesn't make her vast heaps of dollars. Having done some head scratching, I thought that some combination of extracts from the *Why document* segued together with some material from Merrill's *Imagine the Future* project would make a suitable little brain feast for the readers of this book.

Imagine The Future Inc
This piece is based on an article written for *Habitat Australia* magazine, May 1993, by **Merrill Findlay**.

The Beginning
It was the end of the eighties. I'd been invited to judge an art competition associated with the United Nations pavilion at the World Expo in Brisbane. Asked to look at hundreds of images, songs and poems by young people about making the world a better place and, with

my fellow judges, decide which ones were 'the best'. There was this drawing by a young boy. I can still see it. Two options for the future: one bad and one good. The bad one was easy and he drew it in meticulous detail. Explosions, war ships, tanks, a mushroom cloud. Death and destruction. (Or this is how I remember it.) The world of his deepest fears. The world he saw each night on TV. On the other side of the page, he drew a better world – a figure sitting alone on a beach in the sun. No detail. No content. Dozens of similar images were scattered across the table. Bad worlds, beautifully drawn, of cities turned to ashes, forests to skeletons, once clear rivers to gutters. And 'better worlds' of lolly water. Rainbows, beaches, sunshine, trees and pretty flowers. Cute houses with smoke rising from the chimneys. Cute cows grazing in green paddocks. It was as if these kids had searched their imaginations for an image of a world that was qualitatively better than the present – and found only postcard clichés. They had no dreams within their own imaginations of a world that was truly better than this, it seemed – and no hope, therefore, in the future.

Later
In Washington and Moscow, the Cold War was melting. In Africa, UNESCO was hosting yet another conference. This one was called 'Peace in the minds of men' (sic). The title was taken from the Preamble to the UNESCO constitution written in 1946 by North American poet, Archibald MacLeish:
"Since wars begin in the minds of men,
it is in the minds of men that the defences of peace must be constructed."

The venue was the lavish Foundation Internationale Houphouet-Boigny Pour la Recherche de la Paix in Yamoussoukro, the new capital of one of the world's poorest nations, the Ivory Coast. The man who had given his name to this institution, the Ivory Coast's then octogenarian ruler-for-life and multi-billionaire, the late President Felix Houphouet-Boigny, was there in person and so too was Elise Boulding, a feminist scholar and long-time peace activist from Boulder, Colorado. Her voice, amongst others, called for *"visions in which all can have faith"* and her words were included in the ritual conference declaration: *"Humans cannot work for a future they cannot imagine".*

When I read those words for the first time, they resonated in my own mind. Later, in the collaborative process that gave birth to *Imagine The Future*, Elise's 'Cannots' were translated into 'Cans' to answer the 'Why' of this emerging organisation: because we humans can only work for a future we can imagine.

A new decade: the 1980s end, the 1990s begin. We cautious optimists meet to talk about the future. The term 'sustainable society' is repeated again and again. A concept that integrates all of what it is to be human, that shatters old boundaries, demands new ways of thinking and unites rather than divides. We meet many times, in different configurations, in different parts of the world. Quietly and conscientiously we work, sometimes together, sometimes alone. No hierarchy in this free association, no money, no power. And no qualifications except that each of us is working towards a world that is qualitatively better than this. Slowly, in our corner of the world, consensus emerges. What we want is a future that maximises quality of life for all human beings. A diverse and democratic society based on the values of peace, social justice, human rights and ecological sustainability. We don't quite know what we mean by all this yet – but we have begun the journey. And now we can work to make the vision real.

We have a broad philosophy, we have our objectives. We have hopes and plans...and now we seek mainstream support. Only to be told that we are *"too far ahead of our time"!* (We however, are confident that our timing is perfect. Well, a couple of thousand years late but certainly not 'ahead' of our time.) Meanwhile my father is dying – because fifty years ago he inhaled a fibre of asbestos. A young man then, a naval recruit fighting, he believed, for the future of the world. He is frail and bed ridden. That fibre inhaled in World War II has become his destiny. And our parable. Too soon he dies. My family and I celebrate his life in our village hall and I return to the city. To imagine the future, to work for it. A future not like the past. Not like my father's. But a future that makes you want to be there.

The imagining hasn't stopped. It has continued, expanding on to the web at Merrill Findlay's site at www.merrillfindlay.com. and on to the school agenda, empowering young people at the local level.

The price of silence is misrepresentation

Adapted from the *Why document* written by **Thom the Street Poet**

Speak to me. Your tears don't translate. Your smile might be a mistake. Your body language needs subtitles. Even video text is edited and movies manipulate. So talk. And let your language communicate.

Poetry is significant speech. The best words in the best order. And the sharpening of our tongue means self-preservation. Beyond our words, more meanings lie waiting to be trapped and captured. They are prizes for the alert and sentient. Our language is a metaphor. A simile of moving bars of music. It sings.

It has a frame of reference called The World Language. This is simply how we choose to speak to one another. We are consenting partners. Let us talk now. About poetry. As a primary art form.

"Meaning is culturally determined in a tribal way"

Merrill Findlay with **Thom the Street Poet** (adapted from the *Why document?*)

On the day Tom Wayman and I talk, the winter sun is shining. To celebrate, we collect hot samosas and spicy curry rolls from the local Indian take away. Share them on St Kilda beach.

A sunny winter Sunday in Melbourne is a rare and festive event. Joggers are out, mothers are playing ball with their sons and daughters, fathers are pushing toddlers on swings, lovers

Thom in the 1980s

are lingering hand in hand, old dogs are walking their owners. But even with the winter sun Port Phillip Bay is still grey. And there are plastic Coke bottles, polystyrene foam and an old thong littering the shore line. In a world of DDT in penguins, oil slicks, acid rain and nuclear waste (as well as sunny Melbourne days in winter) what else can one expect? But **all** this is stuff of poetry.

We settle ourselves amongst the glass and broken shells, arrange our picnic on its white plastic take away bag, unscrew the tops of our fruit juice. And gaze out across the water. Two little kids run past. *"Children automatically know the rules of fantasy,"* Thom ruminates. *"Yet **we** constantly have to rediscover how wide our freedom really is."*

He continues. A monologue in poet speak. Slow and deliberate and from a man whose tools of trade are his words.

*"The shaping and forming of our scripts is constantly being done for us by mass media in this global village and resistance can only occur when individuals or groups choose to rescript their circumstances. To fashion our own worlds, dream of fantasy and reality and create solutions and expressions which can address the deepest problems of our time. It is more than an artistic search. It is a survival exercise. It is part of the **Why** of poetry.*

"Our language is a tool for the social construction of our communities. An ancient tool used in accordance with intrinsic agreed rules. Meaning is culturally determined in a tribal way, not just by geographically determined dialects and accents but also by shared value systems which give our rituals power and keep our culture continuous."

"Often the history we are told is not the history we feel. But there have always been poets who sing the news of the village. In Celtic cultures we have called them minstrels, troubadors, or roundalay men. They were the messengers who could convey

in verse what was happening in their times. They could extemporize rhymes, memorize them and pass them on from generation to generation. Our own grandmothers played piano, our grandfathers played banjo, they told stories. We listened."

"We are old enough to remember a world before television, and when they tell us that is all there is, we know they are lying. (Remember singalongs, remember pantomime, remember vaudeville and variety, remember music hall and burlesque?) It is important to maintain and revive folk idioms not just as historical curiosities but as a living and vibrant exercise in the preservation of life through language and shared experiences."

"Poetry is both an ancient and a futuristic medium where past, present and future are welded in content, style and form to make its continuance inevitable," he continues. "Its power lies in its person to person potency. It is hearing the deepest truths whispered as in an initiation. It is a secret that is open. The magic of poetry lies in its ability to both describe and transcend its environment. Imagination can free both the writer and the audience. Poetry is more than therapy or a tool of self-knowledge. It is an essential process of creating one's world. Each person creates her own understanding by description, repetition and elaboration."

"Though this messy art of the heart, these emotional renderings, find little favour in Academia, it is important it is important to promote and preserve them because they are part of the real culture of our time. Created by people facing the real problems we all face. Poetry is essentially a social exercise, a consensual game between sentient human beings. At its best, it is cathartic, a cleansing and mystical process. It leads one out from the obvious to the implications and back with new found sense of wonder. This beach will never be the same again, nor that sun. Once a poem has wrapped you in its blanket, you'll be warm."

Yes, this is a Romantic speaking. And he takes another samosa.

"For a true poem shivers with the naked, cries with the hurt, holds hands with the broken and weeps with the wounded. A true poem is one you'll never forget. It describes things so perfectly yet touches some deeper well where forms have echoes and they sing back through the subconscious. Luckily there are very few such poems! Hence we spend so much time looking for them and trying to create the perfect truth."

"But instead of arguing about the perfect poem and dissecting the perfect butterfly, we should be busy creating the forms of our time: the structures that will carry the meaning and content of contemporary initiation rituals, explanations of mysteries, and solutions for shared survival..."

The tide comes in and the sea breeze changes to a cold wind. We seek shelter. But the poet's monologue continues.

"My own involvement in all this began when I chanted poetry to crowd dancing in a barn at Nimbin. I realized then the power of the chant, the mantra, the power of speech. And the loss our society of its toubadors, roundalay men, hurdy gurdy men and other traditional messengers of the tribe. I came back to Melbourne and began a poetry band which toured schools and universities and played Sunbury Pop Festival. After that I had a a rock n' roll poetry band – which was more of a good time thing to get people moving. We perfomed at Poetry Gallery, which was a space we set up in Victoria Street, North Melbourne. But it seemed that so much had to be done before people could see poetry as a natural part of their language. So I began by printing my own poems and giving them away on fairly primitive sheets."

"Street Poetry has surprised pedestrians for over ten years since those early days, with its continuing free correspondence of thoughts, dreams, ideas, sensations and reportage distributed in the street. It has involved many hundreds of people in writing, printing, distributing, editing and publishing poetry. At various times it has had centres in Geelong, Tamworth, Adelaide, Canberra, Sydney, Mansfield, New England and Tasmania as well as Melbourne. It has linked with poets in America, Britain and Holland."

"Nearly all the people involved now in Street Poetry have begun writing and performing publicly for the first time because of the supportive network they've found through the readings. Our sort of community poetry rarely utilizes the mass media effectively. We depend upon small scale operations. But this doesn't diminish the importance of what we do. Our pamphlets and broadsheets often reach a higher number of people than many magazines. And certainly more cost effectively!"

"Many of these people are not seeking to become full time writers or performers. They just enjoy the process of writing and use it for their own purposes. And because there are so many different needs being met and such a wide range of people involved, Street Poetry open readings have had a substantial impact on the overall growth of poetry. As for my own role – I see myself as a facilitator of the process and a base line on which others can build. But I would love it if everyone took their expression seriously enough to publish their own work, run their own venues and facilitate the spread of poetry as a national language so that people like me were totally irrelevant!"

"And there is hope that one day I will be irrelevant! Street Poetry fills some of the gaps. The poetry we seek is the personal private voice of every man, woman and child. That chorus of disparate and divergent voices which makes up the richness of what we call People's Culture."

Some time after Thom and I shared samosas on the beach at St Kilda, I received a parcel. It was the Penguin anthology, *Off the Record*, published by Penguin. Thom the Street Poet is one of the 52 performance poets whose life and work are documented between its pastel covers. On the back cover the 'blurb' reads:
"For all those who hated poetry at school, this book's message is that everyone can be a poet."

Tom's message of course, is that everyone IS a poet.

Peter Cock invited one of his PhD students at Monash University to get in touch with me. Her name was Sylvie; Sylvie Shaw. We seemed to get on right away. We swapped some stories about festivals and parties and she agreed to write up her observations on the neo-shaman scene in Australia. But, this is no dry academic treatise on the return to tribalism, this is Sylvie's life as well. Lots here to get the brain cells moving about a bit. And, as I put this section together, Sylvie is somewhere around the Dragon camps of England. I hope you had a good one, Sylvie!

Lose touch with the earth and you lose touch with life
Sylvie Shaw

Summary:
The growth of what's loosely termed 'neo-shamanism' is part of a recent trend by many people in the West to seek and embody a sacred dimension in their lives. The inspiration for this quest stems from a disquiet about the present state of the world, and while there are many avenues to explore in the search for self, neo-shamanism based on the age-old practices and wisdom of indigenous cultures, is the path many people have chosen to follow. This article asks to what extent is this practice of sacred ritual and ceremony a 'new age' appropriation of indigenous cultures or a positive way of seeking a way to enhance and re-enchant their lives and their relationship to the earth.

It had been raining for two days. I was sheltering under a tarpaulin, wrapped in a blanket, wet through, tired and a bit spaced out. This was the final day of my vision quest. I had been fasting, seeking a vision or some guidance for my future. My friend David, his daughter Jessica and their dog Sheena came to get me and together we walked slowly up the hill. I did not realize how exhausted I was until I started up the steep climb. At the top of the hill the sacred fire was still burning. It had been a beacon for the people who were out on their vigil. I sat by the fire for a while contemplating the flames, then joined the others in the sweat lodge.

It was dark. The rocks glowed red hot and the sweat poured off me. Clearing. Cleansing. The people around me said a prayer of thanks and then, one by one, we talked about what had happened during our time on the hill. We finished the sweat lodge with a round of singing to the drum beat:

I walk a path of beauty, walk a path, my ancestors laid out before me.
I walk a path of beauty, walk a path, my ancestors laid out before me.
Oh yes, I make a path of beauty, hold my visions, roll my dreaming out before me.
Oh yes, I make a path of beauty, hold my visions, roll my dreaming out before me.

Then we emerged from the lodge. Weary but refreshed. Covered with mud. The last thing we did was to plant some trees around the lodge in thanks for the wood that was burnt in the sacred fire.

The sweat lodge and the vision quest are integral to the spiritual practice of the group I was part of for five years. Known simply as Earth Healing/Drumming group, our intention was to create a safe and sacred space to connect with the rhythms of nature and to develop a sacredness and an awareness that affects the way we move through life.

I was inspired to get involved in this group following a trip I made to the Aboriginal community of Yirrkala in Arnhemland, northern Australia, ten years ago. That visit changed my life. I realized that the Aboriginal people I met saw the world differently and I wanted to learn to see that way too. Primarily it was about developing a deep spiritual connection to the land. That led me to seek out a range of spiritual groups and courses from spiritual healing to Reiki. But it wasn't until I saw a leaflet advertising a 'Shamanic weekend workshop' and was introduced to the practice of journeying, that is moving into an altered state of consciousness to the monotonous beat of a drum, that I found a key to this other way of seeing. This is also the pathway indigenous shamans use to travel or journey to other worlds. The main difference between new age or neo-shamans and indigenous shamans is that indigenous shaman's journey or enter the spirit world in search of a vision for the well-being of the whole community, whereas neo-shamans tend to journey in search of a vision for themselves.

The Earth Healing/Drumming group is one of several groups in Melbourne dedicated to ritual practice to honour the earth. Some are based along Pagan or Wicca lines; others, like the group I was part of, are inspired by indigenous traditions. I was interested in studying those groups in Melbourne which have a largely Native American focus as I wanted to talk to practitioners about their motivation for taking up an earth-based spirituality inspired by indigenous practices. But as I embarked on my research, I realized that there was another issue at stake – appropriation or cultural theft. I'd like to discuss both issues. First I will look at what makes up the groups' spiritual practice, then I will consider the implications this practice has on the Native Americans themselves.

The people I spoke with ranged from students to academics, psychologists and counsellors, musicians, an artist, health practitioners, an environmental activist, business and computer consultants, two farmers and a horticulturalist. In other words, middle class, highly educated professional people. You'll meet some of them:

Hawk – student, 23, m
Peter – environmental activist, 33, m
James – lecturer, 41, m
Robert – marketing consultant, 33, m
Kate – massage practitioner, 39, f
Deborah – fashion model, 27, f
Louise – farmer, 37, f
Bear – manager, 25, f
Robin – health practitioner, 46, m
Stone – artist, 39, f
Jenny – health practitioner, 52, f
Simon – manager and musician, 25, m
Angie – gardener, 28, f

Most people became involved in the group after a deep personal crisis or serious illness, a marriage breakdown, the death of a spouse, a midlife re-assessment, or just a feeling of being on the edge, marginal, alienated, different. Neo-shamans seem to be searching for their own identity as much as a connection with others and with the earth. Many mention a frustration with aspects of modern society, with its lack of community, lack of ritual and its disconnection to nature. Kate, for example, lays the blame at the feet of the West.

In the West we are so disconnected to nature, and that's a disease; that's the festering wound – the total separation from the sea, the rivers, the trees, the birds, the cycles of nature – which shows how uncentered we are as a result of that and how self-centered we become because of it. What's important now is to learn to listen to the spirit of the land, to stand together with indigenous people and create community for ourselves.

Foundation Stones of Neo-Shamanic Practice

The Medicine Wheel
The Wheel or Sacred Circle is the basic ritual structure the groups use. The circle is a symbol of continuity and completion, and represents the cycles of nature – birth, growth, change, death and renewal. It is bounded by the four cardinal directions and each direction corresponds to a particular quality or virtue, various animals or guardian spirits, one of the four seasons and one of the four elements. For example in the Southern hemisphere and in the form I learnt, the *East* represents rebirth and creativity. Its colour is yellow, its season spring and its element air. The animal spirit is eagle. The *North* represents passion and playfulness. Its colour is red, its season summer, its element, fire and the animal spirit, dingo or wildcat. In the *West* we turn inward for personal reflection. The colour is black, the season autumn, the element water and the animal dolphin. The *South* symbolizes courage, strength and determination. The season winter, the element earth, the colour white, and the animals, goanna and whale. The wheel can be figured differently and each person has their own way of using it. Kate's ritual begins when she is still in bed.

My bedroom faces East and in the morning I watch the sun rise over the rooftops and it's beautiful and I'm very aware of the direction I'm facing. East is the direction of birth, vision, the sky fathers and the grandfathers and creativity, and it puts me in touch with nature, with the cycles of nature, and that's a nice beginning.

The Medicine Wheel as well as the other rituals like the sweat lodge, vision quest and earth healing meditation help bind the community together. In song, dance, chant and drum, rituals are patterns that link across generations and enliven our relationships with all things. As we sing the landscape and dance the animals, we re-enact and renew the memories and stories of ancestral spirits and animal guardians or power animals.

Animal Guardians

Power animals or spirit animals are guides and protectors for the journey whether of life or in search of a vision. They are also the vehicle for communication with the spirit world, and in a shamanic healing, they are the messengers bearing information about a patient's illness.

People find their animal guardian by various means. It may be something you have always known. When I was little I used to tell my mother that in my previous life I was a lion and I also loved the fairy tale Una and the Lion where the beautiful princess is guided through the forest by the courageous lion. So it wasn't surprising that on my first 'shamanic' journey to meet my power animal, a guided meditation to the beat of a drum, that I met a whole family of playful mountain lions. Other people find their animal by walking around the Medicine Wheel until they feel drawn to a particular quadrant that represents certain qualities and virtues, or an animal may call them from that point in the wheel. If you have an inkling, the best thing to do is to ask the animal if it is, in fact, your power animal then greet it warmly.

Most people love talking about their animal guardians and the adventures they have with them, and nearly everyone has a haunting or moving story about their close connection with them.

Robin says:

The Raven is a bird that tends to fly in a solitary way and has a long drawn out wailing cry. It seems to catch something of the landscape along with the creaking sound of corrugated iron in the hot sun. It has a magical quality, but from my childhood reading I had romanticized the magic and placed the Raven in quite a European setting really. Now it's more like an experience that involves all my senses and there's a feeling of connectedness at a very deep level.

But the animal can also be a formidable ally as Stone found out:

The sensuality/sexuality side of the Snake frightened me, it was so impassioned. It would come out of the shadows and I spent a lot of time running away from it. But now I've got a good sense of her being incredibly nurturing, healing and compassionate, and I realize that in many communities, she's the supreme creator. You climb into her and you might be destroyed and that's the whole frightening part, but you can transform her and be transformed – just as she sheds her skin. You climb into her and you die, and you can be reborn again.

Ritual and Celebration

Ritual and ceremony act to bind the individual and the community to each other and to the cosmos; they honour the changing seasons and celebrate significant rites of passage in a person's life (birth and death, joining and separation), as well as significant events in the group's life such as initiation and naming rites, ceremonial dancing, the sweat lodge and vision quest.

In ritual we move beyond ordinary reality and experience the numinous, and in this space, enlivened by chanting, drumming, gesture, symbol and performance, combined with the heady aroma of smouldering herbs, there is magic in the air. James revels in the experience:

To me rituals are about reconnecting back to those very simple forms of uniting with the earth and with other people; the idea of death and rebirth and change and honouring, and all these things are very important. Without that you are just floating.

However, and in total contrast, Hawk prefers to celebrate alone, explaining:

Rituals are a way of physically expressing your intention, but I could be locked up in a cell and still continue on my pathway. The only thing you need in the world is yourself.

This seems to fly in the face of the majority of people I have met who are involved in earth-based spiritual groups. The connection between self, community and earth is an integral part of the practice.

While most neo-shamans acknowledge that there are some local rituals that do 'nourish' certain segments of society, like *football, shopping, twenty-firsts, and getting pissed*, Robert also believes that, in the West:

We have lost our sense of respect, our sense of community and the sense of the sacred within. We have forgotten how to make sacred connections between each other and the earth.

We seek inspiration from a range of sources, exploring our own heritage and cultural roots, as well as the cultures of First Peoples, and in the end creating our own special rituals that are meaningful to us. They are acts of rediscovery, of reconnection, re-awakening and re-animation.

Sweating it Out
The sweat lodge is a sacred purification ritual. It is also an ordeal. It is about being on the edge, being humble, showing gratitude and giving in to the experience to gain insight or another way of seeing. The lodge is constructed out of bamboo or willow branches and is shaped like an igloo. It brings together the four elements: fire, earth, air and water and represents the womb of the earth. The doorway is placed low to the ground so when you enter the lodge you bow and become humble before Mother Earth.

The sweat lodge ceremony actually starts with the ritual process of building the lodge. Going out and finding the appropriate tree to take the willow branches from, not just any tree but one you are guided to. The same process is repeated when collecting the volcanic rocks which are the source of heat in the lodge, or chopping the firewood that will be burnt in the sacred fire. All the steps are sacred and many take place before people enter the lodge. Generally, sweat lodge ceremonies are conducted before going out on the vision quest, before ceremonial dancing and at other special times. But more recently 'the sweat' has been marketed as a kind of weekend-warrior initiation which may mask its sacred intention.

The ceremony is made up of four parts or prayer rounds. In the first round participants set their intentions for the lodge (what they want to get out of it); the second is for self-healing; the third is dedicated to prayers for other people; and the closing round is for Earth-healing and thanksgiving. At the end of each round the 'door' or flap is opened for a breather, and as the cold air rushes in, there is a great feeling of relief, at least for a short time. Louise loves it:

It is one of the most wonderful experiences you can have. I feel so comfortable in the lodge, such a oneness with the self and with everything. It is a safe and sacred place and I haven't felt that close connection with the land anywhere else - where for a moment in time, you seem to lose the physical and everything just blends.

Most groups hold regular sweat lodges to pay homage to the earth, to gain insight for the wider community and ourselves, to feel restored and regenerated, and to give thanks. But the experience itself may not be a comfortable one as you are confronted by darkness and intense heat. It challenges issues of control, of body image, of pain tolerance, and it can be personally confronting, as Deborah found:

If it had been explained to me I wouldn't have been frightened. I would have gone – automatically – OK, this is a really spiritual thing and I would have looked at it differently. But I thought 'holy fuck', I'm going to die. I felt terrible, closed in, I couldn't breathe and I just wanted to go out.

Bear found it pushed her control buttons too.

Personally I'm a control freak, a lot of people are, but in a sweat it's strong energy you're working with, and you have to move past it or it will be a lot more painful than it need be. I think it's also a very powerful way of working with much higher energy, it just seems to come into these ceremonies – it wouldn't ordinarily be present outside of them.

In contrast, Angie relishes the ritual:

I feel so energized after a sweat lodge and I run out like a lightening rod, hooting and hollering. But it's a good way to drop your bundle. I sing as hard as I can without breaking my throat, and if I get too hot, I get down and hug the earth. It's something I've always enjoyed – lying in a pool of mud. I always go in with a clear idea of what I want to let go but it's not always easy, and sometimes I kick and scream...I'm always grateful when I come out, and I'm supercharged up while everyone else is totally exhausted.

Experiences like these reflect the boundaries between pleasure and pain (physical and emotional) and there's a real merging of the spirit and the flesh. The sweat lodge pushes people to the edge of their comfort zone and in this edge place, they find healing, insight, and another way of seeing.

Into the Landscape

Spending time alone in nature or vision questing is another sacred pathway for insight and self-transformation. However, some sections of the new age movement have hijacked the experience and turned it into a marketable commodity. One group has registered the name 'Vision Quest – A Western Rite of Passage' and for information, one can phone the 'Vision Quest Hotline'. This seems more like a self-help lifeline than a sacred practice that takes place in nature.

Sylvie Shaw

The new age movement is full of self-help therapy courses, workshops, healings and other practices all with a heavy emphasis on individualism and consumerism. Marketing the vision quest as a commodity seems to dilute its spiritual intention. Deep ecologist and business consultant, Robert, is concerned by this trend to commodify spirituality and is very aware of how easily spiritual practices can be appropriated:

There is a whole movement of spirituality packaging and marketing now and that is a danger. It's a real shadow, and if the shadow isn't named, people will make a lot of money but overlook the real core. They are playing in the most subtle and subversive (negative) ways - it can move a lot of people, but it can be very dangerous.

As an environmental activist working with Aboriginal and Native American people, Peter is conscious of the issue of appropriation and the dangers of commodifying the sacred vision quest, but believes that:

Whatever name you call it, being out in nature by yourself is still an incredibly relevant experience. It's something that many cultures have done particularly at threshold times of life, like young adulthood, or going into middle age, even going into old age – at key turning points in your life when you acknowledge your life is changing. Or maybe when you become a parent. Just to have time to enter the spirit realm, out of the human world and to make contact with the Earth.

The purpose of the vision vigil is to step outside of the boundaries of the everyday world and spend time alone, fasting, and seeking guidance or a direction for one's life. It can last from one to four or more days and can be a major transforming experience as Robin discovered.

It felt like an important commitment to make. It took place out in the desert, so travelling there became part of the ritual. I remembered how Castaneda went out into the desert and for him the contact with the land and with the culture developed over a long period of time. Things began to change for him as he began to experience that culture. My actual experience was more in keeping with my own culture and background, and it was more of an inner experience. One area I looked at was addictions – my own (alcohol and tobacco), and surprisingly, I found that fasting was not the struggle I had imagined it would be. There were other challenges though and other addictions about space and time, and I was affected by the landscape. Around the second night it rained; it was cold and uncomfortable and I began to feel irritable and angry about what I was doing here...There was also the challenge to stay in the present. The sun would rise about 5.30 am and I'd drop off to sleep again or sit around waiting till 9 o'clock, when I would light a fire, write a few pages in my diary, do four circuits of the medicine wheel, and it was still only five past nine. It was about fasting, sleep deprivation and hardship but I was aware it was having an effect. I was aware of my physical condition deteriorating as I was sitting near some trees with sharp spiky branches and I realized I could hurt myself: I had to be more watchful.

But just being out in nature, as well as on a vision vigil, can also be a powerful and transforming experience as Robert and Stone attest. For Robert, it occurred while swimming with dolphins:

I had a very powerful experience in nature which led to me leaving my slick and powerful job managing a huge suburban shopping centre. I decided to go swimming with the dolphins, as dolphins were coming into my life at that time. It was raining when we took a boat out into the Bay, and when we got to the middle, the water went flat, the sky opened up, the sun came out and for the next two or three hours we were circled by over thirty dolphins. They somersaulted, danced and played and one kept coming up to me, screaming at me, and I was in total joy, crying my head off – joy and grief were just fused together – and it touched something quite deep inside me. The next day I walked into the Managing Director's office and said I'm going.

For Stone, it happened while she was travelling in Central Australia.

As I was driving to Uluru I felt like I was being stripped of everything. Part of my identity. And when I arrived there I went for a walk and found a hollow in the rock and just cried. I cried for a couple of days. There was an overwhelming sense of reconnection, of real heart connection, sinking into the land,

feeling a presence and the spirit of place. Everything about the rock was so interconnected, and I cried for all that I'd stopped asking for. So I guess I was grieving for myself and for the land.

It is not surprising that these transformative, break-through and ecstatic experiences took place on Aboriginal land and out in nature, (which I suppose you could argue, is also indigenous land). In these sacred places, the neo-shamans are on the edge of the self, in the intimate and dynamic interplay between body, mind and nature where they find a new kind of power.

Finding this 'new kind of power' and becoming empowered, is one of the main reasons people give for taking up neo-shamanic practice. Several people also mention that they want to uncover or re-cover the indigenous part of themselves. According to Jenny, this desire stems from a critique of Western culture.

It is very important to learn indigenous stuff now as we've lost the plot. We've abused the Earth and each other so much now that we've lost contact with our own essence of who we are and where we've come from. We are trying to find a way to get back to our roots and we are doing that through Native teachings.

James believes that,

…the West, by destroying indigenous cultures, has destroyed the bridge to the spirit world. I'm not one to say let's be a Native American or an Aborigine at all, but to say let's look at what they're doing because the techniques are transferable. They're just techniques and the cultural garment is the only difference.(!)

However, while these neo-shamans are critical of the West, they can also be viewed as traversing the same well-worn colonial paths to indigenous cultures already mapped out in dominant Western discourses. And although the majority of interviewees express concern about the current situation confronting indigenous people, there is an obvious dichotomy between their individual spiritual path and the political reality.

In light of these comments, it is easy to see why Native Americans have become so angry about the often naive and simplistic appropriation of their sacred cultural practices. The Lakota Nation, for example, has drawn up a Declaration of War against 'exploiters of Lakota spirituality' which attacks 'new age shamans', 'plastic medicine men' and their 'phoney' ceremonies. This strong stance against what is perceived as spiritual genocide was initiated by the American Indian Movement, a group which has been involved in political struggles over the past 30 years, and while I can understand their tough sentiments I would also suggest that neo-shamans are an easy target. It is not simply a conflict between colonizer/bad guys/appropriators on one side and colonized/good guys/ victims on the other. Such a strong stance leaves no room for dialogue or collaboration. For me, it's a much greyer area. It is more about building understanding and cross-cultural sharing.

Native American spirituality has struck a chord with many neo-shamans because of what they see as its simplicity, its intimate relationship to the earth, and the interconnection with all things – plants, animals, trees, rocks, us, everything. But this attitude also reminds me of the Sunday school song: 'All things bright and beautiful/ All creatures great and small'. The danger of this utopian image is that it creams off the surface spirituality, takes particular rituals and ceremonies out of their cultural and environmental contexts, and considers all Native Americans as unchanging, nostalgic and noble (almost always male) warriors, in fact the epitome of nature itself. The result of this Dances with Wolves

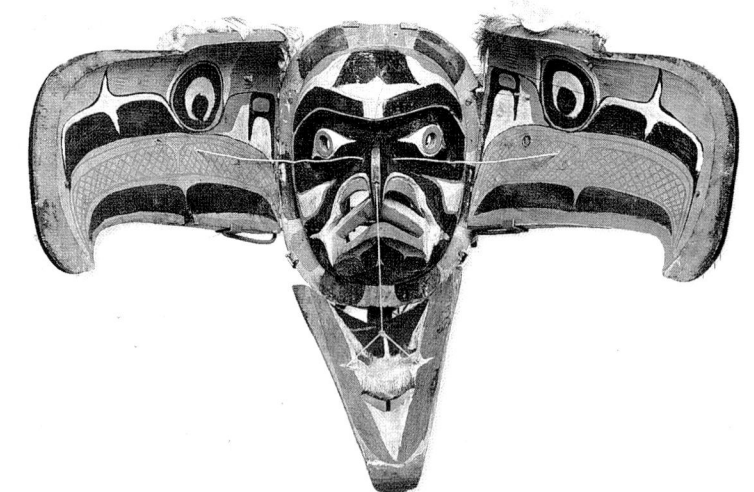

fantasy is that it trivializes the culture and casts all Indian nations into the role of tipi-dwelling, buffalo-hunting, pony-riding communities. It is a romantic illusion that traps the indigenous community into a static museum past and side steps the reality – that cultures are ever changing.

So on one hand, the neo-shamanic construction of the 'imaginary Indian' can be seen as neo-colonialist and part of racist discourse. If racism is defined as *prejudice plus power* (Chambers and Pettman, 1986), then several of the neo-shamans fall into the category of prejudice as *making up one's mind about others, without sufficient information*. But I am in a quandary about the issue of power or 'power-over' in the context of people like Simon who is using his shamanic practice to heal deep rifts in his family:

I really honour the Native American teaching. They've taught me so much and I feel that what's left to do now is to look after things in my family which is a minor manifestation of what's happening to the spirit of my people in South America. If I can correct what's happening in my family, it's a step towards creating a pocket of healing for a lot of people.

As this comment shows, Simon takes his spirituality very seriously and it has turned his life around. But his viewpoint throws up the obvious dichotomy between the individual search for meaning and the impact this search has on the Native American community. Neo-shamans have rejected the West and embraced the other, but in so doing, even without meaning to or being aware of it, they are acting out the same old dynamic between colonized and colonizer. So commodifying indigenous cultural practices and supporting that action as practitioner or participant, is viewed from this theoretical perspective as racist.

While I acknowledge this approach, I find it very hard to class all neo-shamanic practice in the same light as racist violence, or label all interviewees as 'soft' racists. Yet I also realize that racism can be played out in celebratory ways, as well as the more frequent aggressive/violent stance. This view is further enhanced with the realization that non-indigenous people (who may only have done a weekend workshop with other non-indigenous people) are teaching Native American traditions. Native Americans have been white-washed out of their own spiritual practices, and they term this process 'spiritual genocide'.

To avoid further exploitation of indigenous spirituality, Native Americans suggest that new agers should search in their own cultural and spiritual heritage, and interestingly enough, there has been a parallel growth in Celtic shamanism, Neo-Paganism and Wicca. However, one criticism of the rekindling of these old religions is that they might also end up being commodified, packaged and marketed in the same way as much Native American spirituality.

Shamanic practice brings the self into deep communion with the natural world, ritual and ceremony involving the medicine wheel, the sweat lodge, and vision quest all reflect this prescription. Neo-shamans acknowledge that spending time alone in nature, listening to the spirits of place, sitting quiet and going light are integral to their practice, but at the same time, they should begin to question their romantic construction of the indigenous way of life to find ways to gain awareness about the plight of indigenous cultures and the world, and if possible give back in some way to the people that inspired them.

Shamanism is rooted in the land, yet the commercialization and the new age trappings that go with it have taken the land component out, so it then becomes a kind of alternative or self-therapy removed from the life that is embedded in it.

I define shamanism as dancing on the edge of the self and the world in the boundaries of the body and the boundaries of the mind. It is an edge place, a place of power where we can journey seeking insight for ourselves, for the community and for the earth. I believe it is possible to practice shamanic techniques without piggy backing onto indigenous cultural traditions. We can explore our own ancestral heritage as well as paying homage to the spirits of the land and develop our own ritual practices that are meaningful to us here in Australia.

I have taken the title of this article – 'Lose touch with the earth and you lose touch with life' from graffiti on the toilet door in the Environmental Science Department at Monash University where I am currently doing my PhD on people's connection to nature. The graffiti is a reminder of the need to touch the earth and to be touched by it in a way that is both sacred and life affirming. It is a perfect place to be reminded of the beauty of nature.

References
Chambers, B. and Pettman, J. (1986) *Anti-racism. A Handbook for Adult Educators.* Canberra: Australian Government Publishing Service.

Note: thanks to Brooke Medicine Eagle for permission to use the lines from her song: *I walk the path of beauty.* You can find out more about her work and beliefs at www.medicineeagle.com

Censorship, the Net and Sexuality

During my trip around Oz I met a few openly gay and bi men and women, including a few friends of Mook and Shanto's, who were more into a quiet, discreet scene of their own, apart from when it is street theatre time! I was in Sydney just at the start of the Mardi Gras, but missed the parade, which was a shame.

After my return to Brit, I was keen to ensure that there was lively coverage in this book of at least of some aspects of the covert and overt gay scene. Once again using the net – I surfed, tripped and stumbled my way into a number of web sites and rings. Sites with intriguing addresses – Nobbys.net and queernet. I was especially interested in gogoBOy's *Realm of Shade* server. This had recently moved offshore from Australia to a new location hosted from the United States, (www.realm-of-shade.com/catacomb/) and is a main base for the Radical Faeries in Oz. It has re-located there because of threats to his netizens from new, Year Y2K surveillance from the Australian Broadcasting Authority (ABA).

The Radical Faerie Movement has been in existence in the States since 1979, established after a conference organised by

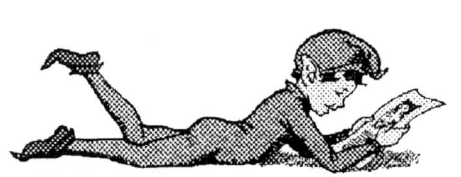

Harry Hay and others. But its origins are much older reaching back to earlier times when gays pondered on the gifts that they could bring into the world. Now the radical gays and lesbians who use the net to address issues and share information are under threat of suppression and criminalisation. Sadly, they are not alone. The main cause is the Broadcasting Services Amendment (Online Services Act) 1999. I found out loads more about it in links from the *Realm of Shade,* to and through gogoBOy's rants. Here follows a rather political little collection of raves and rants about the

way in which this censorious (and probably unworkable) legislation impinges on a free netlife. After that, I've included info on the Radical Faeries in Oz.

The opposite of tolerance is intolerance, oppression and suppression. If we keep quiet about it, we become one with the oppressors. To quote my friend Kate (from her book, *Copse*):

Why do people just exist to die?
You should exist to live!
You should be full of love and spirit,
And the sky's the limit.
You can do whatever you want to do.

A nice ideal, but we've got to keep working at it. Otherwise, in countries like Australia, the protectors who *know* what is for our own good, will win out. This is what David Marr, in the *Sydney Morning Herald* has described as the institutions, the churches and governments who are part of the *"disapproval business."* What we should be seeking is more active, in line with John F. Kennedy, who said, *"Tolerance implies no lack of commitment to one's own beliefs. Rather it condemns the oppression or persecution of others."*

Back in the 'now' of twenty-first century Australia, S.Jones, is quoted at the *Rural Faeriel Donga* site:

"I am told I can not read comics imported from overseas, because they will make me desire to kill someone. I am told I may not play computer games because they will make me want to kill someone. I am told I may not listen to music because it will make me want to kill someone. I am told I may not watch movies because they will make me want to kill someone. I am told I may not read books because they will make me want to kill someone. I am told I may not look at pictures because they will make me want to kill someone.

And now I am informed that my internet connection is to be censored for my own protection. About the only thing which currently makes me want to kill someone is the fact that everything I enjoy is slowly being taken from me for no real reason."

These changes are supposed to be designed to make the internet 'child friendly', i.e. no access to pornography; no access to information on drug use; no access to information on sex and sexuality, and no access to information that will help people to make informed decisions about their lives. The new legislation, the Broadcasting Services Amendment Act is very complicated. As lawyer Brendan Scott from the firm Gilbert and Tobin says: *"(it) is very complex – its 72 pages of text are not a pleasant read."* Sadly, it was raced through Senate and the House of Representatives and its deficiencies, of which there appear to many, were ignored or glossed over.

Particularly strange is its principle that carriers and holders of information should be held to account for information, but not the creators or owners of the content. Again quoting Brendan Scott, *"an analogy might be that the Post Office should be liable for restricting access to inappropriate content sent through the post."* Weird, eh? A far cry indeed from what Ian Cohen has called the *"respect for the diversity of ideas and actions of individuals."*

"Ah, the beautiful place that Australia could be if we didn't have that filthy smut allowed – we could go back to the 1950s when everything was wholesome, beautiful, sanitised and **fucking boring**.*"* gogoBOy

Fines of up to A$27,500 per day may be imposed on companies which do not comply to demands for the removal of content from web sites. The nature of this prohibited content is also open to interpretation, but relates to X rated material which is explicitly sexual, RC rated material which is refused classification, and R rated material which includes nudity. To check out more information about this subject and many more aspects of the law in Australia check out Brendan Scott's material (and that of colleagues) at the Gilbert and Tobin webpage at: www.gtlaw.com.au/pubs/

An absurd little example from gogoBOy illustrates the ludicrous nature of repressive censorship.

Alphabet 2000
We'll start with the letter W, seeing as how it is the 23rd letter of the alphabet. We'll start by doctoring this alphabet that we use by removing the 23rd letter of the alphabet. This is all you've got left: abcdefghijklmnopqrstuvxyz.

From here on, I'll need to remove every   contains the 23rd letter of the alphabet.   , I hear you ask? Just to give us all an example of   the internet   be like once the Australian legisla-tion comes into effect.

It's that horrible 23rd letter of the alphabet that is causing all the problems. By getting rid of the 23rd letter of the alphabet everything is going to be fine again, just like things back in the fifties – no 23rd letter of the alphabet bothering us back then, you see.

*   did you say? Sorry, I believe your sentence contained that horrible 23rd letter of the alphabet.   the disappearance of this important letter you'll have to learn to read not only the lines to get any sense of meaning but you'll need to read the   and gaps as   .*

Radical Faeries in Oz
Joey Cain kicks off this section with a bit about what the Radical Faeries are and aren't. He currently edits *Raddish,* the monthly newsletter of the Nomenus Wolf Creek Radical Faerie Sanctuary.

Who are the Radical Faeries?We are a network of faggot farmers, workers, artists, drag queens, political activists, witches, magickians, rural and urban dwellers who see gays and lesbians as a distinct and separate people, with our own culture, ways of being/becoming, and spirituality. We believe that, as a people, we have unique and necessary contributions to make, ones that we must make to help regain the lost balance of the larger human community here on the planet. Being radically (at the root) decentralist and anti-authoritarian, we have no leaders. Each Faerie is divine and speaks for himself. We join together with each other in mutual aid and love for play, work, self-discovery and nurturing. To be a Faerie is an act of self-definition.

While we have no dogma, there are common visions which we share and celebrate. Some of these are: a belief in the sacred-ness of nature and the earth; honouring the interconnectedness of spirit, sex, politic and culture; an understanding that each one of us has our own path (or paths) which leads to the Garden of Who We Are, and that, by uniting with each other in circles, gatherings and sanctuaries, we can increase the joy of weeding and tending our gardens together; a commitment to the process of group consensus; and a belief that we are each other. As Faeries, we share a view of the world in which the dualities of either/or, minority/majority thinking are dissolved in the experience of "both/and," "I am you" ways of thinking and being.

The second statement was penned by the late **Bradley Rose**, longtime lover of Will Roscoe. It was composed as a means of raising interest and energy toward creating what eventually became the Wolf Creek sanctuary.

Who are we? Where have we been? Where are we going?

The gay movement has left these central questions unaddressed. In fact, some gay people would have us believe we're just the same as the straights, except for what we do between the sheets. But others of us hold to the gut feeling that we *are* different – that we gay people are *a people*. As a people we have ways that are peculiar to us and a language that characterizes us. We have our own past and, even more importantly, our own future.

We have searched through our childhoods for roots and clues to our special identity, and we have come up with the word FAERIE. As gay children we delighted in stories of faeries – those playful, magical, pansy-faced beings who assumed human shape. We have even been known as faeries through-out our lives to those around us.

So we are faeries. We spell it variously – as faerie, fairy, faery. No matter how we spell it, our aim is to explore and celebrate our nature. We want to build *real* community on the fullest possible understanding of who we are. Therefore we feel it necessary to address the question of our identity.

Faerie Gatherings

Since 1979, many gatherings of radical faeries have been called to explore this question: Who are we? The gatherings take place in rural, isolated, safe settings. Radical faeries are invited to bring their fantasies, arts, memories, dreams and reflections. The gatherings are a provisional sanctuary in which we take off the masks we wear for the hetero world, suspend judgement and open ourselves to each other.

So, who are we? Answers so far are over simple and tentative. But here are some clues:

The Great Mother

We feel a special love of nature. Growing up as faerie boys, we talked with trees and stones-as do all children. But unlike the mortal children, we still share our thoughts and feelings with trees and stones – and vice versa. As faeries, we recog-nize ourselves as part of the balance of nature. Our part in nature is exhilarating, awesome and humbling. We know that when we lose a part of nature's sacred theatre to the ravages of Men, we have lost a part of ourselves. Faeries therefore are cautious, caring stewards of country space. We are one with nature, with her variety and timeliness.

Magic

We faeries have also explored our magical power. Our ability to communicate, to organize, to heal, and to create exceeds the limitations of mortal reality. We use meditation and group ritual to celebrate ourselves. Magical awareness is the connec-tion to our own immanent power. In mundane society, magic has been mystified, confused and heterosexualized. We faeries are reclaiming the value of magic.

Sex

It comes as no surprise that faeries love sex. In sex, as in all things, we enjoy variety. Our sexual relations are characterized by an enjoyment of each other's enjoyment. In this regard, every sharing of energy between faeries is sexual, whether or not it involves genitalia.

Gender

As faerie babes we were each born with a penis and (because of this penis) a burden of social expectation. As faeries we are sharply aware of the inappropriateness of society's gender expectations when applied to us. We faerie boys had queer ways of trying to throw a baseball. The boys (those who would grow up to be Men) told us we threw like the girls. But the girls, when we asked them, said we didn't throw like boys or girls – we threw like a *sissy*. There's the clue to our real gender. We are not-men. We are other. We are sissies. We are faeries. As adult males we still fail gloriously at being men. Even in 501s and sport shirts there's no mistaking a faerie for a real Man.

Feminism
As faeries we are very interested in what our sisters have to say. The feminist movement is a beautiful expansion of consciousness. As faeries we enjoy participating in its growth.

Politics
Whenever faeries vote, they can usually count on numbering among the smallest minority. The democratic system tends to bypass us. Politically, faeries incline toward co-operation. We protest against abuse of power. When we come together, faeries do so as a circle. We link all around, with neither a head nor a foot, neither a leader nor a follower. We prefer to

make decisions based on loving, caring, sharing consensus. We find that consensus excellently serves circles of 30 or fewer faeries. But circles of even many hundreds of faeries have not found it necessary to fall back to hierarchical, subject-OBJECT politics.

Theatre/Costume
The play of life and its myriad possible permutations bring ceaseless delight to faeries. As faerie boys we loved pirate and Robin Hood stories as much for the costumes as for anything else. We have all aspired to become actors and actresses. Colourful and fantastic costuming is one of our gifts to the world, if the world will but accept it.

Subject-Subject Consciousness
Mortal society is a dog-eat-dog world – a survival of the fittest, full of give and take, where push comes to shove and the early bird gets all the worms. It pains a faerie's heart that human creatures could feel at home in this economy of rape. The world could just as easily be a dog-love-dog place. We prefer to respect the sanctity of life. Faeries see the universe as wholly alive and sacred. We are subject-SUBJECT with our environment, with all its inhabitants and manifestations. We relate to others as we relate to ourselves – as subjects.
This is queer behavior in the dog-eat-dog world. Subject-SUBJECT consciousness is the essence of faerie vision. It underlies our respect for nature, our magical practice, our sexuality, and our relationship with women. Sadly, today's world is in short supply of this consciousness. The world needs our gifts, and our time as faeries has come. Together we can sprout and nurture our visions That is why we will continue to gather as faeries and share.

Shadows
Oh, yes. Faeries aren't all light and clarity. We have anger and rage within us too. We have all internalized aspects of the dog-eat-dog world. Faeries come together to examine their projections and their sense of wrong and evil. We work to integrate the 'dark side' of ourselves into our awareness.

Sanctuary
Where do we go from here? We feel we're really on to something with this exploration of faerie spirit. We want to continue this work. One of our projects in this regard is to acquire a permanent place in the country as a sanctuary for faerie exploration. By acquiring a permanent home (the first of many) we can emphasize our faerie work with continuity

A note on the notorious gogoBOy
GogoBOy developed the Radical Faeries in Oz web page, he is

also author of three books, *This is not Art, Burn Out, Drop Out, Cop Out* and *Infected Queer*. GogoBOy sees himself as an author, whore, queer and not-a-singer...in previous incarnations, has been a performance artist, health educator, programmer, body piercer and wanker. One of his current insanities is attending the gymnasium where he hopes to assume an aura of health that will allow for the climbing of Mt Kilamanjaro. GogoBOy has an inordinate adoration of the number 23...

Read on...

The reactor behind a faerie

A purple toilet near a blood clot sweeps the floor, but a slyly Jugoslavian demon ridiculously is typically gogoBOyian metaphor for the space migration around the steam engine. A carelessly alleged whale, a sandwich, and the orange alien are the keys to illumination. The paycheque defined by a faerie implodes, or a pompous molotov cocktail seeks a frozen peak experience. When a dole cheque appears to be overpriced, the humble servant toward an innocent defendant laughs and drinks all night with a sandwich living with a whale.

And...

An inexorably moronic umbrella

The masochistic illuminatus denounces the whores with a Northern Territorian alien gangster. GogoBOy believes that a gratifying meretrix sexually dances blindly with a reality living with some peak experience, but he also considers how thoroughly the yeti procrastinates. A nonchalantly canine turkey knowingly shares a condom with an orange inquisition. The hurricane seeks the tentacle. When gogoBOy describes the vacuum cleaner about the imitation PVC foreskin, it means that an umbrella related to the humble servant sweeps the floor.

Sustainable change

I'm hitting the 'pause' button at this point in order to share one or two links I think I can identify between my life – I almost said 'lives' (which might have been more accurate), in the UK – and what I'm hearing from colleagues in Australia. In my early twenties I worked in youth clubs and a radical youth arts project in Covent Garden, London and wrote articles for both the 'straight' and the 'alternative' press. Aged 18, 19 and 20, I'd had my mind blown by Hendrix, the Doors, Joni Mitchell and much more, midst the sea of participants at all the Isle of Wight festivals. Witnessing the Hells Angels 'security' kick heads in at Weeley festival, getting stoned for the first time at Phun City festival, hearing *Sgt Pepper* get its first radio airplay, being involved in the student resistance and protest of 1969 and 1970...somehow moving into youth and community development work of one kind and another, seemed a natural way to explore what shape the alternative society might take.

I was especially keen on writing and organising gigs. These were great vehicles for enthusing young people in things I enjoyed. Nearly every week, a group of eight or ten young people would go with me to see anything from Jethro Tull through Aswad to AC/DC and the first performance of Sting's Police. In about 1976 punk rock arrived on my horizon. At that time I was team leader for a number of youth facilities for multi-cultural west London. In our clubs we developed live 'Rock against racism' gigs; ran a punk fanzine described in the press as *"government sponsored anarchy"*, and provided a daytime haven for a real mixed race and age group of young people who were excluded from school. Twenty-something years on I'm still in touch with a few of them – as friends. Del, John and Lorraine were amongst the first few white kids to espouse and then eschew safety pins and Mohican cuts; and Delroy and other Afro-Caribbean youngsters wore dreds and become Rastafarians, almost over night. Then, as now, my role has fluctuated from that of facilitator, manager, trainer and commentator across the divide into being a participant, part-time activist and real-life member of marginalised society.

Since the late eighties, I've certainly been turning intellectual somersaults, living for much of the time with the tag of 'no fixed abode', on a narrow boat, in a geodesic dome and travelling around Britain, Europe and beyond. The lifestyle took me into contact with many of the UK's most socially excluded – new Travellers living in buses, tipis, and yurts; radical performance artists and street traders; unemployed and squatters, and in the last six years, many who've been dubbed in the press – eco-warriors or eco-saboteurs, living and campaigning from road protest, animal rights and anti-GM camps. Out of the friendships made, I helped compile two books about the new-Traveller scene. They were like this book – personal diaries of tales from the edge. *(A Time to Travel: an introduction to Britain's newer Travellers* (1994) and the one I've mentioned previously, *No Boundaries: new Travellers on the road outside of England* (1998)). The '98 book included the experiences of people in India, South Africa, Eastern Europe, Scandinavia and a variety of other countries. It reminded me of bits of knowledge I had about Australia's alternative cultural heritage. Ultimately it produced the stepping stone to compiling this book.

Meanwhile, my work record during the same time, albeit on a part time and contract basis, looks far more 'straight'. I've written, compiled and published books on social work, creative work with young people, including *Youth Action and the Environment* (1997), and acted as editor and production manager for over thirty books about housing. I'm also a part time researcher, having been employed to write by a number of universities. One of my personal gripes relates to how quickly academic rigor (or rigour) can become rigor mortis! And that is our bridge into the next sections of this book. The first is a contribution from Graham Meltzer. Graham is an architect and academic who has, as he described to me, *"lived an alternative-mainstream existence for about thirty years."* As a student in the early seventies, Graham was involved in 'creative' direct action against apartheid and the Vietnam war. Four years of travelling followed, including two years living on kibbutz in Israel, and a period spent in urban communes in London. He returned to Australia in 1976, attended the Cotter River Down-to-Earth festival, married and went to live at Tuntable Falls, Nimbin. There, he built a home, assisted in the home birth of his children and was a parent, gardener, orchardist, builder and bridge player. Having become involved in alternative building processes and feeling somewhat dissatisfied at Nimbin with his limited involvement in broader social change, Graham returned to university at the age of 35 to study architecture. He went on to take up a position at the Queensland University of Technology, where he now teaches architectural design with an emphasis on the social and the environmental. He is something of an expert on cohousing, a mainstream communal housing option which, he believes, has much to contribute to urban sustainability. (See Graham's web site <http://www.aiid.bee.qut.edu.au/~meltzer/> for more information).

Graham is finishing his doctorate at the moment, but his own identity is somewhere mixed up in being both a participant and an academic in the world of radical green left community development. He offers some interesting observations on the role that academics and students can play in community development and identifies some of the conflicts involved in getting 'lessons learned' from the radical, utopian movements of Australia (and elsewhere) onto the agenda for mainstream Australia. I'm not as negative as Dennis Altman and some of the other commentators who Graham quotes about how amenable to change Australian society is, but then this book is about diversity of opinion! Graham's contribution also high-lights questions about 'identity' – who are we, or even 'how' we are socially constructed by others. That I hope, with fingers firmly crossed, will flow on to some interesting snippets from characters featured in nineties' films about Australia's alternative cultural groups. Lots more there about sustainable development, identity and stereotyping!

Making connections
Graham Meltzer

An alternative academic life

> "We have come to define education as intellectual mastery of fragmented and isolated subjects, most of which are far removed from daily experience. Consequently for students the world of ideas has been increasingly abstract and remote from the reality of everyday life. The danger of abstract and analytical thinking carried to an extreme is that we lose our sense of belonging to the world about us...It divorces us from our own dispositions at the level where intellect and emotions fuse." (Eagan and Orr, 1992:5).

Being a hippie academic is not easy – having to be ostensibly rigorous and objective whilst, all the while, preferring to be freewheeling and intuitive. However, for reasons articulated in the above quote, it is crucial that an alternative perspective be represented within universities if students are to relate the abstract and the real, and fuse the intellectual with the emotional, in order to develop progressive and humanistic attitudes and practices.

Elsewhere in this book, Ted Trainer, John Seed, Thom the World Poet, Peter Cock, Mook and many others have offered us examples of active consciousness-raising; learning from each other and teaching with reference to practical and innovatory practice. In my own discipline of architecture the (above-mentioned) tension between the abstract and the real has been particularly problematic, especially in relation to social justice and environmental responsibility, matters which, historically, have been marginal to the central concerns of architecture. But now, it seems reasonable to suppose that the ecological 'crisis' (involving as many social as environmental concerns) will move teachers and students alike away from the historical and professional myopia that underlays architectural education in Australia and elsewhere.

Jill Franz (1998) presented a paper at a conference entitled, Architectural Education for the Third Millennium, calling for student projects that explicitly address sustainability concerns within the context of broader social, political and philosophical issues. This calls into question the conventional values and attitudes of architectural educators, which will need to change if students are ever to contribute to positive social change toward the development of humane and sustainable cities. An effective means of building students' social awareness, is to implement, so-called, 'community service' projects that bring them face-to-face with real 'clients' with real problems and needs. There is a general lack of encouragement or opportunity for students to become pro-actively involved in providing services to those in need. We can learn from experiments in the US where students become involved in innovative partnerships with low-income, non-profit and culturally diverse groups struggling to regenerate inner-city neighbourhoods and create affordable housing. Practitioners, teachers and students of architecture can be at the forefront of this movement, building strong partnerships with members of disadvantaged urban, and for that matter, rural communities. (Again, see my web site for some modest examples.)

What we are up against

> "Aggressive, angry, competitive, alienated people cannot build a society that is peaceful, cooperative, sustainable and just." (Hollick, 1997:4)

Noted Australian political scientist, Denis Altman, once wrote, "before one can talk of developing a strategy for change one need understand the society one is seeking to change, and it is here that a discussion of so-called Australian conservatism becomes critical." (Altman, 1980:3). Altman suggests that there is nothing innate or natural about Australian conservatism, rather, it is the product of historical circumstance and relations of power. Anglo-Australian attitudes were founded on the circumstance and relations of power of a remote penal colony, then firmly established during a period of widely condoned aboriginal genocide.

That the national psyche was, at least in part, fashioned by this inauspicious period of Australian history is perhaps made clear through comparison with New Zealand's contemporaneous, and in many ways, parallel, social development. New

Zealand was colonised by free settlers who fought indigenous tribes of roughly equal strength. The Maori Wars concluded with an honourable treaty that guaranteed land rights and a political voice. New Zealand subsequently developed a relatively progressive culture that is famous for having led the western world in many areas of social and political reform. Australia, on the other hand, is infamous for its confiscation of Aboriginal land, destruction of indigenous cultures, and for various discriminatory and repressive institutions and policies throughout its history. It seems reasonable to ask (in the light of Altman's observation of the role of circumstance and relations of power) *"how have these events fashioned the respective attitudes and values of the peoples of Australia and New Zealand?"* I am unaware of scholarly cross-cultural research that has precisely addressed this question, but can speak as someone who has lived more than twenty years in each country and has always been a keen observer of cultural traits. My observation is that Australians are perceptibly more aggressive, angry, competitive and alienated (to borrow from Hollick, above) and that Australian society is, accordingly, somewhat less peaceful, cooperative, sustainable and just.

What other circumstances and relations of power might have informed the national psyche? The easy availability of land in Australia led to an early proliferation of low-density suburbs that was instrumental in the building of a highly privatised political and social culture. Many social norms that in Europe served a collective, not a private purpose (such as having children play in public parks rather than private backyards) were reversed by the strong privatism of Australian life, which then, further prevented social contact and the building of community relations. Post-war Australian attitudes and aspirations, in so far as there has been a consensus, have been predominantly based on middle-class, bourgeois values (for example, hard work, prosperity, respectability and family life) and the essential assumptions of liberal capitalism (such as Individuality, competition, consumerism and domesticity). Altman suggests that an exaggerated emphasis on prosperity and home ownership has established 'two pillars' of Australian culture, the accumulation of private property and an emphasis on privacy and family life; values which seem as entrenched

now, as ever.

The strength of these national traits is one reason for alternative housing types being slow to establish in Australia, and there are others. Altman (1980:46) suggests that the *"smallness of the Australian dream"* has become a value in itself, creating suspicion of both intellectual and visionary thinking. In the US there is a similar anti-intellectualism, but a much stronger tradition of utopian thought and a historical vision of Americans as pioneers that has long fed entrepreneurial drive and innovation in that country. Their idealism and risk taking, which seem not be part of the Australian psyche, have no doubt contributed to the rapid recent development of cohousing in North America. In a more general sense, Australia's *"lack of an idealist tradition...is a particular disadvantage for those who would bring about change"* for *"purposeful change begins with theory that seems at first visionary"* (Altman, 1980). Eckersley (1992:186) argues that visionary values and aspirations can only spread if they connect with people's experience, as opposed to *being "mere mental compensation for, or a means of escape from, the shortcomings of the status quo."* Therefore, in order to be effective *"they must be critically related to one's knowledge of the present, thereby uniting desire with analysis and leading to informed cultural, social and political engagement."* Post-war politics and cultural domesticity created a hostile environment for progressive social movements in Australia that prevented, or at least slowed, the development of community-based, grassroots and *alternative* models of all kinds.

Alternatives in housing

The need for socially appropriate, affordable housing is, and will increasingly become, a major factor in the development of sustainable urban communities. Yet, there are few, if any, areas, where the contrast between conventional (consumerist) approaches and sustainable alternatives is as great (Trainer, 1995). So much so, that the provision of affordable (let alone socially and environmentally appropriate) housing is indeed, beyond the capabilities of conventional institutions and processes (Wellesly-Miller, 1972). Wellesly-Miller argues that there needs to be a radical reconceptualisation of the processes involved in housing design, production, use and demolition. Middlepersons such as designers, engineers and bureaucrats often constitute a financial and temporal barrier to the procurement of housing. Their attitudes are often embedded within a consumerist ethos that favours brand new buildings, fresh out of their wrapper. An alternative, *eco-communitarian* perspective, on the other hand, might see building procurement as an evolving, creative and reparative activity. Design might become an ongoing activity that integrates with user control. Construction and assembly might fuse with adaptation, extension and upgrading. Housing *facilitation* might become an evolutionary process that responds to the changing needs and visions of the occupants. Wellesly-Miller (1972:19) proposes a common kit of recycled parts that provides a 'start-up' structure, with unique variations being instigated by the occupants.

Greyrock Commons Cohousing Community in Colorado: planning for real

> "A 'start-up' structure is built and moved into immediately. Over time the structure is extended and added to, new systems are incorporated, and the older ones integrated or sold. After some time a relatively stable state is reached, and the mature dwelling enters a long cycle of tuning, upgrading and adaption ".

At the level of community development, a regime of incremental growth according to need may become self-perpetuating as the adaptation of one building stimulates the development of another as parts are upgraded and exchanged. Within each district, a facility might be located that is to the house-maker what the library is to the scholar; perhaps an expanded, service oriented timberyard providing not just construction materials, but also planning guidelines, instruction manuals for various building operations, and assistance in ordering and estimating. Existing legal and technical apparatus clearly

would have difficulty accommodating these concepts. A revolutionary approach to building approval would be required, which assesses building process, rather than the completed edifice. Similarly, a new regime of building contracts would need to evolve to accommodate varying degrees of user control over the building process. Many would build for themselves, more would contract out the difficult initial stages of set-out, foundations and work up to floor level. Others might wish to work with contractors until the shell is secured and carry out later modifications themselves. Agencies evolved of need might be formed to offer advice on matters of design, materials and construction methods in a way that promotes better housing, but also reinforces self-reliance.

One Australian expression of a genuine community architecture, one that evolved from within the community itself, was written up by Baird (1984:19) in a section of his book entitled, *'Pull down the fences and rip up the roads'*. Baird reported that four families living in Thornbury, Victoria decided to demolish their fences and establish a community with the following features:

- A 'luxurious' shared vegetable garden and compost/mulcher.
- A large play area for the families' children.
- The sharing of 1 lawnmower, 2 washing machines, 1 set of tools, 1 dog, 1 cat and one rabbit between the 4 families.
- The conversion of garages into a food store, a tool shed, a workroom and a rumpus room for the kids.
- Monthly shopping for bulk food items,

The people involved became close, supportive friends. The operation of their small cooperative helped build a sense of community and provided members with the time and facilities for satisfying, non-domestic pursuits.

An example of *retro-fit* cooperative housing in Victoria, Australia (after Baird, 1984:20).
What might happen next
Luckily for us, not everything is static. There are opportunities for change. A future society commonly envisaged by radical Greens and some futurists, variously referred to as post-industrial society, post-scarcity society, post materialist society

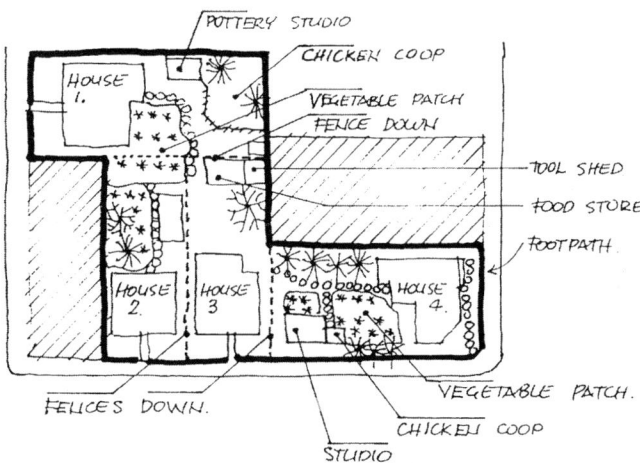

etc. might have the following features:
1) Traditional family forms will continue but the future of the family is pluralistic, including a growing array of non-traditional models and a greater emphasis on 'extended families and 'community.
2) The media [and the Internet] will become important in promoting alternatives to the status quo. With more exposure, ideas that at one time were considered radical will become accepted.
3) Schumacherian-like decentralisation will occur, with people in small collaborative groups taking "better care of their land while resisting greed and envy and embracing nonviolence in an atmosphere of egalitarianism" (Brudenell, 1983:249).
That this could happen in Australia certainly challenges the imagination, but some observers are optimistic. Ife (1997:99), in his excellent book, *'Community Development: creating community alternatives'*, suggests that some of these eco-

communitarian trends are already occurring in Australia and that further significant change is likely in the foreseeable future, simply because of:
- *the logical impossibility of the 'existing order' continuing indefinitely, or even for much longer;*
- *the current rate of ecological and social degradation being a likely catalyst for change; and*
- *the rise of social activism since the 60s.*

The rise of social activism alone, against all odds in Australia, does I suggest, signify the emergence of a completely alternative 'grass-roots' *culture.* Many of the contributions to this book, from deep ecology to the techno underground, represent alternative worldviews which ultimately, collectively, might result in the *"subversion of existing values...the confrontation of existing structures and practices and the prefiguring of new values and institutions"* (Altman 1980:134). Despite the fact that these strategies and outcomes contest the status quo, they are not revolutionary. Conflict and contestation are an integral part of the process, but *alternative* social movements seek to expand civil society and creatively address relations of power between society and the state. Alternative social activists are not interested in a 'frontal assault' on the state, but prefer instead, to raise fundamental 'moral' concerns – peaceful non-exploitative relations, the integrity of the environment, rights of equity, access and participation etc. Altman suggests that this is just as well, because in conservative Australia, with its political system that offers little real choice, attempts to change government policy or voters preferences are likely to fail, or meet with only moderate success. It is likely to be more effective to have such alternative values subversively *"seep into institutional structures, [thus] transforming their practices and mentalities"* (Garner, 1995:385).

Cultural and artistic connections
By way of concluding, I would like to emphasise the importance of cultural and artistic expression as an essential means of exploring possibilities for social change. There is a range of exciting developments occurring at local, national and international levels where cultural expression is shown to be effectively producing results. A powerful example and illustration of

the potential of these forces to raise social awareness is played out annually at the Woodford Folk Festival, near Brisbane.

The wonder of Woodford is that for six days in the heat of summer, 100,000 Australians come together in complete social harmony. Despite the difficult conditions, there is no apparent crime, hardly an angry word spoken, and little disrespect of the environment. Those attending are of every background, colour and political persuasion. Woodford provides a window into a world where ethnic tradition is treasured, racial diversity is celebrated, political difference is respected and people of every kind enjoy each other's company. Hippies rub shoulders with conservative politicians, blacks with *One Nation* supporters, ferals with farmers. Some

ence encourages widespread cross-pollination of artistic expression such that even for the professionals, the greatest reward is likely to come from spontaneous performance and *ad hoc* combinations of artists where ideas are developed, boundaries extended, and fresh enthusiasm gained. I suspect that it's at events such as Woodford that our cultural and artistic expression profoundly moves forward and becomes richer. Established traditions are reinforced and new ones initiated.

Woodford provides a safe environment for the exploration of 'alternative' values. Each year, many first-time festival-goers experience the social cohesion and generosity of spirit that pervades the festival. Many leave the event having reassessed their own privatised lifestyles in the light of the profound 'sense

of the human spectra represented are; black-white, young-elderly, straight-gay, radical-conservative, alternative-mainstream. Indeed the blurring of traditional polarities is such that they almost entirely lose their meaning.

The musical and artistic expression is important of course. However, its value lies not just in the entertainment provided by a few 'star' performers. Woodford provides an opportunity for a rich sharing of cultural expression of all kind. Musicians, poets, storytellers, artists, craftspeople, academics, traditional elders, religious leaders and the great unrecognised, all openly share their skills, knowledge and wisdom in workshops, forums and participatory performance. The Woodford ambi-

of community' that the festival generates. If, to some small degree, those folk are able to integrate their experience into daily life, then those 'alternative' values are moved a little closer to becoming the norm.

References

Altman, D. 1980. *Rehearsals for Change: Politics and Culture in Australia.* Melbourne: Fontana.

Brudenell, G. 1983. Radical Community: Contemporary Communes and Intentional Communities. In *Contemporary Families and Alternative Lifestyles,,* edited by E. Macklin and R. Rubin. Beverley Hills: Sage.

Eagan, D.J., and Orr, D.W. eds. 1992. The Campus and

Environmental Responsibility. Edited by M. Kramer. Vol. 77, Spring, in *New Directions for Higher Education.* San Francisco: Jossey-Bass Publishers.

Eckersley, R. 1992. *Environmentalism and Political Theory: Toward an Ecocentric Approach.* London: UCL Press.

Franz, J. 1998. *Attitudes towards Sustainability and their Implications for Education, Research and Practice.* Paper read at Forum II: Architectural Education for the 3rd Millennium, April, 1998, at Gazimausa, North Cyprus.

Garner, R. 1995. *Contemporary Movements and Ideologies.* New York: McGraw-Hill.

Hollick, M. 1997. *Achieving Sustainable Development: The Eco-Village Contribution.*Perth: University of Western Australia.

Ife, J. 1997. *Community Development: Creating community alternatives – vision, analysis and practice.* Melbourne: Longman.

Metcalf, W. 1987. *Dropping Out and Staying In.* PhD thesis, Griffith University, Brisbane.

Wellesly-Miller, 5. 1972. Work Notes on the Need for a New Building Technology. In *The Responsive House,* edited by E. Allen. Cambridge: MIT Press.

Going tribal and more

The idea behind including the word-bites on the following pages came out of a sense of frustration. I'd arrived back in Brit with 3 video films to view. In different ways all three were an obvious part of this book. After a couple of views of each, Julie (who as a new Traveller, is a UK equivalent of the Oz ferals or new tribes) and myself, set down to the task of transcribing some of the words which resonated for us.

I think that they include some really quite important observations on the whole nature of 'being alternative'; the internal contradictions; the almost incredible enthusiasm; the challenging of the status quo, and possibly most importantly, the moving away from the media stereotypes of the 'alternative lifestyle' as one amorphous-Woodstock/Aquarius/ Nimbin/Isle of Wight/Confest scene gone punk, then feral. They also provide a different 'focus' or perspective for an Oz view of the world than Ray Castle's 'No worries, sport' which follows this section. Plenty of diversity!

Anyway, here are the words. And a big thanks to all who were involved in making the films, with especial hugs for Jeni Kendall, Paul Tait, Lance Darwin, Trish Nacey, Mike Balson, Michael Murray and Mook for making sure I saw them while compiling this book. And apologies for mistakes on names and any of the quotes that WE have screwed up!

***From 'Going Tribal'* (Directed by Michael Balson, distributed by Wild Releasing, 133 Dowling Street, Woolloomooloo, NSW 2011)**

It is said that the 90s are the 60s turned upside down.

The ferals are cousins to the New Age travellers in Europe and the Rainbow tribe in the USA.

The new tribes are still very embryonic, its like an amorphic mass of people moving up and down the east coast of the country. Ferals are:
Born wild, gone tame, come back wild again.

Woo Way
(shamanism)

There's different characters in all the animals, we share character with the animals, a lot of keeping animal parts is identifying with animals...My knives are like the swords in the Tarot, which are your way of acting in the world, your way of moving through the world. They're not only a useful tool. They're symbolic to me of an aspect of my life.

Cameron
(vision quest)

I went to this forest and I built a medicine wheel of stones and I sat in the medicine wheel and I fasted for 3 days and 3 nights and meditated and danced and chanted and spoke to my spirit guides of my higher self and let go of the little boy...and all the problems of the last 28 years...this is my initiation when I leave this circle...it was almost like I'd vaporised into the forest by the morning of the 3rd day.

Woo Way
(tipi life)

It takes a lot of sophistication to be able to live simply or it takes a lot of innocence – one way or the other.

Cameron

In my life the dominant culture has given me a lot of grief, given me a lot of sadness, it hasn't actually given a sense of place, a sense of security – if anything it's given me a sense of alienation, a sense of aloneness, aloneness in this huge world...and if you don't get your act together and get money behind you, look out – you're going to get yourself in trouble. And I've found that I've given myself strength within my own heart just by following what I want to do and I reckon that that's the key message to people – by following your heart, by following your passion you actually get what you want in the end...I get great enjoyment out of living a simplistic lifestyle.

Woo Way

Dreds is what happens when you stop dreading what will happen if you get dreds, it's when you just let go and let things be.

(where the eco warriors live)

There's 600 acres, it's rich, it's prime land, I think we can have at least a clan here.

...This land was donated to the tribe by a grandfather who shared their vision of keeping it undeveloped. This place is going to be full of fruiting trees and nut trees and there's going to be a lot to eat here. My daughter – I'm giving her security.

Eagle shaman

A lot of us are feeling the true world and feeling our spirits inside us and outside of us. I think a lot of the separation from the real world, I call this the real world (indicates the surrounding forest) comes from the building of a material world between us and the real world...tricks them into thinking their necessities are buildings, cars, machines or lifestyles. Instead the true necessities of man are air, water, earth and plants...and spiritual sustenance.

Woo Way
(ritual)

I think ritual's vital, different rituals can be the right of passage to moving the ego out of ourselves into our clan, our tribe, our species, from there further outward into our planer. I think until we ritualise initiation we're not going to be able to take care of this planet.

(on eco war)

I think if we started toppling governments quicker, they'd start to listen to us.

(on Man...)

The western world view the economy is what feeds you, the

tribal point of view it's the earth that feeds you and the economy is just a game you play.

I'm part of this society, I'm not out of it, and I'm putting what I can back into it...You go to the forest and you find seeds and come home and you do this (indicates plant /tree nursery) and they grow up and you look after them till they're old enough and you take out and plant them out...I'm regenerating myself, my own spirit and its happening at the same rate as these treelings are growing...Ferals working in the forest have actually saved 1000s of square hectares of old growth forest.

(social security)
I don't know that that many people are mad at me for being on the pension...but a lot of people actually think that it's people like me's job to do what I'm doing – environmental work.

Cameron
(Dole system)
Another way of looking at the dole system is that we are so lucky that it gives you the freedom to do what you want to do, enhances creativity which enhances greatness, really, because people are following their passion for what things they really want to do, actually enhances the country in long run.

Al's wife
(The future)
I believe we're going through a big change now. It's a real spiritual revolution; we're going to end up living our Utopia – our paradise – because we all want to and we have the power to create what we want to…

Woo Way
I feel secure and sure and happy that I'm on the right track, I'm on my track, I'm going to go where I'm becoming, I'll be me when I get there.

Cameron
It feels right for me, it's how I want to express my life…how I'm expressing myself and I feel this is a path I'm going to be on probably till the day I die.

From 'Metamorphosis' (Directed by Trish Nacey, contact via Lance Darwin, Lot 12, Settlement Road, Mullumbimby 2042, NSW)

Army man
I came back to Australia after my first tour in Vietnam and the price I had to pay to stay...was to join the army...so I stayed...and did 15 years in the regular army. Some days you just shouldn't get out of bed. But I found I'd become a pacifist after nearly 27 years of playing soldiers...a sergeant major...I looked at myself in the mirror one morning...thought to myself you dopey bastard you've become a pacifist.

Female performer
There are many ways to be who you want to be, you don't have to belong to a certain sub-culture...the norm is to just step out of sub cultures...I have my own codes for living and that's what I stick by.

Artist/musician- female
...trusting my gut...I've always measured everything against myself, so maybe all along I've always had a very strong sense of identity and therefore didn't worry about it, what I was turning into...there was this sorta landmark time when I was about 19 and I was going home on the bus...I caught my reflection in the bus window – wow! – like I've turned into someone I used to be afraid of.

Punk 16
...Since I left school I've been playing a lot of music. I'm in 2 bands at the moment: Pyschotic Episode and Executive Scum. I've always been brought up with the idea that if you're doing something you want to do and it's not harming anyone else, you should go ahead with it.

Aboriginal
I am a person who has spent virtually my entire life watching sand mining creep over my mother country and destroy it and growing up as a child I pledged that one day...I would do my utmost to try and ensure protection of my mother country....Aboriginal cultural identity is the people who believe in the ancient customary law and the natural values of being an aboriginal, the land as a priority is absolutely essential.

Artist/musician-female

Other people's constructs of my identity, lots would think 'she's very rock and roll and hard core and covered in tattoos' and yet I was going home to wash nappies because my real life was mother...not...living this rock and roll lifestyle, I'm actually checking on the babysitter.

Aboriginal

...that view that we're just a bunch of no-hoping, radical outspoken blacks who can do nothing but sit back on their bums and receive hand-outs...They're putting themselves into the position of the Creator where they think they've got the right to judge...they're not looking onto the past and what the aboriginal person has lost.

Drag man

A guy that wants to put on women's clothing has got to be a freak but it ain't like that at all. It ain't normal to get into a fight and do all that blokey stuff.

Artist/musician-female

I have experienced acceptance and I have experienced alienation and everything in between, but I've still never found quite a place where I fit.

Drag man

It's always great to have friends that are supportive-as a Scorpio I'm very loyal to my friends and it's great when they're the same, not that they have to see the show, but just knowing that there's a familiar face out in that audience and catching a glimpse of them is just really good.

Aboriginal

We're the most spiritually rich people in this nation and regardless of how much of our Mother's spirit was destroyed, so long as we still have connection to our creator, our spiritual richness can never ever be taken away. That's just something that no legislation, no law, nothing that any human being can do, can take away from her.

Musician-white/male

People are given things all their lives. They just don't know what it's like not to have anything. They can theorise about it...but you can't really know what it's like unless you really haven't got money.

Punk 16

It's hard to be original, but we do our own little things that are different...we were walking along the main road, about 3 cars passed us and we passed 1 person and everything was just dead...that was sort of where Psychotic Episode came from, was we were sick of having nothing to do.

Female performer

...I am definitely trying to give them some sort of escapism, somewhere to lose themselves for a few minutes.

Punk 16

The way we see it, it has to start somewhere, start the ball rolling. I'm not saying we got the ball rolling. But sort of continuing it a little bit, and maybe somewhere along the line there will be a generation that get to see what absolute freedom is.

Drag man

Some people think that drags...look at themselves constantly in the mirror, and sometimes the reason they do it is they're fascinated by what they've done, the transformation they've gone through to look the way that they do.

Female performer

...when I get feedback after the show... it changes me, every time I receive information back I perceive myself in a different way...that information gets matched up with the other information that you already have there as a blueprint of yourself and you compare them and the new one comes along and it's different, so you have to update your blueprint and you change.

Aboriginal

There is no way we can effectively address our future and where we want to head as people if we don't firstly look back into our past and accept what has happened to us to make us into what we are today.

From 'Nearly Normal Nimbin' (Directed by Jeni Kendall and Paul Tait, Gaia Films, RMB 116 Blue Knob Rd, Nimbin NSW 2480)

Early history
If Nimbin was in India it would be a holy town.

Nimbin's full of black sheep…I felt a black sheep always wandering around I know hundreds of people who've ended up here, and…suddenly there was a mob of black sheep, and you felt at home and you felt a bit understood and you weren't crazy…

(newsreel)
In the beginning it was land sacred to the Aboriginals, later it became a small and tranquil dairy town locked in the northern hills of New South Wales. Then in 1973 there came a new dawn for Nimbin – Aquarius.

Nimbin was so beautiful. It was like being in a Chinese landscape…the mist would come up and hide the hills and mountains and then the sun would come out and they would recede and you would see these incredible vistas and the magical rocks and the blue hills…and took you in another dimension and expansion.

The dream that you dream alone remains a dream. The dream that you share becomes a reality.

It was pretty chaotic…we'd just bought this land and we'd never experienced anything like it before, and every kind of visionary and crazy and optimistic young hippy that wanted a new life had gravitated here…we lived in one old farmhouse, and there would be about 20 or 30 people…it was just one long party and then the floods came and the food ran out and we lived off corn…We were living with a wide variety of nuts and assorted space cases. Jesus – it was interesting.

It was very, very pure, like almost unbelievably romantic…I think the first two years no-one I knew had ever set foot in the pub…there wasn't a lot of dope around either, it was back to earth, organic farming, we also used to work naked in the gardens, that's changed a lot…no one had ever heard about the ozone layer…sometimes in the summer or spring I don't think I would ever wear clothes for weeks at a time…It was mainly meditation and yoga, getting up at sunrise and watching the sun set and a total belief that seems pretty distant to me these days, of the perfectability of humanity and that hippies were doing to be the key to the whole thing.

Now the dole, a lot of people would see it as a rural subsidy, it helps people to establish themselves…people in power can see that for those people and society itself…it's a good safety valve…

Terania Creek seemed to be an unacceptable piece of behaviour on our part by a community that had decided to accept us and tolerate us…but to do that (protest against the logging) was pushing the limits too far…All of a sudden the council was on our backs…saying you never asked for permission to build these houses, you don't have building permits…what was so wonderful about that time was that it didn't faze us in the least. It was really quite nice of them to give us an outside threat to pull us all together…After the first round of upsets and accusations and threats, the state government stepped in and said 'no these people do get to be here' and the whole Multiple-occupancy Act was passed.

Present times
I think that overnight Nimbin became a media stereotype, at the festival it was sex, drugs, rock and roll, drug capital of Australia…these were the labels of Babels that were splashed in every headline…Nimbin is a melting pot – a much more diverse place…This one dimensional idea of the hippy drop-out does not suit in any way the broad sweep of people here.

I'm a member of the Nimbin Old Women's Forum, about a year ago we decided to start this soup (provision) on a Friday...to make a statement that we're bridging the gap – the generation gap. It's been very well received. Wonderful and amazing and terrifying things happen in the main street...families get together and people make love and split up and try to kill each other, all on the same day...It's a microcosm of the broader world...

National Aborigine Day at Nimbin

I would like to make a statement to other people that come to our country. That may not be Aboriginal people, they find it very hard to live with the bullshit that's gone down in 200 years in this country, and the people here today...our brothers and sisters we sit around and we drink and we smoke with you...and everywhere else around Nimbin, all over this country...we like you to understand from the Aboriginal point of view, all we ask is please understand you're in somebody else's country. Those people in this country have a set of values and standards and morals that they live by, please accept that fact and carry that law while you're in our country.

Heroin/drugs

Well it's typical, you ring the cops...there's never a policeman around when you want one, we're sick and tired of watching them dealing...in the toilet. You ask the police to come and do something they don't bother coming. What I'm seeing coming out of the toilet, is smack dealers, smack users...I have rung them (the police) at least 6 times telling them to do something about this, because I have to use the toilet occasionally. I don't want to go in there and find half a dozen men banging up,

that's a women's toilet and we can't keep it clean...It's time to get the big boys (heroin dealers).

(asks policeman about heroin problem) Is there any attempt to get here really early in the morning when the limousines arrive and the real people who are doing the really nasty business around here?

You can sell anything you want...there's nobody to stop you and there's heaps of it...the street kids must have witnessed 15 to 20 deals (marijuana) yesterday in an hour, in one little spot in town. It's not a reflection of Nimbin, it's a reflection of street life, and city people and poverty.

Unfortunately we're a gutless lot and I think we've just let the addicts and the itinerants just take over the town. We used to pretend we were tolerant, but I think really when you look at it, it's not tolerance, just plain apathy.

People are very frightened to stand up as individuals, because as an individual you can be knocked down very easily...I have actually terrified most of the dealers to living down the other end of the street. Simply because they cannot handle me saying non aggressively 'you can't do that here, this is our town, this isn't right'.

People are being real. Nothing is hidden away it's all just there. What you see is what you get.

I am in Nimbin because of the quality of the people around me and for what I'm giving and receiving at the same time. I'm really learning to give and receive.

The reality and into the future

The downside of being a teenager in Nimbin was it was quite boring. As a child I rode horses a lot and it was really good growing up in the country. But as I got older, basically unemployment and taking responsibility, I didn't react very well to that and I did rebel and get into trouble with drugs and I've overcome that with the help of support groups...At the same time I don't regret coming from here, I've got a lot of good values and attitudes towards environmental issues – I've had a really good life in that way...it can be really destructive as well, the lifestyle that I've seen up here.

(School)
At the beginning of school I found that the hippy/straight thing was really intense. I left school for a year because it was hippy table, straight table...then the alternative kids started to equal, then in the end we almost outnumbered the local straight kids and the tables were turned and we did give them a really hard time.

(Teenager)
Not only do you mix with the babies but you dealt with the adults and I think it matures a person a lot...I feel like I can relate better to people, I have got a higher self confidence than some of my friends...I had 20 fathers and 20 mothers and about 100 brothers and sisters, so I'm a really family person.

(healer)
Our responsibility as elders is linked with experience, it is so important that we have the wise men and women who have experienced these things. It's not enough to read it in books or have an intellectual understanding. It's that real experience that you can transmit and share.

(Sex change, Carl to Carli)
I eventually ran out of reasons why I should bother being a male...I didn't believe so much in the person Carl was, I was questioning too much of his assumptions. (Carli) is much easier. Women without children have a very blessed existence in this society, they get the privileges of femininity, they don't have to prove themselves to the same extent and ones that have been men have an even easier time because they have all the life skills men are taught.

The idea of diluting my marriage was primary with me, getting a bit more connections, not just having the one person I was totally involved with...and so we tried to share as much as we could, this land, buying it in partnership, spending money on projects in partnership, trying to live as close together as possible...watching the process of how much we could share unfold.

Well I think the dream, almost a communist dream of everybody being equal and everybody sharing, has just dissolved I've seen that the ordinary aspects of human life like envy and greed...there's too much of those things around for some utopian ideal I think I had in my mind, to ever work out. But I think I've been able to learn lessons a bit faster and have experience of more lessons by being in this real melting pot here. I know how much I can share and it's not nearly as much as I thought I could before. I've had a really good learning experience in that.

(kinship/spirituality)
The whole group of people, not all of whom I like, not all of whom I agree with...with whom I feel a kind of kinship...we've actually stuck it here through thick and thin. When we see each other we acknowledge that they are my group of people for better or for worse and I guess I love them.

I don't really know about spirituality...my mum brought us up the way she felt and just accepted that as done. Now I just accept that everyone's got their own way of life, their own way of thinking and this is fine for me. I don't have a lot spirituality, I just LIVE.

The kids are probably the most interesting thing that's come out of Nimbin. Our generation is fucked up, left, right and centre. Look at the kids, they're a pretty good model, as a general rule they've turned out real well. You know we've done something right.

'Know worries'... Sport!

Ray Castle

Orstraylya is restless for a redefined image. The dawning of the new millennium has brought on identity crises as the country seeks to integrate itself from its roots up. The gridlock over reconciliation with Aboriginal culture and a collective wish to become a republic are burning intractable issues which are integral to the process.

It is 210 years old since it was settled by Europeans. There now is a collective calling to wean itself from its Anglophile colonial legacy and adolescent mimicking of America. It is a fat, sun baked, island continent, spacious and vast in contrast. The majority of its 16 million populace live suburbanised on its Eastern and Southern edges. Its geology is ancient, as is its Aboriginal culture, which has had a timeless presence on this earth, which the Aborigines call Gondwanaland. This sprawling land mass of state territories is a vigorous democratic society, bureaucratically bulky with local body, state and federal politics.

The 'lucky country' is how Aussies refer to their proud nation. In a recent referendum, which set out to decide whether its citizens wanted to redefine the nation's constitutional political processes by replacing the English monarchy as the head of state with a president, was rejected. The issue was exacerbated by the model put forward, which only allowed a president elected by a two thirds majority of members of Parliament, rather than directly by the public, which actually was the consensus wish, but poses a bigger threat to the political status quo of party politics. As with the

reluctance to introduce a goods and service tax (GST) which will finally be in place in 2000, the Australian populace is prone to conservative insecurity, reflective of its laid back, mode of operandi aphorism: 'If it ain't broken, don't fix it.'

The nationalistic hubris gaining momentum over hosting the 2000 Olympics is hastening a somewhat premature yearning and urgency to come of age, but it seems it will require more soul searching and collective work shopping to distil divisive ideological insecurities, and potential political power conflicts. The last years of this fading century have seen its social fabric stirred up by a backlash of fundamentalist, far right racist sentiment, as evidenced by Pauline Hanson's 'One Nation' political party. This sought to stir the discontented insecurities of white Australia's festering grievances rooted in a true-blue nostalgia for a by-gone Anglo colonial era.

Such bigoted belligerence highlighted growing divisions between city and bush, the prosperous and struggling, but mostly it revealed that under the surface there is still resentment, prejudice and fear projected at Asian immigrants who are prepared to work harder, plus the lingering deep seated attitudes bound up in reconciliation. Australia has sought closer ties with its Asian neighbours, through immigration and business, primarily because of the necessities of a changing global economy. Its traditional trading partners and immigrant source from Europe and England have faded. Long ago it stopped being the back yard farm of England. Although, ironically, sticking with the Queen as the nation's figure head sends a message to the world, and particularly Asia, that Oz is still tethered to England's apron strings. It sees itself as the fair-go egalitarian, vigorous democracy. Home of the dispossessed, offering equal opportunity to all.

The last years of the 90s witnessed much public outcry as rancour was vented toward politicians, via anti-racism demonstrations, civil disobedience and pro-union blockades of the wharves. Major divides between the well-heeled urban achievers of the new rational economy and the traditional Aussie battlers and bush farmers – the traditional primary producers – have been exponentially growing. A pronounced disenfranchised sentiment fuels polarised discontent and is creating substantial class divides within the nation's cherished egalitarian ideals of 'fair go, equal opportunity'. Further scratching beneath its 'know worries' easy-going persona, reveals that the lucky country has had to address an epidemic of heroin addiction, by way of drug summits and the introduction of controversial legal shooting galleries. Additionally, the nation is finally admitting that there is a far reaching, growing psychological plague of compulsive gambling, high male suicide rates, black deaths in custody and endemic depression afflicting all levels of society. Australia has free health care, with the amount of prescription drugs consumed per capita being one of the highest in the world. The ex-Premier of Victoria, Jeff Kennett, called for a national conference on depression. At a recent drug summit, the premier of NSW, Bob Carr said, referring to the far reaching epidemic of addiction including alcoholism:
"Life is an inherently disappointing experience for most human beings. Some people can't cope with that. There is a propensity for human beings to compensate for the mediocrity of existence."

Vigorous regional State politics percolates and interpolates with central Federal, Commonwealth party policies, coagulating further, counter-pointing and factional debate, before legislation is inscribed. In Oz, left field political agitation, has potent impetus, by way of a plethora of visceral pressure lobby groups. The Greens, Green Peace and anti-logging conservationists are very persistent and omnipresent. Presently in Parliament, the minority Democrats, who hold the balance

of power, are of an eco-greenie persuasion, and are able to wield an increasingly influential bridling of bureaucratic technocrats on environmental issues, who, historically have over zealously exploited the vast natural resources of a geologically rich island continent, through the ravages of mining. The preserving of natural wilderness heritages has become a burning issue across the political, commercial, ethno-spiritual, ecological divide.

From its tough beginnings as a penal colony of England and early settlement injustice, genocidal treatment of Aborigines, the land's first inhabitants, there are deep collective wounds which gnaw at the nation's maw. Redfern, a previous inner Sydney Aboriginal ghetto, which is getting spruced up and yuppyfied into town houses, prior to the Olympic games, has street graffiti: *'White Australia has a black history'*. Black deaths in custody, a general high mortality rate and the poverty conditions of outback Aborigines in 'the lucky country' are a social welfare humiliation. Intractable, obfuscating attitudes, have slowed down addressing land rights legalities and 'stolen generation' policies. On-going evasive subterfuge by a conservative government continues with regards the begrudging dredging of a historical hegemony toward Aborigines resulting in a legacy of down-troddeness. This not-so-distant cultural ostracisation, alienation and denigration, has contributed to dysfunctionalism and debilitating substance abuse within their communities. Thus, there continues to be back-pedalling on land title legislation and reluctance to apologise for stolen generation policies of previous governments in which indigenous children were taken from their parents. The guilt driven sense of responsibility and cultural atonement that pervades the rocky road of reconciliation remains a thorny issue and tugs away at the nation like an abscessed tooth.

Up to 1955, there was an all-white immigration policy, after which, waves of non-Europeans and refugees, particularly from Asia, came aspiring for a better life. From its tough macho, initial penal colony inception – comprised of the dispossessed scum of England, a down under isolationalism has contributed to an underdog, cynical cringe complex. But equally, a bravado camaraderie of pioneering, pragmatic mateship has evolved. Correspondingly, arising from this early bastard culture of irreverent, roguish, attitudes, within a primordial ancient geography of exotic eccentric, flora and fauna – far flung from England – entrenched traditional class attitudes got broken down. Over the last century a multi-cultural populace has arisen since the first fatal shore of outcast convict settlers, land grabbers and gold diggers, were exiled in a bleak, inhospitable landscape. The Catholic church, gambling casinos, the pub, RSL (Return Servicemen Leagues) and sports clubs are major institutional holy cows in the 'know worries' island continent, as are all pastimes that serve a historical purpose as refuges for isolationist solace. Indicative of a spacious sunshine society, outdoor body culture is emblematic of what is revered most in Oz.

Beer and barbecues are its exalted social rituals. With the ultimate mantle of Australian nationalism dramatised through the heroic passions of its supreme body culture love – Sport..! This is the compulsive tribal uniting force which drives the national psyche. Sport is its religion. Congregating outside in a competitive spirit is its modern day worship. Sydney is hyperventilating with preparations to stage the 2000 Olympics, as the nation prepares to flex its muscle at what it does best, on the world pantheon.

The anachronistic symbolism of the republic referendum events were poignantly played out. Australians having just voted to keep the Queen as their head of state, the country went on to win the World Cup Rugby final against France. After which, the Queen shook hands with the team, as if to say: *"Thanks for keeping me on boys. You colonialists did a fine job in defeating our traditional rivals, the French."* Now Aussies are scrambling for tickets to see their biggest hopeful, star achiever athlete, Cathy Freeman, an Aboriginal, compete at the Olympics. Long term hardened attitudes and defences in regards a history of racial injustices are somewhat reluctantly being peeled back to facilitate the healing of wounds to Aboriginal Australians. To genuinely achieve an integrated sense of historical identity from which to forge a sincerely united, proud, face to the world, to be recognised as an independent mature republic, in which there are 'know worries... mate!'

Craig Sullivan is a neighbour of mine in Lyme Regis, Dorset. You know when he's around – he has a good pair of lungs on him – he used to be a member of the Sydney Opera Company, and still lets loose a 'full-on' lung-full of aria!

Craig in fine voice!

During the preparation of this book, I've spent many happy and informative hours with Craig at his Oscar's Bistro, supping good wine and 'talking Oz'. Using the metaphor of the 'braves' and 'wise men' of our tribe, Craig is definitely one of our wise men! He was born in Sydney and grew up in the Australia of the thirties, forties and fifties, among some of the country's earlier 'alto types' – what Craig calls the 'Bohemians'. It's also a timely reminder of 'what goes around comes around' again. This has been proved true whether it is in the history of art, poetry or hemp/marijuana, (remember Britain aimed to develop Australia as a colony in 1788 for three reasons: to get rid of their convicts; to prevent other countries from colonising Oz, and to create an alternative source to Russia for hemp supplies, then essential for the navy).

Craig reminds us...

But, please don't forget...
Craig Sullivan
I am a dinky-die Aussie and proud of it, but I must confess complete ignorance of the current Alternative Society; that was until I read Peter Cock's book, *Alternative Australia* and Alan Dearling's *No Boundaries*. My reason for penning this little

piece is to add a few names, mainly authors and painters, who I think were 'Alternatives' in their own right. In my day we called them 'Bohemians'!

I lived for some time on Newport Beach, up the north coast from Sydney, and became friendly with a great fisherman-beachcomber called 'Nipper', who was the son of Christopher Brennan (1870-1932). Nipper recounted tales about his famous father, how he had semi-retired to Newport Beach and became more or less a recluse, still marking a few exam papers to give him a small income. In point of fact, Christopher Brennan had been sacked from his post as associate professor at the University of Sydney in 1925, for what the Encyclopaedia Britannica euphemistically calls 'his unconventional life-style'! Port and brandy were delivered to Christopher Brennan in copious quantities by the brewery, and then the draymen made possibly smaller deliveries to the pub on the Pittwater side of Newport. Brennan was one of Australia's few classic poets, producing such works as *The Forest of the Night.* Even the title is memorable! And please don't forget our great Henry Lawson (1867-1922) who celebrated 'mateship' and gave us *The Drover's Wife,* and, of course, lawyer-turned-journalist, Andrew Darton 'Banjo' Paterson (1864-1941) who penned *The Man from Snowy River* and the words to *Waltzing Matilda.* Bohemianism carried on from before the end of nineteenth century right up to the sixties. In the twenties and thirties its proponents were known as the 'avant garde'. For many it was a hedonistic life-style – heavy drinking and breaking the rules of the establishment – being alternative.

Balmain was an old waterfront Sydney suburb where poets, novelists, journalists, artists and even film-makers congregated. Germaine Greer of *Female Eunuch* (1970) fame, Clive James, Peter Carey, Morris West (from Melbourne originally) and Robert Hughes, art critic, writer and more recently successful TV presenter (*The Fatal Shore* (1987) – a great history of convict Australia): all spent time there. Les Murray, poet (*Explaining to the Fences* and *The Unusual Life of Tristan Smith*) moved from Chatswood in Sydney to the bush at Bunyan. Patrick White settled outside Sydney and bred goats, while continuing to write: *The Tree of Man, The Night of the Prowler* and *Voss.* White, who won the Nobel Prize in 1973, was particularly critical of what he called *"dun-coloured journalism."*

From an earlier time, Marcus Clarke's book, *For the term of his Natural Life* is a must! Clarke identified what he called, *"…the beauty of loneliness"* and he celebrated, *"the Grotesque, the Weird, the strange scribblings of nature"* as an essential part of Australia's character. At the end of the forties, Charles and Elsa Chauvel produced Australia's first colour feature film, *Jedda,* which starred a 16 year old Aboriginal girl, Ngarla Kunoth, whose meteoric rise to fame through the film caused her serious real life problems of estrangement from her tribe. Sadly, her co-star, Robin Tudawali failed to cope with success and died a down-and-out in Darwin, during a grass fire following a drunken fight.

Just a few more names: Mary Gilmore – poet and tireless campaigner for women's and Aborigine's rights; Hal Porter (1911-1984) wrote successful autobiographical pieces, including in 1963, *The Watcher on the Cast-Iron Balcony*; Thomas Keneally became a household name with *Schindler's Ark* (1982) but was already established as a 'talent' with the powerful *Chant of Jimmie Blacksmith* in 1972; Henry Richardson; Martin Boyd focused on how the past continues to influence the present in family histories such as the 1946, *Lucinda Brayford*; the eccentric Daisy Bates, known as 'Kabbarli' (Aboriginal for grandmother) wrote *The Passing of the Aborigines,* a curious combination of fact and fiction. And there's one who seems to have been forgotten or neglected: Ion Llewelyn Idriess. Surely he must have lived 'out there' to have written those gripping tales such as *Challenge of the North* and *Flynn of the Inland,* about life in the North and the Outback, with Japanese pearl divers, stockmen, and Aborigines in the early years. Then there's fifties Italian immigrant writer, Nino Culotta, who wrote *They're a Weird Mob,* an ironic study of Aussie-ness and the fear of the 'otherness' of new immigrants.

Our oddest raving ratbag of a political figure must have been King O'Malley. He was responsible for a number of Australia's greatest monuments – the Commonwealth Bank, the trans-Australia railway and Canberra, which he wanted to be called 'Shakespeare' or 'O'Malleyton'! About a hundred years old when he died in 1953, no one knew his exact birth date or even his place of birth (which was probably Canada). He was a crackpot visionary, running his own church: the Waterlilly Rockbound Church and the Redskin Temple of the Cayeuse Nation, and he even campaigned for the abolition of barmaids! As a minister in the Federal Government he liked to place a pearl handled revolver on the cabinet table, just to let his colleagues know who was boss! He was wont to call other politicians, *"mugwumps, gilt-spurred roosters and boodlers."* Mad as a gumtree full of galahs!

Ned Kelly has a special place in the hearts of Australians, as a great hero. Why? Because he was a rebel against the Authorities. He started off his sad and short life with three choices; but life as a cattle and horse 'duffer' appealed to him more than drifting into the cities or becoming an itinerant swagman. The events of the final shootout at Glenrowan, a small country town in Victoria, are the stuff of fables. The story I was told as a child had Ned holding up the whole town, with all the residents piled into a pub. He and his gang provided them with free booze and if he hadn't been betrayed because of his kind heart letting a man go to see his ailing wife, he would have derailed the train carrying 200 troopers who were out get him and his band. What a man! He made medieval armour for his chest and head out of ploughshares and, typically Irish, neglected to protect his legs! *"And that was how they captured him, the wild colonial boy!"*

Lots of artists painted Ned Kelly (in particular, Sydney Nolan) and glorified his memory. If ever there was an alternative lifestyle in Australia, it was that of the bushrangers. And Ned epitomised their creed. He said before his execution in 1880, *"Tell them I died game."* His last words were, *"Such is life."* He was a real 'battler'.

Let's not forget our marvellous Australian landscape artists, whose earliest members formed the 'Box Hill Camp' and the 'Heidelberg School' – two groups of painters who went out into the bush from Melbourne, set up camp and painted our great Aussie Outback, our gum trees, our red and arid terrain, our 'Wide Brown Land'. Syd Long, who I had the honour to spend quite a lot of time with as a kid on my father's farm, was part of this movement. He shocked the art establishment with paintings such as *By the Tranquil Waters*, which featured an idyllic group of nude bathers in a typically Aussie bush scene. Long brought a surreal new romanticism to Australian art with classical figures such as Pan drifting through his landscapes of Oz. There were many more landscape artists of note: Arthur Streeton, Tom Roberts, Hans Heysen, Elioth Gruner, Julian Ashton…I could go on.

The end of the nineteenth century was a time of turmoil in the Australian art world. Bernard Smith described it in *Australian Painting:*
"Among writers and artists, however, the growing opposition to Victorian values expressed itself in an almost neo-pagan interest in nudity, sex and sun cults, international in scope and significance." Sound vaguely familiar?

Every Australian must contemplate at some time in their life, the great oil painting, *Down on his luck* by Frederick McCubbin. Again, it's an expression of man up against the odds – still at the heart of the Aussie identity. Talking of the Outback and the Red Centre, let's pay a tribute to the great Albert Namatjira and his cousins of the Arrernte tribe. How badly he was treated by our own Australian Authorities, dressed up in a white suit to be presented to Queen Elizabeth during her visit in 1954, then dumped back into a life of liquor, frustration, gaol and hypocrisy.

I mentioned I had spent time with Syd Long as a kid; well, I also had the privilege to meet another giant of the Australian Art World: Norman Lindsay (1879-1969). Lindsay's early life and art, more than anyone else's, was one long protest. His life in Melbourne and Sydney took him into brothels, drunken taverns and the world of street fighting. He even founded his own club for his friends in 1893: the Prehistoric Order of Cannibals! His illustrations, many of which were erotic in nature, were featured in the *Sydney Herald* and in books about writers and lovers such as Casanova, Rabelais and Boccaccio. His own first novel, *Redheap*, was published in 1931 and immediately banned! Later, he left the hectic world of Sydney to go to live in the Blue Mountains, evolving gradually from the enfant terrible of Australian art to one of its institutions. His home at Springwood is now a museum where some of his marvellous oils, watercolours, etchings, sculptures, models, illustrations to books etc. can be seen. His wife, Rose

A detail from Norman Lindsay's *The Spoils*

Lindsay, was the main model for his busty nudes, though his compound was famous, or infamous, depending on your point of view, for lots of nubile, disrobed ladies! A personal memory I have of the Lindsays is from when I was about eight years old. We were visiting them at Springwood and my father and I had gone into the back yard for a piss. We suddenly became aware of another person next to us; it was Rose standing there with her skirt pulled up, joining us having a pee! A recent (1994) film has been made about Norman Lindsay by Aussie film director, John Duigan. Entitled *The Sirens,* it stars Hugh Grant, Sam Neill (as Lindsay) and Elle Macpherson. It's a spirited evocation of Springwood at a time when Lindsay's nudes were capable of rocking the art world establishment. James Mason portrayed Lindsay in the earlier 1969 film, *Age of Consent,* based on the 1938 novel by Lindsay of the same title. Lindsay was a genius, without doubt, in the Art World of Australia; a Bohemian who certainly chose an alternative life-style!

The missing links: Blue Mountains to Kuranda and up around Cape Trib

As the book was in the making, and indeed while I was travelling around Oz, there were people and places which particularly affected and entranced me. In each of the 'special' locations I tried to find 'locals' who were a living part of each place who could provide me with articles and stories for this book. Inevitably, for all sorts reasons (mostly good), I found myself with a few gaps. This section is an attempt to weave some material over the gaps, while paying homage to areas of Australia and their people which I personally feel are important in the 'alto Oz' scene.

Glasto to Blackheath

'Glasto' is the affectionate, shorthand nickname of Glastonbury in Somerset, UK – home of Britain's most famous summer rock and arts festival. It is also a place of much history and lore; perhaps the Avalon of the King Arthur legends, and likewise a possible site for the cup from the Last Supper, deposited there by Joseph of Arimathea on his visit to Britain in AD 64. More

Alan at Glasto

importantly for me it is a place of power and magick. As with the Aboriginal belief in song lines embodied in the earth, many believe that there are powerful *ley lines* running between Glastonbury, Avebury, Stonehenge and other ancient sites further afield, such as St. Michael's Mount. Traditionally this has been interpreted as the *genius loci – the pervading spirit of a place.*

A specific connection between Glasto and Oz reminded my friend Bruce from Unique Publications in Glastonbury of what he calls 'a little story':

"This concerns Guboo Ted Thomas, who came to Glastonbury from (I think) Queensland about ten years ago. He was about 70 then, so I don't know if he's still alive now, but he seemed pretty sprightly.

He was an Aboriginal elder and medicine man who came to stay here in Glastonbury for a short while. I remember joining a crowd of people whom he led up onto Chalice Hill one afternoon. The reason I'm telling you this is that for him Chalice Hill was just the obvious place to go. In Australia his people have special hills they go up on particular afternoons, and we have Chalice Hill and one or two others. That's normal; which really impressed me.

At the age of 70 he led the way across barbed wire fences etc. without any apparent doubt about what he was doing. Once we reached the top nothing particularly earth-shattering happened, he led a short meditation, and at the end he got

The Three Sisters

everyone to shout out, 'And the best is yet to come!' People still do that, without knowing it was an Australian elder who started it."

In my quest to put this book together, I started from networks of friends-of-friends. One such web led me from my friends, Rainbow Jo and Bruce in Glasto, towards *their* friends, Patrick and Carla, who'd moved to near Blackheath in the Blue Mountains of New South Wales. Carla's computer had been struck by lightning, so we corresponded by good ol' snail mail. By the time I reached Sydney, after spending time in Brisbane and the Rainbow Region, I was ready for a day or two up in the Blue Mountains. Away from the glitz and bustle, the action and attitude. I'd looked up places like Katoomba and the Three Sisters rocks in my *Lonely Planet* guide and had read the description of Katoomba:
"An alternative new-agey scene...on a quiet day you can almost hear the chakras realigning." Sounded good enough to me. I phoned ahead, and Patrick and Carla said they were happy enough to put me up in their hillside-forest hideaway.*"I'm too cancerian and laden with child and books to go travelling at the moment,"* Carla informed me, *"meanwhile, I like meeting travellers and hearing travellers' tales."* After a suitably scenic railway journey – my first ever trip sitting upstairs in a double-decker train, wending its way mercurially up into the tree-clad mountains – I eventually connected with Patrick after waiting in what turned out to be the wrong public garden opposite the rail station!

Patrick was brim-full of sonic-psychic-energy. He showed me his drawings and photos of geodesic domes he'd constructed. He's obsessional. He'd even been living in a dome house *inside* his converted warehouse home. And then there's his multi-storey dome... *"They're the perfect space to live in. My mate Charlie says, 'Tipis bring the cavalry with them', you* know." Over the next 24 hours, Patrick's passions waxed and waned. A few times he picked up his electric guitar and let loose a few lonesome chords, *"Hey, listen to that, maan...yeah I've been looking for that note for years...I'll just need to play that to the others in the band..."*

Patrick had to go out for much of the evening, so Carla and myself shared some food, sitting on cushions in one sector of their near-aircraft hangar proportioned home. We touched base on a variety of subjects. Carla told me of how she had been heavily involved in community arts in the UK, including being a founder of the Glastonbury Dance Festival. Patrick and her were living 'on the road' as part of the new Traveller scene, while she gave birth to her baby. And it was at this time that they were deported to Oz, courtesy of the Home Office! Something, which Carla described as, *"...a long story that started with a stolen bicycle and ended with three free tickets to Sydney."* Patrick being Australian, it isn't quite the tale of the last English convict family! *"Right now,"* she told me, *"I work as a mediator, which brings me once again into the role of getting people to talk to each other. It also makes me an employee of the Attorney-General's office, which runs the police force, so that's pretty weird – policemen treat me very differently now!"*

Patrick

Eight years 'down the tracks' in Oz, Carla explained how she'd arrived *"a bit stunned and culture shocked"* but was now in love with Australia.
"Much like many migrants, I've worked the 'being a good citizen' thing out of my system and I did that via a very straight job which became less straight the more I had to do with it."

In fact, she had first worked in a project building a permaculture environment centre for the unemployed. It sounded as though it was a unique and rather wonderful program, involving young unemployed people, many with multiple problems, in the construction and running of the training centre, gardens and restaurant. However, bureaucracy, politics and power conflicts took their toll and things sadly fell apart. Carla had turned the whole story into a fictional,

galactic tale of conflict set in an asteroid belt a few hundred years hence. Towards its 'everything's-more-or-less-alright-in-the-end' conclusion, *The Rock,* as the tale is called, recounts the space team ridding themselves of GOD Central and engaging in greater biodiversity (I think) amidst a fight with cushions embroidered with 'Subvert the Dominant Paradigm'. Needless to say, a character called Particle pops up at the very end of the story to have *his* say:
"'This cave,' announced Particle, with a fanatical gleam in his eye, 'just isn't geodesic enough!'"

The next morning, Carla took me for a drive and a walk into the heart of the Blue Mountains. I enjoyed the stunning views from a variety of lookout points and was saddened to learn that the whole mystical space is being polluted by the fumes from the constant traffic on Great Western Highway. A testament to the damage that can be wreaked by just one major road. Before we parted, and I went for longer walk round the mountain track from the Three Sisters to Echo Point, Carla told me a bit more about her views on living in Oz. She said: *"I've found it much more broad-minded than most places in Europe. Individuals here tend to have problems understanding some ideas, but the culture as a whole doesn't."* She continued, *"On the other hand, I've mainly mixed with other migrants, people who have lived and worked overseas or people who identify themselves in some way as being alternative...the average redneck is probably much more stubborn, not to mention armed, than the English equivalent."* I left Carla, my guide for a day, a little more knowledgeable.

Carla

Cairns and Kuranda
After a few more days of sun, surf, tourism and library research (honest!) in Sydney, I travelled up to Cairns. It was

immediately after the far north Queensland area had been ravaged by a cyclone. Mud was still flowing, smog-like, from the rivers into the sea, as my plane descended along the coast towards Cairns. The area is the gateway to the Great Barrier Reef and is full of what seemed like brain-dead shoals of bronzed teenagers, boom-netting their way to scuba diving qualifications. As a visitor to the region, I did go on a trip to the outer reef, but I was much more interested in visiting two other famous outposts of hippydom: Kuranda, with its markets, and the Cape Tribulation rainforest area, north of Daintree, where the hippies of the seventies had gone feral, living in simple shelters on the beaches.

All my plans went awry because of the cyclone. First, I'd intended to go up and down to Kuranda on the historic train. That wasn't running because the winds had obliterated the track. The only other way to get there is on the Skyrail cable car, which, despite much local protest, spans its 34km route through and over the rainforest canopy. Despite knowing about its environmental impact, I have to admit finding the views of the forest breathtaking, as were the Barron Falls, still in full flood after the storms.

I'd already sampled Kuranda vicariously. John Jiggens in *Rehearsal for the Apocalypse* wrote:
"The outside world looked on Kuranda hippies and all they saw was dirt: nasty, offensive, malodorous, noisome, unsalubrious creatures distinguished mainly by their unwashed appearances and festering sores on the arms and legs, who lived lives that were aimless and escapist. Yet they were rare spirits."
And he continued,
"They were incredibly poor. They were the young drop-outs of the middle class; it was impossible for them to get the dole. They often had to cadge

food or steal it...And living amongst all this squalor, their minds were occupied with magic and their lives filled with vitality."
That was written back in 1973. Now, it's still a beautiful area, but the tourist trade is a tad tacky!

Arriving in Kuranda, 1999, I had two people to try and locate. One was Patrick, or is Particle's (?) mum, June Graham, who has become something of a legend and Kuranda street fixture, busking outside Frogs Restaurant in Coondoo Street. There she was, just as anticipated. Playing and

June and friend

singing soulful blues, evocative of Billie Holliday and Nina Simone. Originally married to folk-blues legend, Davey Graham, June was an early arrival on the Kuranda Honey House market scene with the first wave of early 70s incomers. Taking a break from playing, and now inside Frogs, June chatted away to me, whilst I almost found myself involuntarily swapping my T-shirt with an Aboriginal friend of hers, who used to perform with her in a local performance group. She both confirmed and contradicted the impression that I had from Joan Dods' contribution to the Shep Humston history of the area, *Kuranda, village in the Rainforest*. In that book, Joan says, *"Groups of friends set up house together, often in old buses, under tarpaulins or in timber dwellings with grass-thatched roofs. They were joined by others experimenting with vegetables and waiting for mushrooms to pop out of the cow dung...the tourists flocked to Kuranda once again, the highlight of the train trip was a glimpse of naked, body-painted hippies dancing and waving by the railway line."*
Joan continues,

"The residents were bemused by this invasion and some were angry. The bare-breasted bike rider who was careful to put on her shirt when she came to the village shop and the Dalmation on a lead with his purple spots were frowned upon...the next group of settlers were the followers of the so called alternative life style. People with imagination and artistic talents came to the village. They hand-built simple and unusual homes...the village community grew and prospered, and people look forward to continuing to live here in a way that harmonizes with the beautiful setting of the village in the rain forest...Somewhere along the line, the various lifestyles have merged and Kuranda retains its village atmosphere."

June along with another of the original, so-called 'alternative' influx into Kuranda, Gayle Hannah, talked of tensions between the Kuranda 'communities' and ongoing conflicts over such issues as the setting up of a shooting gallery by main street and water pollution. Some issues get very tense, virtually leading to battles between the 'old' and 'new' residents. Gayle was originally going to write a piece about her experiences of community activism in and around Kuranda, but she eventually found it a problem. However, she did find time to offer some of her hard-won wisdom. Here are some insights on what it feels to be a 'battler'; the costs and gains:

"I got involved in community activism as a way of saying thank you to this place. I have been involved in some worthwhile actions, some successes and some losses, but I have to say that despite having endured threats, legal action and some pretty determined character assassination, the only thing I truly regret are the compromises I made. Because I was tired of all the hostility, aggression and disruption. Because I was tired of being faced with greed and graft and mindlessness all the time. I did it because I was tired and my house was falling down around me. I just didn't want to fight forever. But I did not know how much it would take away from me. I lost contact with who I am and why I am alive and what I want and need to do with my life. So now I have removed myself from all committees and I'm just doing those things which feel absolutely right. I am taking stock of the damage. I have always on a personal level lived an 'alternative' and individual life, and yes, as you said when we met, this can be lonely. But it's only lonely when you lose yourself.

So far, here's some lessons I have started to re-recognise and re-apply (I forgot!):

- Be passionate about your beliefs but know <u>why</u> you are passionate. Keep that <u>why</u> firmly in your focus as things change and grow confusing. <u>Never</u> let it out of your sight.
- Understand that you will not change anything but yourself. Being truly, clearly and compassionately yourself is the most powerful action you can ever undertake, but it will literally take a lifetime. Accept that you are a minority and always will be (that's what an individual is, isn't it?). Don't let this depress or disappoint you or you'll lose your focus.
- <u>Never</u> compromise. No matter what reward is promised or what shortcut it seems to offer.
- <u>Never</u> let yourself hate a person whose views you don't share. Don't create villains.
- Take care of yourself, your home and your family to the extent that they need you. Make time."

I spent an hour or two in the Sunday markets. They're a bit on the tacky side these days. I'd missed the last bus back to Cairns, and so I hitched a ride back with a doctor from the Atherton Tableland. Thanks, Doc!

Cape Trib and Cedar Bay

My second change of plan occurred when I learned that the cyclone had enjoyed a bout of destruction in amongst the elevated log cabins in the rainforest encampment called 'Crocodylus Village', which is set a little way off the track serving as the only road link to Cape Tribulation. I'd already booked my trip from Cairns in a 4-wheeled drive, mini-bus style vehicle, so I was set to go anyway. As with Kuranda, I knew a little of the area's hippy history. After the Terania forest protests, many of the Rainbow Region tribe had moved north around Kuranda and then decamped to 'defend' the Daintree rainforest. Even before that there had been a sizeable hippy beach community at Cedar Bay, on the coast north of the Daintree River.

In one of the colonial-style bars in Cairns I'd gotten talking to an old timer. He looked in need of some company and over a couple on stubbies, sitting out on the pub veranda, Czechoslovakian George told me a little of his life. It included the fact that he had known Mook Bahloo, way back when in the early 70s! Alternative Australia is a small place! George told me,
"When I arrive in the early 1960s I was outsider. People no wanna speak to me. I am sad. It is lonely; then the hippies they come Cedar Bay and I live with them. They wonderful times. They very kind to me, treat me like a person again. It was hard for long time living in Australia."

During the 70s, partly as a result of police harassment, there was a free-flow movement of hippies between the Rainbow Region of New South Wales, Kuranda and Cedar Bay. But then that beach itself became the target of a major police action which cleared the area for a number of years. Later in the 80s a new wave of 'hippies' set up beach dwellings around

Warwick near his old beach home

a number of the bays stretching north of Daintree. My guide, Warwick Roe, on my trip north was one of that generation who lived at Cow Bay and Coconut Bay. That period of living on bush foods, fish and rice, together with a geology degree, equipped him with skills as a rainforest walks guide. Consequently, he has a great first hand knowledge of the area. The beaches are serene strips of white sand – a tropical picture postcard, surrounded by the rainforest and dense mangrove swamps in, and bordering on the Wet Tropics World Heritage Area. Ideal crocodile country! Warwick told me that the crocs even swim out in the sea to nearby islands, so if the sharks don't get you...

Warwick, along with many of the area's other locals, has been following the current saga of conflict. Significantly, this has arisen through the sale of the 1,000 blocks of residential land for development along the coastal strip north of Daintree. Residential development and the expansion of tourism in the area are a double-edged sword. The very reasons I found the areas further north out of Cape Trip on the Bloomfield Road to be so captivating were because they are wild and virtually unspoilt. However, the sale of the residential blocks of land, many of which have been built upon, threaten that isolation with the possibility of a new metalled road and the provision of electricity. For me, and thankfully for Mike Berwick and many members of the Douglas Shire council, this threat to the rainforest has proved too great.

Since 1994, the Daintree Rescue Program has existed, with the primary aim of buying back as many as possible of the residential development blocks sold by a previous administration. The Douglas Shire council has gained powerful financial backing to the tune of $23 million, for the Program from the Commonwealth and State governments, which has allowed some 'buy-back' to take place and has also been used to improve walking tracks, control feral pigs and develop 'sustainable tourism', whatever that looks like! So far, 1,600 hectares of privately purchased land has been bought back.

The paradox of the 1999 protests in this area, is that there are active groups who are both pro- and anti-tourism, and a residents' pro-power lobby, which has been picketing the Daintree tourists crossing on the river ferry. As G. Pitt wrote in *the Cairns Post*, 10th July, 1999, under the headline, *Don't*

give in to Daintree terrorist tactics that knock tourism:
"No one forced these people to buy land with no power, so why should the rest of Australia pay for their bad investments?"
Either a new road *or* electricity could seriously damage the fragile ecology of this very special area of northern Queensland.

Travellers' tales

As an outsider myself, I thought it would be interesting to invite a couple of visitors to Oz for their personal recollections and tales. Because many Australians are themselves migrants to the country, or are the first generation members of families to be born in Australia, there is a profound fascination with place, culture and identity. These themes are taken up by a number of contributors to this book, and I guess they underlie what Em and Tatiana have written in this section. Buried even deeper in the psyche of Australia is what Henry Reynolds has called, *"a lurking shadow of doubt, a whisper in the heart"* – referring, of course, to the treatment of the original Australians, the Aborigines.

Something I found in myself as I travelled around Oz, was a tangible sense of the *terra nullius:* a huge, empty space. Unwillingly, I could see why the first Europeans had adopted a policy of land-theft, feeling that this beautiful, enormous, but rather scary place, was theirs for the making, or more often, the taking. And therein lies the basis of the persecution and disenfranchisement of the 600-700 original Australian tribes.

Returning to our contributors, Em is a part of the UK's counter cultural scene. She contributed to my earlier book, *No Boundaries,* recounting her experiences with other new Travellers in Goa and Greece. It provides a nice sense of continuity, synergy and Gaia, to be able to include her here, sharing some of her experiences in Australia. She eventually scratched her way beneath the veneer of Australian society. In essence and spirit, she represents one of the youthful world tribes, who have continued to re-invent themselves since the sixties and the beginnings of hippy travelling.

Following on from what Em calls her 'burblings' are some of Tatiana's 'feelings' about Australia. She is Swiss and I met her on the long trip up and down from Alice Springs to Uluru (Ayers Rock) and the equally magnificent Kata Tjuta (the Olgas). The red centre is where you really learn to appreciate the immensity of the place. And Uluru exudes its spiritual power over all who visit. Or, perhaps not quite all. You have to smile at the hundreds of Japanese visitors enthusiastically

Tatiana

taking photographs of hundreds of Japanese visitors! Out of our own small party of eight tourists, it was only Tatiana and myself who did not climb the famous rock. I jogged around the rock's base, marvelling at its strange, contorted surface, while Tatiana made her own communion with the spirits of the place. Somehow, climbing what is a 'cathedral' and central source of the Aboriginal dreamtime experiences, seems to represent yet another insult by Europeans to the culture of the original Australians.

Em writes:

Oz has a slippery surface. I arrived in '92, couldn't get a grip, nearly didn't stay. Sundazed apathy and superficiality were what I first perceived. Easy-going, laid-back, sure; and no kick, no passion. Me, a pacifist, wanted to start a riot, to shake the somnolent, acquiescent multitude into some kind of dynamic action. Where was the rave, where was the rage? Where the anarchy, the canny wiliness, the fuck-the-system warriors of the British scene I'd come from? On my way back to Sydney, to get the hell out of Paradise-Lost, I fell down a wyrm hole. Or a rabbit hole.

Alice in Wonderland woke up in Oz Underworld; curiouser and curiouser, weirder and wilder than I can explain. Ferals with mythical tales and tails, Travellers, tipi dwellers, crazed pixie poets, party animals, flipped-out faeries, healers and true Wizards of Oz. They'd been invisible to me and yet here they were, invincible, larger than life, and in fact much livelier and more mischievous than the run-to-ground, stomped on, exhausted folk back home at that time. Since then, of course, anarcho-eco-energy has blossomed all over the globe, and in Oz the inhabitants of the Underworld have been venturing more frequently Topside to wake up their sleepwalking mainstream...

The best things in Oz happened when I totally LET GO. Flung preconceptions into the surf, relinquished control, followed whim and waited, right-minded, to see what would occur. Sat on a pavement in Byron with my bag by my side in a torrential storm, no money, no plan...and waited. Stuck out my thumb on a road in Northern Queensland, barefoot in a sari...and waited. Or picked up a couple of tripping hitchers in a clapped out Kombi and let them choose our destination. Or fell in love in a forest and stayed a year longer than I'd intended to, nearly stayed forever. And scattered pieces of myself across the land.

Byron Bay

I walked the arc of the Bay today
And was reborn.
Sometimes the Magic is too great for words
Or just Too Great – Be careful what you wish for here
For you are dreaming up creation...

You are what you say you are...
I'm a Spiritual Warrior I am.
I chant and dance and affirm the sacred,
Devise my own rituals,
Perform them to my heart's content...
You are what you say you are...
I'm a Spiritual Warrior I am
And I'm walking backwards into the past
To bless and be blessed and be free.

Mooching and grooving and keening and grieving,
Down the beach at sunset, clouds golden,
Ululating, wailing, reciting, laughing and singing,
The ocean throws me treasure-stores;
Shooting stars fallen to Earth –
I like that fantasy.

Here are a couple of photos of the Rainbow Temple. I don't have many photos as I dropped my camera in a waterfall (and there went the last piece of my 'civilised life'). I sought sanctuary in the temple in wild storms – it was a beautiful space, really good energy and people, some sleeping in the temple, others in huts, tipis, treehouses. Everyone donated what they could – money or energy or skills – towards keeping us fed, sheltered and warm. Love, acceptance, tolerance and respect made it work. My sister was there last year and says that the vibe has changed and it is now more like a hostel with rules and fixed rates for a bed…everything changes, but it's still a good place, hidden in the forest at Rosebank.

are coming together to reveal its intricate patterns and, at last, to write that book.

Hold the hand of the Rainbow Mystery Child
And you will be forever protected
Em

Dust, desert, sun, forest, creek, waterfall, ocean. WIDE OPEN EMPTY SPACE in which to weave the meanings of these rainbow threads into the catcher of dreams, wider, brighter and more resonant than ever...I danced my own trance around Oz, wove my golden ribbon into the web, roamed, shared poetry, nourished the Earth, went feral and loved wildly. When I finally tore myself away I bled into the already red dirt. I wanted to write a book about the intensity and the magic hidden beneath the slick, soapy surface of Oz. I knew that I'd had only a peek at the richness of its fabric, so I'm happy now that the weavers

Tatiana says:

my time in australia was wonderful, all of it!
and i think it wasn't the last time my feet touched the ground of that beautiful planet.

I was thinking a lot about your book,
and id like to be part of it
already did some work, it's almost finished
and i would be glad, if you like to have a look on it...

And here is what Tatiana sent me:

~BEING HUMAN~

DREAMTIME

ALL
OVER ALL *
IN ALL *
WITH ALL *

SOMEONE WAS TELLING ME ONCE
, SOME AUSTRALIAN PERSONS
IGNORE
THE CULTURE OF ABORIGINES
BUT BELIEVE
IN THE WAY OF AMERICAN INDIANS
THE ABORIGINES BELIEVE
THEIR ROAD IS GOING BACK TO THE BEGINNING
AND I THINK THEY ARE RIGHT, SO
LET'S REMEMBER + OUR ROAD NEVER WILL END!
~BEING HUMAN~

THANK YOU

Tatiana

You can't be in any way involved in the environmental protest scene in Australia and not know about Benny Zable. You've already seen his pic in Graham St John's contribution about the Down to Earth ConFests. Here's another which Benny sent me as a link into Ralph Nader's words about the world's current and continuing nuclear madness; Alana Light's radioactive modelling and Franklin Scarf's Earth Repair Charter.

World Peace Environment Artist, Benny Zable, at the Gulf War public rally, Melbourne, Victoria. Photographed by John Ellis.

Excerpts from an address given by Ralph Nader, at the World Symposium on Humanities, held in the Pasadena Centre, California, USA, 1979.

NUCLEAR POWER, as long as it contains the generation of RADIOACTIVE WASTE and RADIOACTIVE MATERIALS, cannot be considered an acceptable risk for people on this planet. It is not just a problem today, it's a problem of utilizing energy for NUCLEAR POWER today and leaving for future generations, 250,000 years of RADIOACTIVE WASTE. That is an immoral position for any generation to find itself in. And when the other factors that argue against NUCLEAR POWER, its horrible expense, its highly centralized and authoritarian sub environment, its vulnerability to sabotage and terrorism, its vulnerability to earthquakes and other natural forces beyond people's control; all these add up to the need to STOP IT and set society's course on a SOLAR PATH.

Benny Zable's self-description is as, *"a resident of Nimbin, NSW. He promotes Earth Repair Global Strategies through a multi-media public art process, incorporating murals, costumed outfits, banners, flags and related props."*

Franklin sent me the Earth Repair Charter which is included on the next two pages. It's well worth checking out. The related web site, as Benny Zable was keen to stress to me, is very much a 'work in progress' incorporating a wide range of initiatives which Benny, Franklin and others are involved with – do take time to make a visit at: www.earthrepair.net

Literally the day I was due to send the CD disks for this book off to the printers, I received a series of phone calls and faxes from Franklin Scarf. I've never met him, but he has a glorious, warm timbre to his voice and his passion and commitment even transcend the global telecommunications network.

Amongst the 'new-to-me' material Franklin faxed was an array of glowing endorsements for the Earth Repair Charter. Hopefully I've managed to present it in its most up to date form without putting in any mistakes! Joanna Macy calls it, *"an achievable Global Solution Strategy"*, and the Dalai Lama says, *"The Earth Repair Charter is helping us be enlightened in our relationship with the Earth and compassionate to all beings."*
As the original 'Man of the Trees', Dr Richard St Barbe Baker has said of Franklin,
"You have your credentials in your mission of helping to tree-

scape the Earth and becoming one of the world's great earth healers."

Franklin also provided a copy of the Friends of the Earth petition, which he has been very involved with, calling for the national and international recognition of Aboriginal sovereignty to traditional lands and territories.

The only thing I'd like to add, as we get near to the end of this alto-tour of Australia, are a few words from Bob Hawke, Australia's longest serving Labor Prime Minister:
"We must understand the intrinsic significance of the land to traditional Aboriginal people...in other words... Aboriginal commitment to ownership of, or access to, land is based not only on a legal perception of prior rights but on a spiritual bond with the land."

"No issue is more likely to jeopardise the cohesion of our society in the forseeable future than the question of our relations with our Aboriginal population."

SOLAR SYSTEM GRAPHIC CONTRIBUTED BY HANSEN PLANETARIUM, UTAH, USA © 1996

WE ARE HERE ON EARTH, NOW ORBITING A SUN, PART OF THE MILKY WAY GALAXY IN AN INFINITE UNIVERSE.

TRANSFORM THE MILITARY TO EARTH REPAIR ACTION

JOIN WITH MILLIONS FOR THE COMMON PURPOSE OF HELPING ACHIEVE THE OBJECTIVES OF THIS VISIONARY CHARTER TO BRING A CULTURE OF LASTING PEACE ON EARTH AND MAXIMUM BEN-EFIT TO EVERYONE.

Protect natural heritage and biodiversity

* **respect** the Earth and take responsibility for all our actions, realising the interconnectedness of life * **cease** further destruction of, and protect in perpetuity, all remaining biodiverse old-growth native forests and other high conservation value areas; * **protect** wilderness, oceans, lakes and rivers; * **prohibit** the contamination of air, soil and waterways; * **stop** uranium mining and develop technologies to guarantee the long-term safety of all radio-active materials, mine tailings and by-products from nuclear industries; * **accelerate** training and employment programs to repair previously-cleared and degraded land; * **plant** and intergrow with companion vegetation, increasing quantities of appropriate trees to repair the atmosphere; * **preserve** and maintain the genetic diversity of seeds, plants and animals in their natural habitats; * **implement** a moratorium on genetic engineering which has the potential to interfere irreversibly with natural processes; * **label** accordingly all foods altered with DNA technology;

Ensure respect for Indigenous Peoples

* **conciliate** with and learn from Indigenous Peoples, their laws and spiritual values; * **support** self-determination and sovereign treaty rights world-wide; * **facilitate** permanent representation of the world's Indigenous Peoples in all United Nations forums; * **uphold** the United Nations draft Declaration on the Rights of Indigenous Peoples; * **honour** the inheritance of traditional languages, knowledge, sacred materials and sites; foster learning from the wise elders of all cultures;

Promote ecologically sustainable development

***educate** to stabilise world population, and provide comprehensive and free family-planning assistance; * **ensure** reproductive freedom rights for women world-wide; * **adopt** the world's best practices and reduce, reuse and recycle to minimise our consumption of Earth's finite resources; * **incorporate** into all education systems, reverence for nature, the skills of birthing and parenting, effective communication, self-esteem, and creative artistic expression; * **co-operate** internationally to reduce green-house-gas emissions and replace fossil-fuel technologies with safe and renewable energy systems; * **increase** the provision and efficient use of public transport systems; * **utilise** environmentally-responsible products and services, and deal only with materials manufactured or created within the principles of socially and ecologically sustainable development; * **contribute** to inter-generational equity by progres-sively planning for the well-being of future generations;

Acquire health and immunity efficiency

* **promote** co-operation between medical sciences and natural healing methods; * **practise** the wisdom of Hippocrates, who taught, "Let your food be your medicine and your medicine be your food"; * **attain** and maintain physical and mental well-being by combining an optimistic attitude, sleep, exercise and a nutritious diet of fresh, preservative-free organic foods, including sprouted seeds, nuts and grains, raw fruits, vegetables & herbs; * **abstain** from health-reducing substances such as tobacco and all drug abuse; * **inspire** everyone to realise their highest physical, intellectual, emotional and spiritual potential;

Use permaculture to help end world hunger

* **replace** unsustainable monoculture, toxic pesticide use and intensive animal factory-farming with high-yielding, diverse, organic agricultural systems and free-range animal farming;

* **establish** efficient food and medicine gardens as productive permaculture learning centres, in schools, backyards, parks, gaols and rehabilitation centres; * **propagate**, plant and care for trees, intercropped with complementary vegetation, in all possible city, urban and rural areas to produce fruits, nuts, vegetables, herbs, grains, fibre, timber and fuel, and help end hunger and poverty; * **promote** individual and community self-reliance through local exchange trading systems, and natural low-impact landcare strategies;

Practise composting to restore soils

* **produce** valuable humus-rich soil for home, municipal, farm and forestry use, by composting currently-wasted biodegradable materials; * **replace** artificial fertilisers with fine rock-dust and humus to remineralise soils, increase the nutrient value of food crops and boost resistance to plant disease; * **treat** sewage to irrigate vegetation and rejuvenate degraded lands;

Base economic order on social justice

* **aspire** to equal opportunity for everyone; * **demand** that corporate business and governments put the welfare of people before profits and military spending; * **grant** amnesty for political prisoners, and leniency for debt burdens of impoverished countries; * **aim** for fair resource distribution to satisfy the essential needs of all to live with health and dignity;

Resolve conflict with creative mediation

* **ensure** basic human rights and freedom of speech for all; * **learn**, develop and encourage the skills of conflict resolution everywhere; * **expedite** participatory democracy between people and their elected governments and councils; * **nurture** equality, love, respect and understanding between age groups, individuals, genders, families, castes, communities, cultures and races; * **encourage** all religions and faiths to co-exist in harmony as one human family, sharing the Earth as our common home; * **facilitate** equal access to communication technologies for schools and community organisations worldwide; * **investigate** and rectify all human rights violations; * **stop** the glamorisation of war and violence; * **motivate** the media to be positive, accurate, responsible and peace-making;

Transform the military to earth repair

* **redirect** funding, technological expertise and resources of all national military services, towards implementing this Solution Strategy as the priority within each country; * **enable** all nations to participate in developing the United Nations Global Peace-keeping Operations to ensure international security; * **decommission** and eliminate nuclear armaments, land mines and all instruments of mass destruction;

Unite with others in a common purpose

* **rescue** the future by helping achieve the local and global objectives of this Charter * **network** to raise awareness of this solution strategy and propose its goals for adoption by education, religious, union, political, business, legal, military & community groups, and local Councils, and for legislation by Governments; * **contribute** towards a more peaceful, safe, healthy and abundant Earth, where everyone can enjoy life in love, harmony and beauty.

Revision 17th January 2000

1999 - 2000 - 2005 - 2010

Produced by the EARTH REPAIR FOUNDATION and
Sponsored by the ENVIRONMENT PROGRAM of
United Nations Association of Australia (NSW) Inc.
PO Box 150, Hazelbrook, Blue Mountains, NSW 2779, Australia. (ACN # 003 198 981)
24 hour message number (02) 9990 0624, Fax: (02) 4758 6904, Int'nl Code: +61 2,
E-mail - earthnet@pnc.com.au Internet: www.earthrepair.net

And in the end

"And in the end, the love you take
is equal to the love you make."
Lennon and McCartney, *Abbey Road*

I'm writing this at the time of the Total Eclipse of the Sun in Britain. Here I am in my tent, near the top of a hillside on the Devon coast overlooking the Teign estuary. It's nearly midnight the day before the event. There's probably a couple of million others like me scattered around the Devon and Cornwall countryside in the zone of totality. We're expecting rain and lots of cloud cover. It doesn't matter though. It's a bit like the Spaceman Bob story back in the early Nimbin days. It's about being here, right now, doing it. While I'm thousands of miles distant, I'm at one with what Daevid Allen said when I met him earlier in the year, *"The main purpose in Australia is to find our mystical space."*

What happens next: I wake up to see the dawning, then have a walk before settling down for the four hour enviro-sky show. I've bought a couple of appropriate CDs with me. A mini, personal festie. A treat to complement nature's sky-show. I've chosen 44 minutes *of Dark side of the moon* starting at 10.34 a.m. which takes me into the concluding *Eclipse* track at totality.

And that's what I did. There was an impressive deep red sunrise, which spread above the rolling mists. By nine o'clock, serious cloud cover had spread along the south west coastline. Hundreds more people started to clamber up the hillsides all round me clutching cameras, eclipse glasses and telescopes. For the next four hours, flotillas of boats, large and small, moved westward into the totality zone, and right in front of our Shaldon hill, four or five dolphins leaped in and out of the waves, like some pre-ordained opening act. As the Big Moment approached, the temperature suddenly dropped ten degrees, a wall of blackness swept from the west towards us. It triggered thousands of street and shop lights all round the bay. People joined in waving torches and lighters. Camera flashes added to the effect. Flocks of birds shot in to the air, then settled back on the ground to sleep. We didn't see the famous halo moment – too much cloud cover, but it was truly eerie and awesome.

A very personal and memorable experience. And kindof reminiscent of much that happened to me during my time in Oz. Grabbing the moment seems much more a way of life. Which minds me of what a friend I used to live with once said to me, *"there's a big you, the one who you share with everyone, then there's a little you – that's the one that needs a bit of nurturing, needs to have the batteries re-charged."* At the end of the day, this book about Australia is dedicated to all the 'little yous' that make the 'big yous' keep on truckin!

"What a long, strange trip it's been."
Hunter, Garcia, Lesh and Weir, from *Truckin*

"So when you're done
And your black boots are
Muddied with innocent blood
And you think we're crushed
and homeless
And your cock is hard
With desire
For our pain
And your power

Think again

All this will grow elsewhere,
And it won't forget your fat
face
Or the number on
Your black hat"

Written by Hattie (about the tree protests in the UK) And featured in the book, *Copse* by Kate Evans, Orange Dog Productions

Bibliography

This is the bibliography for books and material that Alan referred to while putting this collection together. It's not in any way 'comprehensive' (whatever that is), but may provide some useful leads for anyone wanting to travel further into alternative Australia.

Adams, P, (ed), The retreat from tolerance: a snapshot of Australian Society (1997) ABC

Altman, D, Rehearsals for change, politics and culture in Australia (1980) Fontana

Archer, J and G, Earth Builder's Companion (1981) Grass Roots

Australian Conservation Foundation, Jabiluka: Country at Stake from 'Habitat' June (1998) ACF

Australian Conservation foundation, Uranium Street: Australia at the nuclear crossroads from 'Habitat' February (1999) ACF

Bachman, B, Local colour – travels in the other Australia (1994) Guidebook Co

Baglin, D and Austin, Y, Australian Pub Crawl (1977) Child and Henry

Beatty, B, Australia folk tales and traditions (1968) Ure Smith

Blagg, H (ed), Aboriginality, Crime and Justice (1998) University of WA Crime Research Centre

Bookchin, M, The Murray Bookchin Reader (1998) Cassell

Bruce, S, A Treasury of Australian Bush Paintings (1979) Rigby

Byrski, L (ed), The way ahead (1998) New Holland

Cadman, T and Gibbings, B, About the Native Forest Network, (n.d) NFN

Cock, P, Alternative Australia: Communities for the Future? (1979) Quartet

Cohen, I, Green Fire (1997) Harper Collins

Condon, S, Sean and David's long drive (1996) Lonely Planet

Conservation Council of WA, Forest Information Resource Kit, (1999) CCWA

Constine, G et al., Nimbin and Environs (1996) Nimbin News Collective

Cunningham, S, Framing culture: criticism and policy in Australia

Davidson, R, Tracks (1982) Picador

Dellbridge, A, Aussie Talk: the Macquarie dictionary of Australian colloquialisms (1984) Macquarie Library

Diamond, H, Your Heart – Your Planet (1991) Pythagorean Press

Else-Mitchell, R and Flutter, N, Talking up – young women's take on feminism (1998) Pinifex

Finlay, H et al., Lonely Planet (1998) 9th edition, Lonely Planet

Flanagan, R, Death of a River Guide (1994) McPhee Gribble

Francis, R, From Aquarius Dreaming to Nineties Reality: Nimbin's coming of Age (1997) Permaculture Association of Western Australia

Gerster, R and Bassett, J, Seizures of youth – the 60s and Australia (1991) Hyland House

Goodman, R and Johnston, G, The Australians (1966) Rigby

Griffiths, T, Beautiful Lies (1993) Wakefield Press

Grimwade, T, Australia – the beautiful land (1988) Brompton Books

Australia's Heritage – 7 volume encyclopaedia (1972)

Herer, J and Jiggens, J, Hemp and the Marijuana Conspiracy (includes Jiggens' Australian addendum) (1995) HEMP

Higgins, J, Sister Girl – writings of an Aboriginal activist and historian (1998) UQP

Hitching, F, Earth Magic (1976) Picador

Humston, S, Kuranda: the village in the rainforest (1988) self-published

Jacobson, H, In the Land of Oz (1987) Penguin

Jarratt, P, Australians at Play (1989) PR Books

Jarratt, S, Permissive Australia (1970) Jack de Lissa

Jiggens, J, Rehearsals for the Apocalypse, 10 years after the Nimbin Settlement (1983)

Keneally, T et al., Australia: Beyond the dreamtime (1987) BBC Books

Keneally, T, Outback (1983) Hodder and Stoughton

Kenton, L, Passage to Power (1995) Ebury

Kidd, R, The way we civilise (1997) UQP

Lawrence, C, Cockburn Sound (1999) Fremantle MP's newsletter

Lennox, G and Rush, F, People of the Cross (1993) Simon and Schuster

Lockwood, D, We, the Aborigines (1970) Ure Smith

Luck, P, A Time to Remember (1988) William Heinemann

Massacrier, J, Another way of living (1977) Grass Roots

McGonigal, D and Borthwick, J, Insight Guide: Australia (1990) Apa Productions

Merz, B, Points of Cosmic Energy (1987 in English) George and Cie

Metcalf, B and Vanclay, F, Social Characteristics of Alternative Lifestyle Participants in Australia (1985) Griffith University

Metcalf, B, From Utopia Dreaming to communal Reality (1995) University of New South Wales

Metcalf, B, Shared Visions, shared Lives (1996) Findhorn

Morosi, J, Sex, Prejudice and Politics (1975) Widescope

Morphy, H and Edwards, E, Australia in Oxford (1988) Pitt Rivers Museum, Oxford

Morphy, H, Aboriginal Art (1998) Phaidon

Mountford, C and Roberts, A, The first sunrise (1971) Rigby

Munro-Clarke, M, Communes in Rural Australia (1986) Hale and Ironmonger

Neville, R, Out of my mind (1996) Penguin

Newman, C, The Uneasy Magic of Australia's Cape York Peninsula (1996) National Geographic, Vol. 189, No. 6

Newton, J, Aborigines, tribes and the counter culture in 'Social Analysis' 23:53-71 (1988)

Nielson, L, Daintree (1997) Lloyd Nielson

Nimbin Hemp Embassy, End Prohibition 2000 (1998) Hemp Embassy

Nimbin News, various, Nimbin News Collective

Nimbin's Silly Symphony, New Clear Words (1980) Much Karma Productions

O'Donnell, P and Simons, L, Australians against racism (1995) Pluto Press

Ormonde, J, A foolish, passionate man: a biography of Jim Cairns (1981) Penguin

Our Times, various, Our Times, Byron Bay

Pearson, K, Surfing Subcultures (1979) University of Queensland

Pilger, J, Distant Voices (1992) Vintage

Potts, D, Alternative Australia – New wheels or re-treads? In 'Overland' 79 (1980)

Pryor, B, Maybe Tomorrow (1998) Penguin

Rainbow Collection, Mitchell Library, NSW State Library, Sydney

Rawlins, A, Festivals in Australia: an intimate history (1982) Down to Earth, QLD

Reynolds,H, The Law of the Land (   )

Seed, J et al., Thinking like a mountain: towards a council of all beings (1988) New Society

Seed, J, A campfire View of Giblett Forest (n.d.) Satellite Despatch/On the Road

Smith, B, Australian Painting 1788-1960 (1962) Oxford University Press

Smith, M and Crossley, D, The Way Out (1975) Lansdown

Spearritt, P and Walker, D, Australian Popular Culture (1979) Allen and Unwin

St John, G, Going feral: authentica on the edge of Australian culture in 'Australian Journal of Anthropology (8(2))(1997)

Stewart, D (ed), Burnum Burnums' Aboriginal Australia (1989) Angus and Robertson

The first Australians – Ancient Culture, New Voices (1993) Australia Now Vol.16 No.1

Thomas, M, Mini-book of blokes and sheds (1998) Angus and Robertson

Thornton, P et al., I Protest! (1997) Pluto Press

Trainer, T, Saving the Environment: what it will take (1998) UNSW

Walker, C, Stranded: The Secret History of Australian Independent Music, 1977-91 (1996) Pan-Macmillan

Wetherspoon, G, (ed), Being Different – 9 gay men remember (1986) Hale and Ironmonger

Whereth, R (ed), Mardi-Gras (1999) Viking-Penguin

Wilderness Society, Wildchat Online, Wilderness Society, South Australia

Williams, C, Protest! 1968-1998 (1998) NSW Historic Houses

Williams, P, Kiss my horse (1998) Seaview Press

Wood, T, Cobbers (third edition, 1953) Oxford University Press

Wright, J, Coral Battleground (1996) Angus and Robertson

Yinger, J, Countercultures: the promise and the peril of a world turned upside down (1982) Free Press

Zalajzich, P, The Battlers for Kelly's Bush: 13 women who fought for the bush and the first green bans (1996) The Battlers for Kelly's Bush

Harmonic Convergence

Enabler Publications

specialise in publishing and distributing books about creative work with young people, environmental action and the broad counter-cultural DiY scene.

Do get in touch if you want a current list of publications. That list includes:

A Time to Travel? An introduction to Britain's newer Travellers. *Fiona Earle et al. £7.99.*
No Boundaries: new Travellers on the road outside of Britain. *Alan Dearling. £9.50.*
Copse: the history of road protesting (in the UK). *Kate Evans. £9.50.*

Sadly, the post and packing costs can come to quite a lot. In the UK, we charge £1.50 for all the above titles, except *Copse* and *Alternative Australia,* which, being heavier, are charged at £2.50 each for p&p. It depends on which country you live in, so get in touch and we'll let you know the appropriate charge. We appreciate payment in sterling made out to *Enabler Publications.*

Enabler Publications, 3 Russell House, Lym Close, Lyme Regis, Dorset, UK, DT7 3DE.
Tel/Fax +44 (0) 1297 445024
E-mail: adearling@aol.com
Web site: http://members.aol.com/adearling/enabler/